Living and Working with the New Medical Technologies

This stimulating collection of essays is the product of face-to-face
dialogues among anthropologists, sociologists, and philosopher-
historians, all of whom focus their attention on newly created biomedical technologies and their application in practice. Drawing on
ethnographic and historial case studies, the authors show how biomedical technologies are produced through the agencies of tools and techniques, scientists and doctors, funding bodies, patients, clients, and
the public. Despite shared concerns, these essays reveal that the
authors have achieved no consensus about the objectives of their
research and deep epistomological divides remain – making for provocative reading.

MARGARET LOCK, ALLAN YOUNG, ALBERTO CAMBROSIO
McGill University

MARGARET LOCK is a professor in the Departments of Social Studies
of Medicine and of Anthropology at McGill University. She is the
author of *East Asian Medicine in Urban Japan: Varieties of Medical
Experience* (1980) and *Encounters with Aging: Mythologies of Menopause
in Japan and North America* (1993). She has also co-edited five books,
including *Pragmatic Women and Body Politics* (Cambridge, 1998).
ALLAN YOUNG is Professor of Anthropology in the Department of
Social Studies of Medicine, McGill University. He is the author of *The
Harmony of Illusions: Inventing Post-traumatic Stress Disorder* (1995).
ALBERTO CAMBROSIO is Associate Professor in the Department of
Social Studies of Medicine, McGill University. He is the co-author,
with Peter Keating, of *Exquisite Specificity: The Monoclonal Antibody
Revolution* (1995).

D0596816

Cambridge Studies in Medical Anthropology

Editor

ALAN HARWOOD *University of Massachusetts, Boston*

Editorial Board

Medical anthropology is the fastest growing specialist area within anthropology, both in North America and in Europe. Beginning as an applied field serving public health specialists, medical anthropology now provides a significant forum for many of the most urgent debates in anthropology and the humanities. It includes the study of medical institutions and health care in a variety of rich and poor societies, the investigation of the cultural construction of illness, and the analysis of ideas about the body, birth, maturity, ageing, and death.

This series includes theoretically innovative monographs, state-of-the-art collections of essays on current issues, and short books introducing main themes in the subdiscipline.

1. Lynn M. Morgan, *Community Participation in Health: The Politics of Primary Care in Costa Rica*
2. Thomas J. Csordas (ed.), *Embodiment and Experience: The Existential Ground of Culture and Health*
3. Paul Brodwin, *Medicine and Morality in Haiti: The Contest for Healing Power*
4. Susan Reynolds Whyte, *Questioning Misfortune: The Pragmatics of Uncertainty in Eastern Uganda*
5. Margaret Lock and Patricia Kaufert, *Pragmatic Women and Body Politics*
6. Vincanne Adams, *Doctors for Democracy*
7. Elisabeth Hsu, *The Transmission of Chinese Medicine*

Living and Working with the New Medical Technologies

Intersections of Inquiry

Edited by

Margaret Lock
McGill University

Alan Young
McGill University

Alberto Cambrosio
McGill University

PUBLISHED BY THE PRESS SYNDICATE OF THE UNIVERSITY OF CAMBRIDGE
The Pitt Building, Trumpington Street, Cambridge, United Kingdom

CAMBRIDGE UNIVERSITY PRESS
The Edinburgh Building, Cambridge CB2 2RU, UK
http://www.cup.cam.ac.uk.
40 West 20th Street, New York, NY 10011–4211, USA   http://www.cup.org
10 Stamford Road, Oakleigh, Melbourne 3166, Australia

First published 2000

Printed in the United Kingdom at the University Press, Cambridge

Typeset in Monotype Plantin 10/12 pt. [wv]

A catalogue record for this book is available from the British Library

Library of Congress cataloging-in-publication data
Living and working with the new medical technologies/edited by Margaret
Lock, Allan Young, Alberto Cambrosio.
     p.   cm. – (Cambridge studies in medical anthropology; 8)
ISBN 0 521 65210 3 (hardback). ISBN 0 521 65568 4 (pbk.)
1. Medical technology – Social aspects. 2. Medical innovations – Social aspects.
3. Medical anthropology.
I. Lock, Margaret M.   II. Young, Allan, 1938–   . III. Cambrosio, Alberto,
1950–   . IV. Series.   V. Series: Cambridge studies in medical anthropology;
8.
[DNLM: 1. Anthropology – trends. 2. Technology, Medical – trends.
W1 CA4539R v.8 2000/W1 CA4539R v.8 2000]
R855.3.L58 2000
610′.28 – dc21
DNLM/DLC
for Library of Congress   99-24537   CIP

ISBN 0 521 65210 3 hardback
ISBN 0 521 65568 4 paperback

Contents

Contributors

ALBERTO CAMBROSIO, *McGill University*
VEENA DAS, *New School for Social Research, New York*
JOSEPH DUMIT, *Massachusetts Institute of Technology*
PATRICIA KAUFERT, *University of Manitoba*
PETER KEATING, *Université de Quebec à Montreal*
MARGARET LOCK, *McGill University*
ILANA LÖWY, *Hopital Necker-Enfants Malades*
ANNEMARIE MOL, *University of Twente*
HANS-JÖRG RHEINBERGER, *University of Salzburg*
PAUL RABINOW, *University of California, Berkeley*
RAYNA RAPP, *New School for Social Research, New York*
ALAN YOUNG, *McGill University*

1   Introduction

Alberto Cambrosio, Allan Young and Margaret Lock

Use of the term "intersections" in the title of this book undoubtedly evokes impressions of postmodernist rhetoric, yet it is also a term long used by symbolic interactionist sociologists to analyze "intersecting" lines of action and social worlds.[1] This interplay of postmodernity and tradition is precisely one of the "intersections" we undertake to explore in this volume. Further intersections arise between the various analytical approaches exemplified by the authors represented in this book, and also between the human actors, the tools, the entities and the bodies that are constitutive of the new medical technologies. How these intersections relate to each other, in other words, how new biomedical objects and subjects call for new kinds of analyses, is one of the issues raised by the present collection of articles.

As indicated by the book's title, one can work with the new medical technologies, and we all live, directly or indirectly, with them. Some of the contributors tend to focus on the "working" side of this equation, others on its "living" side, while all struggle, more or less openly, to bring these two sides together. The authors display many differences in their choice of topics and approach (two not entirely independent elements). However, they share an understanding of "body politics" that, instead of rejecting or accepting recurring dichotomies such as that between Nature and Culture, looks at how dichotomies are produced. Yet, rather than focusing on either differences or commonalities, it seems more interesting to us to look at intersections, that is, temporary convergences that can lead to advances on some particular problem, with no pretence of providing a comprehensive world-view or a theoretical manifesto.[2]

The book was born then from an attempt at a dialogue across disciplinary fields that took place at a three-day conference held in July 1996 at Cambridge University, England. The fields represented were (medical) anthropology and science studies, although the latter can hardly be considered a disciplinary field but, rather, a loose connection of scholars focusing on a problem area. Reference to a "dialogue across

1

disciplinary fields" is not meant to imply that organizers and participants took for granted disciplinary demarcations, nor that most of them claimed allegiance to a clear-cut disciplinary identity, though this is evidently the case for some contributors. Rather, the conference could be said to lie at the intersection of two domains that, in spite of their interest in the same substantive area, differ in the ways they conceive of their analytical objects. This neat divide into two camps does indeed capture some of the dynamic of the meeting, but it also oversimplifies it, as it soon became apparent to all participants that "science studies" does not present a united front but, rather, a diversity of approaches mobilizing sociology, epistemology, history, and anthropology itself. Similarly, an anthropology of medicine, while the culture concept is usually retained as one of its central concepts, nevertheless draws on insights obtained from history, sociology, and so on.

Conception of the conference can be traced back to ongoing discussions over the last few years among the three book editors, two anthropologists and a sociologist who, while belonging to the same academic department, operate in different, though intersecting, disciplinary and professional networks. By resorting to a somewhat trite metaphor, one could argue that the conference and book grew out of the need, on the editors' part, to explore and clarify some of the perceived relations and tensions, both within and between their department microcosm and their professional macrocosms. Yet, we would resist such a description, for the problem, as we frame it, is less one of drawing parallels between different "levels" of generality, than one of understanding the production of generalities out of local situations.[3]

As the conference progressed, discussions started to crystallize around a few intersections including agreements on what the disagreements are. Simultaneously, attempts at increasing the generality of the discussion by mobilizing a disciplinary rhetoric were replaced by more concrete references to a diversity of audiences, the actual or ideal readers of our work. To talk of audiences has the advantage of stressing the agency of researchers, their active shaping of discourses to interest colleagues, the subjects they study, funding agencies and so on. To talk of audiences also immediately evokes a potential multiplicity and heterogeneity of individuals and groups. In our case, they ranged from academic colleagues across various social science fields, to the researchers and clinicians in the biomedical field who were the objects of, but also often the collaborators in, our inquiries, to the patients who redefine their identities and properties by interacting with the new technologies of the body.

It seems fair to argue that at the conference the (real or perceived) challenge came from science studies – a relative newcomer to the academic world – and it crystallized around the notion of "black box." Briefly put, from the point of view of science studies, mainstream work in well-established disciplines such as anthropology or sociology, even when purportedly dealing with medical or scientific matters, generally ignores the production of clinical and laboratory objects and procedures, thus treating them as "black boxes." The "opening of black boxes" is often seen as (one of) the specific task(s) of science studies, with the proviso that there is no agreement on what would constitute a proper "opening" of the boxes. The counter-argument raised by several anthropologists at the conference was that a focus on the opening of the black boxes leads to a neglect of the "broader context" within which scientific and technological objects evolve in practice, and translates into little interest in their fate once they leave the scientific laboratory – a point to which we will subsequently return.

Numerous articles could be cited to validate both sides of this argument, but the contributors to this book make it clear that such a dichotomous, oppositional setting apart of medical anthropology and science studies does not apply here. On the contrary, most of the authors, precisely by focusing their interpretations on intersections among the activities of a range of actors and objects, overcome, to a degree, the dilemma posed by black-box or broader context. This is not to suggest, however, that some kind of rapprochement was achieved; on the contrary, as the essays make clear, deep epistemological differences remain among the authors of these essays.

Problematics of Medical Anthropology

Over the last twenty-five years, medical anthropology – as a field clearly defined by distinctive professional associations, journals, symposia, programs of graduate training, and so on – has emerged from insignificance to become one of the most conspicuous anthropological specialties. During this period of expansion, medical anthropology has likewise grown more variegated, both as to its subjects – international health, psychiatry, indigenous systems of medical practice, new biomedical technologies, and so on – and its perspectives and epistemologies. Until the 1960s, anthropologists interested in medicine tended to accept the goals set by Western medical institutions or, alternatively, to follow an ethnographic tradition that located sickness and healing as subjects within the circle of witchcraft, sorcery, magic and religion. Today anthropologists can choose from an assortment of orientations – from anthropologies of suffering, experience and the body; from anthropologies that identify themselves with the interests of Western medical institutions; and from anthropologies that seek to demonstrate how values, interests and bias are integral to all medical knowledge and practice. Because of these developments and the divisions to which they have given birth, one should not assume that writer and reader share a consensus regarding the meaning of this term "medical anthropology."

Despite these various orientations, the term "medical anthropology" is sometimes understood to imply that anthropologists interested in sickness, healing, bodily consciousness and similar subjects, constitute an autonomous subdiscipline, and that they rely on methodologies and theories that are particular to medicine and substantially different from those employed by social and cultural anthropologists. We reject this proposition, at least as far as it refers to the kind of work represented in this volume; "medical" ideas, practices and responses ought to be approached in the same way, *mutatis mutandi*, that anthropologists concern themselves with other domains of life.

The anthropology of medicine is free to follow many paths. One path is *interrogatory*. It seeks solutions to the puzzles stemming from people's claims about events and objects in the material world – their ideas about witches, surrogate motherhood, and pathogenic (traumatic) memories, for example. It rejects what can be called the "idea of cognitive generosity" – the notion that inconsistencies and contradictions in people's accounts of the world are merely apparent, rather than real (Lukes 1967; Sperber 1985: chapter 2). The starting point of the interrogatory path is the assumption that goal-oriented human behavior is guided by reason (rationality). Evidence to the contrary can be interpreted as the failure of the observer (anthropologist) to completely understand the perceptions, beliefs and desires of the individual actors. But what exactly does "reason" mean in these circumstances? At the very least, it would imply an ability to apprehend contradictions, inconsistencies and emotionally charged input to debate. But the idea that we all, anthropologists and the people whom anthropologists study, can spontaneously agree on what constitutes a contradiction or an inconsistency is precisely the problem. Of course, there is a wide range of perceptions on which anthropologists will generally agree with our informants. For example, both of us will be able to pick out individuals afflicted with severe psychoses as different from other people. But spontaneous agreement is missing in many instances, including the puzzling events that we frequently encounter while studying the diagnosis and treatment of sickness in other societies. And the reason is clear: the conditions that determine whether a belief or a claim is a contradiction and/or an "inconsistency" are cultural and not universally evident.

How do we account for the orderliness of people's medical behaviour unless we assume that they are rational? And if we cannot claim a shared rationality with our informants (minimally the ability to agree on what constitutes a contradiction), then how can we claim to understand and interpret their life worlds and their cultures? The solution is not to renounce reason, but rather to *relocate it* – moving it out of the minds and brains of individuals and into the social institutions, technologies and practices through which individuals interact with one another and with other elements of the material world. Instead of using this term "reason," which brings with it unwarranted assumptions about the tendencies and powers of the human mind, it would be clearer if we substituted for it another term, *styles of reasoning*, borrowed from the philosopher Ian Hacking (1992). Where "reason" suggests something unitary, universal and constant, styles of reasoning suggests variation – that is, ways of making facts and meanings that change from society to society, and from venue to venue within a given society.

This version of an anthropology of medicine has many historical sources, but the most obvious place to begin is with J. G. Frazer's familiar observations on magic, science and religion. Frazer identified religion with the propitiation and supplication of natural and supernatural powers, and he identified magic with the coercion of these same powers. In Frazer's version, magic resembles science more closely than it resembles religion. To grasp the significance of his point, one must understand his ideas about reasoning. Like his great predecessor, the empiricist philosopher David Hume, Frazer believed that human cognition is guided by principles of *association*. Mind is initially a blank slate upon which experience leaves its impressions. In the course of further experiences, these impressions are associated into complex concepts, through relations based on resemblance and contiguity.

According to Frazer, beliefs and practices connected with magic are based on two kinds of associations: resemblance or "sympathy," where like is seen to produce like, and contiguity or "contagion," in which things once in contact continue to influence one another after the contact is ended. Scientific reasoning is based on similar associations but, in this case, they are constrained and controlled. In contrast, the cognitive processes underlying magic are characteristically confused. Nonetheless, magic and science are connected genealogically: science is the product of a progressive refinement in thinking rather than a discontinuity.

Frazer's account is individualistic and cognitive. In it, systems of beliefs and practices are displaced by the perceptions and mental operations of solitary thinkers; psychology is treated as the queen of the human sciences (see Ackerman 1987: 40, 51, 157–8). In other words, he is writing about reason rather than styles of reasoning.

E. E. Evans-Pritchard's famous monograph on magic and medicine, *Witchcraft, Oracles and Magic Among the Azande* (1937), departs radically from Frazer's work. The Azande book is the product of intensive ethnographic research conducted in the language of the local people, while Frazer's research consisted of collecting vignettes from unsystematic and fragmentary literary accounts. During his lifetime, Frazer's work was described as being "comparative"; today we are inclined to see it as being merely "anecdotal."

Evans-Pritchard's investigations of sickness and witchcraft led him to the oracles through which the Azande construct their disease etiologies, manage their sickness episodes, choose their interventions and identify targets for vengeance magic. By Western standards, the oracles appear to be "so much nonsense," and Evans-Pritchard makes this his starting point. Evans-Pritchard's achievement was to put the apparent nonsense into a context, that is, a *system* of ideas, perceptions, technologies and social relations. And, following this, he proceeded to demonstrate the system's underlying coherence.

In the context of his book, "coherence" refers to two things. First, it refers to a formal property of the system, its capacity to reproduce itself over time. For example, the Zande system is organized in such a way that oracles provide an endless supply of "witches," thus perpetuating the Zande inclination to consult witch-catching oracles when someone falls sick or suffers misfortune. Second, coherence implies the existence of a thinking subject (the typical Zande) and a standard against which the subject's words (and the thoughts and perceptions that they ostensibly mirror) and behavior can be measured. In other words, the system is coherent in the sense that its elements meet a standard that has been set for them by Evans-Pritchard and by his ideal reader.

Beneath the surface of this text, Evans-Pritchard is engaged in conversation with Westerners who would question the rationality of the Azande. His book is simultaneously an ethnography and an interrogation in which the Azande are made to account for logical inconsistencies and contradictions. This represents a mode of discourse that is not only foreign to Frazer's evolutionary associationism, but is also hostile to the principle of cognitive generosity.

Sixty years after its publication, *Witchcraft, Oracles and Magic Among the Azande* remains a monument in the history of the anthropology of medicine. Contemporary readers may find parts of it rather old fashioned, specifically where Evans-Pritchard introduces science into his discourse. "[W]e need to judge to whom we can appeal for a decision when a question arises whether a notion shall be classed as mystical." This judge or standard is science – according to Evans-Pritchard, a development of common sense that is distinguished from the latter by its superior techniques of observation and reasoning, most notably its fidelity to "experiment and rules of Logic" (Evans-Pritchard 1937: 12). Some of these same readers might object to the way in which Evans-Pritchard characterizes science, as a highly refined form of rule-governed rationality. Science, they will want to argue, is a powerful and successful system of reasoning, a historically determined assembly of objects, technologies, social relations and language games. Indeed some readers will want to go even further in this respect, to ask whether it is possible to employ the term "science" in any useful sense other than the plural; not science, but rather the "sciences," each deploying its particular system of reasoning. And which of these systems did Evans-Pritchard have in mind as his standard: medical science, biological science, psychiatric science, particle physics?

If we dispense with the idea of a unitary rule-governed science and a correspondence theory of knowledge, is it possible to continue to interrogate cultures in the way that Evans-Pritchard interrogated Zande oracles? This is a serious question, because its answer will determine not only how we will interpret *Witchcraft, Oracles and Magic Among the Azande* from this point on, but likewise how we will study and describe our common subject, whether it be medicine, sickness or madness.

From Representations to Practices

The "science question," that is, the question of whether or not science should be considered as a socio-cultural endeavor and analyzed as such, has not only been a key issue to anthropologists interested in investigating biomedicine, but has also been instrumental in the development of the field known as "science studies." And here is another intersection. Evans-Pritchard's book that, as argued in the previous section, should be considered "a monument in the history of the anthropology of medicine," also appears to be a persistent trope in many early science studies texts, in particular those originating from the Edinburgh-based "strong program."[4] The choice of the Azande's poison oracle as a key example in Barnes's and Bloor's manifestos for a new sociology of science was of course not an innocent one, since that same example had been mobilized by philosophers engaged in normative analyses of science. In the particular reading of the strong programers, the poison oracle thus became at the same time a resource against and a terrain on which to confront attempts at a demarcationist philosophy of science, one that is aimed at developing logical, a priori criteria, such as "falsifiability" and a universal understanding of "rationality" for establishing a distinction between scientific and non- (or pseudo-) scientific knowledge. According to strong programers, social, rather than logical processes, grounded all sort of beliefs, including those labeled as scientific, and thus a sociology, rather than a philosophy of science, was called for to account for the content of science.[5]

Yet, in spite of the excitement that it generated and still seems to generate in some quarters, it soon became apparent that the claim that scientific knowledge is socially produced is a far less interesting one than attempts to investigate *how* that same scientific knowledge is (re)produced. And, following up on this insight, it also became evident that the socio-cultural reductionism advocated by strong programers was a mirror image of the logical or technological reductionism advocated by their philosophical counterparts and, as such, untenable. As a way out of this dilemma, one had to shift the focus of inquiry from knowledge to practices, thus completing the ethnographic turn by looking at the "material culture" of science, at how scientists perform things, rather than at the frozen products of those performances. Interestingly enough, after Evans-Pritchard, it was yet another scholar of the 1930s, Ludwik Fleck, who can retrospectively be said to have first shown how to go about doing precisely these kinds of analyses.

Fleck, the author of a masterful account of the development of the Wassermann reaction to diagnose syphilis that antedates the publication of Evans-Pritchard by two years (1979[1935]), is presently credited with having written the very first monograph dealing with the content of scientific knowledge from a thoroughly sociological point of view. Fleck's contribution, however, initially attracted far less attention than Evans-Pritchard, and even today Fleck is often perceived as a mere "precursor" of Kuhn. This is how, for instance, Barnes (1982) presented Fleck's work.[6] Yet, another reading of Fleck is possible (not to speak of another reading of Kuhn![7]), one that chooses to emphasize not so much Fleck's claim that facts about syphilis were actively shaped by thought-styles or paradigm-bound collectivities, but, rather, his detailed description of how "practice," understood as a series of ongoing interactions between researchers, tools, instruments, resources and other elements of biomedical networks, accounted for how the Wassermann test was developed and accepted as a reliable diagnostic procedure.

So here, it would seem, we could find another intersection between anthropology and science studies, insofar as the ethnographic analysis of the material culture of collectivities is something science studies practitioners share with anthropologists. Yet things are not so simple, since "practice," as seen by the latter, is intimately linked with or shaped by culture, while for at least some of the former, a practice-oriented or "performative" approach (such as the one exemplified in Mol's chapter in the present volume) represents an alternative to cultural analysis. Traces of this opposition are easy to find in the present book, but it should quickly be added that the demarcation line between these different approaches does not run smoothly between anthropology and science studies; rather, it cuts across each field, especially in the case of science studies, a state of affairs once again readily detectable in this collection of essays.

The papers in Part II of the present volume point to the existence of these intersecting, yet diverging paths. Ilana Löwy's chapter clearly lies on the "culturalist" and "contextualist" side of the debate, insofar as its twin goals are to show how clinical trials for anti-HIV drugs were shaped by a long-established, pre-existing culture of clinical experimentation evolving out of cancer research – an argument that profoundly qualifies claims about the alleged decisive role played by the intervention of AIDS activists (Epstein 1996) – and to argue instead that a specific political and economic context constrained their design and performance. In contrast, Annemarie Mol adopts a "performative" approach that replaces the dichotomy between "disease" and "illness" (the medical and the social) with an ethnographic understanding of the material realities (the plural is important) of diseases. As a result, the picture of a culturally and cognitively homogeneous biomedical model facing the lifeworld of patients – or the constraining powers of context-defining institutions – is replaced by the pragmatic intersection and juxtaposition of "differences" (Berg and Mol 1998) that proliferate on both sides of the alleged divide. The chapter by Peter Keating and Alberto Cambrosio also questions socially or culturally determinist accounts by examining competing classifications of nosological entities. Rather than reducing differences to the incommensurability of social worlds or professional segments, the authors stress the formal and informal regulatory activities that allow a variety of perspectives and practices to co-exist and unforeseen options to emerge. Regulation, in this sense, is not restricted to the organization of consensus. By making hierarchies and choices explicit and consistent across laboratories, it leads to the production of new, unexpected events and highlights the emergent qualities of any resulting scheme. Finally, Allan Young's chapter examines the multiple styles of reasoning – epidemiological, statistical, clinical and experimental – that intersect in psychiatric science and clinical practice through technologies of traumatic remembering and forgetting. The chapter traces the transformation of these technologies over the past half-century, in relation to the biologization of mental illness (and developments in psychopharmacology, neuroscience, and imaging technologies), the rise of population-based epidemiological research, and the creation of the National Institute of Mental Health.

It can indeed be argued that a source of disagreement between the various authors represented in this book relates to the question of whether or not a notion such as that of "context" (be it cultural, social or whatever) should be invoked to account for the topic under investigation. The answer to this question depends, in part, on what one means by the term "context." For instance, the term is often used to argue that in analyzing biomedical innovations one should look not only at the biomedical setting from which they emerged but also at their subsequent fate in relation to patients, medical insurance companies, the popular press, and so on. In spite of possible disagreements on how this is actually to be done, this interpretation of the "context" clause is not *per se* very controversial, for all can agree that a detailed ethnographic analysis of new medical technologies should include the extended network that is co-substantive with their definition. However, talk about context can also be interpreted to mean that a priori-defined cultural, social, economic and political factors should be included in the analysis of scientific and clinical work. Yet, whether scientific or clinical laboratories can be equated with some sort of subsystem contained in a larger social setting and open to outside cultural and social influences is an open issue. To think in this way, to mobilize this kind of "container metaphor" (Lakoff and Johnson 1980), is to engage in a profoundly asymmetrical endeavor, treating scientific and medical notions and practices as open to investigation while taking for granted sociological and anthropological understandings of society and culture. To the criticism that one should not treat scientific and clinical research as if they were taking place in a social and cultural void, it could be countered that the point is not about whether biomedical practices take place within or outside a sociocultural space but, rather, to ask which tools should be used to account for those very practices. Rather than using society to explain nature (or vice versa) one should investigate the co-production of nature and society.[8]

In this last respect, Hans-Jörg Rheinberger (1997: 37) espouses a clear-cut stance, when he claims that "[i]t is not, in the end, the scientific or the broader culture that determines "from outside" what it means to be a laboratory [. . .]. It is "inside" the laboratory that those master signifiers are generated and regenerated that ultimately gain the power of determining what it means to be a scientific – or a broader – culture." If this is so, one can indeed be led to argue, as Rheinberger does in the first chapter of the present collection, that the advent of genetic engineering and its application to medicine corresponds not

simply to a radical transformation of biomedical practices and representations, but also, more generally, to a collapse of ontological distinctions
between nature and society, one that will require, among other things, a
profound redefinition of the tasks of the social sciences. Paul Rabinow's
chapter contains a sharp criticism of Rheinberger's argument, and of
the germane argument by Latour (1993), that he characterizes as epochal and metaphysical. Rabinow urges us to desist from these kinds of
totalizing categories and to focus on a more restrained research strategy,
one intent on developing a series of limited concepts that will simultaneously avoid pseudo-entities such as "culture" and "science" and
allow for the naming of things that had previously to be left unnamed.

Technology and Human Subjects

The constitution and transformation of physical bodies and individual
identities through technological practices is a concern of several of the
anthropological contributors to this volume. It is at sites of practice,
particularly policy-making arenas and clinical settings, where most
attention has been paid to the way in which, following Foucault,
biopower is performed. Certain feminist anthropologists have taken up
the problem of the microphysics of power where Foucault left off and,
going beyond the original argument about subjugated knowledge and
the work of repression, have made the accounts and experiences of those
on whom technologies are practiced central to their investigations. In
science studies it was recognized that non-human actors have agency
and are not merely passive entities, they are part of the production of
knowledge and practice. Similarly, whereas earlier theorizing about
relationships of power, hierarchies and repression tended to constitute
those on whom power was enacted as passive recipients, in recent years
an emphasis on individual agency – including a range of responses to
new technologies, from a wholehearted embrace of them, to a pragmatic
acceptance or rejection, to an ironical distancing – has replaced the
former picture of a technological manipulation of subjects (Ginsberg
and Rapp 1995; Lock and Kaufert 1998). In part because the subjects
of technologies are themselves situated at intersections – of the medical
world, individual interest, and family obligations, to name a few – their
co-production of technological practice makes for an important part of
the analysis. To this it should be added that while the transition from
the embrace of medical technologies to a distancing has characterized
work in both the anthropology of medicine and in science studies,
several workers in the latter field (some represented in this book) have,
by now, opted for a different approach. Instead of aiming at a critical

sociology of medical technologies, one, that is, that provides implicit or explicit criticism of those technologies, these writers' goal is to produce a *sociology of criticism* – a symmetrical analysis of the resources mobilized by scientists, clinicians and lay people to assess and use those same technologies.[9]

When analyzing medical, as opposed to other forms of technologies, another site of agency must, of course, be kept in mind, namely that of the material body. In keeping with a commitment to an approach that acknowledges the co-production of nature and society, technologies of the body are not, therefore, conceptualized as things-in-themselves by the book's contributors. Medical technologies are independent neither of the agency of scientists and medical practitioners, nor of the individuals on whom the technologies are practiced. Further, medical practice cannot be conceived independently of the material body of the patients. Here, however, different approaches can be, once again, adopted. Some scholars maintain that while the body has indeed been neglected by historians and sociologists of medicine and has thus to be "put back in place," that body has to be conceived of as a material, ahistorical, biological entity in which cultural practices can be grounded, but that is not in itself cultural. Other scholars, on the opposite end of the spectrum, see the body as yet another socio-cultural or discursive construct. Yet other scholars, think that both alternatives have to be rejected and that this can effectively be done by looking at the practices through which bodies are performed.[10] It is at these complex intersections that the majority of the authors of this book have worked to reveal how we all live and work with the new medical technologies.

Rayna Rapp highlights the gap between epidemiological description, clinical services, and individual and family understandings of illness, and argues that technologies of diagnosis, therapies of intervention, and systems of support are all enacted and interpreted in this gap. However, her essay which focuses on Down syndrome, more than any other in this collection, is concerned with how families perceive and talk about this gap. Like Kaufert, Rapp is sensitive to the unstable, expansive area of expert knowledge. She shows how identities of families with Down syndrome children are "resculpted" as a result of their exposure to support groups and the medical world, akin to what Rabinow (1992) has termed as "biosociality." However, she argues throughout her essay for "doubled discourses," in which scientific discourse is contested from various domains of popular knowledge and is dispersed unevenly into the lives of those directly affected by this disorder.

Joseph Dumit also analyzes how new biomedical technologies are articulated with the production of new biosocial identities, but, in his case, by focusing on patients suffering from "new socio-medical disorders," i.e. ill-defined, overlapping syndromes such as Chronic Fatigue Syndrome and Attention Deficit Disorder. The existence of these disorders is highly contested (for instance by the companies that some patients hold responsible for the onset of their disease) and, in an interesting twist, while social constructivist arguments are used by corporate lawyers and company experts to deny the reality of the disorders, new biomedical technologies such as brain imaging are seen by patients as a major tool for validating their claims. The production of new nosological entities thus takes place in a virtual space governed by controversy and inhabited by the courts and the media (including the Internet) as well as by doctors and patients, and the resulting realities are temporally and locally contingent.

In her chapter, Patricia Kaufert discusses the creation of clinics for the screening of two "hidden" diseases – cervical and breast cancer. Following Foucault's lead, Kaufert understands the idea of screening for disease as reflecting a particular view of health and disease, one in which the body, in particular the female body, must be thought of in need of constant monitoring and surveillance. Kaufert contests the idea of a truth in numbers, and shows convincingly how interpretations by epidemiologists and radiologists are made on the basis of vastly different perceptions of the meanings of numbers. Similarly to Rapp's doubled discourse, Kaufert writes about "two conversations" that take place simultaneously, but "in different tones and languages." The first, about risk, cost-containment, survival times and so on, is rational. The second deals with emotion, faith, morality, fear and death. These two conversations can never be reconciled, and neither can one ever replace the other.

The chapter by Margaret Lock is concerned with the reconfiguration of the margins between culture and nature, in this instance life and death, as a result of intensive care technologies developed over the past thirty years. Her comparative ethnographic work in Japan and North America shows how in these two locations meanings attributed to brain-dead bodies are not the same, with significantly different outcomes for clinical practices, including the organ transplant enterprise in these two settings. Lock does not argue for a straightforward contrast between Japan and North America based on cultural difference, but presents a complex argument in which heterogeneity and disputes in both settings are recognized.

Veena Das traces the multiple genealogies – the set of practices – that result in the object of study for her essay, namely the transplant world in India. Das shows how the political representation of individuals is co-produced with scientific knowledge, and she gives emphasis to how international discourse, with its rhetoric of a "shortage of organs" is reinterpreted in the "local" setting of India. On the basis of ethnographic data from India, in which it is clear that structural violence is implicated in the unequal distribution of and access to organs, Das is able to generate a critique of a bioethics grounded in the ideas of autonomy and individual rights.

The chapters presented here are the product of a challenge to communicate successfully across disciplinary boundaries. The reader may judge whether or not the authors have risen to the occasion.

NOTES

The Cambridge conference took place under the aegis of the Committee on Culture, Health, and Human Development of the Social Sciences Research Council, New York. In particular we wish to thank the Committee Program Director, Frank Kessel PhD, for his unwavering support and personal contribution to the conference. We are also very grateful to Diane Colbert for carrying out the arrangements for the conference on our behalf. The SSRC also provided funds to support this endeavor, as did the Wenner Gren Foundation for Anthropological Research, New York.

1. See, e.g., Strauss 1993, esp. pp. 39–40 and 233.
2. On this topic, see Rheinberger's notion of "concatenation" in Rheinberger 1997: 21–23.
3. For a fascinating discussion of "increases in generality," a central topic of the "new" French sociology, see Boltanski and Thévenot 1991, and Boltanski 1990a, esp. Section III.
4. See, for instance, Barnes 1974 and Bloor 1976; see also Collins and Pinch 1982 as well as Law and Lodge 1984. By breaking the hegemony of US-based functionalist approaches over the sociology of science, the "strong program" effectively led to the establishment of the science studies field. For a stimulating analysis of ritualistic accounts of the demise of the "old" sociology of science and the rise of a "new" one, see Lynch 1993: chapters 2 and 3.
5. For early attempts to apply this approach to medicine, see Wright and Treacher 1982.
6. For those who appreciate Canguilhem's warnings against the "myth of precursors" in the history of science, it is particularly ironic to see Fleck labeled as a "precursor" of Kuhn; see Canguilhem 1968.
7. For a discussion of two possible readings of Kuhn's work, one that matches Barnes's reading and one that focuses on practice, see Rouse 1987: chapter 2.
8. For more on this issue see, for instance, the debate between, on the one side, Collins and Yearly and, on the other side, Callon and Latour in Pickering 1992.
9. On this issue see Boltanski 1990b.

10. These issues were the focus of a recent conference on "Theorizing Bodies in Medical Practices" held in September 1998 in Paris and organized by the Centre de Sociologie de l'Innovation (CSI) of the Ecole Nationale Supérieure des Mines and by The Netherlands Graduate School of Science, Technology and Modern Culture (WTMC).

REFERENCES

Ackerman, Robert 1987 *J. G. Frazer: His Life and Work*. Cambridge: Cambridge University Press.
Barnes, Barry 1974 *Scientific Knowledge and Sociological Theory*. London and Boston: Routledge and Kegan Paul.
   1982 *T. S. Kuhn and Social Science*. New York: Columbia University Press.
Berg, Marc and Annemarie Mol 1998 *Differences in Medicine. Unraveling Practices, Techniques and Bodies*. Durham and London: Duke University Press.
Bloor, David 1976 *Knowledge and Social Imagery*. London and Boston: Routledge and Kegan Paul.
Boltanski, Luc 1990a *L'amour et la justice comme compétences*. Paris: Métaillié.
   1990b "Sociologie critique et sociologie de la critique." *Politix* (3ème trimestre): 124–34.
Boltanski, Luc and L. Thévenot 1991 *De la justification: les économies de la grandeur*. Paris: Gallimard.
Canguilhem, Georges 1968 "L'objet de l'histoire des sciences." In *Études d'histoire et de philosophie des sciences*. Paris: Vrin.
Collins, Harry M. and Trevor Pinch 1982 *The Social Construction of Extraordinary Science*. London: Routledge and Kegan Paul.
Epstein, Steven 1996 *Impure Science: AIDS Activism and the Politics of Knowledge*. Berkeley: University of California.
Evans-Pritchard, E. E. 1937 *Witchcraft, Oracles and Magic Among the Azande*. Oxford: Clarendon Press.
Fleck, Ludwik 1979[1935] *Genesis and Development of a Scientific Fact*. Trans. Fred Bradley and Thaddeus J. Trenn. Chicago and London: University of Chicago Press.
Ginsberg, Faye and Rayna Rapp 1995 *Conceiving the New World Order: The Global Politics of Reproduction*. Berkeley: University of California Press.
Hacking, Ian 1992 "The Self-Vindication of the Laboratory Sciences." In A. Pickering (ed.), *Science as Practice and Culture*. Chicago: University of Chicago Press, pp. 26–64.
Lakoff, George and M. Johnson 1980 *Metaphors We Live By*. Chicago: University of Chicago Press.
Latour, Bruno 1993 [1991] *We Have Never Been Modern*. Trans. Catherine Porter. Cambridge, MA: Harvard University Press.
Law, John and Peter Lodge 1984 *Science for Social Scientists*. London: Macmillan.
Lock, Margaret and Patricia Kaufert 1998 *Pragmatic Women and Body Politics*. Cambridge: Cambridge University Press.
Lukes, Steven 1967 "Some Problems about Rationality." *Archives Européannes de Sociologie* 8: 247–64.

Lynch, Michael 1993 *Scientific Practice and Ordinary Action: Ethnomethodology and Social Studies of Science*. Cambridge: Cambridge University Press.

Pickering, Andrew (ed.), 1992 *Science as Practice and Culture*. Chicago: University of Chicago Press.

Rabinow, Paul 1992 "Artificiality and Enlightenment: From Sociobiology to Biosociality." In Jonathan Crary and Sanford Kwinter (eds.), *Incorporations*. New York: Zone (distrib: MIT Press), pp. 234–52.

Rheinberger, Hans-Jörg 1997 *Toward a History of Epistemic Things: Synthesizing Proteins in the Test Tube*. Palo Alto and London: Stanford University Press.

Rouse, Joseph 1987 *Knowledge and Power: Toward a Political Philosophy of Science*. Ithaca: Cornell University Press.

Sperber, Dan 1985 *On Anthropological Knowledge*. Cambridge: Cambridge University Press.

Strauss, A. L. 1993 *Continual Permutations of Action*. New York: Gruyter.

Wright, P. and A. Treacher (eds.) 1982 *The Problem of Medical Knowledge: Examining the Social Construction of Medicine*. Edinburgh: Edinburgh University Press.

Part I

Epochal transitions? Biomedicine and the
transformation of socionature

2 Beyond nature and culture: modes of reasoning in the age of molecular biology and medicine

Hans-Jörg Rheinberger

The argument

In this short chapter, I examine what I perceive as the historical relation between molecular biology, gene technology and medicine, and I touch on some aspects of its consequences in the context of the human genome project. I argue that the prevailing momentum of early molecular biology resided in creating the technical means of an extracellular representation of intracellular configurations. As such, its medical impact was not different from traditional biological chemistry. With the advent of recombinant DNA technologies, a radical change of perspective ensued. The momentum of gene technology is based on the prospects of an intracellular representation of extracellular projects – the potential of "rewriting" life. Its medical impact is virtually unlimited, although at present rather constrained. As a result, I question the very opposition between nature and culture. I argue that the "natural" and the "social" are no longer to be seen as ontologically different.

Introduction

Is there one culture, are there several different cultures of biomedicine? This conference seems to be based on the assumption of the latter. In the context of attempting an anthropology of knowledge, Yehuda Elkana stated almost two decades ago: "There is no general theory of culture or of a cultural system" (1981: 8). This is an apodictic statement, indeed; but it leaves room for crossing boundaries between scientific disciplines, systems of practices, and social contexts, just as molecular biology has overturned the boundaries of the traditional biological disciplines and their academic containment over the past decades. It allows me to follow the "molecularization" of biology with respect to some aspects of medicine, of medical care, and to the concept of health.

In his marvellous book The *Pasteurization of France* (1988[1984]),

Bruno Latour describes the rise of microbiology, its articulation with, and its takeover in the realm of medical practice, of urban sanitation, and of a first wave of biotechnology in *fin-de-siècle* France that quickly swept over Europe as a whole. The movement became tightly connected with the name of Louis Pasteur (and Robert Koch in Germany). Latour describes the process as an extended chain of translations: "At one end, France; at the other, those who in their laboratories make the microbes visible; in the middle, the hygienists who translate the data from the laboratories into the precepts of hygiene" (1988[1984]: 56). The possibility of the Pasteurian takeover of medicine was grounded in a "shared misunderstanding" (Latour 1988[1984]: 120). Applied microbiology promised the *prevention* of illness, not just cure, for the whole population. Once successfully disseminated, shared convictions, with their inherent simplicity, turn into misunderstandings. However, it is precisely such misunderstandings that constitute the vehicles for historically effective cultural movements.

Latour's structural description of the Pasteurian revolution comes surprisingly close to the translation chain which characterizes the current project of sequencing the human genome: at one end, the tens of thousands of fragments of the human chromosomes chopped up in pieces and kept in the refrigerators of the research laboratories; on the other, the competition of the biotechnology companies for leadership in molecular engineering; and in between, the hospitals, the health agencies, and the criminologists who convert the data of the laboratories into the precepts of a molecular medicine and a DNA-based recognition of health and treatment of illness. The possibility of the molecular takeover of medicine is grounded in another shared misunderstanding: healthy genes, not just cure, for the whole population. Whether this emerging new misunderstanding delivers a realistic picture of the causes and the distribution of diseases in contemporary Western societies is not a matter of discussion in this chapter. It is clear, however, that the prospect of "molecularizing" diseases and their possible cure will have a profound impact on what patients expect from medical help, and on a new generation of doctors' perception of illness. Its effects will by far transcend such major transformations in medical practice as the "Pasteurization" of Europe in the late nineteenth century, or the "antibiotization" of anti-microbial therapy beginning with the Second World War. At any rate, the identification of a mutated gene such as that thought to be responsible for Huntington's disease, on the upper arm of chromosome 4, and other comparable genes, have a good chance these years of covering the front pages of major newspapers. The Huntington disease gene took ten years to be identified. Although the search for such a gene started long before the genome project took shape, it was quickly perceived as one of the achievements of the project. This is the result of the recursive powers of such an endeavour.

Molecular Biology, Gene Technology, and Molecular Medicine

In 1949, the already world-famous, somewhat eccentric protein chemist and Nobel laureate Linus Pauling published an article in *Science*. In this article, he and his colleagues Itano, Singer and Wells from the California Institute of Technology in Pasadena traced back to an electrostatic charge difference in the oxygen-transporting molecule haemoglobin, what physicians had long since known under the phenomenological term of sickle cell anemia. Pauling accompanied this publication with the publicity-demanding, triumphant announcement that sickle cell anemia was a "molecular disease" (Pauling et al. 1949). The publication date of this article is often quoted as the birth date of "molecular medicine." Biomedicine promised to open its own, genuine atomic age.

A little less than fifty years later, at the time of this conference, the encompassing project of sequencing the whole human genome is well under way. Conceived around 1985 in the United States, this daunting, molecular genetic piece of big science has meanwhile been capillarized, has grown into a worldwide network, and has spawned additional genome sequencing projects. The whole effort has been budgeted to amount to no less than $3 billion. In view of the diversification of projects, and sources accordingly, that has already taken place, no one will any longer be able to count how much it will have cost in the end. The project itself has set in place a mechanism for dissemination and changing its own boundaries. To paraphrase Latour's characterization of the Pasteurian program, a century earlier, for fighting against microbial diseases: "It is not a question of ideas, theories, opinions. It is a question of ways and means" (Latour 1988[1984] 47). Like the Pasteurians, the molecular biologists and the project managers of the National Institutes of Health and the Department of Energy, who initiated the program of molecularizing human medicine, "placed [their] weak forces in . . . places where immense social movements showed passionate interest . . . [They] followed the demand that those forces were making, but imposed on them a way of formulating that demand to which only [they] possessed the answer, since it required [men] of the laboratory to understand its terms" (Latour 1988[1984] 71). Those molecular biologists engaged in human genetics attempt to precisely localize all human genes and to sequence the three billion or so building blocks of our genetic heritage in their entirety. One of the most outspoken advocates of the project(s), Nobel prize winner and co-discoverer of the DNA double helix, James Watson, justifies the venture with the following argument: "For the genetic dice will continue to inflict cruel fates on all too many individuals and their families who do not deserve this damnation. Decency demands that someone must rescue them from genetic hells." And he asks: "If we don't play God, who will?" (Watson 1995: 197). Who is "we"?

Between roughly 1940 and 1970, a new paradigm had been established in biology: molecular biology. In 1948, one of the founders of cybernetics, Norbert Wiener, in a truly visionary gesture, drew a résumé of the history of biology in modern times. The organism of the seventeenth and early eighteenth centuries, he said, was a mechanical automaton. The organism of the nineteenth century was a steam engine. The organism of the twentieth century, however, according to Wiener, had become a medium of communication and control, pervaded by the crucial concepts of message, noise, information and coding (1961[1948]: 62–9).

So far, historians of biology disagree whether the development of information theory and cybernetics in the 1940s had a direct influence on the take-off of the "New Biology" as advocated by Warren Weaver (Judson 1979; Kay, in press; Keller 1995). They agree, however, on the basic argument that with molecular biology, a paradigm shift has occurred that involves the notion of information. Indeed, this would be hard to deny, although there have been arguments to the contrary (Sarkar 1996). I find it safe to state that biologists and physicians engaged in basic medical research have started to view the organism under a new perspective. They have come to envision the fundamental processes of life as based on the storage, transmission, change, accumulation and expression of genetic information. According to this view, there is a genetic program entrenched in the punctuated sequence of the DNA building blocks of the chromosomes. The development of the organism as well as its overall metabolism is regulated by means of a differential retrieval of this genetically enshrined instruction, that is, its transposition into biological function. As a result of this process, the proteins (and some RNAs) govern, either as structural elements or as biocatalysts, that is, enzymes, the life phenomena of the cell and of whole organisms. The "central dogma" of molecular biology, explicitly formulated in 1958 by Francis Crick (1958), has pervaded all of contemporary biophysics, biochemistry, cell biology and genetics, and has provided it with a new super-slogan: DNA makes RNA, RNA makes protein. The material basis of the genes is DNA which duplicates with every cell division, a process called replication. RNA carries the genetic message gene by gene from the nucleus to the cytoplasm in a process called transcription. A very sophisticated molecular machinery with the ribosomes in its center is said to translate the sequential information of messenger RNA into molecular prescriptions that are realized through the three-dimensionally folded proteins in metabolism.

The basic insights into these molecular processes were gained in the years between 1953 and 1965. The work of Maurice Wilkins, Rosalind Franklin, Francis Crick and James Watson exposed the double-helical structure of DNA and immediately suggested a possible mechanism of gene duplication. Paul Zamecnik and Mahlon Hoagland, and Jacques Monod and François Jacob identified the two RNA-molecules that mediate between the genes (DNA) and the gene products (proteins), transfer RNA and messenger RNA, respectively. Monod and Jacob also provided a first model for gene regulation. Heinrich Matthaei and Marshall Nirenberg as well as Severo Ochoa and his co-workers clarified the relation between these two basic categories of biological macromolecules: the genetic code. (For detailed overviews see Judson 1979; Morange 1994.)

It is extremely compressed but probably fair to say that the essential epistemic achievements of this first phase in the history of molecular biology basically rested on two conditions which at the same time constituted its early drive. First, the transition of a small group of researchers to simple, biophysical, biochemical and genetic model systems; and second, the development – by far not all of them in the context of molecular biology! – of a series of biophysical, biochemical and genetic technologies. Examples of the former are bacteria, viruses and finally macromolecules. Examples of the latter are, just to mention a very few of them, X-ray crystallography, analytical and preparative ultracentrifugation, electron microscopy, radioactive tracing, more and more sophisticated sorts of chromatography and electrophoresis, as well as the experimental tools of phage and bacterial genetics. It goes without saying that these two series of events interacted and evolved in interplay by becoming combined.

Indeed, these techniques and their results were crucial for the coming into being of molecular biology. But despite much public praise and hope, they were of quite limited immediate influence on medicine and its practices. In many cases, the results, in the form of molecular representation they took on, simply did not lend themselves to therapeutical application (as in the case of sickle cell anemia). In other cases, they basically sanctioned a practice that was well under way and had developed without the direct impact of molecular biology, as in the case of antibiotics, which revolutionized antibacterial therapy in the late 1940's and early 1950's. In still other cases, molecular techniques expanded diagnostic potentials, but did not qualitatively change, much less revolutionize the possibilities of metabolic correction. Examples are nuclear medical screening and enzyme tests.

The advent of gene technology, genetic engineering or, as some prefer to say, applied molecular genetics, since the beginning of the 1970s has effected a decisive prospective change in the relation between molecular biology and medicine. Gene technology developed in three waves. The first was marked by the identification of restriction enzymes and the construction of recombinant plasmids at the beginning of the decade. The second was characterized through the development of novel DNA sequencing techniques towards the end of the 1970s. The third set the stage for the big genome projects around the middle of the 1980s and included pulsed-field electrophoresis, artificial chromosomes, partially automated DNA sequence analysis with fluorescent probes, automated DNA and RNA synthesis, and the polymerase chain reaction (PCR). Within a timespan of less than twenty years, molecular geneticists have learned not only to understand the language of the genes in principle, but to spell it. In other words, they have learned to read, to write, to copy and to edit that language in a goal-directed manner. These are, of course, metaphors. But today, there exist precise and powerful functional equivalents to each of these analogies of language and of writing, and they have neatly been installed in the form of special and more and more easily manipulable techniques. Those are the procedures of DNA sequencing (reading) and of DNA synthesis (writing), both automatized in recent years; DNA multiplication in the form, for example, of the polymerase chain reaction (copying); and the arsenal of operations resulting in changes in the molecular structure of the genes such as site-directed mutagenesis and refined restriction and ligation, deletion and inversion of bits and pieces of DNA (editing).

The emergence of these so-called "recombinant DNA technologies" has created a new situation, and with that, has led back to higher organisms. The central tools of recombinant DNA work – such as restricting, transcribing, replicating and ligating enzymes; plasmids, cosmids, artificial chromosomes, and other molecular transport systems – are not sophisticated analytical and electronic machinery. They are themselves macromolecules that work and perform in the wet environment of the cell. With gene technology, the central technical devices of molecular biological intervention have themselves become parts and indeed constituents of the metabolic activities with which, at the same time, they interfere. The scissors and needles by which the genetic information gets tailored and spliced are enzymes. The carriers by which it is transported into the cells are nucleic acid macromolecules. This kit of purified enzymes and molecules constitutes a "soft" technology that life itself has been evolving over a period of some three billion or even more years, according to the recent estimations of paleobiology. It is able to function and is adapted to operating within the proper confines and in the milieu of the intact living cell. With gene technology, informational molecules are constructed according to an extracellular project and are subsequently implanted into the intracellular environment. The organism itself transposes them, reproduces them, and "tests" their characteristics. With that, the organism as a whole advances to the status of a locus technicus – that is, to the status of a space of representation in which new genotypic and phenotypic patterns are becoming probed and articulated. This technique is of potentially unlimited medical impact. For the first time, it is on the level of *instruction* that metabolic processes are becoming susceptible to manipulation. Until that point was reached, medical intervention, even in its most intrusive physical, chemical and pharmacological forms, was restricted to the level of metabolic *performance*.

With the possibility of manipulating the genetic production program of an organism by its own, unmodified and modified components, the molecular biologist, as a molecular engineer, abandons the working paradigm of the classical biophysicist, biochemist or geneticist. He no longer constructs test tube conditions under which the molecules and reactions occurring in the organism are analyzed. Just the other way round: he constructs objects, that is, basically, instruction-carrying molecules which no longer need to pre-exist within the organism. In reproducing them, expressing them, and screening their effects, he uses the milieu of the cell as their proper technical embedding. The intact organism itself is turned into a laboratory. It is no longer the extracellular representation of intracellular processes, i.e., the "understanding" of life that matters, but rather the intracellular representation of an extracellular project, i.e., the deliberate "rewriting" of life. From an epistemic perspective, this procedure makes the practice of molecular biology, *qua* molecular engineering, substantially different from traditional intervention in the life sciences and in medicine. This intervention aims at *re-programming* metabolic actions, not just interfering with them. As Leroy Hood, one of the leading biotechnologists at Caltech, has put it: from now on biologists will work on models whose appropriateness will be "*tested in biological systems or living organisms*" themselves (1992: 162).

If we are to believe Donald Chambers from the University of Illinois

(Chicago), the editor of a recently published *Festschrift* on the occasion of the fortieth anniversary of the DNA double helix, the new biology that resulted from this crucial transformation has effected "dramatic advances in the biomedical sciences. Molecular medicine is not a vision for the future, but is at hand as our intrepid gene hunters identify genetic lesions of disease, develop new diagnostics, and achieve mechanistic understandings that will yield new, rational, molecular therapies" (1995: 413). In the same volume, Sir Walter Bodmer of the Imperial Cancer Research Fund in London prophesies that essentially all human genes, estimated to be in the order of 100,000, will be found, sequenced and localized on their respective chromosomes within the next forty, if not the next ten years. This knowledge, he conjectures, will be summarized in a "book of man" (1995: 423). Others, such as Walter Gilbert, Nobel laureate and Harvard professor, speak of a "vision of the grail" (1992: 83).

Let me just mention a few of Bodmer's examples that, not to count diagnostic procedures such as restriction fragment length polymorphism (RFLP), will be the outcome of "molecular medicine" within the next four decades: "corrective measures" for the carriers of the Huntington gene, Alzheimer's disease, and some 5,000 clinically diagnosed diseases with a genetic component; drugs and diets for the large risk group of people prone to suffer from heart diseases; preventive measures for populations with an elevated risk of genetically induced cancer; specific forms of immune suppression for patients suffering from genetically determined allergies, including hay fever and asthma; cures for specific deficiencies in behaviour or performance such as dyslexia for which a genetic basis is assumed; an effective vaccination against HIV; DNA-based cancer therapies as well as vaccines against certain forms of cancer. The list could be prolonged. In any case, Bodmer leaves no doubt that the practical medical benefit of the genome analysis projects for efficiently fighting diseases, for which there has been no cure so far, will be enormous and indeed unprecedented.

Moreover, Sir Walter Bodmer is of the opinion that this overall information on the human genome "will enable genetic analysis of essentially any human difference" (1995: 414). In view of this easy and gliding linguistic transition to a new genetic determinism, one might ask what at all, in the long run, might remain outside the realm of "molecular medicine." We are not hearing here the voices of isolated propagandists of a new eugenics, we are hearing the virtually unified voice of an international elite of the biomedical complex. None of these experts, to be sure, is supposed to plead for eugenically motivated measures on the level of the population. Since the end of the Second World War, medical genetics in the Western countries has increasingly become oriented towards the sick person, the individual that carries a potential genetic burden. It is oriented towards individual counselling and bound to respect personal decisions. But precisely here, the dilemma is located. Not only diseases are genetically inherited. Essentially normal, as well as very trivial, characteristics are also genetically inherited. What will then count as normal? Consequently, Bodmer asks himself: "Will alterations ever be offered? Will germline therapy ever be accepted?" (1995: 424). Just to take a very simple example: shall parents, in the future, have the right to decide what kind of eye colour their child will have? Bodmer is quite outspoken about the fact that the decision as to whether to allow such interventions "will become entirely a social and a political . . . rather than a scientific decision" (1995: 425). But if so, then we urgently need a serious discussion about the social and ethical dimensions of a molecular or, as Thomas Caskey from the National Institutes of Health puts it, "DNA-based medicine" (1992: 112). To leave such discussion about the scope and limit of genetic intervention and action to the biomedical experts alone will then be plainly counter-indicated.

Today already, we are witnessing a global, irreversible transformation of living beings, animals and plants, towards deliberately engineered beings. Future natural evolution will appear as insignificant in this perspective. The usual objection at this point, especially from scientists, is that the adoption of the viewpoint of such a radical break produced by molecular genetics is not justified. After all, it is said, evolution itself has invented and practiced the means of horizontal gene transfer, and the cultivation and breeding of plants and animals by the enhancement of mechanisms of genetic change goes back to the Neolithic civilizations. I disagree with this view of smooth transition. To this argument, I would like to oppose a quotation of David Jackson, a former student of James Watson at Harvard and Paul Berg at Stanford, who chose a career in industry and became an investigator of the American Pharma Trust DuPont Merck:

I would argue that the ability to read, to write, and edit DNA is functionally unprecedented in human history. All we have ever been able to do before is to select among the various combinations of genes that the mechanisms of genetics have presented to us. And, while we have developed very powerful and very sophisticated selection procedures, selecting from among a set of alternatives over which one has almost no control is fundamentally different from being able to write and edit one's own text. (Jackson 1995: 364)

That is, from the point of view of the practitioner, what molecular biology and medicine enables us to do. Who is "us"?

Writing and reading, as forms of calculation, instruction and legislation, have profoundly shaped the social body and political power structure of Western societies from their pre-Greek inception in Mesopotamia through the Gutenberg galaxy of the Renaissance and the expansion of printing during the Industrial Revolution to the microchip industry of today, with DNA-chips on the horizon. What is new about molecular biological writing is that we now gain access to the texture, and hence the calculation, instruction and legislation of the human individual's organic existence, that is to a script which until now it has been the privilege of evolution to write, to rewrite and to alter. What Darwin called "methodical", or "artificial selection" has barely scratched the surface of this script within the last 10,000 years of human evolution. For artificial selection, in a way, itself still was nothing more than a specific human mode of natural evolution. This has now gone and with it, natural evolution will become marginal. Molecular biology will arrive at inventing the biological future. Once more Jackson: "The ability to write and edit DNA is the basis for a synthetic and a creative capability in biology that has not previously existed" (1995: 364). Toward the end of this millennium, it has moved a big step towards the vision of Robert Sinsheimer some twenty years ago, at the dawn of recombinant DNA technology: "For the first time in all time, a living creature understands its origin and can undertake to design its future" (Sinsheimer 1969).

Conclusion: Beyond Nature and Culture

The more molecular biology has blurred the contours of what genes might be on a molecular level (Fischer 1995), "genes for such-and-such," as public icons, have become more abundant than ever. What is at stake in the current public discourse of molecular biology, as Evelyn Fox Keller rightly observed, is a profound "transfiguration" of the long-standing question of "genetic determinism" (Keller 1992: 288). An optimistic version of this observation would be that the quest after a "genetic analysis of essentially any human difference" will finally result in an inflation of the argument from genetics. In view of what has been said above, it can at least be stated that the traditional dichotomy between "nature" and "nurture," between "biology" and "culture," is about to collapse. One of the leading narratives of Enlightenment philosophy in general and of the modern sciences in particular has been to conceive of the development of human society as liberating (wo)mankind from the constraints of nature. It has been trying to draw a clear distinction between natural history on the one hand, and social history as superseding and replacing the former, on the other hand. It is intriguing to argue that molecular biology, as one of the results of this process, definitely subverts the perception of history from which it originated. It makes us realize that the result of its scientific conquest is not to supersede, but to change our natural history, that the very essence of our being social is not to supersede, but to alter our natural, that is, in the present context, our genetic condition. We come to realize that the *natural* condition of our genetic makeup might turn into a *social* construct, with the result that the distinction between the "natural" and the "social" no longer makes good sense. We could say as well that the future *social* conditions of man will become based on *natural* constructs. The "natural" and the "social" can no longer be perceived as ontologically different. They are no longer useful concepts to describe what is going on at the frontiers of the present "culture of biomedicine." We become aware that we live in a world of hybrids for the characterization of which we run short of categories. As Latour says, in claiming that we have never been modern – at least not in the sense of successfully separating culture from nature: "Instead of always being explained by a mixture of the two "pure" transcendences, the activity of nature/society making becomes the *source* from which societies and natures originate" (Latour 1992: 282).

NOTES

This paper makes use of two earlier articles:
Rheinberger, Hans-Jörg 1995 "Beyond Nature and Culture: A Note on Medicine in the Age of Molecular Biology." *Science in Context* 8(1): 249–63.

1996 "Molekulare Medizin als Paradigma? Gentechnologie im Blick von Wissenschaftstheorie und medizinischer Ethik." In Heinz Schott (ed.), *Meilensteine der Medizin*. Dortmund: Harenberg Verlag, pp. 555–61.

REFERENCES

Bodmer, Walter 1995 "Where Will Genome Analysis Lead Us Forty Years On?" In Donald A. Chambers (ed.), *DNA: The Double Helix, Perspective and Prospective at Forty Years*. New York: New York Academy of Sciences, pp. 414–26.
Caskey, Thomas C. 1992 "DNA-Based Medicine: Prevention and Therapy." In Daniel J. Kevles and Leroy Hood (eds.), *The Code of Codes*. Cambridge, MA: Harvard University Press, pp. 112–35.
Chambers, Donald A. 1995 "The Double Helix: Prospective. Introduction." In Donald A. Chambers (ed.), *DNA: The Double Helix, Perspective and Prospective at Forty Years*. New York: New York Academy of Sciences, p. 43.
Crick, Francis H. C. 1958 "On Protein Synthesis." *Symposia of the Society for Experimental Biology* (London) 12: 138–63.
Elkana, Yehuda 1981 "A Programmatic Attempt at an Anthropology of

Knowledge." In Everett Mendelsohn and Yehuda Elkana (eds.), *Sciences and Cultures: Anthropological and Historical Studies of the Sciences*. Dordrecht and Boston: Reidel, pp. 1–76.

Fischer, Ernst Peter 1995 " 'How Many Genes has a Human Being?' The Analytical Limits of a Complex Concept." In Ernst Peter Fischer and Sigmar Klose (eds.), *The Human Genome*. München: Piper, pp. 223–56.

Gilbert, Walter 1992 "A Vision of the Grail." In Daniel J. Kevles and Leroy Hood (eds.), *The Code of Codes*. Cambridge, MA: Harvard University Press, pp 83–97.

Hood, Leroy 1992 "Biology and Medicine in the Twenty-First Century." In Daniel J. Kevles and Leroy Hood (eds.), *The Code of Codes*. Cambridge, MA: Harvard University Press, pp. 136–63.

Jackson, David A. 1995 "DNA: Template for an Economic Revolution". In Donald A. Chambers (ed.), *DNA: The Double Helix, Perspective and Prospective at Forty Years*. New York: New York Academy of Sciences, pp. 356–65.

Judson, Horace F. 1979 *The Eighth Day of Creation: Makers of the Revolution in Biology*. New York: Simon and Schuster.

Kay, Lily E. (forthcoming) *Who Wrote the Book of Life?* Stanford: Stanford University Press.

Keller, Evelyn Fox 1992 "Nature, Nurture, and the Human Genome Project." In Daniel J. Kevles and Leroy Hood (eds.), *The Code of Codes*. Cambridge, MA: Harvard University Press, pp. 281–99.

1995 *Refiguring Life. Metaphors of Twentieth-Century Biology*. New York: Columbia University Press.

Latour, Bruno 1988[1984] *The Pasteurization of France*. Trans. Alan Sheridan and John Law Cambridge, MA: Harvard University Press.

1992 "One More Turn After the Social Turn." In Ernan McMullin (ed.), *The Social Dimensions of Science*. Notre Dame: University of Notre Dame Press, pp. 272–92.

Morange, Michel 1994 *Histoire de la biologie moléculaire*. Paris: Editions la Découverte.

Pauling, Linus C., A. Harvey Itano, S. J. Singer and Ibert C. Wells 1949 "Sickle-Cell Anaemia, A Molecular Disease." *Science* 110: 543–8.

Sarkar, Sahotra 1996 "Biological Information: A Sceptical Look at Some Central Dogmas of Molecular Biology." In Sahotra Sarkar (ed.), *The Philosophy and History of Molecular Biology: New Perspectives*. Dordrecht: Kluwer Academic Publishers, pp. 187–231.

Sinsheimer, Robert 1969 "The Prospect of Genetic Change." *Engineering and Science* 32: 8–13.

Watson, James 1995 "Values from a Chicago Upbringing." In Donald A. Chambers (ed.), *DNA: The Double Helix, Perspective and Prospective at Forty Years*. New York: New York Academy of Sciences, pp. 194–7.

Wiener, Norbert 1961[1948] *Cybernetics, or Control and Communication in the Animal and the Machine*. New York: M.I.T. Press and John Wiley & Sons.

3   Epochs, presents, events

Paul Rabinow

Epochs

Ethnographically, it is a distinctive fact that the field of the social studies of science is peopled by first-rate practitioners. These practitioners are frequently solicited to take meta-positions on the state of our present age and/or on the nature of things. Today, characteristically, these practitioners are responsive to such solicitations. This response is not so surprising when one considers the fact that the field arose in part to modify previous understandings of science as a rather atemporal, disembodied and theory-driven practice. Science studies in its plural manifestations has developed a dense and rich set of methods to study claims to knowledge, to analyze their embeddedness in fields of power and discourse, and to diagnose current pathologies of understanding (of nature, society and the self). There is but a small step to be taken from formulating a diagnosis of the state of the present to proposing a therapeutics. To devote oneself to the enterprise of studying the producers of the most valued forms of knowledge in our contemporary world places one in a position to pose questions about the status of all knowledge. In the light of this state of affairs the question I want to explore here is: what to make of a disjunction between the successful conceptual ground-clearing as well as often exquisite case studies that the field has contributed and some of the larger categorical meditations its leading practitioners put forward? What is at stake is an exploration of what the most encompassing analytic categories should be. Epochs? Cultures? Civilizations? Events? In order to reflect on that issue, I take up two examples of analysts who have both forged important conceptual tools for understanding scientists in action as well as taken a well articulated stance on these more encompassing issues.

Let us begin with a conceptual discussion, one involving ideas, theories and opinions. Hans-Jörg Rheinberger, in his article "Beyond Nature and Culture: A Note on Medicine in the Age of Molecular Biology," identifies and conceptualizes a recent crossing of a threshold in the biosciences. He characterizes the older period, the one being left behind, as follows:

Classical biophysical, biochemical, and genetic techniques can all be seen as aiming at the construction of an experimental environment in which it is possible to replace the milieu of the living cell in such a way that, starting with "model" organisms, cellular structures and/or metabolic processes can be isolated and analyzed. (Rheinberger 1995: 251)

The goal of such "classical" scientific practice is "the extracellular representation of intracellular configurations" (Rheinberger 1995: 251). In this classical frame, organisms and their parts are things in the world; science, using appropriate means, represents them in conventionalized and disciplined forms. The things of the world and the practices used to analyze and represent them are ontologically separate but epistemologically congruent.

Across the Rheinberger threshold lies a different relationship between the living being, the milieu in which it exists, and the scientific project and practices that engage it. "With gene technology," Rheinberger argues in this volume, "the central technical devices of molecular biological intervention have themselves become parts and indeed constituents of the metabolic activities with which, at the same time, they interfere. . . For the first time, it is on the level of *instruction* that metabolic processes are becoming susceptible to manipulation" (p. 25). First remark, Rheinberger characterizes the transition in temporal, even epochal terms: the life sciences passed from a historical period in which the work of modeling adequate representations of life's functions changed into one in which the project became one of intervening in natural processes at the level of basic informational codes. It is consistent with this interpretation to claim that the science of living beings has undergone a distinctive inflection from molecular biology (in the 1930s) to biotechnology (circa 1980). Second remark, this epochal transformation may well extend beyond the life sciences; this transformation is identical or homologous with transformations occurring in other domains such as social relations. One could recast Rheinberger's schema by saying that an epochal threshold has been crossed once the constituent (functional) elements of living beings are themselves taken up as technical things to be treated technologically.

Heidegger (1977a, 1977b) identified a similar epochal transformation from "The Age of World View" in which knowing and gazing subjects stand outside of and in front of a world they represent, to "The Question Concerning Technology," where Heidegger posits that our understanding of being has moved from this representational frame of subject and objects to a thoroughly "technological" understanding of being, one that takes nature (all things, both human and non) as a "standing reserve" of resources waiting to be put to use. The things of the world in this understanding of being include subjects as well as objects. Furthermore, Heidegger underscores that, "the essence of technology is not technological." Rather, the essence is a clearing or space in which things appear as "standing reserve." For Heidegger epochs are different and sequential understandings of being within a general history of metaphysics.

Rheinberger basically seems to follow Heidegger in claiming we have had two qualitatively different clearings in which practices have emerged producing two different types of subjects and two different types of objects and two different types of relations between subjects and objects. If, in the first instance, life scientists sought to fabricate *mimetic* models of nature, in the second, the representation of nature is secondary to an intervention using (recontextualized or reconverted or customized) natural materials to serve our purposes. The units to be worked on (and with) did not need to have pre-existed *per se* within the organism as functional units; the requirement is only that they be compatible with the functioning within the organism now understood as an assembled milieu. For example, the polymerase chain reaction (PCR) takes certain qualities of polymerases (enzymes essential to the reduplication of DNA) and turns those potentialities to other ends thereby modifying the qualities themselves. Potentialities are unhinged from the entities and sites in which and for which they had evolved; they are put to work in the service of what Rheinberger calls the "intracellular representation of extracellular projects" (p. 19). However, this phrasing is ambiguous as clearly all previous scientific understanding of living beings was carried out on the basis of an extracellular project.

Rheinberger presents what appear to be two mutually incompatible conclusions. First, he approvingly quotes Bruno Latour's assertion that understanding science "is not a question of ideas, theories, opinions. It is a question of ways and means" (Latour 1988[1984]: 47 in Rheinberger 1995: 253). Rheinberger had indicated a change in telos from representation to intervention; such a change appears to involve ideas, theories and opinions as well as ways and means. However, there does exist at least one consistent answer to the question "ways and means to what?" that escapes this seeming contradiction. That answer is "ways and means to ways and means" – *techne* as its own goal, mastery for its own sake, technology for the sake of more technology. It follows that leading practitioners of the social studies of science, while claiming to be offering a comprehensive understanding of things that escape from the previous metaphysical interpretation of science as epistemologically adequate knowledge, have escaped this metaphysics only by embracing and embodying a technological understanding of being. Rheinberger, following Heidegger and Derrida, knows he is doing this but seeks to make the most of it. Latour does not seem to take it into account and within the framework of network builders and resource maximizers, it is not obvious that the conceptual means of doing so are available.[1] Consequently it is perfectly consistent that Latour does not employ epochs; he has universalized the present understanding of being. In his ontology all things (human and non) have always already been doing the same thing, being is and always has been a strategic network of ways and means. Latour writes in *We Have Never Been Modern*:

All nature-cultures are similar in that they simultaneously construct humans, divinities and nonhumans . . . If there is one thing we all do, it is surely that we construct both our human collectivities and the nonhumans that surround them . . . The collectivities are all similar, except for their size . . . there are indeed differences but they are differences in size. (Latour 1993[1991]: 107–9)

Today we have a handle on this metaphysics and can mobilize happily ever after. History, which had never really begun, has now come to a true end. Or it will once enough actants have been mobilized (and immobilized) in this new (old) (atemporal) cause.

However, "epoch," understood as one of a series of distinctive "historical" periods, is a contemporary idea, integral to "The Age of the World Picture." Hans Blumenberg, in *The Legitimacy of the Modern Age* (1983[1966]), identifies epochal self-understanding as one of the linchpins of modern self-consciousness. He demonstrates that it was roughly at the time of Napoleon that the concept of epoch underwent a reversal from a term that designates an event in the present to one which designates an extended period of time of which the event is only an indicator. The etymology of the word indicates its primary meaning as punctuate. Blumenberg writes:

The Greek word "epoche" signifies a pause [*Innehalten*] in a movement as well as the point at which a halt is made. For ancient Skepticism, this root meaning gave rise to the application that commanded restraint in the movement of cognition and judgment . . . For the technical language of astronomy, the epoche was a special point at which to observe a heavenly body, its transit through its zenith or its greatest proximity to or distance from another star. (Blumenberg 1983[1966] #28: 460)

This punctuate, positional view began to give way in Western philosophical self-understanding in the period following the French Revolution to historical epochs understood as complex unities, states, configurations. For Goethe, Napoleon revealed the end of one epoch and the dawning of another. Blumenberg argues that the concept is an unstable and basically untenable one: eventually one must make an arbitrary choice between the real or nominalistic characteristics of the criteria chosen to pick out and define these periods of time. He argues that the realist's decision to choose definite starting points always leads to irresolvable problems. Detailed historical examination dissolves the sharp breaks revealing precursors and continuities. Blumenberg is a partisan of the older sense of epoch. "It is not history but this contemplator of history who halts at a resting place so as to survey what happens before and after" (1983 [1966] #28: 478). A consistent nominalist would likely agree with Blumenberg that "Man does indeed make history, but he does not make epochs" (1983[1966]: 478). One might modify this claim by saying we make and are made by events and forms.

So let us desist from Latour's metaphysics by accepting that Rheinberger's claim is a standpoint, a punctuate halt and temporary stocktaking: ways and means in molecular biology have been changing rapidly in the last two decades, accelerating and often making possible a space of experiments not previously available. But, of course, why one did these experiments or developed those techniques, or posed one set of questions rather than others, are interrelated phenomena. In molecular biology in recent decades, one distinctive event has been the rapid transformation of concepts into objects into technologies into experimental systems into concepts and all the permutations thereof. *Quidity*: What is a way? and What is a mean? are constantly at issue and can't fruitfully be determined a priori by dicta about the omnipresence of ways and means.

Intervention: Experiments

In that spirit, we can ourselves take stock of Rheinberger's second conclusion. "With DNA technology, molecular biology has turned, in less than twenty years, from a mode of discovery into a praxis of invention" (Rheinberger 1995: 256). We encounter here another strong epochal claim. Taken as such, it runs into the problem that Blumenberg argued all realist epochal claims must encounter. The project of an effective mode of intervention into living matter – defiantly refusing a telos of conceptual guidance – is significantly more than twenty years old. Philip Pauly in *Controlling Life: Jacques Loeb and the Engineering Ideal in Biology* (1987) documents how Loeb, a friend and colleague of John Dewey, had striven for a mode of approaching living beings that might be called "mechanical" (or perhaps "disciplinary") intervention. Beginning in the early 1880s, disdaining any craftsman-like pieties towards nature's pre-existing and telic forms and functions, Loeb sought to redefine biology as a question of control. In so doing, he recast the object, the mode of action and the acting subject. "Experimentation," Pauly writes, "gained significance beyond its ordinary function of providing determinate answers to definite problems within a hypothetical-deductive schema. The activity of experimentation took on value in itself, and experiments became demonstrations of the manipulative power of biologists" (Pauly 1987: 5). Loeb's project was to find ways and means to activate nature's triggers and levers. He conceived of experimentation as a type of disciplinary technology.

Loeb represented himself as an unsentimental and courageous purifier, a modernizer. To advance, biology had to overcome (even to obliterate) older, obfuscating distinctions in order to advance down the road to transforming living matter into the kind of object upon which men could attain "the achievements of the technology of inanimate nature" (Pauly 1987: 199). Foremost among these conceptual obstacles was the distinction between the natural and the pathological. Militantly refusing this hierarchy, an engineering approach to biology took all products to be of potentially equal interest. Older normative and metaphysical ideas of the primacy of understanding, of the organism as a whole, etc. would yield, Loeb wagered, to the primacy of ways and means. "The control of a phenomenon was the explanation of it" (Pauly 1987: 116). Hence a new normative and metaphysical order, fully modernist in its utopianism, its search for new beginnings, its discursive self-purification, its triumphalism over history (i.e., the evolutionary past of specific organisms).

Among the consequences of a project of biology practiced as engineering, Pauly notes

that nature was fading away. As biologists' power over organisms increased, their experience with them as "natural" objects declined. And as the extent of possible manipulation and construction expanded, the original organization and normal processes of organisms no longer seemed scientifically privileged; nature was merely one state among an indefinite number of possibilities, and a state that could be scientifically boring. This transformation was not the result of a "mechanistic" view of life – something that could be defined, discussed, and proven correct or not; rather, it was a generalization from biologists' practice as they saw the extent of the artificialization taking place in laboratories. Nature was disappearing, not as the result of argument, but through trivialization; not through disproof, but displacement. The natural became merely one among many results of the activity of biological invention. (Pauly 1987: 116)

Pauly's claim is somewhat too broad. For example, this period was simultaneously one of great exaltation of nature as wilderness, in the growth of the national parks system in the US, not yet Disneyworlds, the sublime antedated the virtual. Hence it is more precise to say that Loeb was part of a transformation of one set of understandings of nature and a corresponding set of representations in a specific domain of disciplinary practice. That practice may have been cast as overcoming theory or metaphysics but that self-representation was a project. It never became a fully embodied practice. Loeb's experiments were unsuccessful and did not produce long-lasting insights, techniques or experimental systems. Seen from one standpoint in the present, Loeb's project can be taken up as a moment in "the engineering ideal in biology," as long as we insist that what we mean by "engineering" and "biology" have changed over the course of the last century and that "ideals" are normative and internal to the constitution of a practice. Seen from another standpoint in the present, Loeb's work was a relatively minor event. Relative, that is, not to changing world-views or epochs but to other events.

Presents

It is hard to resist the demand that seems, hydra-like, to be omnipresent today to provide a world-view: scientists do it (usually after hours or after their active scientific life has wound down), pseudo-scientific fields are founded by propagating world-views (evolutionary morality), science journalists do it from time to time, and many of the leaders of those who study the producers of scientific knowledge are doing it as well, today. What does the world look like these days to producers of world-views? Let me in the briefest and most schematic of terms look at how Latour and Rheinberger are viewing these days. To that end, Michel Foucault's (1984) presentation of Immanual Kant's "What is Enlightenment?" provides some helpful distinctions. In November 1784, Kant was one of a series of thinkers asked by a German newspaper to share their views on the topic of Enlightenment. Kant cast his answer in terms of the attitude one might adopt towards the present, the present as a possible exit point towards maturity. Foucault, in passing, provided a typology of other stances previously adopted towards the present as a philosophic category. The typology is not very important *per se* but the question is a good one.

In addition to Kant and Foucault's attention to the present, there is a further set of distinctions that I find consistently heuristic. Norbert Elias in his famous essay that opens *The Civilizing Process* (1978), draws a distinction between civilization and culture and identifies the former with a dominant strand of Enlightenment thought in France and the latter in Germany. "Civilization," Elias writes, "refers to a process or at least the result of a process. It refers to something which is constantly in motion, constantly moving forward ... French writers desire to improve, modify, adapt. The French imply that the false civilization ought to be replaced by a genuine one" (1978: 5, 40). To this processural and reformist current whose drive is to encompass all aspects of society, Elias contrasts an ideal type of the "German concept of *Kultur* [that] refers to human products that are there like flowers of the field. To works of art, books, religious or philosophical systems, in which the individuality of a people expresses itself. The concept of *Kultur* delimits" (1978: 5). It delimits the important from the unimportant, it demarcates and values the truly special things in a base world. Elias quotes Kant's 1784 *Ideas on a Universal History from the Point of View of a Citizen of the World* where he wrote of his contemporaries: "The idea of morality is a part of culture. But the application of this idea, which results only in the similitude of morality in the love of honor and in outward decency, amounts only to civilizing" (Kant 1784 in Elias 1978: 8). The opposite of such false civilizing airs, to these Protestant German bourgeois, was culture. Elias observes that the German *aufklärer*, as opposed to their French equivalents, were far removed from political activity, typically located, as was Kant, in provincial cities. They thought abstractly about politics and tentatively about nations and their missions, focusing more on subjects and universals. Their legitimization, Elias concludes, "consists primarily in intellectual, scientific, or artistic *accomplishments*" (Elias 1978: 4). The civilizing process versus cultural accomplishments provides a helpful commonplace. Not coincidentally, the two thinkers under discussion here, Latour and Rheinberger, are French and German. Elias's contrast helps to situate their work not to explain it – after all, Blumenberg and Elias were Germans and Foucault, French and I am using their work to destabilize these categories.

A New Constitution: Bruno Latour

Foucault identifies one stance towards the present as follows: "The present may be represented as belonging to a certain era of the world, distinct from the others through some inherent characteristics, or separated from the others by some dramatic event" (1984: 33–4). The example Foucault gives is that of Plato's *Statesman* in which the interlocutors recognize that the world is in a period of backward turning with all the negative consequences that implies. There is a common destiny manifesting itself. The task of the philosopher is to identify the current state of the world and to propose action based upon that understanding of how things are and where they are going. Bruno Latour ends his major philosophic work, *We Have Never Been Modern*, by asking

Is it too little simply to ratify in public what is already happening? Should we not strive for more glamorous and more revolutionary programmes of action, rather than underlining what is already dimly discernible in the shared practices of scientists, politicians, consumers, industrialists and citizens when they engage in the numerous sociotechnological controversies we read about daily in our newspapers?... We scarcely have much choice. If we do not change the common dwelling, we shall not absorb in it the other cultures that we can no longer dominate, and we shall be forever incapable of accommodating in it the environment we no longer control. Neither Nature nor the Others will become modern. It is up to us to change our ways of changing. (Latour 1993[1991]: 145)

And so it is today, in the present, with what Plato referred to (and we can imagine Latour endorsing even though in almost all other respects he is not a Platonist) the herd of free bipeds.

For Latour, we have, for some time now, already crossed over into a certain state of things but we have been in a condition of mis-recognition towards it. Overcoming the mis-recognition of the natives, their *illusio* in Pierre Bourdieu's terms (1982), making the break with common sense, is the hallmark epistemological *rite de passage* for French thinkers, their guarantee that they are doing science – even when they are deconstructing the category. Latour's project is to show us where and how we have erred, so that we can correct our course, put ourselves in harmony with the way things really are (and have been). If we follow Latour in making this fundamental break, we will understand the workings of heaven and earth, we will cease our futile bickering, we will be in a position to write and enact, in statesmanlike fashion, the best Constitution for the world. Then, and only then, seeming contradictions will be overcome, theory will be reconciled with practice, Nature with Culture, Science with Society. False consciousness will drop away, true practice will be unfettered and a more just situation will unfold. Once the correct understanding is taken up, then the achievement of a common destiny will become possible, a new era will be with us and, correctly assessing it, we would recognize ourselves as belonging to it. In *We Have Never Been Modern*, Latour writes:

In order to sketch in the nonmodern Constitution, it suffices to take into account what the modern Constitution left out, and to sort out the guarantees we wish to keep... Every concept, every institution, every practice that inter-feres with the continuous deployment of collectives and their experimentation with hybrids will be deemed dangerous, harmful and we might as well say it – immoral. (Latour 1993[1991]: 139)

And "It is time, perhaps, to speak of democracy again, but of a democracy extended to things themselves" (Latour 1993[1991]: 142). Plato's visit to Syracuse was rather disappointing, will Latour's voyage to America achieve better results? Will the new Constitutional Convention and its Committee of Enlightenment draw together all things in motion? Will Latour be the Lucretius of global democracy? A viril Gaia? Will we see Committees of Public Virtue extended to all things, human and not? Will civilization reign? Are we on the edge of a "dramatic event"?

To the Epistemic Things: Hans-Jörg Rheinberger

Foucault characterizes another stance towards the present as follows: "The present may be interrogated in an attempt to decipher in it heralding signs" (Foucault 1984: 33). The name Foucault provides as an exemplar of this position is St. Augustine. The examination of the self, its practices and conscience, opens a path towards the greater understanding of the true path to knowledge of the self, of the meaning of the world's signs, of the telos of examination. Hans-Jörg Rheinberger, in his astute and fashionable book *Toward a History of Epistemic Things: Synthesizing Proteins in the Test Tube* (1997), takes up a position towards the present similar to that of Heidegger's "The Question Concerning Technology," updated by Derrida's theorization of writing. Rheinberger states:

My aim is to emphasize the dynamics of research as a process of the emergence of epistemic things. Such an endeavor involves unfathoming the basic question of how novel objects come into existence and are shaped in the empirical sciences. The consequences of such a shift of perspective from the actors' minds and interests to their objects of manipulation and desire lead us toward a history of epistemic things. . . Stated simply, we deal here with an economy of epistemic displacement, such that everything intended as a mere substitution or addition within the confines of a system will reconfigure that very system. (Rheinberger 1997: 1, 4)

In his epilogue, Rheinberger concludes:

Our modern world, with all its postmodern amoeboid protrusions, is shaped and dominated by a plexus of rhizomic technical systems. We rightly speak therefore of a technological civilization. It is not the sciences that have been the founding forces of modern technology. Just the opposite: it is a technological form of life that gave that particular epistemic activity we call science its historical impact and its quasi-irresistible drive. In the last instance, scientific systems derive their importance, their dignity, and their valuation from that superspace. (Rheinberger 1997: 228)

We live in a technological civilization. Rheinberger answers the question concerning technology, not like Heidegger with a patient waiting for a new god to appear, but with a certain excitement and respect for the special practices and products of the technological form of life.

It is striking that Rheinberger employs the Kantian word "dignity," distinguishing it, as he should, from "importance" and "valuation." Rheinberger, however, along with most practitioners of science studies, is a post-humanist, and therefore it is not too surprising that he departs from the neo-Kantian tradition in identifying the subject to which these qualities are attributed, not a transcendental subject but certain practices in the Superspace. It seems legitimate to draw the conclusion that this Superspace is closely related to Heidegger's clearing, *lichtung*, the space of illumination in which worlds appear. Today, the present is a space of signs, traces and writing. Different epistemic objects are made and circulate, fractally, perhaps. They compose, and are composed by, a form of life, in their molten and moving difference. We are called to interrogate ourselves as to how things are; the answers appear only in the Superspace. This imperative searching and the possible answers it produces are constrained both for protein chemists and for (post)-semioticians, whose narratives alternate chapters in Rheinberger's text. Reconfigurations are never innocent and never quite what they seem to be. Our present is presently that form of being, that deferral and that quasi-irresistible drive. Knowing this, we are freed from (previous) metaphysics as much as one can be.

Hesitations

Today, there are demands to make our knowledge do things, important things, just as there are demands to name the true significance of our age. I am uneasy about Latour's eagerness to be the New Statesman, in general. More specifically, his Constitution is metaphysical in a double sense. (1) Everyone else in the last two centuries was wrong about nature, society and politics. Latour repeats the ultimate modern move, to bring forth a new and better Leviathan. (2) Unlike Hobbes, Latour claims to base that new order on true knowledge, his knowledge that finally reveals the ultimate status of all that is and has ever been. Modern to the hilt, Latour claims no ancestors, all thinkers who preceded him were in error. With this claim, Latour joins a distinguished group of modern men who claim to have thought themselves into Truth. Like Kant or Husserl or Descartes or Comte or Saint-Simon, Latour has found the truth and has convinced himself on the basis of his own demonstrations that he can see how truth will assure that future forms of life can proceed on a sure basis to an improved future. Surely, to be blunt, there is something pathetic about claiming actor-network-theory as the foundational knowledge for (yet another) new totalizing regime of power and knowledge. Latour's stance, I observe, takes its place in a long line of French civilizing projects, aptly characterized by Hans Blumenberg as sharing a "missionary and didactic pathos" (1983 [1966]: 10). The pathos arises when the world fails to see, to heed, to correspond, or even ultimately to appreciate the civilization on offer.

How can one not be hesitant over epochally diagnostic claims about the ultimate distinctiveness – dignity – of our civilization? Rheinberger has written a highly original, finely documented, and thoughtful monograph about experiments with protein synthesis and transfer RNA over the course of several decades. In the book, he juxtaposes detailed accounts of one laboratory's work with dense material-semiotic readings of the meaning of these experiments. This form is unprecedented in science studies. From these extraordinarily specific circumstances, rendered in language sharply divergent from one community of practitioners to another, and surely approaching untranslatability between these communities, Rheinberger draws claims about the "saving power," to use Heidegger's term, to be found within technological civilization. At the very least, this move would seem to be obliged to answer why it has not committed that most basic of the ethnographers' category mistakes "my village = the world." Clifford Geertz, in his "Thick Description: Toward an Interpretive Theory of Culture," poses the issue with his usual sauciness: "The problem of how to get from a collection of ethnographic miniatures . . . to wall-sized culturescapes of the nation, the epoch, the continent, or the civilization remains unsolved" (Geertz 1973: 21).

He continues:

The notion that one can find the essence of national societies, civilizations, great religions, or whatever summed up and simplified in so-called typical small towns and villages is palpable nonsense. What one finds in small towns and villages is (alas) small-town or village life. . . The locus of study is not the object of study. (Geertz 1973: 22)[2]

Obviously, we all know (well, most of us) that what one finds in biochemical laboratories is biochemists doing biochemistry. How, if at all, the local findings relate to, or illuminate, Science, or Technological Civilization or Science Studies would be well-served with more interpretive or material-semiotic work.

Events

The classification game rapidly grows tiresome. Consequently, as the reader no doubt expects, I will close by quoting myself. By so doing, my work too is made available for scrutiny. At the end of the Preface to *Essays on the Anthropology of Reason,* one finds:

Today, knowledge-producers are faced with two types of relentless, omnivorous and insatiable, demands. The first demand is to be "effective." In the human sciences, this generally means "operationalizable," good for something else. Although the things produced under this imperative are often imaginary, they can have very real effects, e.g. the creation of a prosperous bio-ethics community. The other demand is for "meaning"; America has a thriving world-view industry. One response to these demands is to accept one or the other or both. Another is to resist them. I am trying to do neither. Rather, Max Weber's provocation that leading a life of science foregrounds "self-clarification and knowledge of inter-related facts" and "a sense of responsibility" remains, for me, the general demand of the day (Weber 1946). However, as one never encounters a general demand, the problem of where to look, how to proceed, and what to do once one gets there, is persistently present. (Rabinow 1996a: xiv)

I have adopted a research strategy that is more restrained and limited in scale than Latour or Rheinberger. Recently what has interested me is the emergence of (partially) new objects, sites and forms. Thus, in the work that resulted in *Making PCR* (Rabinow 1996b), I concentrated on a new site of production of knowledge and value, a founding instance of the American biotechnology industry, Cetus Corporation. I had gone to Cetus not because it represented the spirit of the age, or the essence of technological civilization, or the ultimate in hybridity. Rather I had gone there in a kind of ricochet from the Human Genome Project at UC Berkeley's Lawrence Berkeley Laboratory which was in disarray. That project had cast itself in epochal terms, and that representation had succeeded in achieving funding for multiple well-equipped sites and a great deal of bureaucratic politics. Cetus turned out to be interesting in part because certain other things had happened there, some successful, some not. There was no inevitability to the place, it was not obviously emblematic, either then or now. It was, however, significant.

At Cetus, a very powerful and important technique had been invented during the mid-1980s – PCR, or the polymerase chain reaction, a technique that enabled researchers to identify specific strings of DNA and then to amplify them millions of times, turning genetic scarcity into genetic bounty. The technique turned out to be very valuable, and to receive symbolic recognition with a Nobel prize rapidly awarded in 1993. Cetus management, keen analysts of the demands of the day, bet the company's future on cancer therapeutics. These efforts largely failed. PCR emerged in their shadows. That is not a general lesson; other companies invented what they set out to invent. Others failed altogether.

Neither Cetus, nor PCR, need be over-interpreted for their meaning. First, what is intriguing about both the site and the technique is their singularity, their specific temporality. Their moments of triumph were short. The effects were diverse and manifest. A great deal of routinization followed. There was certainly something American about the company, and the official inventor of the technique, and the way the company was financed, and how the inventor was educated, and the way many of the other scientists and managers and scientist-managers approached things. There was certainly something capitalist about the whole enterprise. There was something unquestionably modern in the desire and project to capture bits of living matter and manipulate the contexts in which they were found and the ways in which they worked and could be reworked. There was something ultimately poetic, for a time, in the making of the site and the technique. Bureaucratic prose soon followed. The site disappeared. Today, PCR is a pervasive, flexible and unsurpassed tool, mandatory in laboratories doing this genre of work.

In this ethnographic work at Cetus as well as in the subsequent field project at the central French genome mapping laboratory, the *Centre d'Études du Polymorphisme Humain*, I gradually came to understand that the object of study that intrigued me was the "event." Obviously there are a plurality of events at any one time. However, from time to time, new forms emerge that have something significant about them, something that catalyzes previously present actors, things, institutions into a new mode of existence, a new assemblage, an assemblage that made things work in a different manner. A manner that made many other things more or less suddenly possible. Such happenings are not reducible to the elements involved any more than they are representative of the epoch. Nor are such events mysterious and unanalyzable. It is only that so much effort has been devoted in the name of social science to explaining away the emergence of new forms as the result of something else that we lack adequate means to conceptualize the event of new forms as the curious and potent singularity that it is.

The present is a good time to desist from employing totalizing categories like epoch, civilization, culture, society (or, at the very least, hesitation, scrutiny, pausing and pondering are in order). These notions are in conceptual ruins contributing in no small part to the disarray of disciplines like anthropology, sociology and history that were built around them. Science studies has been instrumental in inventing and testing new analytic categories that have proved to be powerful in the sense of extending and enlivening our capacity to understand things. Latour's articulation of actor-networks or immobilized mobiles, like

Rheinberger's explorations of experimental systems, are unquestionably advances. In part, they are advances because they pick out things we did not have adequate means of naming before. In part, they are advances because they have found a means to avoid focusing on unanalyzable pseudo-entities like culture, or, for that matter, science. I trust it is clear that I am not proposing yet another return to empiricism, only a form of nominalism. I am advocating a larger and more refined series of limited concepts, that will enable richer modes of intellectual work. Why? Because if the goal of such labor is understanding, then our concepts and our modes of work must not be only useful and meaningful although at times they may be that as well – but good to think with, that is to say, capable of making something new happen in a field of knowledge.

NOTES

1. Pierre Bourdieu, who holds a similar position to Latour, attempts an escape by claiming that his sociology is scientifically true, allowing him to escape from the *illusio* that all other social actors are caught within (Bordieu 1982).
2. Note the use of "culturescape."

REFERENCES

Blumenberg, Hans 1983[1966] *The Legitimacy of the Modern Age*. Cambridge, MA: M.I.T. Press.
Bourdieu, Pierre 1982 *Leçon sur la leçon*. Paris: Les Editions de Minuit.
Elias, Norbert 1978 *The History of Manners. Volume 1. The Civilizing Process*. New York: Pantheon Books.
Foucault, Michel 1984 "What is Enlightenment?" In Paul Rabinow (ed.), *The Foucault Reader*. New York: Pantheon Books, pp. 32–50.
Geertz, Clifford 1973 "Thick Description: Toward an Interpretive Theory of Culture." In *The Interpretation of Cultures*. New York: Basic Books, pp. 3–30.
Heidegger, Martin 1977a "The Age of the World Picture." In *The Question Concerning Technology and Other Essays*. New York: Harper and Row.
    1977b "The Question Concerning Technology." In *The Question Concerning Technology and Other Essays*. New York: Harper and Row.
Kant, Immanuel 1784 *Idea for a Universal History from a Cosmopolitan Point of View*. Trans. Lewis White Beck in *Kant on History*. Bobbs-Merrill Co. Inc.
Latour, Bruno 1988[1984] *The Pasteurization of France*. Trans. Alan Sheridan and John Law. Cambridge, MA: Harvard University Press.
    1993 [1991] *We Have Never Been Modern*. Trans. Catherine Porter. Cambridge, MA: Harvard University Press.
Pauly, Philip J. 1987 *Controlling Life: Jacques Loeb and the Engineering Ideal in Biology*. New York: Oxford University Press.

Rabinow, Paul 1996a *Essays on the Anthropology of Reason.* Princeton studies in Culture/Power/History. Princeton: Princeton University Press.

1996b *Making PCR: A Story of Biotechnology.* Chicago: University of Chicago Press.

Rheinberger, Hans-Jörg 1995 "Beyond Nature and Culture: A note on Medicine in the Age of Molecular Biology." *Science in Context* 8(1): 249–63.

1997 *Toward a History of Epistemic Things: Synthesizing Proteins in the Test Tube.* Palo Alto and London: Stanford University Press.

Weber, Max 1946 "Science as Vocation." In H. Gerth and C. W. Mills (eds.), *From Max Weber: Essays in Sociology.* New York: Oxford University Press.

Part II

Laboratories and clinics: the material cultures of biomedicine

4 Trustworthy knowledge and desperate patients: clinical tests for new drugs from cancer to AIDS

Ilana Löwy

Transforming the "Art of Healing" into a Science: Origins of the Controlled, Randomized Clinical Trial

This chapter discusses a "soft" biomedical technology: the randomized, controlled clinical trial. Clinical trials of new drugs were often presented as "transparent devices," a non-problematic, and thus non-problematized way to evaluate new therapies. The development of the "controlled randomized trial" in the 1940s and 1950s was according to the official histories of this technique a step that moved the "art of healing" from a "pre-scientific" to a "scientific stage." It eliminated the subjective element in the evaluation of new treatments, and replaced it with quantitative and objective data, radically separating the "hard" scientific aspect of healing from its "soft" social and cultural aspects (Bloom 1986). Doctors were always aware that their healing activity has a "non-scientific" dimension. In his book, *The Principles of Medical Knowledge,* published in 1902, the Polish philosopher of medicine, Edmund Biernacki, distinguished between the "science of diseases" and the "art of healing." The science of diseases (physiology and pathology), he explained, can claim scientific status because it is based on objective observations and on experimentation. Therapies, however, cannot be considered an exact science. They were, as a rule, developed through empirical bedside tinkering while their results were intrinsically "non-scientific" because they depended on the highly individualized and idiosyncratic patient–healer relationship and were influenced by the patient's (and doctor's) belief that a given therapy would work.[1] "Suggestion can bring better mental equilibrium and better feeling, and can influence in a positive way even the most material perturbations of vegetative functions of the organism" (Biernacki 1902: 297). In order to develop a scientific way of testing treatments, one should therefore have two series of sick individuals: one receiving a therapy "with suggestion," and the other "without suggestion." But, Biernacki explains, this is an absurd proposal: how can one administer therapies without suggestion?

The controlled clinical trial aims, precisely, to dissociate "therapy" and "suggestion." The need to develop a method to evaluate and compare therapies increased with the number of available (and presumably efficient) drugs on the market. The development of the chemical industry (mainly aniline dyes industry) in the second half of the nineteenth century, opened the way to the synthesis and marketing of new therapeutic substances such as anti-pyretic compounds. The manufacture of drugs was at first seen as a way to diversify the output of the chemical industry and to open new markets to its products. However, it rapidly became a new industrial branch, interested not only in the synthesis of new molecules, but also in the development of other therapeutic means such as antisera (Travis 1992). In the twentieth century, the consolidation of the links between research laboratories and the clinics and between research laboratories and industry, accelerated the production of new drugs. Moreover, while the old "materia medica" was often perceived as useless (Warner 1986), drugs such as aspirin, arsenophamine (salvarsan), anti-diphtheric serum or insulin had a solid reputation of efficacy. Doctors confronted with the increasing flow of new therapeutic substances were faced with the dilemma of how best to make their patients benefit from these new developments without falling victims to marketing strategies. They looked, therefore, for an objective and impartial way of evaluating and comparing therapies.

Harry Marks traced the path which led from the first, mostly unsuccessful attempts to organize large-scale comparisons of therapeutic regimens conducted in the interwar period, to the establishment, circa 1950, of the "gold standard" of clinical trials: the controlled, randomized trial (Marks 1987a). In order to introduce such trials, doctors needed to give up part of their power as experts. They needed to recognize the authority of an external specialist – the statistician – and to acknowledge the superiority of "objective measures" of the clinical status of patients (such as results of laboratory tests) over evaluations grounded in the individualized and embodied skills of the practitioner (Marks 1987b). This difficulty, strongly present in the interwar period, diminished during the Second World War. During the war numerous doctors worked in state-directed research agencies (such as the Office for Scientific Research and Development (OSRD) which coordinated the war-related research in the US) and became accustomed to large-scale operations controlled from above. Two additional elements facilitated the introduction of controlled clinical trials in the post-Second World War era: the increased involvement of the state in biomedical research and (in Europe) in the organization of health care, and the growing importance of "academic medicine" – doctors and researchers linked to major medical schools and teaching hospitals. The growing dependence of medical research on public money increased the need for medical researchers to deflect accusations of sloppiness or, worse self-interested moves and unholy alliances with drug producers. Such accusations could not have been refuted by developing quantifiable and objective methods of selecting therapeutic regimens.[2] On the other hand, the "scientifization" of therapies strengthened the alliance between biomedical researchers and academic physicians and increased the power of the latter. Controlled clinical trials were, as a rule, conducted in leading teaching hospitals (or at least under the direction of doctors who worked in such hospitals) confirming the importance of these institutions as the main sites of therapeutic innovation (patients who wish to obtain "state of the art" therapy must go to a teaching hospital), and reducing the relative power of non-academic practitioners.

The central element in a controlled therapeutic trial is randomization, that is, the random distribution of eligible patients in a test group which receives the tested therapy, and a control group which receives either a placebo or a reference treatment. The randomization, if made correctly (and supervised by competent statisticians) ensures the equality of the two groups, making possible statistically valid comparisons. A second important element is double blind treatment: neither the patient nor the treating physician know if the patient belongs to the treated group, or to the control group – an efficient way of eliminating the role of "suggestion" in therapy. The third important principle is the "objectivation" of results.[3] Thus in the "classical" example of a controlled clinical trial, one which tested the efficacy of streptomycin as an anti-tuberculosis drug, the statisticians who organized the trial decided that the clinical progress of the patient would be evaluated exclusively through the reading of their X-ray films by outside experts. Certain doctors who at first willingly enrolled their patients in this trial, later rebelled, claiming that X-ray films alone did not provide an adequate measure of the patients' progress (or lack of it) and that they should be combined with more extensive clinical evaluations which should be made by the best qualified person – the physician who followed the patients from the beginning of their disease. Their "rebellion" failed, however, and the trial's organizers decided to stick firmly to the principle of external evaluation advocated by statisticians (Marks 1987b).

From the 1950s on, leading medical researchers strongly advocated the use of randomized, controlled clinical trials to evaluate new therapies and introduced such trials into their practice. The most important contribution to the "officialization" of the status of controlled clinical trials was, however, the importance accorded to these trials for the acquisition of marketing permits for new drugs. Doctors do not have to submit the already approved therapies to new scrutiny, or to extensively test methods that do not involve licensing (say, new surgical techniques). By contrast, manufacturers of drugs are obliged to prove that their products are not harmful and that they are efficient. The first requirement is an older one and is related to legislation on food quality. The second is relatively recent. For example, the first law aiming at safeguarding the US public from dangerous drugs was promulgated in 1906. This law also established a governmental agency – the Chemistry Bureau – to control drugs (later this task was delegated to the Food and Drug Administration). The US law was amended in 1938, and again in 1951, to tighten control over the prescription of potentially dangerous and/or habit-forming drugs, but it did not deal with the evaluation of drug efficacy until 1962. Only then, in the aftermath of the thalidomide scandal, the Kefauver-Harris amendment imposed the testing of the efficacy of new drugs before the granting of a marketing permit (Lasagna 1989; Swann 1994). Other countries developed similar legislation. Thus, the French Authorisation de Mise sur le Marché (AMM) system dates from 1972 (Steru and Simon 1986). While national regulatory laws are not identical, all Western laws now include the principle of verification of lack of toxicity and efficacy of drugs, and they all consider controlled clinical trials as the appropriate way to test efficacy (Lasagna and Werkö 1986).

The recent focus on cost/benefit considerations in medicine enhanced the role of clinical trials in the study of the efficacy of therapies. Adepts of "evidence-based medicine" propose to enforce stringent rules for evaluating all therapies based on the widespread use of randomized controlled clinical trials as a way of reducing medical expenses. Advocates of this approach, such as David Sackett, head of the National Health Service (UK) Centre for Evidence-Based Medicine, at Oxford University, see clinical trials as the only way to develop a rational and cost/benefit effective medical practice (Vines 1995; *The Lancet* 1995). However, not all doctors view controlled clinical trials as a valid method for verifying their practices.[4] Clinicians who criticize this technology argue that randomized trials are centered on diseases and disease-related variables rather than on patients and patient-related variables ("objective indicators" such as shade on an X-ray film or a blood count do not necessarily reflect the patients' feelings about their disease). They also contest the wholesale transferral of methods developed to study laboratory animals to the clinic (Hellman and Hellman 1991; MacKillop and Johnston 1986). Clinical trials, they explain, are usually modeled after artificially crafted and excessively simplified situations, and are incapable of supplying answers to complex questions physicians face in an ordinary clinical situation (Feinstein 1987). A different criticism reflects the point of view of the drug manufacturers. These critics argue that the process of evaluation of new drugs is disproportionately costly, burdensome and inefficient. Claiming to defend patients' interests, regulatory agencies such as the FDA made arbitrary choices which are not justifiable on statistical grounds, such as preference given to trials against placebo and for "the intent to treat" analysis (in which subjects are always considered as belonging to the original group to which they were assigned, even if the drug was not administered long enough for its effects to be made manifest). Useful drugs are therefore slow to reach the market – and sometimes remain stuck on the company's shelves – unnecessarily increasing the patients' suffering (Lasagna 1989).

The latter argument closely recalls the accusations brought against the FDA by representatives of the AIDS associative movement in the late 1980s ("red tape kills"). Their activism led to changes in the process of testing and licensing new anti-AIDS drugs, such as the speeding up of the administrative process, increased enrollment of patients in trials of promising drugs, the development of less restrictive criteria for recruitment of participants in clinical trials of anti-AIDS therapies, and compassionate distribution of non-licensed drugs outside official protocols ("parallel track"). The intervention of the AIDS associative movement was seen as an unprecedented inclusion of non-experts in the process of the establishment and validation of scientific knowledge, and thus as a radical change in the ways scientific knowledge is developed and stabilized (Epstein 1993, 1995). The inclusion of patients in deliberations on clinical trials was indeed unprecedented. But how well-established was the "scientific knowledge" they reportedly subverted? A close look at the development of therapy for another category of "desperate patients" – those who suffer from advanced cancer – reveals a different picture: one of numerous exceptions to the "gold standard" of randomized, controlled clinical trial. One may indeed argue that in the domain of therapies for "desperate patients," the exception became the rule.

AIDS is an infectious disease, and at first the only links between cancer and AIDS were limited to the search for a therapy for Kaposi's sarcoma, a cancerous growth often associated with AIDS. Cancer therapy started, however, to be perceived as having affinities with AIDS, when (circa 1987) this pathology was redefined as a chronic rather than acute disease. The putative similarity between cancer and AIDS was accentuated when (circa 1990) the development of full-blown AIDS in HIV-infected individuals started to be perceived as a result of the break-

ing down of a dynamic equilibrium between the retrovirus and cells of
the immune system (cancer is seen by some specialists as resulting from
the "escape" of some malignant cells from "immune surveillance").
This similarity was also accentuated by the observation that HIV
may develop resistance to anti-retroviral compounds such as AZT
(malignant cells tend to develop resistance to anti-tumor drugs and this
phenomenon is a major obstacle to the development of efficient chemotherapy for cancer).

Two categories of anti-AIDS drugs were developed: anti-retroviral
drugs and drugs directed against opportunistic infections. These two
categories are, however, often lumped together under the general heading "therapies for AIDS." This may be confusing because the rules that
govern the tests for drugs employed to cure opportunistic infections
(and often developed independently of AIDS), are different from those
which govern the search for specific anti-retroviral agents. For methodo-
logical reasons (the discussion of clinical trials of drugs used to fight
opportunistic infections in AIDS patients will bring us to the vast subject of testing anti-bacterial or anti-mycotic compounds) this chapter
will deal with the latter category only, that is, with the search for a "cure
for AIDS." This search, my thesis is, was partly modeled on the search
for the "cure of cancer," and therefore on patterns of clinical experimentation with anti-cancer drugs established in the US in the 1950s
and 1960s.

Experimentation in the Clinics as an Organizational Innovation: Chemotherapy of Cancer at the NCI, 1945–1975

The intensive effort to develop anti-cancer drugs after the Second World
War was in some ways a consequence of the industrial development of
penicillin as part of the Allies' war effort. The penicillin success stimulated efforts to uncover other "miracle therapies", and it showed that
an efficient way to achieve this goal was the development of large-scale
cooperation between scientists, physicians and industrialists, coordinated by a governmental agency (Neushul 1993; Liebenau 1987;
Heffland et al. 1980; Hobby 1985). Summing up the achievements of
Second World War research the chairman of OSRD (an institution
which coordinated penicillin production), Vannevar Bush, explained
that "penicillin reached our troops in time because the government
coordinated and supported the program of research and development
of this drug. The development moved from the early laboratory stages
to large-scale production and use in a fraction of time it would have

taken without such leadership" (Bush 1945:9). His colleague, Chester Keefer, the president of the Committee on Chemotherapeutic and Other Agents, of the National Research Council (an institution which supervised the clinical tests of penicillin and its distribution to civilians) also explained that the production of penicillin during the war "was the finest example of what can be accomplished by collaborative effort in research and development in the medical sciences when proper leadership is available" (1948: 722).

The first important search for anti-tumor compounds, through massive screening of chemical compounds, was conducted by Cornelius (Dusty) Rhoads, former head of the Medical Division of the Chemical Warfare Service of the OSRD. The development of the first successful chemotherapy, the treatment of lymphoma by nitrogen mustard indeed stemmed from studies on war gases (nitrogen mustard, or iperite, is a war gas used during the First World War). Rhoads became familiar with the therapy of lymphoma with nitrogen mustard through his work at OSRD, and was quick to grasp the opportunities of the new therapeutic approach. At the same time, during his years at OSRD, he became enthusiastic about "big science," big budgets, centralized planning and coordinated cooperative efforts. He was soon given an opportunity to organize a "big science" effort in oncology. After the war, Rhoads, a cancer specialist, was appointed the director of Memorial Hospital, New York, an institution which treated numerous cancer patients. In 1945, Alfred Sloan, the president of General Motors, pledged one million dollars for a cancer research institute at the Memorial Hospital. The institute, directed by Rhoads, and named after Charles Kettering, the director of the Research Division of General Motors, set as an explicit goal "the organization of industrial techniques for cancer research." Mass screening of chemical compounds fulfilled this goal (Bud 1978).

At the same time, a second screening program was developed at the National Cancer Institute (NCI) by Murray Shear. Shear started his studies of anti-tumor compounds (at first, natural compounds, such as bacterial toxins and then synthetic chemicals compounds) in the 1930s. His was a small-scale program in which a few chemists collaborated with selected clinicians. After the war, however, Shear became convinced that only a large-scale scientific endeavor could lead to a therapy for cancer. He explained that, "it is already apparent that much careful thought will need to be devoted to the relationships between organizational units and among human elements if such large ventures are to be productive to justify large expenditures" (1951: 580). Such large-scale efforts, he added, should be inspired by industrial organization. Consequently, he started a screening program at the NCI, parallel to the Sloan

Kettering Institute program directed by Rhoads. Both programs were efficient in rapidly screening a large number of substances in the test tube and in cancer-carrying mice but both were severely hampered by their limited capacity to test anti-cancer compounds in patients.[5]

Screening programs for anti-cancer drugs were modeled on screening programs for sulfa drugs, and for antibiotics. It is, however, relatively simple to rely on *in vitro* models and experiments made in laboratory animals when testing anti-microbial products. A micro-organism is different from a mammalian cell and it is not too difficult to find substances which selectively harm bacteria but not the body's cells. By contrast, a malignant cell is quite similar to the normal cell from which it is derived. Researchers failed to identify important structural or metabolic differences between normal and transformed cells. The only significant importance between these two types of cells was their rate of division. Malignant cells multiply fast, but so do some categories of normal cells, like bone marrow cells or epithelial cells. It was thus difficult to find compounds that selectively eliminated malignant cells only, and the differences between effective doses and toxic doses of these compounds were generally very narrow. This difficulty could not be solved in a test tube or in animal models of cancer (which in any case were seen as imperfectly representing the human disease). Thus researchers relied on clinical trials to calibrate the doses of anti-tumor drugs and to find the conditions to maximize their usually limited therapeutic effects. Moreover, large-scale clinical trials were necessary to ensure the calibration of toxic and not very effective drugs. The Cancer Chemotherapy National Service Center (CCNSC), founded in the US in 1955, aimed to answer this need and to coordinate pre-clinical and clinical testing of anti-cancer drugs (Zubrod 1979).

The CCNSC was created as a result of direct political pressure. In the 1950s the faith in "miracles of modern science," boosted by the rapid arrival of new and efficient antibiotics on the market, the considerable increase in biomedical research funding and of the activities of specific lobbies (e.g., the American Cancer Society lobby, or "Mary (Laskar) and her little lambs"), increased the interest of the US Congress in cancer research. Finding a cure for cancer was a popular political goal while recent scientific developments such as the use of nitrogen mustard in the therapy of lymphoma or of folic acid analogs in the therapy of childhood leukemia, indicated that this goal was a feasible one (Patterson 1987). Cancer patients were not, at that time, a specific pressure group, and the politicization of cancer was done by congressmen who wanted to please their constituents, and by cancer charities (which often viewed themselves as speaking on behalf of the cancer experts rather than of patients). These were, however, efficient ways of politicizing the issue of cancer, and the decision, made in the US in the mid-1950s, to dedicate relatively large sums of money to the search of a "cancer cure" (CCNSC's budget was $5.6 million in 1956, $20 million in 1957, and $28 million in 1958) was basically a political one.

The aim of CCNSC, according to Dr. Gordon Zubrod, who headed the leukemia task force of CCNSC, was "to set up all the functions of a pharmaceutic house run by the NCI" (1984: 12), while the CCNSC chairman, Kenneth Endicott, emphasized that a cure for cancer would be found when the industry–government cooperation in the pharmaceutical area were as efficient as it was in the military area (1957). CCNSC was seen, above all, as an organizational innovation: an efficient way of coordinating the activities of numerous professional groups. The activities of the various panels of CCNSC – the screening panel, the chemistry panel, the endocrinology panel and the clinical trials panel – were coordinated by a central structure, the Cancer Chemotherapy National Committee, which also mediated between the CCNSC, governmental agencies, charities and industry. One of the official goals of CCNSC was the reinforcement and the diffusion of standards of good practices in pre-clinical and clinical research. The homogenization of pre-clinical practices was an easier task. One of its important elements was the highly codified standardization of laboratory animals (at first exclusively mice) and tumors used in screening tests, and the codification of toxicity tests for drugs. The CCNSC established strict guidelines for screening and then enforced adherence to these guidelines through an elaborate control system (Sessoms 1959–60). One of the foremost activities of the program was to develop relationships with industry. An important part of screening activities and of the production of animals was delegated to industrial and semi-industrial settings. In addition, the CCNSC established close collaborations with numerous pharmaceutical firms, and developed detailed instructions for how these collaborations were to be conducted (*Cancer Chemotherapy Reports* 1966).

The homogenization of clinical studies was more complicated. It was conducted by the Clinical Trials Panel, which in 1956 established ten collaborative study groups which included physicians in about 100 hospitals. The number of collaborative groups and hospitals rapidly expanded: in 1959 the network included 19 groups and 149 institutions, and in 1961 these numbers grew to 25 groups and 171 institutions (Walkers 1962). Members of the panel surveyed the application of protocols and the quality of laboratory analyses of other members of the cooperative study group, and they saw to the uniformity of criteria of clinical evaluation. These measures were justified by the need to raise the standards of cancer diagnosis, and by the low efficacy of the tested therapies which were not expected to produce dramatic effects like antibiotics did (Endicott 1957). The CCNSC program was later criticized for its low efficacy. Indeed between 1956 and 1964, the program successfully screened tens of thousands of natural and synthetic compounds, but it did not uncover a single new family of anti-tumor compounds. This program had, nevertheless, a key role in the establishment of organizational patterns for large-scale screening of chemicals, and for the cooperation between the laboratory and the clinics and large-scale coordination of the testing of new drugs. As one of the chief investigators of this program, Isidore Ravdin, put it:

The chemotherapy program has gained the confidence and active collaboration of a large segment of the pharmaceutical industry. It has stimulated, more than ever before, the synthesis of unusual compounds in amounts necessary for widespread clinical trial. It has established, here and there, new facilities for preclinical pharmacology and toxicity testing... The organized Cooperative Chemotherapy Clinical Studies have continued to yield quantitative data in a much shorter time than any single institution could possibly have achieved alone. It had stimulated the interest and cooperation of many internists and surgeons in the possible advantages of the chemotherapy of patients with advanced malignant disease. It had in several areas continued to organize a national standard reporting system of end-results with uniform standards of clinical appraisal. It had continued to develop excellent biometrics units in a number of our medical schools and in other institutions, to provide statistical consultation... The gains, therefore, have been substantial and you will hear of them. We have not achieved the goal we originally set out to achieve. Our adversary is tough and elusive. (Ravdin 1962: 8)

One may argue that the "negative result" – the proof of the absence of anti-tumor activity of tens of thousands of tested compounds – was, in itself, an impressive organizational achievement. The greatest practical success of the CCNSC, the engineering of a cure for acute lymphoid leukemia (ALL) in children, was also, to a large extent, a triumph of efficient organization. In the early 1960s several drugs were found to induce temporary remission of ALL, but children treated with these drugs invariably relapsed and died. In 1961 Dr. Zubrod proposed to create an Acute Leukemia Task Force with the implicit aim to find a cure for this disease. The idea to create a task force was inspired by industrial strategies and the CCNSC staff visited IBM to learn more about the organization and the function of "single-objective" task forces (Zubrod 1984). The new approach was highly successful and an aggressive pursuit of a single goal, combined with intensive cooperation among experts led, in the mid-1960s to the first cures of ALL. This cure was achieved thanks to the development of successful multidrug regimen, and to the development of efficient ways to follow up patients (elimination of residual malignant cells in the spinal fluid, prevention of hemorrhages and infections). It was obtained in "single-arm" clinical experiments, that is, in trials in which treated patients were compared with historical controls. This rule applied not only to the cure of ALL, but to all the clinical trials of chemotherapy of cancer sponsored by the CCNSC (Zubrod et al. 1977).

The success of the ALL cure (and the concomitant success of therapy for Hodgkin's lymphoma) led to the proliferation of institutional structures which coordinated cooperative trials of new cancer therapies. The high hopes linked with the large-scale diffusion of these trials were not fulfilled: no efficient cures were found for the common cancers affecting adults. In contrast, these trials had important organizational consequences. The new professional segment of medical oncology (physicians specialized in cancer chemotherapy) was organized around the carrying out of multicenter clinical trials. Such trials promoted homogenization of diagnostic and therapeutic procedures, and were a privileged site for information exchange and the accumulation of professional prestige. They also were a preferential site for intensive interactions between the laboratory, clinics and industry (Cassileth 1979). On the other hand, the "trial-centered" orientation of medical oncologists transformed clinical experimentation into a quasi-routine therapy for cancer which was proposed in leading cancer treating centers to nearly all the patients who failed to respond to standard therapies. The multiplication of clinical trials for cancer subverted the traditional argument that entering a clinical trial made it impossible to adapt a therapy to the individual patient's needs. The opposite argument was advanced for trials of anti-cancer therapies: the large number of such trials facilitates the adaptation of the best therapy to the specific disease of an individual patient (Gagnon 1994; Fintor 1991).

One of the consequences of the development of medical oncology as a "trial-oriented" professional segment was the increased need for the standardization of the criteria for the evolution of malignant disease and the agreement on what was to be considered a success in a therapy of this disease (Gehan 1960). "Objective criteria" of therapeutic success are relatively unimportant in individualized patient–doctor interaction (it is enough that the patient and the doctor agree that a treatment was successful), but they are crucial for the development of large-scale multicenter trials. Clinical trials of anti-cancer therapy revolved around the notion of "measurable response": in hematological tumors, the number of abnormal cells in the blood or in bone marrow; in patients who carried solid tumors, the size of the tumor(s) as visualized by palpation, X-rays films, and later also new visualization techniques such as NMR or CT scanners; in tumors associated with the presence of specific (e.g. hormonal) markers, the level of the marker in the serum. An "objective response" to a therapy was thus dissociated from considerations on symptoms or quality of life (Karnofsky 1961). This dissociation was based on the assumption that such "objective measures" were directly correlated with the clinical evolution of a malignant disease (or, to be more precise, that the multiplication of transformed cells reflected in the tumor's size was the malignant disease). Thus a report of a joint FDA/NCI Task Force on experimental therapies of cancer (which was prepared following a congressional investigation on the alleged inefficacy and abuses of chemotherapy) argued in favor of the patient's right to seek a treatment which holds out a hope of clinical benefit, however slim, adding that the "overall response" of phase I trials of anti-cancer drugs was 9.5 percent, and that this response rate was enough reason for many patients to enroll in a clinical trial of a new therapy. The report did not explain, however, that a 9.5 percent "objective response" did not mean that about 10 percent of the patients had lasting remissions, or long-term disappearance of symptoms, only that the size of their tumor decreased temporarily (Joint Task Force on Anticancer Drugs 1982). Experts recognized the problematic aspect of studies based on evaluation of "objective responses" to anti-cancer drugs. Thus Marvin Schniederman, a biostatistician who in the early 1950s collaborated on the first NCI clinical trials in acute leukemia and solid tumors and who later helped to develop statistical centers which collaborated with the cooperative clinical trials program of the CCNSC noted in 1967, that the excessive use of "objective measures" when evaluating anti-cancer drugs may lead to a "third type error," that is to the finding of correct answers to the wrong questions (Schneiderman 1967). The criterion of "objective responses," evaluated through visualization and laboratory measures was maintained, however, probably because it was the most efficient way of comparing results and developing large-scale collaborations.

Phase I (dosage finding) and phase II (preliminary efficacy testing) of clinical trials of new and promising cancer therapies were as a rule non-randomized, while phase III which compared the efficacy of a new therapy to "reference therapy" was randomized (if there was no "reference therapy," the tests were often transformed into a non-randomized phase II–III trial). This principle is linked to the development of CCNSC. The very first clinical trials of chemotherapies, at the NCI, organized by Dr. Zubrod before 1955, were randomized, and the NCI (on Dr. Zubrod's recommendation) hired a biostatistician (the above mentioned Dr. Schneiderman) to supervise these trials. With the founding of CCNSC, the programs' directors, who wished to accelerate and to streamline the testing process chose to make phase I and II trials single-arm trials and then to promote randomized phase III trials (if a reference therapy was available) and phase IV trials (the follow-up of molecules which obtained marketing permit) (Rothman and Edgar 1992). The National Chemotherapy Program which, in 1965, replaced the CCNSC, adopted the principle of non-randomization in the early stages of the testing of anti-cancer compounds. The program selected and coordinated a network of "agreed cancer treatment centers" which tested new drugs. These drugs were first made available to a small number of selected centers, then, if promising, were distributed to a larger number of institutions and physicians sponsored through NCI grants and contracts, who often conducted phase II–III tests. Drugs found to be efficient in the NCI network later went through a regular procedure of FDA approval, received a marketing permit, and became available for all medical practitioners. The free distribution of new and promising anti-cancer drugs in the US was controlled by clinical trial networks, and supervised by the NCI. From the early 1970s on, experimental drugs (the so-called group C drugs) were thus distributed to cancer patients who were treated by doctors within the NCI network (Chalmers et al. 1972).

In all the early stages of this process the clinical trials were modeled on the ALL therapy and were single-arm trials. The rationale behind the absence of randomization was that where no known therapy existed, randomization was useless. This reasoning was challenged later. Indeed, when the patient is expected to die soon, no efficient treatment exists and the therapy is potentially life-saving, randomization and tests against placebo may seem highly unethical. But what if the patient has a chronic, potentially fatal disease, which has a complicated and often unpredictable trajectory and in which the proposed treatment would in all likelihood at best reduce symptoms or induce temporary remission? The expansion and "routinization" of cancer chemotherapies and the recognition of their limited therapeutic efficacy for the majority of (adult) patients suffering from advanced cancer, raised the question of the need to continue the unusual patterns of testing of these drugs established during the "pioneering days" of chemotherapy. Some experts proposed to abandon these patterns and to align clinical trials for anti-cancer drugs with clinical trials for other drugs (Chalmers et al. 1972). This opinion did not prevail, however. Cancer specialists continued to argue that randomized trials of new anti-cancer drugs were unethical and, moreover, not necessary. Randomized trials, they proposed, should be limited to later phases in the evaluation of a drug and to the comparison between two accepted therapeutic regimens (Gehan and Freireich 1972).

To sum up, clinical trials of anti-cancer therapies in the US (and, later, in other Western countries) established a pattern of centralized, multicenter trials, which involved close collaboration between research laboratory, industry, and clinics. They also established the principle of cost-free distribution of promising drugs without marketing permit through a network of agreed physicians coordinated by a government agency. They promoted the use of "single-arm" (non-randomized) clinical trials of these substances (phase I–II or phase II–III trials) to test drugs intended for "desperate patients" and the principle of reliance on "objective markers" of disease progress in these trials. Moreover, the rapid extension of clinical trials of anti-cancer drugs transformed clinical experimentation into a quasi-routine way of dealing with an advanced, incurable disease, one which is often perceived by patients suffering from such diseases as their right (a right to get a promising therapy and to maintain hope). I will argue that many of these elements can be found in clinical trials of anti-retroviral substances produced by major pharmaceutical firms – trials that, from 1988 on, dominate the search for a "cure for AIDS."

The Normalization of Exceptional Practices: the Search for Anti-Retroviral Therapies, 1982–1995

The participation of patient representatives in the decision concerning clinical trials of anti-AIDS drugs, some observers claim, transformed these trials into a path-breaking event (Edgar and Rothman 1990; Feenberg 1995). The involvement of patients' spokespersons in decisions concerning their therapy is indeed an important innovation. It is related to the specific fate of AIDS as a "mass-mediated epidemic," and to the unique role played by the organized homosexual movement in this epidemic. In the last part of this chapter, I will propose that the main effect of the participation of patients' representatives in decisions concerning the testing of anti-AIDS drugs was a political one: organized AIDS patients removed the testing process from the hidden realm of medical expertise and submitted it to the critical public gaze. Other changes such as the redefinition of what science is, or the change in the meaning of being a patient, were the direct or the indirect consequences of the political move of displaying the social background and the normative aspect of a biomedical technology named "clinical trial."[6] If one agrees with this hypothesis, one may argue that here again we could benefit from comparison with cancer chemotherapy, because the development of anti-cancer drugs in the 1950s and 1960s was strongly shaped by political considerations. The important differences between clinical trials for anti-cancer and anti-HIV drugs can be ascribed to the differences between the political forces which influenced the regulatory process in each case, namely the shift from politicians (as representatives of the lay public) and the "traditional" associative movement (as representing consensual agreement between the public and the experts) to a non-traditional associative movement (suspicious of experts and of governmental agencies), and "lay experts," who represent patients.

In order to understand the rise of the "lay experts" and the involvement of the AIDS associative movement in the design of clinical trials of anti-AIDS therapy, two sets of distinctions are necessary. The first is the distinction between the "heroic" (or "rebellious") phase of the involvement of the AIDS associative movement in the search for new treatments (roughly, until 1988) during which desperate patients tried a wide variety of "parallel" therapies and organized "unofficial" testing of these therapies, and the "institutionalization" phase during which the associative movement relied on pharmaceutical firms and official (if modified) circuits of drug testing. The second is the distinction, mentioned earlier, between the search for therapies for opportunistic infections and the search for anti-retroviral treatments. Both distinctions are arbitrary. In the 1990s AIDS patients (and patient associations) tend to look to the development of anti-retroviral therapies as the main hope for developing a cure for AIDS, but they also continue to use "unofficial" and "parallel" therapies. In addition, while the development pattern of anti-retroviral compounds was usually different from the development of drugs which fight opportunistic infections, some of the clinical trials of drugs against these infections (especially those which are found almost exclusively in AIDS patients), are very similar to trials for anti-HIV therapies. Nevertheless, these rough distinctions are important to the understanding of changes brought by AIDS epidemics to the testing and relapse of new drugs and the role of AIDS associative movements in these changes.

The role of the AIDS associative movement was not the same in changing patterns of testing drugs against opportunistic infections, and in influencing the testing and licensing of anti-HIV drugs. The associative movement usually did not radically change the ways drugs against opportunistic infections were tested. Its efforts mainly contributed to the change of the status of this category of drugs and their transformation from "normal" to "emergency" drugs. Thanks to this change, drugs which were diffused in the usual and slow way (say, drugs which fight tuberculosis or herpes infection) could be tested and released through the (previously existent, but seldom used) special procedures such as "fast track" and "compassionate protocol" (and, in France, ATU, or 'autorisation temporaire de l'utilisation'). Anti-retroviral compounds, that is to say specific anti-HIV substances, were tested differently, because these compounds were developed solely as a response to the AIDS epidemics. The AIDS associative movement made "opaque" (or visible) the previously "transparent" (or invisible) parts of the process of testing and licensing anti-retroviral drugs, it promoted specific, patient-oriented changes in the trial's design, and occasionally influenced the power balance between the main actors (scientists, clinicians, drug producers and governmental regulatory agencies). It did not, however, challenge the essential characteristics of clinical trials, or the fact that the fate of new drugs is mainly dependent on industrial and governmental policies.

The AIDS militancy (which started in the US in the early 1980s) grew out of the organized homosexual movement. Its origins shaped its attitude to medical experts and to the US government. Homosexuals have good reasons to distrust the medical establishment which, for a long time, defined homoerotic sexual orientation as a pathology. It also had good reasons to distrust the Republican majority (those were Reagan's conservative revolution years), which labeled them as "deviants" and "sinners." AIDS activists assumed that doctors and politicians were slow in looking for a cure for a disease which selectively killed homosexuals, drug-users, Haitians, and inner city dwellers, and decided to take the task of anti-AIDS treatment into their hands. Several popular studies provide a colorful description of the "heroic period" of AIDS therapy in the US (roughly 1985–88), during which militants of the associative movement smuggled illegal drugs from abroad and diffused them through "buyers' clubs," and, with the complicity of a few physicians and medical researchers, started "parallel" clinical trials of "unofficial" therapies (Arno and Feiden 1992; Nusbaum 1991). Information about "parallel" (and "official") therapies for AIDS were circulated in publications such as *AIDS Therapy News.*[7] This bulletin, one of the main sources of information on anti-AIDS therapies within the associative movement, documents the end of the "heroic period" of AIDS therapy. Its early issues (1986–87) were mostly dedicated to "parallel" medicines – from lecithin to Chinese cucumbers – and to "community-based trials" which test these medicines (alongside the more orthodox ones). However, from 1988 on the bulletin nearly exclusively discussed "official" therapies. It continued to mention community-based clinical trials, but the status of these trials changed: from the belief that they would uncover a "miracle drug" for AIDS, hidden from the prejudiced eyes of the official expert, these trials started to be perceived as the best device to follow the uses of "official" drugs in a "real-life" environment, and as a structure which is especially well adapted to the study of drugs directed against opportunistic infections. The survey, organized by *AIDS Treatment News* in November 1989, illustrates this change. Readers of the bulletin were asked to rate a list of over 100 anti-AIDS therapies, orthodox, semi-orthodox (e.g., dextrane sulfate, lecithin) or non-orthodox (e.g., shitake mushrooms, ginseng) in terms of their perceived efficacy. The result was unambiguous: the best-rated therapies, far distancing all the others, were AZT (the first anti-retroviral compound) and pentamidine aerosol (a drug used for the prevention of Pneumocystis carinii pneumonia, a common and dangerous opportunistic infection) (James 1989: 411–16).

The discovery of the anti-retroviral activity of AZT was probably the most important (if not unique) event which gradually led to the termination of the "heroic period" of the search for AIDS therapies and put an end to the "AIDS underground." AZT (zidovudine) is a "classical" drug (a nucleic acid analog), developed by a multinational pharmaceutical company, Bourrough-Wellcome. The first positive results with this molecule were obtained in 1987 and they were confirmed in 1988. At the same time (1987), the National Institute of Allergy and Infectious Diseases (NIAID), a subdivision of the NIH, established the AIDS Clinical Trials Group (ACTG), to coordinate clinical trials of AIDS drugs in the US. In November 1989, patient representatives were for the first time allowed to participate in ACTG debates (Harrington 1994). Their participation did bring about specific changes in the organization of clinical trials.[8] One of the first changes was the extension, in 1989, of "parallel tracks" through which patients could gain access to new and unlicensed drugs without having to be submitted to the restrictions of a clinical trial. This innovation, and the rise in compassionate distribution of new molecules, were mainly related to the development and distribution of molecules which fight opportunistic infections. Other innovations, such as the increasing use of "surrogate markers" (biological markers of disease progress) to evaluate performance of drugs, disappearance of trials against placebo and the acceptance of "dirty trials" (that is, trials in which patients had already used, or were using simultaneously other drugs than the tested substances) were usually related to the development of new anti-HIV compounds.[9] The latter trials were also main subjects of discussions and controversies between activists and regulatory agencies, and occasionally between activists and pharmaceutical firms (Epstein 1993).

The development of drugs designed to inhibit HIV replication soon became monopolized by a few big pharmaceutical firms. AZT has clearly shown the way: although some smaller companies tried to develop compounds which were reputed to either inhibit HIV, or to "stimulate the immune system," their efforts were, as a rule, rapidly dismissed as more sophisticated variants of drugs tested in the "heroic times" of "self-help" of AIDS activism (1986–88), such as the Chinese cucumber, Q-compound and lecithin preparation AL-721. Circa 1990, the main anti-HIV drugs tested were produced by major, multinational pharmaceutical companies. These were mostly analogs of nucleic acids – ddI (Brystol-Myers), ddC (Hoffman-Roche), 3TC (Glaxo) and protease inhibitors (RO31-8959 of Roche, and later ABT-538 (ritonavir) of Abbott, and MK-638 (indinavir) of Merck – which acted on a different stage in the virus replication cycle. These drugs were developed in collaboration with molecular biologists, and were named "designer drugs" to indicate that they were devised to interact with a specific point of the virus replication – and also to point to their "high-tech" nature and their direct links with the latest biological knowledge. The development of such "designer drugs" may be contrasted with CCNSC's policy of large-scale and indiscriminate screening of putative anti-cancer compounds, referred to by its opponents as "nothing too stupid to test."

To develop efficient anti-retroviral drugs one needed to understand the viral replication cycle and the natural history of HIV infection in humans. The understanding of the virus replication cycle in the test-tube remained basically unchanged from the mid-1980s on. In contrast, the perception of the natural history of AIDS infection has changed radically in the 1990s, and this change affected the testing and diffusion of anti-HIV drugs. At first HIV infection was seen to begin with an active primoinfection with seroconversion, then passing through a totally silent phase during which the retrovirus was hidden in the cells as an inactive DNA provirus with a very limited activity in the body, and then the gradual (and unexplained) increase in virus load leading to full-blown AIDS (Moss and Bachetti 1989). The main hiding place of the virus during the latent period, at first unknown, was later identified as peripheral lymph nodes (Gerdes and Flad 1992). In 1993, the improvement of quantitative methods to study virus load in tissues and the dynamics of viral replication (in situ polymerase chain reaction, branched DNA signal-amplification technique) led to a new perception of HIV infection as a highly dynamic process with a rapid turnover of virus production and destruction. According to the new view, the puta-tive "latent phase" of HIV-infection was in fact an invisible active phase, invisible that is, to techniques available in the 1980s and early 1990s. A full blown AIDS appears when the immune system is "worn out" by a prolonged and intensive anti-viral activity. At the same time, new tech-niques displayed the – previously suspected but unproven – extremely rapid mutation rate of the HIV. These findings led to precise rec-ommendations concerning treatment strategies: the HIV infection should be treated as early as possible to avoid the exhaustion of the immune system and it should be conducted with multi-drug therapies, which limit the risk of development of resistant mutants which escape therapy (Saag et al. 1992; Nowak 1995; Vella 1995).

Early treatment of HIV infection and simultaneous use of several anti-viral compounds were discussed from 1989 on, but no clear-cut answer was reached on the desirability of these approaches. Some studies indi-cated that early therapy leads to prolonged survival, but other investi-gations did not reach the same conclusions; some authors advocated simultaneous bi- or tri-therapies, others had found that sequential mono-therapies were a more efficient way of dealing with the develop-ment of resistances to drugs (Hammer 1994; Johnston and Hoth 1993). A new perception of the natural history of HIV infection, developed thanks to the use of quantitative PCR and the growing trust of scientists in results obtained with this technique, strongly tipped the scale in favor of multi-therapies. Experts have argued that mono-therapy cannot be successful (Wain-Hobson 1995). This conviction gave an extra impetus to the development of tri-therapies, and to the extensive use of "viral load" in patient's blood as the single important "surrogate marker" and, for some, the only significant measure of the success of a given therapy.[10] This measure can provide a rapid answer, or, to be exact, a rapid nega-tive answer to the question of efficacy of a given drug combination: a therapy which does not lower the viral load rapidly is not worth pursuing (St. Clair et al. 1995b). The possibility of rapidly eliminating inefficient therapies is particularly important in AIDS, because no valid animal model of this disease exists which could serve as an intermediary between observations made in the test-tube and a full-length clinical trial (Lange 1995).

In the 1990s the initiative for designing, developing and testing anti-HIV drugs switched to virologists, molecular biologists, and above all big pharmaceutical firms. This process, which started in the late 1980s was accelerated by the introduction of PCR as an important qualitative and quantitative tool for the study of HIV infection. The routine treat-ment of AIDS patients continued to be important for the well-being of these patients, but in 1996, the prevention and the treatment of opportunistic diseases seem to have become to all, including patient representatives, secondary to the task of the search for a specific "cure for AIDS" (Fontenay and Chambon 1996). This search is now perceived as a highly specialized and complicated enterprise. Multi-drug therapies monitored by sophisticated tools such as quantitative in situ PCR (a technique viewed in 1995 as too complicated and fragile for routine or semi-routine use) were developed through collaboration between virologists, immunologists, clinicians and industrialists. Moreover, pharmaceutical companies need to work together to develop an efficient drug combinations (St. Clair et al. 1995a). The goal of developing a "cure for AIDS," first seen in terms of prolongation of symptom-free survival, is presented now as the elimination of HIV infection, measured (now) as the disappearance of HIV from the bloodstream. This view of AIDS is similar to the shift in the perception of cancer during the clinical testing of anti-cancer drugs when patients' progress, first seen exclusively as the disappearance of pathologic symptoms, was redefined in terms of decrease of tri-dimensional tumor mass, occasionally as a decrease in concentration of tumor markers in the serum, and in the case of hematological cancers, the disappearance of malignant cells from blood and bone marrow. The "culture of clinical experimentation in the AIDS clinics" developed in the 1990s through an alliance with the biology laboratory and with industry. The existence of such an alliance had been postulated before. In practice, however, in the 1980s the relationships between clinicians, industrialists and basic scientists were usually distant, while virologists and molecular biologists recognized that the understanding of the molecular biology of HIV did not advance the understanding of the natural history of AIDS.[11] The development of quantitative PCR facilitated a direct junction between the molecular laboratory and the virology laboratory, the clinics and the pharmaceutical production plant, circumventing the need to develop an animal model of AIDS.[12]

The development of anti-HIV drugs has been, from the late 1980s on, concentrated in the hands of a few multinational pharmaceutical firms (Merck, Glaxo, Abbott, Wellcome) which were able to develop adequate (and expensive) structures for designing and testing such drugs. It depended on industrial moves (which include competition, but also collaboration) and complex interplay between pharmaceutical companies and governmental agencies. The government agencies have played a double role. Agencies such as ACTG of NIAID in the US and ANRS in France coordinate, and in some cases fund or co-fund, clinical trials of new therapies. Other agencies, such as the FDA in the US and the Agence de Médicament of the Health Ministry in France, grant marketing permits for new drugs, and, in countries with a government-sponsored health insurance system, negotiate price and reimbursement of these drugs. The role of governmental agencies in the development of anti-HIV drugs has been the coordination and selective support of industrial efforts, not, as was the case for the CCNSC, the promotion of an entirely new area of biomedicine. Their role may thus be likened to the role of the US and British governments in the development of penicillin – where government bodies such as OSCRD or the British MRC (Medical Research Council) coordinated and co-funded efforts to produce penicillin made by large pharmaceutical companies (Merck, Pffitzer, Squibb, Glaxo, Wellcome, ICI). On the other hand, the development of anti-HIV drugs, like the development of anti-cancer drugs (and unlike penicillin), have been dependent on large-scale clinical trials. Hence the similarities between the two domains, such as the central role of clinical trials in the organization of diagnostic and therapeutic activities, and their transformation into a quasi-routine element of patients' trajectories.

And what about the AIDS associative movement? Activists were present, and vociferous, in the debates on the testing of anti-HIV drugs. One of their main tasks was to give advice to HIV-infected individuals on the choice of the "best" clinical trial for their needs (Sinet 1994). This is important, because in France, for example, the majority of HIV-infected individuals who are in contact with the associative movement, that is all those who are not too marginal to be cut off from organized structure are included in experimental protocols which test an anti-HIV treatment. It is also important because the trial's organizers need to recruit enough patients to make the trial valid. The last consideration is of particular importance when the tested drug already has a marketing permit and the trial's goal is to evaluate a different dosage or a different indication for this drug (e.g., the Concord trial which evaluated the efficacy of AZT in asymptomatic HIV-infected individuals). If the molecule does not have a marketing permit, and if it looks promising, recruitment of patients is less problematic, but these patients often have to make strategic decisions about priorities in enrolling in clinical trials and associative experts may help them to take such a decision. In the opposite case, when access to promising experimental treatment is limited, the associations put pressure on regulating bodies, to widen access and to ensure free or reimbursed supply of the drug. In such cases, the pressure of the associative movement may improve the bargaining position of pharmaceutical companies and help them to shorten the time it takes to receive a marketing permit and to get a better price for their product. The rapid obtention of temporary marketing permits (ATU or 'authorization temporaire d'utilisation') for anti-proteases in France which made possible the wide diffusion of tri-therapies of AIDS (and, as a result, a 60 percent drop in AIDS mortality in 1996) was the direct result of associative movement pressures.

To sum up, the development of anti-HIV drugs is shaped to a large extent by an interplay between pharmaceutical firms and governmental agencies, and, in parallel, is dependent on the willingness of patients to enroll in clinical trials. The associative movement has a greater influence on the second (i.e., AIDS patients) than on the first (i.e., on companies and governmental agencies). Its efforts have been centered therefore on diffusion of comparative information to patients and on the mediation between producers, regulatory agencies and users (occasionally organizing users' pressure on pharmaceutical firms and governmental agencies), a task which may be compared to that of traditional consumer associations. Thus the director of NIAID, Anthony Fauci, explained that: "The scientific community quickly learned the importance of including AIDS activists in the administrative policy-making process . . . AIDS activists became an invaluable resource in the design of clinical trials to make them 'user friendly' to people with AIDS" (Fauci 1995: 71). The supervision of industrialists and of governmental regulatory agencies by users and the transformation of trials in order to better adapt them to the patients' needs, is, one could say, a political task. It is a more complicated task than that of traditional consumers' associations, because the emotional involvement of patients' representatives in the evaluation of anti-HIV drugs is not the same as the emotional involvement of consumers' representatives who test, say, hairdryers, canned soups or computer games. This emotional involvement, together with material considerations (AIDS patients fight for free or fully reimbursed access to efficient therapies) limit their independence from governmental bodies and even from industry. One may suppose, however, that if relatively efficient and relatively standardized anti-HIV therapies were found, the tasks of the AIDS associative movement would become more similar to those of other consumer movements – from those who evaluate consumer goods to those who fight for environmental issues.

Technical Devices, AIDS Activism and Policy

Writing about the social construction of AIDS, the medical historian Charles Rosenberg explained that "if the recognition of disease implies both a biological phenomenon and its social perception, it also involves policy" (1992: 277). This may seem self-evident. Health-care decisions are, by definition, political ones, and historians who wrote about AIDS stressed the importance of political decisions in AIDS. The definition of this disease (that is, the decision as to when an HIV-infected person is classified as an "AIDS patient" and is entitled to receive free medical help and special patient rights), the allocation of funds for AIDS research and the organization of the treatment of AIDS patients, were all shaped by political considerations. Reading the rapidly accumulating AIDS literature (especially that produced by social scientists, historians and policy experts), one may however observe a frequent split between "policy-oriented" publications, which deal with economic and social issues, and investigations inspired by the new trends in science and technology studies, which are focused on scientists' and doctors' practices, and tend to disregard political and economic issues. Such neglect of the (macro) economic and the political is occasionally justified through a reference to new trends in science studies which gave up the previous attempts to link specific bodies of knowledge to the interests of some social or professional groups, and opted instead for ethnography-inspired inquiries into the content of scientific practices (Nukaga and Cambrosio 1997, for example). The presumed opposition between "social determinism" and "study of practices," recently advanced by some investigators who study science is, I propose, artificial. The choice is not (or at least should not be) between culturally sensitive thick descriptions of devices and practices which are conducted in an infinitely flexible world and schematic explanations based on grossly predetermined "group interests" and categories. Both are caricatures: innovations are shaped by and shape their environment, but this environment is not infinitely flexible: it is more or less resilient to change, and this resilience reflects its history. If, as Annemarie Mol proposed, medical innovations have to make room in a "full world," the world is full not only with other devices and practices, but also with cultural, institutional, economic and political constraints (Mol 1993).[13] Das's and Lock's analyses (this volume) make precisely this point. The implementation of life-sustaining technologies in Japan interacts with cultural and religious values, as well as with instruments and tools, with the division of labor in modern hospitals, or with socialization of doctors and nurses. The same act, namely providing an organ from a living donor for transplantation, may have multiple meanings, but its socio-economic context severely constrains the flexibility of its interpretations. In India, it is impossible to disconnect the problem of supply of organs for transplantation from poverty, from violence against the poor, and from their survival strategies.

I understand Rosenberg's injunction to remember that the recognition of disease also involves policy as calling our attention to the existence of "macro" elements and to their constant interaction with "micro" and "meso" levels of representation and intervention. Policies are not conducted "out there", and they may (and often have) very concrete consequences on all levels of human activity. It may be more satisfactory to focus a given study on the (relatively) "clean" micro or meso-analysis of tools and practices, and to leave the (relatively) "dirty" economic considerations for other experts to tackle. This is not always possible, however. Some topics – such as the testing of new drugs – are intrinsically "contaminated" with political and economic considerations, and this "contamination" spreads to every level of practice: to borrow from the AIDS activists' language, there are no "clean" clinical trials. One may argue that there is no such thing as "pure science," and development of knowledge about new drugs is but a special case which illustrates this general rule. On an abstract level this may well be true. In practice, however, some areas of scientific activity are more isolated from the pressures of the external world than others: paleontologists are usually not subjected to the same kind of pressures as forensic scientists are, and the search for new varieties of snails has much lower visibility than the search for new therapies for cancer or AIDS.

Social scientists who became interested in the changes brought to the methods of testing new drugs by AIDS epidemics traced the ways organized patients influenced the definition of experts and expertise, of objective knowledge, and of the tasks of medicine. This is an important point, because the highly visible AIDS activism indeed attracted attention to the role of patients in the constitution and validation of medical knowledge (Epstein 1995; Feenberg 1995). I believe, however, that these accounts tend to exaggerate the extent of the change brought by AIDS activists to an established biomedical technology, and to underestimate the continuities between the trials of anti-HIV drugs, and trials of drugs for other potentially fatal diseases, such as cancer. The "patient-centered" perspective of these studies is related, I propose, to the absence of analyses of strategies of the pharmaceutical industry from studies which attempt to analyse the development of anti-AIDS drugs.[14] Why were the pharmaceutical companies – undoubtedly a key actor in the production and diffusion of new drugs – overlooked or trivialized in these analyses? One possible explanation may be related to the reluctance of social scientists to deal with (for some) self-evident and thus "uninteresting" issues. The pharmaceutical industry may be perceived as an "uninteresting" actor driven (mainly) by a wish to manufacture sellable and profitable products. Another explanation may be related to the difficulty in studying industrial strategies. It is easier to gain access to academic scientists, clinicians or government officials than to indus-trialists. The latter frequently have a strong and direct interest to keep their recent moves secret. Industrial strategies are therefore an easier research topic for a historian than for a sociologist.[15] The industrial secret is a serious problem for students of biomedicine, and this chapter too may be rightly criticized for insufficient analysis of industrialists' activities. One should not confuse, however, the difficulties of a given inquiry, amplified by the shortage of funds and of time and by personal preferences, with an intrinsic lack of interest in a given subject. If the AIDS epidemic is indeed, as Paula Treichler (1987) proposed, an "epi-demic of signification," this term may indicate, among other things, that symbolic interpretations of a disease affect power relationships.[16] Power relationships are, however, affected by other elements as well, for example by technical devices, institutional structures or economic con-siderations. None of these elements is totally stable and predetermined, but their degree of stability and influence may be very different.[17]

The story of AIDS drugs testing illustrates, I propose, both the flexi-bility and resilience of institutions of biomedicine and the technologies they produce. The flexibility makes room for the intervention of users of biomedical technologies: the rigidity reflects the role of history in shaping and consolidating institutions and structures. AIDS activists attempted first to modify radically the evaluation of new therapies for this pathology, then to adapt the existing technology to what they per-ceived as the specific needs of AIDS patients. The second strategy was more successful than the first. Patient representatives were coopted to official decision-making bodies and they successfully changed some of the parameters of clinical trials of AIDS drugs. The patient-inspired changes established the important principle of the right of users to influence medical technologies. The clinical trials for anti-HIV drugs maintained, however, the basic principles of drug testing for potentially fatal diseases established during the trials of anti-cancer drugs. More-over, the introduction, from 1995 on, of a combination of anti-proteases and other anti-HIV compounds led to a partial return to more "tra-ditional" forms of organizing clinical testing of new anti-HIV drugs.[18] The latter phenomenon may be related to the fact that these anti-HIV drugs are produced nearly exclusively by large multinational pharma-ceutical firms which negotiate directly with major governmental regulat-ory agencies. It may also be related to the development of new technol-ogies, such as quantitative PCR, which make it possible to quantify HIV in the patient's blood, and to observe the effects of administration of anti-viral drugs on circulating virus particles. The new technologies homogenized the criteria of evaluation of the efficacy of anti-HIV drugs (an efficient drug combination is the one which lowers the concentration of HIV in the blood below detectable levels), making this process more akin to the evaluation of anti-cancer drugs (Pearlson 1996).

More than a hundred years of close interaction between medicine and the pharmaceutical industry consolidated the role of the biomedical-industrial complex in shaping scientists', doctors' and patients' activities.[19] It is not very surprising that AIDS activists were not able to transform biomedicine's structures radically and permanently. Steven Epstein, who in his thesis of 1993 focused on the role of AIDS activists in the modification of scientific practices, ended the book version of his thesis (published in 1996) in a more sober tone:

> the fact that various dimensions of social hierarchy . . . crisscross and intertwine with politics of expertise only complicates the story and imbues it with additional poignancy. These considerations suggest the true dimensions of the problem: it is unlikely that knowledge-making practices can be substantially democratized, except when efforts to do so are carried out in conjunction with other social struggles that challenge other, entrenched systems of domination. (Epstein 1996: 352)[20]

The direct influence of AIDS activists on the structure and validation of biomedical knowledge was real but limited. This chapter proposes that the most important change brought by AIDS activists lies elsewhere: their action displayed the way norms and power relationships are incorporated into specific biomedical technologies. AIDS activists influenced medicine in the same manner that the anti-nuclear movement activists influenced energy policies: by pointing to the social underpinnings of the previously unchallenged technology and by submitting it to public scrutiny. This is an important change, and one which affects in many ways our understanding and evaluation of biomedicine. The interaction between the AIDS associative movement and the drug regulatory process in the years 1985–95 may thus be seen as an apt illustration of Salomon Neumann's statement of 1847: "medical science is intrinsically and essentially a social science" (Neumann 1847 in Taylor and Rieger 1984).

NOTES

This work was supported by ANRS research grant no. 711–104. I am indebted to Alberto Cambrosio, Margaret Lock and all the participants in the "Cultures of Biomedical Technologies" conference as well as Jean Paul Gaudillière for critical discussion of an earlier version of this paper.
1. Isabelle Stenghers discusses the problematic notion of "efficacy" in Western medicine (1995). George Weisz (1994) has studied the ways nineteenth-century French doctors tried to evaluate therapies and shows that in certain

unambiguous cases (e.g., life-saving surgical procedures) it was possible to make comparative studies and arrive at unambiguous conclusions.

2. On the role of quantification in deflecting suspicion see Porter, 1995. Porter points out, however, that some groups of scientists, such as nuclear physicists, successfully negotiated (relative) independence from public scrutiny, and convinced the fund-givers (nearly always public institutions) that only inside experts are able to judge the quality of their work. It is easier, however, to convince the public that it should not be interested in details of the working of sub-atomic particles than in the development of new treatments for heart disease.

3. On the principles of controlled clinical trials see Hill 1937, and on the implementation of the first controlled trials, see Hill 1990: 77–9 and Lock 1994.

4. Thus trials conducted in the 1970s had shown that treatment in intensive care units did not improve the survival following an infarctus, but these results were not taken into account by doctors who considered it unfair to deprive their patients of the advantage of being in intensive care (Hill 1978; Matter et al. 1976).

5. As a rule, screening programs used mice grafted with a transplantable tumor, a much cheaper model for cancer than spontaneous tumors developed in genetically homogeneous lines of animals. The Sloan Kettering program used a single animal model, the S-180 sarcoma of albino mice.

6. The argument about the reconstruction of meaning of medical science was proposed by Epstein (1995). Feenberg (1995) explains that AIDS patients' activism replaced the technocratic organization of medicine by an attempt to recover its symbolic dimension and caring functions.

7. James started to publish *AIDS Treatment News* in May 1986.

8. Steven Epstein (1993) studied in detail the different stages of the involvement of AIDS activists in the regulatory process in the US.

9. Experts were convinced by activists that the acceleration of the drug approval process need not hamper the quality of testing (Merigan 1990; Young 1995).

10. Such a point of view was expressed for example, by the World Health Organization expert, Joep Lange (see Cotton 1994 for quote) and by the French activist Xavier Rey-Coquis, from the Association Actions-Traitement, who specialized in the follow-up of clinical trials of AIDS therapies (*Le Journal de la MGEN* 1996).

11. David Baltimore and Mark Feinberg stated that "we are rapidly learning about the role of each of HIV's approximately 10,000 nucleotides, but remain largely ignorant of rudimentary aspects of the process underlying the development of AIDS in humans" (1989: 1673).

12. Animal models of cancer were, one may note, an important intermediary in the development of the culture of "clinical experimentation in oncology" in the 1950s and 1960s.

13. See also Berg and Mol 1998.

14. Radical activists of the AIDS associative movement did acknowledge that the capacity of the associative movement to influence the powerful

international infrastructure of pharmaceutical companies is often limited (Lestrade 1966).

15. Thus the industrial development of penicillin during the Second World War has became an object of study from the 1980s on (Hobby 1985; Liebenau 1987; Neushul 1993).

16. In democratic countries power relationships are often directly affected by symbol-laden discourses. To take a recent example, the important political consequences of the supposition that a cattle disease may in rare cases be transmitted to humans may probably be related to the fact that this pathology was called "mad cow disease" rather than, for example, "prionosis."

17. Automatic assumptions about the possible outcome of force trials are a poor social science, but a systematic neglect of pre-existing power relationships does not necessarily make a better one. Thus it is impossible to know what the consequences of a specific confrontation between, say, a group of migrant workers and French officials will be, but this does not mean that in such confrontation both sides have identical ability to construct long and efficient networks or to redefine the meaning of basic terms, such as "policeman," "judge" or "illegal migrant."

18. Harold Edgar and David J. Rothman explained in 1990 that the deregulation brought to the fore by AIDS activists will probably lead at some point to counter-reaction, and that the pendulum will swing again to more rigorous supervision of new drugs. However, they attributed this possibility of change in policy to an accumulation of failures which will result from multiplication of drugs produced by small biotechnology firms, rather than the concentration of the production of new drugs in the hands of a few major pharmaceutical companies and the elaboration of unofficial agreements between drug producers and the regulatory agencies (1990: 139).

19. On this history, see, for example, Pickstone 1993.

20. Epstein refers here to stability of social, cultural and political structures (e.g., those which maintain racist attitudes). He does not discuss explicitly in this context the role of stability of biomedicine.

REFERENCES

Arno, Peter S. and Karyn L. Feiden 1992 *Against the Odds: The Story of AIDS Drug Development, Politics and Profits.* New York: HarperCollins.

Baltimore, David and Mark B. Feinberg 1989 "HIV Revealed". *New England Journal of Medicine* 321(24): 1673–5.

Berg, Marc, and Annemarie Mol 1998 (eds.) *Differences in Medicine. Unraveling Practices, Techniques and Bodies.* Durham and London: Duke University Press.

Biernacki, Edmund 1902 *Zasady Poznania Lekarskiego* (The Principles of Medical Knowledge). Warsaw: Wende and Company.

Bloom, Bernard S. 1986 "Controlled Studies in the Measurement of the Efficacy of Medical Care: A Historical Perspective." *International Journal of Technology Assessment in Health Care* 2: 299–310.

Bud, Robert F. 1978 "Strategy in American Cancer Research after World War II: A Case Study." *Social Studies of Science* 8: 425–59.

Bush, Vannevar 1945 *Science, The Endless Frontier: A Report to the President.* Washington, DC: US Government Printing Office.

Cancer Chemotherapy Reports 1966 "The Cancer Chemotherapy Program, 1965: Analysis of contract activities." 50: 403–51.

Cassileth, Barrie R. 1979 "The Evolution of Oncology as a Sociomedical Phenomenon." In Barrie R. Cassileth (ed.), *The Cancer Patient: Social and Medical Aspects of Care.* Philadelphia: Lea & Febiger, pp. 3–15.

Chalmers, Thomas C., Jerome Block and Stephanie Lee 1972 "Controlled Studies in Cancer Research." *The New England Journal of Medicine* 278: 75–8.

Cotton, Paul 1994 "Many Clues, Few Conclusions on AIDS." *Journal of the American Medical Association* 272: 753–6.

Edgar, Harold, and David J. Rothman 1990 "New Rules for New Drugs: The Challenge of AIDS to the Regulatory Process." *Millbank Quarterly* 86(1) Supplement: 111–42.

Endicott, Kenneth M. 1957 "The Chemotherapy Program." *Journal of the National Cancer Institute* 19: 275–93.

Epstein, Steven 1993 "Impure Science: AIDS Activism and the Politics of Knowledge." Ph.D. dissertation, University of California.

    1995 "The Construction of Lay Expertise: AIDS Activism and the Forging of Credibility in the Reform of Clinical Trials." *Science, Technology and Human Values* 20(4): 408–37.

    1996 *Impure Science: AIDS Activism and the Politics of Knowledge.* Berkeley: University of California Press.

Fauci, Anthony S. 1995 "AIDS: Reflections on the Past, Considerations for the Future." In Caroline Hannaway, Victoria A. Harden and John Parascandola (eds.), *AIDS and Public Debate.* Amsterdam: IOS Press, pp. 67–73.

Feenberg, Andrew 1995 "On Being a Human Subject: AIDS and the Crisis of Experimental Medicine." In Andrew Feenberg, *Alternative Modernity: The Technical Turn in Philosophy and Social Theory.* Berkeley, Los Angeles, London: University of California Press, pp. 96–120.

Feinstein, Alvan R. 1987 "The Intellectual Crisis in Clinical Medicine: Medaled Models and Muddled Mettle." *Perspectives in Biology and Medicine* 30(2): 215–30.

Fintor, Lou 1991 "Patient Activism: Cancer Groups Become Vocal and Politically Active." *Journal of the National Cancer Institute* 83(8): 528–9.

Fontenay, Franck and Jean François Chambon 1996 "La conférence de Washington: L'indavir et le ritonavir relancent l'intérêt pour trithérapies." *Le Journal du Sida* 82 (February): 4–11.

Gagnon, Eric 1994 "Médicine scientifique et médicine de l'individu." *Sciences Sociales et Santé* 2: 4.

Gehan, Edmund A. 1960 "Use of Medical Measurement to Predict the Course of Disease." *Monographs of the National Cancer Institute* 3: 51–8.

Gehan, Edmund A. and Emil J. Freireich 1972 "Non Randomized Controls in Clinical Trials." *New England Journal of Medicine* 278: 75–8.

Gerdes, J. and H. G. Flad 1992 "Folicular Dendritic Cells and their Role in HIV Infection." *Immunology Today* 13: 81–3.

Hammer, Scott M. 1994 "Early Antiretroviral Therapy: Controversy and

Consensus." In J. P. Coulard, J. J. Pocidale, G. Saimot, F. Vachon, and J. L. Vilde (eds.), *Perspectives therapeutiques de l'infection par l'HIV en Stade Precoce.* Paris: Arnette, pp. 87–97.

Harrington, Mark 1994 "La crise des essais therapeutiques." *Journal du Sida* 62 (May): 16–20.

Heffland, W. H., H. B. Woodruff, K. M. H. Coleman and D. L. Cowen 1980 "Wartime Industrial Development of Penicillin in the United States." In John Parascandola (ed.), *The History of Antibiotics.* Madison, WI: American Institute for the History of Pharmacy, pp. 122–47.

Hellman, Samuel and Deborah S. Hellman 1991 "Of Mice and Not of Men: Problems of the Randomized Clinical Trial." *New England Journal of Medicine* 324(22): 1585–9.

Hill, Anthony Bradford 1937 *Principles of Medical Statistics. The Lancet.*
    1990 "Memories of the Streptomycin Trial of Tuberculosis: The First Randomized Clinical Trial." *Controlled Clinical Trials* 11: 77–9.

Hill, J. D., R. D. Hampton and J. R. Mitchell 1978 "A Randomized Trial of Home Versus Hospital Management of Patients with Suspected Myocardial Infarction." *The Lancet* (I): 837–41.

Hobby, Gladys L. 1985 *Penicillin: Meeting the Challenge.* New Haven, CT and London: Yale University Press.

James, John J. 1989 *AIDS Treatment News* 1.

Johnston, Margaret I. and Daniel F. Hoth 1993 "Present Status and Future Prospects for HIV Therapies." *Science* 260: 1286–93.

Joint Task Force on Anticancer Drugs 1982 *The NC Development and FDA Regulations.* Washington, DC: National Cancer Institute, Food and Drug Administration, US Department of Health and Human Services.

Karnofsky, David A. 1961 "Meaningful Clinical Classification of Therapeutic Responses to Anticancer Drugs." *Clinical Pharmacology and Therapeutics* 2(6): 709–12.

Keefer, Chester 1948 "Penicillin, a Wartime Accomplishment." In E. C. Andrews et al, (eds.), *Advances in Military Medicine.* Boston: Little Brown, pp. 719–22.

Lange, Joep M. A. 1995 "Triple Combinations: Present and Future." *Journal of AIDS and Human Retroviruses* 10(1) Supplement: 77–82.

Lasagna, Louis 1989 "Congress, the FDA and New Drug Development: Before and After 1962." *Perspectives in Biology and Medicine* 32(2): 322–43.

Lasagna, Louis, and Lars Werkö 1986 "International Differences in Drug Regulation Philosophy." *International Journal of Technology Assessment in Health Care* 2: 615–18.

Le Journal de la MGEN 1996 Interview with Xavier Rey-Coquis.

Lestrade, Didier 1966 "L'impact du movement militant." *Transcriptase* 43: 5–7.

Liebenau, Jonathan 1987 "The British Success with Penicillin." *Social Studies of Science* 17: 69–86.
    1990 "Paul Ehrlich as a Commercial Scientist and Research Administrator." *Medical History* 34: 65–78.

Lock, Stephen 1994 "The Randomized Clinical Trial, a British Invention." In Ghislaine Lawrence (ed.), *Technologies of Modern Medicine.* London: Science Museum. pp. 81–7.

MacKillop, William J. and Pauline A. Johnston 1986 "Ethical Problems in Clinical Research." *Journal of Chronic Diseases* 39–3(3): 177–88.
Marks, Harry M. 1987a "Ideas as Reforms: Therapeutic Experiments and Medical Practice." Ph.D. dissertation, M.I.T.
1987b "Notes from the Underground: The Social Organization of Therapeutic Research." In Russell C. Maulitz and Diana E. Long (eds.), *Grand Rounds: One Hundred Years of Internal Medicine*. Philadelphia: University of Pennsylvania Press, pp. 297–334.
Matter, H. G., D. C. Morgan, N. G. Pearson et al. 1976 "Myocardial Infarction: A Comparison between Home and Hospital Care for Patients." *British Medical Journal* (I): 925–9.
Merigan, Thomas C. 1990 "You Can Teach an Old Dog New Tricks: How AIDS Trials are Pioneering New Strategies." *New England Journal of Medicine* 323(19): 1341–3.
Mol, Annemarie 1993 "What's New? Dopler and its Others. An Empirical Philosophy of Innovation. In Ilana Löwy, (ed.), *Medicine and Change: Historical and Sociological Studies of Medical Innovation*. Paris and London: John Libbey, pp. 17–127.
Moss, Andrew R. and Peter Bachetti 1989 "Natural History of AIDS Infection." *AIDS* 32: 55–61.
Neumann, Salomon 1847 *Public Health and Property*. Berlin: Adolph Reiss.
Neushul, Peter 1993 "Science, Government and the Mass Production of Penicillin." *Journal of the History of Medicine and Allied Sciences* 48: 371–95.
Nowak, Martin A. 1995 "AIDS Pathogenesis: From Models to Viral Dynamics in Patients." *Journal of AIDS and Human Retroviruses* 10(1) Supplement: 1–5.
Nukaga, Yoshio, and Alberto Cambrosio 1997 "Medical Pedigrees and the Visual Production of Family Disease in Canadian and Japanese Genetic Counselling Practices." In Mary Ann Elston (ed.), *The Sociology of Medical Science and Technology*. London: Blackwell, pp. 29–55.
Nusbaum, Bruce 1991 *Good Intentions: How the Business and the Medical Establishment are Corrupting the Fight Against AIDS, Alzheimer's Disease, Cancer and More*. Harmondsworth, Middlesex: Penguin Books.
Patterson, James T. 1987 *The Dread Disease: Cancer and the Modern American Culture*. Cambridge, MA: Harvard University Press.
Pearlson, Alan S., Avidan U. Neumann, Martin Markowitz, John M. Leonard and David D. Ho 1996 "HIV-1 Dynamics In Vivo: Virion Clearance Rate, Infected Cells Life-span, and Viral Generation time." *Science*: 1593–6.
Pickstone, John V. 1993 "Ways of Knowing: Towards a History of Science, Technology and Medicine." *British Journal of the History of Science* 26: 433–58.
Porter, Theodore 1995 *Trust in Numbers: The Pursuit of Objectivity in Science and Public Life*. Princeton: Princeton University Press.
Ravdin, Isidor S. 1962 "The Clinical Studies Program." *Cancer Chemotherapy Reports* 16: 5–8.
Rosenberg, Charles 1992 "Disease and Social Order in America: Perceptions and expectations. In *Explaining Epidemics and Other Studies in the History of Medicine*. Cambridge: Cambridge University Press, pp. 258–77.

Rothman, David J. and Harold Edgar 1992 "Scientific Rigor and Medical Realities: Placebo Trials in Cancer and AIDS Research." In Elizabeth Fee and Daniel M. Fox (eds.), *AIDS: The Making of a Chronic Disease*. Berkeley, Los Angeles, London: University of California Press, pp. 194–206.

Saag, Michael S, Scott M. Hammer and Joep M. A. Lange 1992 "Pathogenicity and Diversity of HIV and Implications for Clinical Management." *Journal of AIDS and Human Retroviruses* 7(2) Supplement: 2–11.

Schneiderman, Marvin 1967 "Non Objective Art and Objective Evaluation in Cancer Chemotherapy." In Isidore Brodsky and S. Benham Cohen (eds.), *Cancer Chemotherapy*. New York and London: Grune and Stratton, pp. 67–76.

Sessoms, Stuart M. 1959–60 "Review of the Cancer Chemotherapy National Service Center Program." *Cancer Chemotherapy Reports* 1(7): 25–46.

Shear, Murray J. 1951 "Role of the Chemotherapy Research Laboratory in Clinical Cancer Research." *Journal of the National Cancer Institute* 12: 569–82.

Sinet, Marine 1994 "Débat sur l'évaluation des anti-viraux." *Transcriptase* (August): 26–8.

St. Clair, Marty H., Kevin N. Pennington, James Rooney and David W. Barry 1995a "In Vitro Comparison of Selected Triple-Drug Combination for Suppression of HIV-1 Replication: The Inter-Company Collaboration Protocol." *Journal of AIDS and Human Retroviruses* 10(1) Supplement: 83–91.

1995b "Rapid Screening for Antiretroviral Combinations." *Journal of AIDS and Human Retroviruses* 10(1) Supplement: 24–7.

Stenghers, Isabelle 1995 "Le médecin et le charlatan." In Toby Nathan and Isabelle Stenghers (eds.), *Medecins et Sorciers*. Paris: Les Empecheurs de Penser en Rond, pp. 115–61.

Steru, Lucien and Pierre Simon 1986 "French Drug Policy." *International Journal of Technology Assessment in Health Care* 2: 637–42.

Swann, John P. 1994 "FDA and the Practice of Pharmacy: Prescription Drug Regulation before the Durham-Humphrey Amendment of 1951." *Pharmacy in History* 36(2): 55–70.

Taylor, Rex and Annelie Rieger 1984 "Rudolph Virchow on the Typhus Epidemics in Upper Silesia: An Introduction and Translation." *Sociology of Health and Illness* 6(2): 203–19.

The Lancet 1995 Editorial: "Evidence-Based Medicine, in its Place." 765: ii.

Travis, Anthony 1992 "Science as Receptor of Technology: Paul Ehrlich and the Synthetic Dyestuff Industry." *Science in Context* 3(2): 383–408.

Treichler, Paula A. 1987 "AIDS, Homophobia and Biomedical Discourse: An Epidemic of Signification." *Cultural Studies* 1: 263–305.

Vella, Stephano 1995 "HIV Pathogenesis and Treatment Strategies." *Journal of AIDS and Human Retroviruses* 10(1) Supplement: 20–3.

Vines, Gail 1995 "Goodbye to the Dinosaurs: The Rise of Evidence-Based Medicine." *Odyssey* 1(3): 2–7.

Wain-Hobson, Simon 1995 "Virological Mayhem." *Nature* 373: 102.

Walkers, T. Philip 1962 "Current Status of Cooperative Group Program." *Cancer Chemotherapy Reports* 16: 597–602.

Warner, John Harley 1986 *The Therapeutic Perspective: Medical Practice, Knowledge, and Identity in America*. Cambridge, MA: Harvard University Press.

Weisz, George 1994 *The Medical Mandarins: The French Academy of Medicine in the Nineteenth and Early Twentieth Century*. New York and Oxford: Oxford University Press.

Young, James Harvey 1995 "AIDS and the FDA". In Caroline Hannaway, Victoria A. Harden and John Parascandola (eds.), *AIDS and Public Debate*. Amsterdam: IOS Press, pp. 47–66.

Zubrod, C. Gordon 1979 "Historic Milestones in Curative Chemotherapy." *Seminars in Oncology* 6(4): 490–505.

1984 "Origins and Development of Chemotherapy Research at the National Cancer Institute." *Cancer Treatment Reports* 68(1): 9–19.

Zubrod, C. Gordon, Saul A. Schepartz and Stephen K. Carter 1977 "Historical Background of the National Cancer Institute Drug Development Trust." *National Cancer Institute Monographs*, 45: 7–11.

5 Pathology and the clinic: an ethnographic presentation of two atheroscleroses

Annemarie Mol

Hospital Z is a university hospital in a medium-sized town in the Netherlands. It differs in specific ways from other hospitals, but if one wants to study the form modern medicine takes in an affluent welfare state it is no better or worse than many others. In this chapter I will report on a study I conducted in hospital Z. This study was partly ethnographic. For several years I regularly went to this hospital and visited various departments in order to investigate the diagnosis and treatment of atherosclerosis of the leg vessels. The main aim of the study, however, was not to map faithfully what happens in the course of diagnosing and treating this single medical problem. Instead it was philosophical. I wanted to contribute to the crafting of better terms for analyzing the relations between medical knowledge and its objects.

In this chapter I'll present some of my findings – or maybe I should say some of my inventions. More specifically, I will present *knowing* not as a faculty of the human mind, but as an activity of the human body and the instruments it puts to use. This implies a shift in status for the objects of knowledge. Instead of being in the point of focus for a variety of eyes, each with their own *perspective*, they are presented here as objects that are being handled – by hands and knives; by questioning and listening; by coloured dyes and patient files. When analyzed like this, the various ways of engaging in the activity of knowing a single disease, such as *atherosclerosis of the leg vessels*, appear to each have a different object. The term used here to express what having an object might entail is *performance*. The argument is that medical practices *perform* their objects.

The term performance was drawn into sociology by Goffman in the late 1950s for describing the way people stage identities. In the recent social studies of science, the same term has been mobilized again, this time to talk about the way reality is staged (Law 1994; Hirschauer 1998, for example). If I put the term to work here, it is not with the front-stage/back-stage split which pervaded it in Goffman's work. There is no *deeper* real reality behind the one we live with. The reality that counts – or the

82

realit*ies* that count – in our daily lives, lives in the hospital included, are those we are able to perform practically, in one way or another. Thus the disease atherosclerosis of the leg vessels is not a passive reality *preceding* the diagnostic techniques of medicine, but neither is it their *product* (able to live on after medical techniques have retreated from the scene). The term performance nicely catches the coincidence in time between diagnostic activities and the disease they deal with.

Once the relation between hospital practices and diseases are described in terms of *performance* ethnography becomes crucial to the philosophy of knowledge. For instead of listing the conditions under which true knowledge might be acquired, it now becomes urgent for the philosopher to analyze what kinds of objects are performed, how they are performed, and how it might be that while there are large variations in the objects performed that go by a single name (such as *atherosclerosis*) hospital practice does not explode into disparate fragments. Ethnography happens to have good tools for dealing with such questions. This is why I mix the genres here. Doing so, however, leaves neither of them untouched. For it is not only philosophy that alters, but ethnography too. For ethnography, a term like *performance* means that it is now possible to study *disease*.

In the 1950s, the social sciences, ethnography included, gained a foothold in the medical domain by crafting a distinction between *disease* and *illness*. The claim was that, alongside disease, the physical deviances studied by biomedicine, there is another reality, one that will never be exhausted by descriptions that stick to physical parameters. Alongside disease *tout court*, social scientists said, there is such a thing as its psychological and social dimensions. To mark it off, they called this "illness." Different theoretical traditions each made something different out of illness: a sick role; a gradual process of separating out individuals and attributing blame to them; an emotional component that accompanies a physical problem; a lay interpretation of physical impairments and the concomitant life-events; the social problems that follow from disease, and so on.[1] But however, and however much, social scientists got to know about "illness," this did not touch upon the biomedical definitions of "disease."

Recently, a range of scholars have argued that by taking what doctors say about "disease" for granted, a crucial part of medicine is left unanalyzed. The social sciences should not restrict their scope to the emotions and cognitions of patients on the one hand and the organization of health care on the other. The *heart* of medicine, biomedical knowledge, deserves to be studied as well.[2] Many of the first ethnographies of medical knowledge go about their newly set task in a *perspectivalist* way. To an "illness" that equals the patients' perspective on what happens to them, they add a "disease" that equals the physicians' perspective on what happens to their patients. Medical knowledge is thus treated as an assemblage of mental images, as a set of representations, as a growing body of textual and pictorial cultural products.

It is at this point that mobilizing the concept of *performance* makes an important difference. For it allows ethnography to engage with the materialities of diseases, with their fleshiness, their physicality. It allows ethnography to shift its attention from the observing *eyes* of professionals to their *hands* and instruments; from the *group culture* of medical specialists, with their shared languages and mutual rivalries, to the *material culture* of medicine: its hospital buildings, dissection knives, examination tables and artery pulsations. If these shifts are made then perhaps *ethnography* is no longer the most appropriate term for the discipline. Perhaps it would be better to call it *practiography*.

In this text I'll give you a sample of a hybrid genre. Mixing the philosophical aim of crafting theoretical terms with the practiographical style of telling stories, I'll take you to two places in hospital Z: the department of *pathology* and the *outpatient clinic*. In modern hospitals other sites are equally (or in some respects more) prominent in the diagnostic process of patients with atherosclerosis of the leg vessels: the vascular laboratory, where the blood pressure in arms and ankles is taken and blood velocity is measured with duplex machines; and the radiology department where angiographies are made, that is X-rays of arteries in which a contrasting dye has been injected.[3] But there is a special reason for looking at the department of pathology and the outpatient clinic: they are the two extremes of the diagnostic spectrum. That is why I describe them here. They allow me not only to introduce the term *performance*, but to also underscore the *multiplicity* of the disease that I follow from one site to the other: atherosclerosis of the leg vessels.

Getting to Know Atherosclerosis

In order to get access to the way atherosclerosis is dealt with in hospital Z, I asked the local professor of pathology if I could observe it. He sent me to a senior pathologist who specializes in atherosclerosis research, who, after talking with me for a while, handed me over to a resident. This informant happened to be pleased that someone wanted to know about his work. But in the department of pathology leg vessels afflicted by atherosclerosis are not available any random day. The pathology resident phoned me some three weeks after I had explained my purpose to him. "I've got a leg," he told me over the phone. A few days and preparatory steps later we finally saw what I came looking for. Atherosclerosis.

In the small room he shared with two others, books and papers all around, the pathology resident had installed the double microscope for the occasion of my visit. Each of us looked into one of the eyepieces. He focused the image, and pointed out what I should see with an built-in pointer. "You see, there's a vessel, this here, it's not quite a circle, but almost. It's pink, that's from the colourant. And that purple, here, that's the calcification, in the media. It's broken. They have done a bad job with the decalcification. Not done it long enough, so the knife had a problem cutting. Look, all this, this messiness here, that's an artefact from trying to cut calcium, it's hard to cut." He shifted the pointer to the middle of the circle. "That's the lumen. There's blood cells inside it, you see. That only happens when a lumen is small. Otherwise all blood is washed out during the preparation. And here, around the lumen, this first layer of cells, that's the intima. It's thick. Oh, wow, isn't it thick! It goes all the way from here, to there. Look. Now there's your atherosclerosis. That's it. A thickening of the intima. That's really what it is."

There was a little pause and then he added: "Under a microscope."

My endeavor hinges on this last addition. The pathology resident utters it as if he says nothing special. "Under a microscope." But it implies a lot. Without this addition, atherosclerosis is all alone. It is visible *through* a microscope. A thickened intima. There is something seductive about it. To bow one's head over a microscope and let one's eyes be directed by the pointer. If only because a vessel cross-section makes for a beautiful image. With all its pink and purple and its strange forms that slowly come to be discernible if their nature is explained. There's something seductive about it: to use instruments as "mere" instruments that unveil the hidden reality of atherosclerosis.

But when "under a microscope" is added, it is stressed that intimas *depend on* microscopes for becoming visible. And, with that, on a lot more. On the pointer. And on the two glass sheets that make the slide. There is the decalcification that, even when it isn't done for long enough, allows the technician to cut thin cross-sections of a vessel. And there is the work of that technician. The tweezers and the knives. The dyes that turn the various cellular structures pink and purple. Since all these are required in order to get to see a vessel wall, it may be said that atherosclerosis isn't a "thick intima" all alone. It only is a "thick intima" if a lot is added to it.

What to make of this? If thick vessel walls depend on microscopes, we might say they are *constructed* by them. For almost two decades now, the metaphor "construction" has been used in science studies (and many other parts of the social sciences as well).[4] It stresses the historicity of "constructed" entities. It suggests that, like bridges or bicycles, "facts" have not been among us from day one, but have been made. But the analogy with bridges and bicycles also suggests that, once made, facts will pertain for a long time afterwards. The reality "thick vessel walls," however, might well disappear if it were not revitalized time and again. If the dust cover is left on the microscope, the pink and purple cross sections, however impressive they are now, will fade away.[5] It is this requirement of repetitive re-enactment that the theater metaphor *performance* gets across quite well. In pathology, one can say, atherosclerosis is performed as a thick vessel wall. The instruments and skills involved in this performance are not invented from scratch every morning: there are scripts available. These may be followed meticulously or fairly freely; they may be modified and changed. But atherosclerosis *is* the thick vessel wall visible through a microscope only when and where vessels are being sliced, decalcified, colored, put on slides and observed through microscopes.

So this is how we may shift our understanding of what it is to know *and* incorporate "disease" into ethnography: by attending to the activities and materialities on which a disease depends in practice. Instead of going with the suggestion that the reality of atherosclerosis is hidden deep inside the body, it is possible to study the work required to make arterial cross-sections visible. It may not be easy to resist the seduction of the results of all that work, the "final images," but it can be done. Don't forget about the microscope! It is only when they are actively performed as real that thick vessel walls are relevant disease entities. And this is not done by some mind's eye, but by the hands of many people, knives, fluids, glass slides and microscopes.[6]

Getting to Know Atherosclerosis Again

In hospital Z the department of pathology is situated on the fourth floor of wing D. It is not the only site where atherosclerosis is to be found. When I asked the vascular surgeons of hospital Z to show me "atherosclerosis" they took me somewhere else. They did not invite me into an operation theatre right away, to see them open up skins and cut into flesh.[7] First, I was taken along to the *outpatient clinic*. The outpatient clinic of hospital Z is situated on the first floor of wing F. No knives are used there. Neither are there microscopes to look through. In the outpatient clinic atherosclerosis is performed by talking heads and touching hands.[8]

The vascular surgeon walks to the door and calls in the next patient. They shake hands. The doctor points at my presence and says that I'm there to learn something. He sits on a chair behind his desk. The patient, a woman in her eighties, takes a chair at the other side of the desk, clutching her handbag on her lap. The doctor looks in the file in front of him and takes a letter out.

"So, Mrs. Tilstra, here your general practitioner writes you've got problems with your leg. Do you?"

"Yes, yes, doctor. That's why I come here."

"Tell me, then, what are those problems? When do you have them?"

"Well, what can I say? It's when I try to do something doctor, move, walk, whatever. Like, I used to walk the dog for long stretches, but now I can't. I hardly can. It hurts too much."

"Where does it hurt"?

"Here, doctor, mostly down here, in my calf it does. In my left leg."

"So it hurts in your left calf when you walk. Now how many meters, if you walk on flat ground, say, how many meters do you think you can walk before it starts hurting?"

"What can I say? I think it must be, well, some, not a lot, some 100 meters I guess."

"Good. Or not good. Well. And then, can you walk again, then, after some rest?"

"Yeah, if I wait for a while, after that, yes. I can, yes."

What is diagnosed in the consulting room is: "pain in Mrs. Tilstra's left lower leg that begins upon walking a short distance on flat ground and stops after rest." This is what the surgeons call *intermittent claudication*. It depends on a lot of work that is done jointly by Mrs. Tilstra and the vascular surgeon. For Mrs. Tilstra needs the doctor to make her articulate the pain in a clinically relevant way.[9] While this doctor, in his turn, cannot make a clinical diagnosis without the patient. Other elements come into play as well. The desk, the chairs, the file, the patient's identity card, the general practitioner's letter: they all take part in the diagnosis.[10] As does Mrs. Tilstra's dog, without whom she might not even have tried to walk more than the 50 meters which make her left leg hurt.

Studying disease by ethnographic means, is as easy – or difficult – in the consulting room as it is in the department of pathology. The disease performed, however, is different between the two sites. An enlarged vessel wall visible through a microscope in one location, a limited walking distance in the other. The cracking lines of calcium in one site, a story about decreasing mobility in the other. Moreover, even in any single site the patterns are not rigid. There are endless variations.

Even if he has come all the way to the consulting room, Mr. Romer never gets to speak. His wife has come with him. She does the talking. "He's not doing well, doctor, he isn't. He can't do a thing any more."

"So, Mr. Romer," the surgeon says, trying to look the old man in the eye, "what's the problem? What do you come to see me for?"

"It's his legs, doctor," Mr. Romer's wife answers, "He's had a heart attack, he's had two in fact. But now it's his legs. He can't get himself to walk any more. He has too much pain." Mr. Romer looks worn out. And despite the surgeon's stubborn attempt to address him, Mr. Romer doesn't speak. Maybe he can't. Maybe – the surgeon seems to reckon with that possibility – he has given up trying.

A doctor in a consulting room cannot perform intermittent claudication all alone. He needs material support and other people. But the scenario is not that of a machine which stops as soon as a single element breaks down. There is a lot of flexibility.[11] Instead of 100 meters, the walking distance may be 200. Instead of the calf, the thigh may hurt. And if the patient cannot speak, someone else may speak for him. But even so there is a constant here: what is needed, indeed indispensable for clinical diagnosis, is that there be a patient-body. This must be present. And it must cooperate.

The surgeon looks from the file to the Romer couple and back down to the file, where he makes a few notes. Looking up again, he says, "Now, if you please, Mr. Romer, I'd like to take a look. I want your legs, I want to see for myself what they look like. And feel your blood vessels. For you may have a problem with your blood vessels." After having said this in a loud voice, the surgeon turns his head to Mrs. Romer – thereby accepted as a spokesperson – and asks: "Do you think it's possible for him to take his trousers off and lie on the examination table?" It is possible but not for Mr. Romer all by himself. For it isn't easy. The limbs are heavy. Shoes and socks can only be undone when the feet are lifted. The zip gets stuck and the fabric of the trousers is stiff. Then there's the height of the table. But after a while the vascular surgeon holds Mr. Romer's two feet in his hands to estimate and compare their temperature. He observes the skin. And with two fingers he feels the pulsations of the arteries in the groin, knee, and foot. "Can you flex your leg a bit for me, please, yeah, yes, that's it, there you go. Very good."

In their consulting rooms, vascular surgeons add a physical examination to an interview. The patients' answers to the diagnostic questions may make a typical story or a vague one. They may be enough to talk of intermittent claudication straight away, or not quite so. In either case, the performance of intermittent claudication is extended and strengthened by adding the elements a physical examination may yield. Cold feet or one cold foot. Weak pulsations. A thin, poorly oxygenated skin. Revealed through a cooperation of the patient's legs, the doctor's hands, the examination table and the person who helps a patient worn out with age to undo his shoes, and take off his socks and trousers. (See Strauss 1985 for the distribution of medical work over many people, including family and patients.)

Incompatible

When I asked the pathologists in hospital Z to show me "atherosclerosis of the leg vessels" I got to see thick vessel walls through a microscope.

When I made a similar request to the vascular surgeons, they took me to the outpatient clinic to hear patients talk about legs that hurt when walking. Each of these performances comes in varieties, but for now I will focus on the relation between them. How do the "thick vessel walls" of pathology and the "intermittent claudication" and "bad pulsations" of the clinic relate? For a moment it may seem that they do not relate at all. It is a long way from wing D, floor 4 to wing F, floor 1. Maybe it is too far to bridge, for the techniques that make atherosclerosis visible, audible, tangible and knowable in these two places exclude each other.

We walk to the fridge. The pathology resident takes out a plastic bag with a label attached to it. Inside it there's a foot with 28 centimetres of leg. It's been amputated the previous day and routinely sent to the pathology department for inspection. Could the plane of resection, the skin and the vessels please be prepared and assessed under a microscope? As he carries the amputated lower leg to a table, the resident puts his hand on the place where one might expect the dorsal foot artery. "Hah, nice pulsations," he says provocatively. And then he looks at me and adds: "Ain't I horrible?"

In the outpatient clinic surgeons feel the pulsations of dorsal foot arteries in patients whose legs hurt when walking. In the pathology department the gesture of feeling for pulsations is empty. The arteries of dead limbs do not pulsate. It is a sick joke to feel for them. A joke that may have the psychological function of facilitating the resident's entrance in the esoteric world of pathology, where, contrary to most other places, cold human lower legs are things one may take out of a fridge and walk around with.[12] But this same joke also contains ethnographic information: it stresses the fact – banal but crucial all the same – that the requirements for making a clinical diagnosis are no longer met once a patient – or a leg – is dead.

In the department of pathology interview questions cannot be asked either. Does this leg hurt? Even if there were a patient present who might want to answer such a question, it wouldn't make sense. For either an artery is part of the living body of a patient who is able to talk about it, or it is cut out. And however much its absence may hurt, this hurt is no longer caused by the deviances of the artery. Clinical techniques are out of place in the department of pathology. And vice versa. For cutting an artery out of a living leg in order to gather information would cause a far bigger problem than the one the clinician and the patient are hoping to solve. Is it thick, the intima of the femoral artery of Mrs. Tilstra? Nobody knows. And it is unlikely that anybody ever will study slides of its cross-sections.

The practices of performing clinical atherosclerosis and pathological atherosclerosis *exclude* one another. This is not a question of words that prove difficult to translate from one department to the other. When surgeons and pathologists do talk, they tend to understand each other very well. It is not a matter of different perspectives on the same object either. For when a surgeon walks up to the department of pathology and looks through a microscope he'll be perfectly able to discern a thick vessel wall. Every pathologist, moreover, has learned as a student how to interview patients about their symptoms. The incompatibility between pathology and clinic is a practical matter.[13] A matter of body parts that are sectioned instead of patients who speak. Of estimating the size of cells instead of touching a foot to feel how warm or cold it is. Of preparing slides instead of asking the patient to undress. In the outpatient clinic and in the department of pathology atherosclerosis is *done* differently.

Relations

So the practices of pathology and clinic are incompatible. And yet the distance between them is not quite as unbridgeable as this incompatibility suggests. Pathology and clinic do relate with one another.[14]

The pathology resident carries the amputated foot-with-leg that he just took out of the refrigerator, to a table. He measures the length of the leg: 28 centimeters. He makes a note of that. Then he takes a dissection knife out of a drawer. He cuts two small pieces of tissue from the plane of resection, puts them in plastic containers and gives these a number. He scribbles the numbers in his notebook next to a rough drawing, using arrows to show where each specimen was taken from. He does the same with a few pieces of skin. And starts to look for the arteries. It's not easy to find these now that they do not pulsate. But finally he succeeds. He cuts several pieces of each and puts them in containers as well. The containers have holes. They are all dropped in a small bucket that is filled with a fluid that will stop them disintegrating. The next day technicians will turn the preserved pieces of tissue into slides. And in a few days' time the resident and I will be bent over the microscope and see vessels with impressively thick intimas: atherosclerosis. We'll also inspect the cells of the plane of resection. They look alright: not gangrenous. And the skin cells indeed show the signs of long and severe oxygen deprivation. The resident writes this down and takes his notes to his supervisor.

The cross-section that the pathology resident showed to me was of an artery cut out of an amputated leg. This leg once belonged to a patient whose leg hurt badly and persistently and whose skin looked bad. The surgeons did an amputation in order to prevent the development of gangrene, which is deadly. It is the task of the pathologists to judge that operation afterwards. Pathologists also make judgements about the walls of small pieces of vessel that are cut out of poorly functioning circulatory systems in the course of less drastic operations. So pathology has a specific relation to the diagnoses of the clinic: it judges them afterwards.

This judgemental relation is materially supported by the small boxes in which body parts are carried up to the department of pathology. These boxes are accompanied by forms with the patient's name imprinted on them. The pathologist writes down his "final words" on yet another form, that travels back to the treating surgeons. The relations between pathology and clinic involve coordination work. Medicine is full of coordination work. There are so many sites in which disease is done with so many different techniques, that "linking up the incompatible" is essential if a patient is to be given a coherent treatment or comprehensible advice.[15] The specificities of each local practice imply that some links can be made and others not. In the case of pathology and the clinic, a judgemental relation is established. The crucial *missing* link is this: pathology cannot support the vascular surgeons as they seek to design a treatment.

To the pathology resident it is frustrating. He expected pathology to be the science on which medicine is founded and thus to provide a comprehensive understanding of all deviances. But it often lacks the means to even answer simple questions. As he puts it: "I'll never be able to properly diagnose the state of an artery. Never. Not even if I have an entire vessel. In a living patient this is ridiculous of course. But I couldn't even do it in a corpse. For what do you want to know? You want to know the location and extent of the stenosis. That implies that you'd have to make a slide every, say every three centimeters. Or maybe five. Just imagine: over the entire length of a lower leg, an upper leg, an aorta. How many slides is that? Imagine me cutting all the pieces. The technologists slicing them, colouring them, making slides. And then I'd have to assess these carefully, one by one. It wouldn't be enough to say that the wall is thick. But how thick is the wall? How much of the original lumen is left? I'd have to take into account that I look at a lumen that is no longer functioning. It would take ages. It's so time consuming that it's far too expensive. And because there are all these artifacts of death, it's not even certain either. It can't be done."

We've seen this earlier: taking out arterial "material" is a bigger intervention than those the surgeons might take on therapeutically. But the inability of pathology to advise clinicians reveals itself elsewhere. When a patient reports a severely limited pain-free walking distance and physical examination also suggests a poor oxygenation, surgeons consider invasive treatment. But in order to design such treatment they need to know *where* the patient's arteries are bad: in the groin, the knee, the ankles or everywhere? These questions are answered with the aid of the vascular laboratory and angiography. Pathology has nothing to offer, for even *if* a small biopsy were taken it would be taken at a single site and thus not be enough to locate a stenosis. Moreover, even in the absurd case that a pathologist were to have an entire artery at his disposal, the cost of assessing it slice by slice would be much greater than those of the alternatives and the results would still not be conclusive.[16]

Comparing and Finding a Gap

The practicalities of performing pathology and clinic are incompatible and yet relations may be forged between them. If such a relation is indeed established, the "atheroscleroses" performed in two different places *may* map onto each other.

The pathology resident takes his notes to his supervisor. "I've checked everything," he says. "All my cross-sections were of very sick vessels. Thick intimas, hardly any lumen left. Moreover, I've inspected the cells in the plane of resection. They were fine, so they've done their amputation high enough. But the skin cells showed signs of long and severe lack of oxygen. They were in a complete shambles." The supervisor takes the notes. Wants to know a few further details. Comments on the slight misuse of a technical term. And then says: "Okay. I'd better have a last look at your slides and sign the report. They can be happy. They're approved of."

The agony that plagued this patient before his amputation coincides with the thickness of the vessel walls that are made visible afterwards. Here they map onto one another. But the atheroscleroses of the clinic and pathology do not always coincide.

The pathologist: "You, since you're so interested in atherosclerosis, you should have been here last week. We had this patient, a woman in her seventies. She had renal problems. Severe ones, too. So she was admitted. And the next day she dies. Paff, from one moment to the next. The nephrologists were aghast, and so, of course, was her family. So we were asked to do an obduction. It was unbelievable. Her entire vascular system was atherosclerotic. One of her renal arteries was closed off, the other almost. It was a wonder her kidneys still did anything at all. It was hard to see where they got their blood from. And it was more or less the same for every other artery we took out: they were all calcified. Carotids, coronary arteries, iliac arteries: everything. Thick intimas, small lumens. And she'd never complained. Nothing. No chest pain, no claudication, nothing. We phoned her general practitioner just to check. He said she'd been visiting him for coughs and things. High blood pressure. But not with any complaint that made him think of a serious atherosclerosis."

The pathologist remembers this patient well because her condition surprised him. Pathologists expect that when they find bad vessel walls, then the patient will have reported severe complaints earlier on. For this is the story about the relation between pathology and clinic they teach their students: that pathology describes the *underlying* deviances of the tissues, while in the clinic the symptoms of the disease *surface*. But if the findings of pathology and clinic clash, if the atherosclerosis diagnosed in one site is seriously deviant while the other isn't, this story does not work.[17]

Explanations will be sought. Did the patient suffer from pain but never report it? Did she always sit and avoid walking? Had her condition developed so slowly that her metabolism adapted itself to very low levels of oxygen? Sometimes it is possible to answer such questions. The gap between the two "test outcomes" is bridged by an "intervening factor." Thus the coherence between the two different performances of the disease is re-established – in theory. But not in practice. For even if a clash between different "atheroscleroses" can be *explained*, it cannot be *explained away*. If there is an incoherence between various medical performances, one of them will, in practice, be privileged over the other.

Of Primary Importance

There are provinces of medicine in which pathology holds an important place in the diagnostic process. In cancers, the microscopic images of the pathologists, once they are available, overrule clinical stories. Biopsies are taken from lungs, livers, breasts and many other organs in order to inspect small slices of tissue under the microscope. The pathologist sends a diagnostic assessment of these tissues back to the treating physician, who is supposed to refer back to this in all further decisions. In some cases this is even done before patients present complaints to their doctors. In the Netherlands and various other countries, pap smear tests are offered to women of designated ages in order to detect early stages of cancer of the cervix.[18]

But the prominent place of pathology in the assessment of patients with cancer does not follow from the medical "knowledge system." It derives instead from a long list of specificities (the practicalities of diagnosing; the possibilities and risks of treatment; the consequences of leaving people untreated; the organization of health care; political considerations and political pressures, and so on). In other cases such lists add up to a different conclusion. In the itinerary of patients who are plagued by atherosclerosis of the leg vessels, the dominant diagnosis is not that of pathology, but that of the clinic. In vascular surgery the clinical interview forms the entrance to the hospital. If a patient tells a "wrong" story, this forecloses not just a pathological investigation but all further moves along the diagnostic and therapeutic tracks of atherosclerosis.

The vascular surgeon says to Mr. Zender, a man in his early forties: "Now, tell me, what's your job?" Mr. Zender answers with the name of a job I've never heard before. Neither has the surgeon, for he says: "Well, I don't know what that is, but please don't explain it to me, just tell me: do you have to walk a lot?"

"No," says the patient, "it's mostly sitting. But recently, with this pain in my legs, I find myself looking for an excuse to walk. Go to the second floor. That kind of thing."

"So, do you. What if you sit down at home?"

"You see doctor, as long as I do things, it's alright. But like, if we've done the washing up, children to bed, sit on the couch in front of the television, then it starts hurting."

The surgeon summons Mr. Zender to the examination table. And says in the meanwhile: "I'll just have a look to reassure you. So that you won't say I didn't even examine you. But let me tell you one thing. You may have pain in your legs alright. But there's nothing wrong with your leg vessels."

In the outpatient clinic it is clear and distinct. This story isn't "intermittent claudication." For in severe cases patients may have pain even when resting, but then their legs will hurt a lot more when they walk. Someone who looks for an occasion to move his aching legs when resting may be in trouble, but such trouble cannot be eased by the vascular surgeon. The surgeon shrugs his shoulders when asked where the pain may come from, says he doesn't know, and refers the patient back to the general practitioner.[19]

If patients tell a "wrong" story, they are referred back to their general practitioner. If they tell no story at all, but expect doctors to be able to gather all relevant knowledge from silently observing and measuring their bodies, the diagnostic process falters.

I sit in with the angiologist. In the course of the morning, he sees patients with various kinds of vascular problems, not only atherosclerosis. In addition there are patients with problems which the general practitioner couldn't pinpoint. They are likely to have serious internal problems, but what are they? This makes the interview questions more open than they tend to be in the vascular surgeons' clinics. Not: do your legs hurt? But: what can I do for you? Or: what's your problem? Mrs. Vengar comes for the first time, she walks in suffering visibly. When she's seated, the internist looks up at her from his papers. "Well, what is troubling you?" Mrs. Vengar shakes her head, slowly. And then she says: "I don't know doctor, I don't know what it is that troubles me. That's what I come to see you for. Because I don't know."

An answer like that leaves a doctor in an outpatient clinic empty handed. He's been there before. It is an awkward place to be. He has to get her to talk. For a doctor cannot hope to guess where to begin with his further diagnostic work without some significant answer to his interview questions. A clear "clinical picture" is what is needed in order to make a choice among the many further diagnostic possibilities.[20]

Sure, surgeons do not operate on patients on the basis of clinical data alone. They want a clinical diagnosis to be backed up by other data. They want to see the results of blood pressure measurement, and, if this is bad, a duplex and, if this is bad, an angiography.[21] But the intriguing thing is this: if a clinical diagnosis is not bad enough, a patient in hospital Z will never even get any further tests. Patients with good clinical conditions are not treated invasively.

Vascular surgeon: "Sometimes patients are sent in to us, from smaller hospitals. They have bad arteries, we're told – they include the X-ray – could we please operate on them. Well, that's to be seen. I always begin by talking to people. If they have only slight problems, if they can handle their lives without me intervening, I am not going to operate on them."

Only in bad clinical cases is an operation considered. People whose pain does not seriously impair their daily lives are left alone.[22] And a patient who feels no pain upon walking at all, or who does not report it to a doctor, won't be bothered with propositions for treatment at all.

The vascular surgeon: "Oh no. No, we don't dream of it. We'll never go out into the population to find all the bad arteries around. The ones that are bad when you open them up but that nobody complains about. For if we did, and if we then offered an operation to all those patients it would simply cost a fortune. And, more important, we would create far too many victims. For if people have severe complaints you may improve their condition. But if they have no complaints, or just some slight ones, they don't have enough to gain. While they still run risks. Sometimes an operation makes things worse. Or people die. So you're not going to open them up if their lives stand no chance of being improved by it."

This vascular surgeon suggests that what invasive treatment may do is improve a patient's condition. The gain patients may hope for is that their symptoms may disappear so that they are able to walk further without hurting so much. That prospect may make it worthwhile to run the risk of deterioration or – it is a small risk, but it is real enough – of death. Thus someone who has no bad problems is not operated on. In the department of vascular surgery of hospital Z clinical reality is dominant. For it is not just the entrance to the hospital but the very reason for treatment which derives from the clinical picture.[23]

Conclusion

If one gives a philosophical analysis of what it is to know, the shape of an ethnography of practice and the knowledge encountered are very different from that presented in scientific journals and medical textbooks. The difference is not a matter of messiness. The point is not that practices deal with their objects in an untidy and erratic way, while texts tend to be disciplined. Instead the difference is one of coherence. Where in textbooks the various versions of a disease tend to be neatly *aligned* to form a coherent overall picture, in practice there are gaps, fissures and frictions between different performances of any "one" disease. It must be easier to coordinate images and stories of a textbook into singularity, than it is to do this with the materialities of the body and the hospital. For in practice links between various performances are sometimes hard to craft and if they are crafted, even if they go under the same name, the "diseases" diagnosed in different sites, do not necessarily coincide. Instead of being aligned into coherence, in practice reality is *multiple*.

In this chapter the multiplicity of a single disease, atherosclerosis of the leg vessels, was illustrated with a few carefully chosen snapshot stories. These show that ethnography does not need to stay in a symbolic realm, but is capable of expanding itself to a study of *disease*. Such diseases are not a matter of meaning alone, but one of manipulation, too. Interestingly enough, in studying a single specific multiple *disease*, we have come across a version of what used to be called *illness*. The way patients live with their restricting bodies is included *in* the medical performance of atherosclerosis of the leg vessels. For usually it is only if patients consider their painful legs to be a problem that deserves to be presented to a doctor that medical action ensues. Only then may patients be diagnosed as having a disease. So a patient's illness is not (only) located *alongside* the disease diagnosed by doctors. It (also) has a specific place *within* it. And the same is true the other way around. Going to a doctor to ask to be diagnosed with a disease may be a way in which patients live their illness.

The findings and inventions I have presented here do not only have consequences for the academic disciplines from which they emerge and which they try to feed. They also have consequences for what *politics* can be in the highly professionalized and science-oriented field of medicine. I do not develop these consequences here, but point at them. There they are. Under the microscope atherosclerosis is a thick vessel wall. But in the organization of the health-care system the "intermittent claudication" that doctor and patient jointly establish in the consulting room is lived as real. The reality of atherosclerosis does not precede medical technology and the organization of health care, but is intertwined with them. This implies that the impairments of the body and the politics of crafting tools and organizing health care are intertwined as well.[24] If this is so then reality, the physicalities or the psychology of a disease, cannot be the standard by which to assess treatments. The very advantages and disadvantages, the goods and bads, of *performing* reality in one way or another are themselves open for debate. A debate that is political – and simultaneously concerns the very materialities of microscopes, examination tables, paper forms, cold feet and conversations. The politics of the medical field is a matter of organization, but also of metal, and of suffering, and of flesh.

NOTES

I would like to thank all the physicians, researchers, nurses, technicians and patients of hospital Z for allowing me to observe the performance of atherosclerosis in practice; and the Netherland Organization for Scientific Research for the grant that allowed me to study "Differences in Medicine." I am also grateful to participants at the conference on Cultures of Biomedical Technologies in Cambridge, July 1997, especially to Alberto Cambrosio; and to Stefan Hirschauer, Marianne de Laet, John Law, Jeannette Pols and Dick Willems for talking things over. Finally I would like to thank John Law again, for correcting my English.

1. For a classical example of a study departing from a disease/illness distinction, see Helman 1990 (1984). For a good overview of the sociology of illness, see Gerhardt 1989.
2. See e.g. the contributions in Lock and Gordon 1988. Important here is the work of Donna Haraway, who delves into biology with great zeal. Instead of exploring the disease/illness distinction, however, she is primarily concerned to historize and undermine that other, analogous division, the sex/gender distinction (Haraway 1991, for example).
3. For an analysis of the diagnostic process of patients with atherosclerosis of their leg vessels and its relation with decisions about treatment in vascular surgery, see Mol and Elsman 1996.
4. The classic point of reference here is the most famous among the first "laboratory studies": Latour and Woolgar 1979. The first collection of articles (by historians and sociologists) that took up the study of medical knowledge with "construction" in its title was Wright and Treacher 1982.
5. The metaphor of performance is also popular in feminist studies, where it was recently revitalized (Butler 1990). For the argument that a person's *sex/gender* may fade away if it is not actively performed, see also Hirschauer and Mol 1995.
6. This implies that knowledge, however scientific, is not a matter of ideas, but of materialities. It has to do with doing. The most eloquent articulations of this can be found in *Les Microbes* (Latour 1984) on which my text is highly parasitic. With his insistence on practicalities, Latour undermines the philosophers' insistence on the importance of "ideas" and abolishes the high culture/low culture distinction usually made between laboratory science and such mundane practices as farming, cooking and accountancy.
7. In this text the performances followed are diagnostic, they are part of knowledge practices. Therapeutic practices, however, can be analyzed as *performing* some version or other of a disease as well. Thus *cutting* in arteries

performs atherosclerosis as a structure inside these vessels while, say, taking anti-cholesterol medication performs atherosclerosis as a process that gradually develops over time. See Mol, forthcoming. The present text is an adapted version of chapter 2 of that book.

8. I made very short notes on all visits between patients and longer ones in the afternoon or the evening of the same day, or during the next day. My notes are thus full of detail but what I put between " " does not live up to the standards of conversation analysis. (See e.g. Silverman 1987.) Instead of the concern of conversation analysts with the formal structures of conversation, my concern is in what is being said, and also in what is being done. I have adapted the format of my stories to this concern.

9. It has frequently been pointed out that the story patients end up telling their doctors is highly structured by the questioning of the doctor. This is why even what people tell in the consulting room is not quite the "illness" that interpretative social scientists study. Or, as Nicolas Dodier puts it slightly more sharply: the stories patients tell in a consulting room are informed by the physicians' questions, but also by what patients want their doctors to do for them. When they are interviewed by a social scientist, patients do not suddenly reveal "real selves" but shift repertoires and play their part in the social scientific interview-game. See Dodier 1993. For some of the stories the vascular patients in hospital Z were prepared to tell to an outside interviewer, see Mol forthcoming.

10. There are a lot of other relevant "actors" that are not easy to see if one restricts one's observations to the consulting room including, for instance, the Dutch insurance system, that covers all costs for visits to a specialist if the patient has been referred there by a general practitioner. This is linked to the strong position of Dutch general practitioners, who work outside the hospital, and only refer a small percentage of the patients (some 15 percent) who visit them to specialists. Remarking such elements does not require a "macro-perspective" but mobility. To see them, the researcher has to move between sites. For a sympathetic study in which a "single" phenomenon – health economics – is investigated by moving from one site to another, see Ashmore et al. 1989.

11. For a more extensive discussion of the contrast between machine-like *networks* and more viscous, blood-like *fluids*, see Mol and Law 1994.

12. Outsiders have always been fascinated by the rites that introduce those inside medicine into the handling of dead bodies (Good and Good 1993; Lella and Pawluch 1988, for example).

13. The practical incompatibility signaled here, is quite like the *incommensurability* between paradigms that Kuhn talks about. Incommensurability is often presented as a matter of limited understanding, but it may be read just as well as a matter of the use of different techniques, as suggested by Ian Hacking. "New and old theory are incommensurable in an entirely straightforward sense. They have no common measure because the instruments providing the measurements for the one are inappropriate for the other. This is a scientific fact that has nothing to do with 'meaning change' and other semantic notions that have been associated with incommensurability" (1992: 56–57).

14. Despite all the incommensurability "translation" is a continuing activity in hospitals. Studying it reveals patterns quite like those Marilyn Strathern describes in *Partial Connections* (1991) when she talks about comparative anthropology in the fields she studied. The similarities and differences between sites follow complex, fractal patterns. A difference that one may make between two traditions is often to be found in a slightly different way within each one of them. In addition, what is opposed may simultaneously incorporate its other.

15. The question whether such links hold does not just depend on the efforts put into linking, but also on the outcomes of the process. This is illustrated very well by Charis Cussins's (1996) analysis of infertility treatment, which she presents in an article that also marvelously deals with the question of how the patient's subjectivity relates to various medical "objectifications."

16. For the implications of the present approach to the understanding of the introduction of new diagnostic techniques, see Mol 1993. For a further unraveling of what it means to practically link various performances of atherosclerosis, see Mol 1998.

17. If there were never a gap, clinical diagnosis would always be sufficient, while new technical tools may help to change both the width and the nature of the gap. For instance, the recent development of small diagnostic techniques which patients use at home may change their bodily perceptions. See for an analysis Willems 1992.

18. These screening programs obviously have an impressive complexity of their own that I lightly skip here. But see for example Singleton and Michael 1993 and Kaufert (this volume).

19. In the Netherlands, general practitioners have taken it upon themselves to support such patients, no matter what the cause of their complaints. It is not their task to either link a symptom to a cause, or, if that is impossible, to say "there is nothing wrong with you" (as specialists may do) but to say "well, the source of this pain seems not to be located in your arteries, now let's see, how could I still help you." This situates their work in what Dodier (1993) calls a specific *frame of reference*. Dodier calls it a "clinical" frame, but it is of a different, one might say yet more "clinical" kind, than that of "my" vascular surgeons. The Dutch general practitioners have a striking resemblance to the British ones such as they are described in Armstrong 1984. Armstrong, however, prefers to point out continuities and similarities rather than to dig into tensions and differences.

20. The first wave of diagnostic techniques able to measure parameters of silent patient bodies seemed to take away the necessity of even interviewing a patient (Reiser and Anbar 1984, e.g., for this worry). The current proliferation of diagnostic possibilities, however, might as well have the effect of making good clinical interviews indispensable again, if only as a basis for choosing between these possibilities. The most ardent advocates of "scientific medicine," moreover, the clinical epidemiologists, keep on stressing that the value of diagnostic techniques increases when they are not used in random populations, but in clinically selected ones. See e.g. Sacket et al. 1991.

21. The protocol in hospital Z wants surgeons to use their diagnostic tools in

series, from innocent to invasive, in order to never overdo it. As a part of this training in doing research, a medical student held six interviews for my project with Dutch vascular surgeons in other hospitals and two among these told him they prefer to use diagnostic techniques parallel to one another, to spare the patient subsequent visits to the hospital (Van Lange 1994).

22. This finding is quite specific. It doesn't even go for "atherosclerosis" in general. For atherosclerosis in the carotid arteries it is already different. If an atherosclerotic plaque in the carotids dislodges, it ends up in the brain, where it may do a lot of damage. This means that many neurologists and surgeons claim that for the carotid arteries the risks of non-treatment outweigh the risks of treatment even if there are no complaints or these are only slight.

23. However much my ethnography of disease derives from Foucault's analysis of both the knowledge and the materialities of pathology, it is also an attempt to break out of the unificatory powers of the "episteme" (which gains suffocating proportions in the works of people like Armstrong 1984). In the "modern medicine" that Foucault described in *La Naissance de la Clinique* (1963), pathology is presented as modern medicine's foundational discipline. Its investigation of dead tissues directs the clinical gaze that is cast on living patients. My claim is that pathology (or other non-clinical "gold standards") indeed inform the clinic (the judgement of stories as "wrong") *and* that, in its turn, it is sometimes the clinic that takes the lead (in cases where patients have only slight complaints, the condition of the walls of their leg arteries is irrelevant).

24. Working along similar lines, John Law (2000) captures the attentiveness to the multiplicity of reality-performed by talking of the "decentering of the object." And the way reality, technology and organization intertwine, leads him to say that we should attend to, and get involved in *onological politics*.

REFERENCES

Armstrong, David 1984 *Political Anatomy of the Body: Medical Knowledge in Britain in the Twentieth Century*. Cambridge: Cambridge University Press.
Ashmore, M., M. Mulkay and Trevor Pinch 1989 *Health and Efficiency. A Sociology of Health Economics*. Milton Keynes: Open University Press.
Butler, Judith 1990 *Gender Trouble: Feminism and the Subversion of Identity*. London: Routledge.
Cussins, Charis 1996 "Ontological Choreography: Agency through Objectification in Infertility Clinics." *Social Studies of Science* 26: 575–610.
Dodier, Nicholas 1993 *L'Expertise Médicale*. Paris: Métailié.
Foucault, Michel 1963 *La Naissance de la Clinique*. Paris: PUF.
Gerhardt, Uta 1989 *Ideas about Illness. An Intellectual and Political History of Medical Sociology*. London: Macmillan.
Good, Byron, and Mary-Jo DelVecchio Good 1993 "Learning Medicine": The Construction of Medical Knowledge at Harvard Medical School." In Shirley Lindenbaum and Margaret Lock (eds.), *Knowledge, Power and Practice: The Anthropology of Medicine and Everyday Life*. Comparative Studies of

Health Systems and Medical Care. Berkeley, Los Angeles, London: University of California Press, pp. 81–107.

Hacking, Ian 1992 "The Self-Vindication of the Laboratory Sciences." In Andrew Pickering (ed.), *Science as Practice and Culture*. Chicago: University of Chicago Press, pp. 29–64.

Haraway, D. 1991 *Simians, Cyborgs, and Women. The Reinvention of Nature*. London: Free Association Books.

Helman, Cecil 1990 [1984] *Culture, Health and Illness*. 2nd edition. Oxford: Butterworth-Heineman.

Hirschauer, Stephan and Annemarie Mol 1995 "Shifting Sexes, Moving Stories. Feminist/Constructivist Dialogues." *Science, Technology & Human Values* 20: 368–85.

Hirschauer, Stefan 1998 "Shifting Contradictions: Doing Sex and Doing Gender in Medical Disciplines." In Marc Berg and Annemarie Mol (eds.), *Differences in Medicine. Unraveling Practices, Techniques and Bodies*. Durham and London: Duke University Press, pp. 13–27.

Latour, Bruno 1984 *Les Microbes*. Paris: Métailié.

Latour, Bruno and Stephen Woolgar 1979 *Laboratory Life: The Social Construction of Scientific Facts*. London: Sage.

Law, John 1994 *Organizing Modernity*. Oxford: Blackwell Publishers.

    2000. *Aircraft Stories: Technoscience and the Decentering of the Object*. Durham and London: Duke University Press.

Lella, Joseph, and Dorothy Pawluch 1988 "Medical Students and the Cadaver in Social and Cultural Context." In Margaret Lock and Deborah Gordon (eds.), *Biomedicine Examined*. Dordrecht: Kluwer, pp. 125–53.

Lock, Margaret and Deborah Gordon (eds.) 1988 *Biomedicine Examined*. Dordrecht: Kluwer.

Mol, Annemarie 1993 "What's New? Dopler and its Others. An Empirical Philosophy of Innovation." In Ilana Löwy (ed.), *Medicine and Change: Historical and Sociological Studies of Medical Innovation*. Paris and London: John Libbey, pp. 17–127.

    1998 " 'Missing Links', Making Links. On the Performance of Some Atheroscleroses." In Marc Berg and Annemarie Mol (eds.), *Differences in Medicine. Unraveling Practices, Techniques and Bodies*. Durham and London: Duke University Press, pp. 145–65.

    forthcoming *The Body Multiple. Ontology in Medical Practice*. Durham and London: Duke University Press.

Mol, Annemarie and Bernard Elsman 1996 "Detecting Disease and Designing Treatment. Duplex and the Diagnosis of Diseased Leg Vessels." *Sociology of Health and Illness* 18: 609–31.

Mol, Annemarie and John Law 1994 "Regions, Networks and Fluids. On Anaemia and Social Topology." *Social Studies of Science* 24: 641–71.

Reiser, Stanley Joel and Michael Anbar 1984 *The Machine at the Bedside*. Cambridge: Cambridge University Press.

Sacket, D. L., R. B. Haynes, G. H. Guyat and P. Tugwell 1991 *Clinical Epidemiology: A Basic Science for Clinical Medicine*. Boston: Little, Brown and Company.

Silverman, David 1987 *Communication and Medical Practice: Social Relations in the Clinic.* London: Sage.

Singleton, Vicky and Mike Michael 1993 "Actor-Networks and Ambivalence: General Practitioners in the UK Cervical Screening Program." *Social Studies of Science* 23: 227–64.

Strathern, Marilyn 1991 *Partial Connections.* Savage, MD: Rowman and Littlefield.

Strauss, Anselm, Shizuko Fagerhaugh, Barbara Suczek and Carolyn Wiener 1985 *Social Organization of Medical Work.* Chicago: University of Chicago Press.

Van Lange, Bart 1994 *Een verslag van 6 interviews.* Utrecht.

Willems, D. Dick 1992 "Susan's Breathlessness. The Construction of Professionals and Laypersons." In J. Lachmund and G. Stollberg (ed.), *The Social Construction of Illness.* Stuttgart: F. Steiner Verlag, pp. 105–14.

Wright, P., and A. Treacher (eds.) 1982 *The Problem of Medical Knowledge: Examining the Social Construction of Medicine.* Edinburgh: Edinburgh University Press.

6 "Real compared to what?": Diagnosing leukemias and lymphomas

Peter Keating and Alberto Cambrosio

Reviewing the classification of lymphomas in the late 1970s, Henry et al. concluded rather gloomily:

Ten years ago Willis (1967) wrote: "Nowhere in pathology has a chaos of names so clouded clear concepts as in the subject of lymphoid tumors."

We now have a reasonably satisfactory working classification and approach to the diagnosis of Hodgkins disease, but as far as non-Hodgkins lymphomas are concerned[1] there is currently no universally accepted classification. (Henry et al. 1978: 275)

Sixteen years later, having found the original reference for the Willis quote (Willis 1948), Rosenberg figured it was a case of *plus ça change*: "It was Willis who in his 1948 textbook stated, 'Nowhere in pathology has a chaos of names so clouded clear concepts as in the subject of lymphoid tumours.' The situation has not changed today" (Rosenberg 1994: 1359).

Taken separately, each quotation laments the lack of consensus in the classification of lymphomas. Taken together, they seem further to imply that the field itself is advancing at a snail's pace. This, despite the availability of radically new diagnostic tools, borrowed from immunology, cytogenetics and molecular biology. And yet, Rosenberg's somewhat jaded remarks appeared in an editorial criticizing a 1994 proposal for a new classification of lymphomas that incorporated (in addition to traditional morphological and clinical criteria) the latest antibody and cytogenetic techniques and that claimed, as a result, to have finally pinpointed well-defined, real disease entities (Harris et al. 1994: 1361). Produced by an informal international network of nineteen influential pathologists known collectively as the International Lymphoma Study Group (ILSG), the new classification was thus nicknamed REAL (Revised European-American Classification)[2] and deemed so momentous that it was published more or less simultaneously in four different journals (*Blood, The American Journal of Clinical Pathology, Histopathology, Important Advances in Oncology*). Reactions were mixed: some pathologists welcomed the initiative; others criticized it. Among the latter, in addition to Rosenberg, one finds the authors of texts with such titles as "Here We Go Again" (Dehner 1995), "America, You Deserve Better" (Schwarze 1995) and "A Missed Opportunity?" (Meijer et al. 1995).

Meanwhile, in the adjacent field of the leukemias, a year after the publication of the REAL classification, an article entitled "Proposals for the Immunological Classification of Acute Leukemias," appeared in *Leukemia* under the collective signature of the European Group for the Immunological Characterization of Leukemias (EGIL) (Bené et al.). As with the REAL classification, publication of the EGIL proposal was followed by a series of critical replies including some as blunt as those directed at the REAL (van Dongen 1995; Paietta 1995, for example). At the time of the publication of its 1995 proposal, EGIL was only about a year old. EGIL's emergence, however, was predicated upon the prior existence of several national groups devoted to similar purposes, the oldest of which is the French Groupe d'Étude Immunologique des Leucémies (GEIL), created in 1983 and presently composed of members of forty-three French hospital centers.[3] Thus, compared to ILSG, EGIL's undertaking would appear to be less the ad hoc initiative of a limited group of influential clinicians, and to depend more on the systematic accretion of results and practices from a large number of clinical laboratories. Yet, this is probably a matter of degree, since the extent to which EGIL's proposal is in fact grounded in a multinational consensus is open to debate. For instance, while the French representative of EGIL appears to be firmly backed by her national group (GEIL), this is far from clear in the case of her Dutch and German colleagues. Indeed, one year after the publication of EGIL's proposal, a different consensus document was published in *Leukemia* by yet another European group composed mainly of German clinicians but including two of the undersigners of EGIL's proposal (Rothe and Schmitz 1996). Moreover, EGIL's more orderly approach is not necessarily seen as a virtue by clinicians: as we explain below, clinical inspiration and standardization sometimes conflict.

EGIL and ILSG are not alone in their interest in the classification of the leukemias and the lymphomas. Their activities overlap with those of other groups. For instance, the immunological analysis of leukemias and lymphomas, called immunophenotyping, is often carried out with the help of an instrument called a flow cytometer. Users of this apparatus meet to establish norms, guidelines and common nomenclature. The German-based consensus document mentioned in the previous paragraph is devoted to this purpose. On the other side of the Atlantic, following the initiative of a few leading centers, a North American Consensus Conference on the Immunophenotyping of Leukemias and Lymphomas was held in Bethesda in November 1995. The conference allowed representatives of various hematopathology laboratories to compare their practices and to reach a tentative, somewhat fragile consensus. The Bethesda meeting was followed by an International Workshop on Flow Cytometric Immunophenotyping of Human Hematologic Malignancy held in Rimini (Italy) in April 1996, that aimed at international consensus. Accordingly, both the tentative North American consensus formulation and the EGIL proposal (in addition to other proposals) were presented at the workshop, resulting in heated exchanges that, although certainly not reducible to a Europe-USA confrontation, revealed serious transatlantic differences.

Now, why should we, as social scientists, or, for that matter, why should medical practitioners be concerned with classifications? Are they not simply another example of the soft underbelly of medicine that provides so much material for skeptical, social constructivist accounts of medicine? On the contrary, as we will see, classifications of leukemias and lymphomas are not mere epiphenomena of medical practice, they are part and parcel of it. Therapeutic decisions (for instance, the timing and content of chemotherapy) depend on how a given patient is categorized in an accepted classification. In addition, standards of care and clinical guidelines depend upon the equivalencies made possible by shared classifications. This is particularly true when there is diagnostic and therapeutic innovation. As noted by an interviewee:

Lymphomas are very heterogeneous ... so early on there was a necessity for looking at these tumors a little bit more closely than other tumors and classify them, not only for predicting the outcome of that patient but also to develop better therapies ... In the late 60s when people were classifying these tumors all over the world, classifications were extremely complicated, with different names and clinicians were fairly unhappy about the situation because they couldn't try new protocols, it was difficult to compare from one institution to another the results of their therapy because the pathologists were not really agreeing on what to call what and so on. And that was important because we were in the early 70s when the new therapies began to appear, new, very important therapies, both in the area of radiotherapy as well as in the area of chemotherapy. (Interview with a Dr. Raul C. Braylan, Bethesda, MD, 18 November 1995)

The clinical importance of classifications can also be gathered from the amount of criticism generated, both recently and in the past, by the proposal of new classificatory schemes. One of the objections to the aforementioned REAL classification, for example, was that it had too many categories, so many, in fact, that it would be of little use to the clinician (Rosenberg 1994: 1360). In this respect, medical classifications are less a finished product than an active, ongoing intervention on patients or body parts.[4] As an activity, classification is undertaken in the staining of slides and their observation under the microscope, in the flowing of blood through sophisticated equipment and the inspection of the resulting imagery, in the discussions surrounding these activities and in the decision to inscribe a specific disease category in a patient's file. These activities do not follow a linear development, from diagnosis and classification to therapy. In medicine, classification is coincident with diagnosis and the constitution and transformation of both diagnosis and classification follow from and lead to changes in the knowledge of the entities that are diagnosed/classified. Medical classification involves causal claims, either etiologic, anatomical or histopathological, clinical or prognostic. Any or all of these categories may be used in a particular diagnosis.[5] Classification thus occurs at the intersection of individual and generic patients. Even though individual patients are diagnosed within local settings, diagnostic decisions are not simply local events, since, as mentioned above, treating patients requires continuity across time and space.

Dagognet (1970: 162) notes that while classifications are not passive acts of registering reality, the history of classifications can be read as an attempt to get at the principle that corresponds to the ontological truth (the essential elements) of the entities being classified. Classifications, from this point of view, are less the ordering of what we already know than a tool leading to the development of new knowledge (Dagognet 1970: 20–1). Ontological claims may not be very popular in sociology or cultural studies, but they do indeed constitute one of the driving forces behind classification. The aforementioned REAL classification and its claim to display natural disease entities by the correlation through a combination of morphological, clinical, immunological and cytogenetic parameters of the external, visible inscriptions of pathological processes with their underlying causes is just one example of this tendency.

Classifications such as REAL's or EGIL's face a set of similar problems and resort to similar techniques to deal with these problems. We will describe these issues and tactics below. For the moment let us note that, as already mentioned, not all members of the potential audience for the REAL or the EGIL classifications were convinced of their pertinence or necessity. For instance, the editorial accompanying the publication of the REAL article included objections that, taken together, offer an introduction to the problems of instituting a classificatory scheme (Rosenberg 1994). First, the editorialist questioned the existence of a real consensus: true, nineteen pathologists, many of them leaders in this field, had co-signed the REAL classification. But what about other major hematopathologists? It was further objected that the technical skills needed to institute the REAL classification were simply unavailable in many medical centers. Third, established, routine practices (such as the fixing of tissues) were cited as obstacles to the performance of the detailed examinations required by the REAL classification. The gap between clinical practices and the pathology laboratory constituted a fourth criticism: the new classification highlighted biological variables of interest to the pathologist but lacked or was meager or anecdotal when it was a question of clinical course, prognosis or curability that, while scientifically less well-defined, were of obvious concern to the clinician. In other words: clinical data did not (yet) support the classification. Finally, and consistent with the perceived pathology/clinic gap, the classification of various types of tumors (for instance, the inclusion of Hodgkin's disease with non-Hodgkin's lymphomas) was said to run counter to traditional clinical understanding.[6] Social consensus, the distribution of skills, the weight of established practices, the division of labor, differences between thought styles . . . in short: the usual social, technical, cognitive and institutional arguments!

ILSG's rebuttal (Harris et al. 1995b) did not deny the relevance of the issues raised by critics. Rather, the Study Group claimed that while those issues were indeed important, the concerns were unwarranted. There is, in fact, consensus, they argued (this is the largest group of pathologists ever to agree on a lymphoma classification). Sophisticated techniques (immunophenotyping and genetic studies) are available (at least in the United States and Europe) to most practicing pathologists. These techniques can also be applied to fixed tissues, thus meshing with established practices. Distinctive clinical features have been described for most of the disease entities in the new classification. And, last but not least, simplicity, namely the respect of simple clinical groupings, is not a (clinical) virtue if it overlooks distinct clinical entities. As Harris (1995: 111) put it: "This formulation includes a number of disease entities which may alarm those who believe that a lymphoma classification must be simple. The fact remains that these are the tumors that pathologists are seeing and diagnosing, and oncologists must be prepared to deal with them."

In what follows, we will examine, in a more systematic way, some of the issues raised, explicitly or implicitly, by debates such as the one just reported.

The Normal and the Pathological

In *Le totémisme aujourdhui* (1962), Claude Lévi-Strauss tells us that we cannot understand primitive classification systems by looking for outside referents. Primitive classifications, he claims, have an internal structure that give them meaning. In other words, the sense and the referents of the objects of classification cannot be distinguished. The same might be said of scientific classifications; that they are internal to the science in question and that any attempt to make sense of them outside of the confines of the paradigm they created would be a regression to a form of positivism or realism that, today, it would seem, is largely untenable. Unlike a totem pole, however, a medical classification is not a stand-alone technology. Medical classifications have at least two doors to objects and practices on the outside: the clinic and the other sciences. In the case of the classification of the leukemias and the lymphomas, one of the latest doors opened has been immunology (molecular biology is the most recent). While the introduction of immunological categories into the scheme of the hematopathologies may be variously described, for the sake of brevity, we shall describe one route.[7]

It began in the 1950s and 1960s when researchers in immunology set up an experimental system that construed pathology as a technology for the study of the biology of the immune system. By using pathologies or diseases of the immune system as fixed entities, they were able to manipulate the immunological variables of the disease in such a way as to be able to create immunological facts. Robert A. Good and his collaborators, for example, mobilized a long-standing distinction between cellular immunity and humoral immunity according to which viruses were killed by the cellular component of the immune system and bacteria by the humoral component (antibodies) to study a variety of leukemias and lymphomas. Using this distinction as their immunolog-ical variable, between 1957 and 1967 they injected patients with irri-tants, compiled clinical histories and articulated both data sets with animal experiments until they observed that different lymphomas and leukemias displayed differences along the humoral/cellular axis. More precisely, they were able to create generalities: such as that patients with Hodgkin's disease react poorly to viruses and patients with multiple myeloma react poorly to bacteria (Good and Finstad 1968; Hansen and Good 1974).

Since it was already known from pathology that, to continue the example, patients with Hodgkin's lymphoma frequently had enlarged lymph nodes and those with multiple myeloma did not, this meant that it was possible to reclassify Hodgkin's as a pathology of the cells responsible for cellular reactions (known as T cells) and multiple myeloma as a path-ology of the cells responsible for the production of antibodies. This was at once new knowledge of the immune system and a characterization of (at least) two species of lymphoma. This distinction, later translated into the distinction between B and T cells, became universally accepted in immunology (Good 1983: 6–8). However, even though it had used pathology as its technology, its incorporation into the classification of the leukemias and lymphomas was somewhat more problematic.

Classifications of both lymphomas and leukemias had remained until the 1970s the exclusive dominion of anatomopathologists and cytopathologists, who based their analysis on the morphological inspection of patient specimens: a microscope and a few cell stains (complemented with the development of a strong visual memory) was all that was needed (Atkinson 1995). In the early 1970s, a number of new classifications of the lymphomas appeared. Some sought to align themselves with the new immunological knowledge. Lukes and Collins (1975), for example, embraced the latter with a certain sense of abandon basing their new nomenclature almost entirely upon the B cell–T cell distinction. The new classification of lymphomas was termed functional. By redescribing the lymphomas strictly in terms of normal cells, Lukes and Collins were, moreover, able to raise the possibility that the pathological process involved in the production of lymphomas had a parallel in the normal process of the development of the immune system.

Despite this endorsement of a functional immunological approach to the classification of the lymphomas, the subdivisions of the main categories and thus the bottom (diagnostic) line remained firmly based on morphological appearances. For example, B-cell types of lymphoma were divided into small-cleaved and large-cleaved cells. Categorization thus entailed the use of a microscope and the description of a size and not a function. This is not to say that the revision was merely cosmetic. A table comparing a previous leading morphological classification (Rappaport) with their own scheme showed the extent to which their revision constituted a fundamental change in the study of the lymphomas. Categories in the Rappaport classification were in some cases entirely redistributed amongst Lukes–Collins categories. In fact, only one of Rappaport's five categories mapped directly onto the Lukes–Collins classification. In other words, this was more than a translation from an anatomic to an immunologic language. It was a redistribution and thus a redefinition of entities (Good 1983: 24). Moreover, in adopting a functional approach, the dominant categories became invisible to the morphologist: at the time, B cells and T cells were indistinguishable under a microscope.

Now the alignment of the pathological on the normal is not always possible even if it is generally accepted as desirable. The problem was and to some extent still is: how far can the pathological be reduced to the normal? In order to appreciate why this might be a problem for some pathologists, recall that the latter often refer to diseases as pathological entities. By this, they mean both what pathologists create as phenomena in the laboratory and a level of reality distinct from and autonomous to that proposed by the biologists' description of nature. In the past, the autonomy of pathology and clinical medicine (nosography) with regards to biology has often been the case. Since the advent of the cell theory in the 1840s, however, pathologists have tended to name their entities after the closest relative or what is termed the corresponding cell to the diseased cell. The problem here is that the movement from the normal to the pathological has, in the case of the lymphomas and the leukemias, generally been the opposite of what was proposed at the beginning of the 1970s. In other words, pathologists generally named not only the disease but the normal cell that had been corrupted by the pathological process. For some, this was the natural order. For others, it was self-referential. As one of the early adherents to the immunological approach to the naming of diseased cells complained: "the conventional concepts of normal hematopoiesis, which were used by them [the great hematologists] as the scientific basis of leukemia and hematosarcoma nomenclature and classification, was itself almost entirely based on the aspects of neoplastic cells, which constitutes a vicious circle" (Mathé and Belpomme 1974: 81). In other words, even though pathologists had classified according to the putative cell of origin, the determination of the cell had also been within their purview and the criteria for these designations have, more often than not, been those created by microscopy and, consequently, morphology.

Pathologists also act as though their entities need not necessarily have any immediate clinical reality. In the exchange provoked by the proposal of the REAL classification, for example, the guest-editor of the journal *Blood* raised the following objection: "Despite the hope of many, the separation of the lymphoid tumors into B- or T-cell in origin, as major subtypes, is not helpful to the clinician" (Rosenberg 1994: 1360). The group replied: "It strikes us as curiously paradoxical that classification according to a putative cell of origin is intrinsic to virtually all schemes of tumor classification in other systems and yet it is questioned in the United States for lymphomas – the one area in which we actually have objective evidence for the normal counterpart of most of the malignancies" (Harris et al. 1995a: 857).

We would seem to have here a continuing opposition between a scientific basis for the classification of disease entities and a medical or pragmatic basis for that same activity. But the opposition is not so clear-cut. Although the major division of the REAL classification was biology-based, many entities found their justification and their reality in the practice of natural history, the first foundation of clinical medicine and the generator of the entities in question. Indeed, as they pointed out in their original proposal, although lymphomas should ideally be classified according to their normal counterparts, in practice "our current understanding of both the immune system and the lymphomas appears to be inadequate to support a biologically correct lymphoma classification . . . Thus, a lymphoma classification becomes simply a list of well defined, real disease entities. Many of these entities are associated with distinctive clinical presentations and natural histories" (Harris et al. 1994: 1361). More precisely, replying to the criticism that the classification system was too complicated to be of any use to pragmatic practitioners, the ILSG argued that: "A pathologic classification of neoplasms is, by definition, a listing of distinct disease entities, based on features that can be recognized by pathologists: chiefly morphology, buttressed to a variable extent by special techniques. For the pathologists to make the diagnoses, the entities must be defined by these features" (Harris et al. 1995b: 857).

Thomas Kuhn (1993; see also Hacking 1993) has claimed that a science can be characterized by a lexicon that separates it from both past and present practices. Successive lexicons are incommensurable in the sense that the terms and/or kinds described in the preceding science cannot be used in the same way in the new practice, just as vocabularies from one scientific field are not directly transferable to another. The immunological turn taken in pathology would seem to provide a fitting example of incompatible taxonomies. Cells composing leukemias and lymphomas once described according to their structure and their morphological appearance under a microscope are now described according to their immunological function or their molecular biology. The theory of their origin and development is new, just as the technologies used to isolate and display the cells as kinds are radically different. Yet there is no talk of revolution and the incompatible taxonomies not only coexist, but are sometimes used by the same individual. How is this possible?

First of all, despite the change in cellular ontology and technology, many pathological entities have survived intact. The clinical description of Hodgkin's disease remains roughly as Thomas Hodgkin described it, just as follicular lymphoma, which accounts for over 50 percent of the non-Hodgkin's lymphomas, first described by Rappaport thirty years ago, is still diagnosed today. Indeed, whatever one calls the cells composing follicular lymphoma, the clinical symptoms and course remain largely the same. Moreover, non-biological functions (i.e., pathological behavior such as natural history, organ involvement, and microscopic and gross pathology) stand as independent criteria for the differentiation of pathological entities. Secondly, there is a certain artificiality to the opposition between structure and function. Long before the introduction of immunological techniques into pathology, pathologists were able to see function in structure. Thirdly, treating physicians of different age and training who ask for laboratory reports in terms of the classification with which they are clinically most familiar leads to the coexistence of several classifications in pathology reports, a form of ad hoc translation depending on each patient's specific case (interview with J.–J. Prat, Hôpital Lariboisière, Paris, 13 March 1997). Finally, the patients themselves provide for continuity; they cannot be abandoned in the same way that scientific kinds can.

The Quantitative and the Qualitative (Numbers and Pictures)

At the beginning of the 1980s, a new instrument called a flow cytometer became commercially available and was soon adopted by clinical laboratories involved in the immunological diagnosis of leukemias and lymphomas. Here is, roughly, how it works. The cells to be analyzed by the machine are first tagged with fluorescent antibodies specific for particular kinds of cells. Then, the cells flow through the machine that, thanks to laser and computer technology, detects and analyzes the fluorescence attached to the cells, thus measuring the relative proportion of each kind of cell in a patient's sample. In addition to counting T and B cells, flow cytometers enable researchers to identify and quantify cells according to the varying stages of maturation as characterized by the presence, on the cell surface, of distinctive molecules (called markers). For specialists in the diagnosis and classification of leukemia and lymphoma, flow cytometers opened up the possibility of creating a quantitative pathology and thus of attaining a degree of objectivity that would do away with the vagaries of (morphological) visualization. Despite the fact that immunological analysis has indeed become a routine practice in hematology laboratories, this is not exactly what happened.

The lure of quantification depends in part on the type of classification sought. According to one of the authors of the REAL classification, pathologists are not all that keen on quantification (Harris, personal communication). Clinicians, on the other hand, tend to favor a prognostic classification which, when articulated with clinical trials, tends to be quantitative. They want to know what is going to happen to the patient. The patients' survival time can only be quantified if classification proceeds according to prognostic groups and these cannot be identified with pathological entities. Pathologists, hence, are critical of classifications like the so-called Working Formulation devised in the 1970s (see below) and still in use today for its pragmatic, prognostic approach. Proponents of the REAL classification claim: "Overemphasis on survival as a defining feature of a disease, taken to its extreme, could lead to the conclusion that breast cancer and follicular lymphomas need not be distinguished from one another because they have similar survivals" (Harris et al. 1995b: 858).

To understand the problems associated with quantifying pathology consider the following example. In the early 1980s, researchers were able to establish that a well-known morphological entity, acute myelogenous leukemia (AML), could be subdivided into at least four different maturation groups or phenotypes as defined by flow cytometry. Although the four phenotypes tended to agree with the morphological subtypes, each phenotype group contained more than one morphological type of AML (Griffin et al. 1983: 557). Because of the redundancy, both categorizations of the cells in question could not be considered accurate. So, since the quantitative techniques used to generate the subtypes had a "high degree of reproducibility and objectivity of the technique, not always encountered in morphological classification systems in AML" (Griffin et al. 1983: 562), it was suggested that the time had come to abandon the old classification. Fifteen years later, the old classification is still in place. What happened?

Despite the increase in accuracy, even the most dedicated flow practitioners admit that flow analyses sometimes lack clinical specificity. It is one thing to show that a morphological class is phenotypically heterogeneous. But when the heterogeneity runs wild, then, "in view of the vast heterogeneity of AML, subdivisions seem rather arbitrary and academic. Therefore classifications based solely on differentiation, maturation or sublineages may not be worthwhile" (Terstappen et al. 1991). Now, a proposal such as EGIL's does not aim to replace other classifications based on morphology or cytogenetics, but, rather, is meant to be used in conjunction with them. There is, however, no attempt made to integrate morphology, immunology, cytogenetics and molecular biology into a unified, synthetic classification characterized by proposals such as those of the Morphologic, Immunologic and Cytogenetic (MIC) Cooperative Group in the second half of the 1980s (MIC 1986, 1988), and more recently, albeit in a markedly different way, of the REAL classification. The EGIL proposal shares with morphological proposals the common ground of being a classification based exclusively on a single parameter (in this case: immunological).

The debates raised by the introduction of flow cytometric techniques are not limited to the confrontation between different approaches (morphology, immunology, cytogenetics). They also concern issues internal to the immunological endeavor itself. The markers detected by flow cytometry, quantitative though they may be, do not always give the clinician an all or nothing proposition. The numbers are based on fluorescence intensities which in turn must be assessed as markers. If, for example, you tag a sample with an antibody, what do you do if 25 percent of them turn up positive to, say, a B-cell marker? Can you then consider that marker as positive? And can you then use that positive finding to assign the patient sample to a given class of leukemia? These two questions raise the thorny and entangled issues of cut-off points and scoring systems which, in turn, raise an even more fundamental issue often referred to by practicing scientists as the problem of the philosophy underlying different uses of a given technology.

In the EGIL system, the pathological sample to be tested is examined to determine the presence or absence of predetermined markers: in practical terms, this means that the sample is examined with a flow cytometer after treatment with a predetermined set of antibody reagents (a so-called antibody-panel). The cut-off point for a marker to be considered positive was set at 20 percent of cells stained with the antibody (Béné et al. 1995: 1785). The obviously arbitrary 20 percent cut-off point has been harshly criticized. To avoid misunderstanding, it should be noted that the issue is not whether a given patient has leukemia or not. According to EGIL stipulations, all samples being tested have already been determined, by morphological examination, to be from leukemic patients. The point of the cut-off point is to determine the type of leukemia. The question then remains whether one should fix cut-off points or report results as continuous variables, an issue that, as we will see below, expresses the contrast between a will to standardize as a way to achieve a common language and a will to preserve the interpretative freedom of clinicians.

Once a marker is positive, it may then be classified as major (2 points), minor (a half-point) or intermediate (1 point). Adding the scores, one can assign a given leukemia to one of the various types and subtypes of a pre-established classification. The latter is, of course, based on immunological criteria. In fact, a key activity of national groups such as GEIL is to analyze large cohorts of patients in order to produce and periodically revise an immunological classification of acute leukemias.[8]

As with the cut-off point, the scoring approach has come under fire. Indeed, an important difference between the EGIL and the North-American tentative consensus on the leukemias is one of a visual approach versus a scoring system. Flow cytometric analysis can be performed by using either single markers or a combination of different markers (a so-called multiparametric approach). In the first case, one obtains a percentage value and can then decide whether the sample is positive or negative for a given marker. In the second case, one obtains complex two-dimensional or three-dimensional figures that can be used to assess the various pathological cell populations identified by the analysis. This is easier to see than to say, and can best be expressed through illustrations (see Cambrosio and Keating (forthcoming) for an extended discussion of this issue). Figure 1 shows a laboratory report produced by a Texas hospital: the first page contains a summary of the various tests performed on the patient, including a list of the immunological markers and the interpretation of the results; on the second page one finds, on the top of the page, a microscope picture showing the cell morphology and, at the bottom, a series of two-dimensional flow-cytometric images. A skilled analyst can interpret the visual patterns as pointing in the direction of a given type and subtype of leukemia. In other words, the name of the game is to identify the abnormal cell population on a visual display.[9] Figure 2 shows a report corresponding to the EGIL proposal: no images here; instead, we have percentages and the resulting interpretation.

When asked to account for these differences, the practitioners we interviewed resorted to arguments ranging from economics (a multiparametric approach is expensive in terms of equipment and reagents), to questions of skills and standards (the difficulty of regulating laboratory practices increases with the complexity of the techniques used) and to issues of professional training. In France, the latter difference is explained as follows: in most cases North-American laboratories are directed by pathologists, i.e., by individuals who have been trained in pattern recognition by spending years observing tissue slides. These individuals are presently transforming immunological approaches by hybridizing them with their established practice.

A symmetrical explanation is offered by North Americans. They observe that French clinical laboratories in which flow cytometry is performed are not controlled by pathologists (i.e., by people qualified as possessing a synthetic clinical understanding) but by biologists. The latter are accused of replacing clinical understanding with a systematic, algorithmic approach. Interestingly enough, while the French scientists we interviewed do indeed stress the importance of the biologists' role, they also acknowledge the need for interaction with the clinician and thus the significance of clinical understanding. This is precisely why they concur with their North American hematopathology colleagues in criticizing flow cytometry laboratories that are directed by a Ph.D. and

IP95-628   August 22, 1995

Name:

CLINICAL INFORMATION

PSL #: 1354   Age: 1 yrs

Sample Date: Aug 18, 1995   Sample Type: bone marrow   Sex: M   Race: H

Referral Doctor:

Referring Institution: CMC

Referral ID#: 706897

Clinical History: A.L.L.   WBC=28.1 with 20% blasts

LEUKOCYTE MARKER PANEL PERFORMED:

CD61/CD14/CD45	CD5/CD4/CD8	CD71/Glycophorin A/CD45	Intracellular:
CD34/CD13/HLA-DR	CD10/CD19/CD20	m.Kappa/m.Lambda/CD19	Tdt/CD22/CD3
CD16/CD11b/CD45	CD34/CD38/CD19	CD36/CD64/CD34	
CD7/CD56/CD3	CD15/CD33/CD34		

MORPHOLOGY:

Cytospin preparations demonstrate a prominent population of medium-sized blasts with scant to moderate basophilic, focally "cleared" cytoplasm, and nuclei with finely reticular chromatin and little nucleoli. Occasional blasts show sparso azurophilic granulation. In addition to these blasts, abundant lymphoid cells, both mature and immature, are noted. The immature forms are consistent with hematogones.

IMMUNOPHENOTYPIC FINDINGS:

Immunophenotypic analysis reveals a 35% population of medium-sized blasts with a CD13(+), CD33(+), CD15(+), CD11b(partial, dim +), CD64(-), CD16(-), CD61(dim/-), CD34(-), CD36(-), CD14(-), CD10(partial +), CD4(dim, partial +), other lymphoid Ag(-) phenotype. Also noted are 1) 25% B lineage cells, including 13% mature polytypic B cells and 12% maturing B lineage procursors (consistent with hematogones), 2) 1.7% monocytes, 3) 5% mature granulocytes, 4) 9% small T cells (CD4:CD8 ratio = 0.6:1), 5) 3% NK cells, and 6) 8% erythroid precursors.

INTERPRETATION:

The findings indicate an acute myelogenous leukemia without definitive phenotypic evidence of maturation along any of the myeloid lineages (consistent with FAB M0/M1). The unusually high frequency of B lineages is interpreted to represent a (non-neoplastic) "hematogone" hyperplasia. Final diagnosis requires histopathologic, cytogenetic, and clinical correlation.

PATHOLOGIST:

Patient ID:IP95-628   Date:8/22/95

Name:

Age: 1 yr.   Sex: M   Race: H

Specimen: bone marrow

Comments:

Color Code:

Red :: myeloid leukemic cells; illustrated by the 4 larger blasts in the photomicrograph at left.

Blue :: B lineage cells; illustrated by the smaller lymphoid cells in the photomicrograph at left; the arrows in the dot plots below indicate the maturing B lineage precursors (hematogones).

Black :: mature granulocytes

Green :: monocytes

Figure 1.

```
NOM                 :  ███████        Date de l'examen  : 10/ 2/1997
Prenom              :                 Caracteristiques:
No d'inscription    :     3339        Sang=1 moelle=2 autre=3 2
Service demandeur   : MED  A2         Cellules atypiques % 97
```

PANEL D'ORIENTATION

LIGNEE B		LIGNEE T		MYELOIDES		AUTRES	
Membrane (%)							
sIg :	0	CD2 :	95	CD13:	93	Classe II:	0
CD19:	0	CD5 :	0	CD33:	93	CD10 :	0
CD20:	0	CD7 :	0	CD14:	0	CD34 :	0
CD24:	0			CD15:	0	CD41 :	0
Cytoplasme (%)							
c-mu:	0	cCD3:	0	Lysozyme:	..	TdT :	0
cCD22:	0						

PANEL DE VALIDATION

LIGNEE B		LIGNEE T		MYELOIDES		AUTRES	
CD21:	0	CD1 :	0	CD11b	0	CD9 :	0
CD22:	0	CD3 :	0	CD16:	0	CD11a	0
CD23:	0	CD4 :	0	CD35:	0	CD18:	0
Isotype sIg:	00	CD6 :	0	CD36:	0	CD38:	0
Isotype cIg:	00	CD8 :	0	CD65:	0	CD71:	90
		CD25:	9			CD54:	0
		CD26:	0			CD44:	99
		WT31:	0			CD45Ro:	..
						CD30:	0
						CD11c	0
						CD42:	0
						Facteur VIII	0
						Glycophorine	0

```
       Nom autre: cCD79 %  0       Nom autre: MPO   % 90
       Nom autre: cCD13 % 70       Nom autre: BCL2  %  0
```

NOMENCLATURE GEIL: MYELOIDE

```
Pr ████              Dr ████████           Pr ████████
IMMUNOPHENOTYPAGE REALISE APRES ENRICHISSEMENT SUR FICOLL SELON LES TECHNIQUES
DE REFERENCE. SCORING ET SOUS-TYPAGE SELON LES RECOMMANDATIONS GEIL ET EGIL.
```

Figure 2.

that are, in their opinion, technology-driven, as opposed to clinically driven. An undue focus on technology is seen as one of the leading forces behind the trend towards increasingly sophisticated multiparametric analyses.

The contrast between algorithmic versus inspired clinical analyses has also been formulated, in a different form, by one of the critics of the EGIL proposals. According to Paietta (1995), scoring systems, or, more generally, any scheme using a pre-established classification based on a list of markers, has little clinical significance: division into subgroups will only rarely give relevant prognostic information. In her opinion, the a priori definition of theoretically expected phenotypes should be replaced by the retrospective analysis of actually observed phenotypes with respect to their clinical relevance. Individual antigens, rather than a list of marker profiles, should be the focus of immunological analysis. From this point of view, standardization is not a meaningful goal, and experience, rather than convenience, should establish the clinical relevance of a degree of antigen expression.

Professional Tactics

As is evident from the previous sections, there is an uneasy relation between the laboratory and the clinic. This is the case not only for epistemologists or medical philosophers, but also, and more interestingly, for health care practitioners. How this relationship is organized varies from place to place. There is, nonetheless, an underlying similarity and it is this: clinicians see patients in the wards. While their clinical experience gives them a good idea of the specific disease from which the patient is suffering, laboratory results are required in order to confirm, rectify or specify the initial clinical diagnosis. The laboratory used to refer to the morphological inspection of microscopic slides of stained bone-marrow aspirates, blood smears and tissue biopsies. But, as we have seen, it increasingly means the microscopic analysis of those "same"[10] slides treated with specific antibodies that allow one to distinguish between morphologically indistinguishable cells, and/or the use of flow cytometric techniques that replace morphology with entirely different pictures or with quantitative data, and/or the use of cytogenetic and, most recently, molecular biological techniques.

Now, clinicians on the ward, the treating physicians, may be hematologists or medical oncologists: they examine whole patients, ask for laboratory examinations of patient samples (taken by other practitioners – surgeons, in the case of biopsies), inspect the examination results and make decisions concerning treatment. Back in the lab, another sort of clinician, a pathologist, also claims to have patients waiting but these take the form of microscope slides, prepared (fixed, stained) by skilled technicians. Although pathologists do not interact verbally with patients, their diagnosis has an unrivaled aura of scientific certainty. Treating physicians, when sending material to the lab for a so-called consult will very often already have a good idea of what the diagnosis will look like:

their request will often read Confirm AML, Exclude AML and so on, but the final diagnostic word is the pathologist's.

Beyond these generalities, actual arrangements (the clinical division of labor) are markedly different in different countries. While further variation exists within countries, some generalization is possible. In France, as far as leukemias are concerned, hematologists call the shots. Lymphomas, contrary to the USA, are sharply separated from leukemias and fall under the jurisdiction of solid tumor specialists. The hematology laboratory is under the supervision of hematologists but, especially since the differentiation of the laboratory into several sections (immunology, cytogenetics, molecular biology) equipped with advanced technologies, different brands of medical biologists (often, in the case of immunology, people with doctoral degrees in pharmacy) are, in fact, in charge of the laboratory. The increasing specialization and complexity of laboratory results and the diversification of the professional figures in charge of each specialized segment can easily lead to cacophony and the establishment of standardized ways of producing and interpreting results appears as a solution to the problem of articulating differences. This is how we can understand EGIL's support for a classificatory scheme predicated upon the establishment of standardized panels of antibodies, cut-off points and scoring systems.

Lymphomas, on the other hand, are controlled by anatomo-pathologists (so-called anapath), who have been trained in the microscopic examination of tissue slides, a practice relying on the examination of morphology even if, most recently, immunological reagents have been added to the spectrum of dyes used to better visualize cells and tissues. While medical immunology has long had a place in the French hematology system, especially within its most prestigious centers, immunologists have apparently not been very successful in their attempt to penetrate the anapath-controlled domain. Symptomatic of this professional split between the leukemias and the lymphomas is the fact that two key players of the GEIL decided to obtain a *Certificat de maîtrise d'anatomie pathologique générale* in order to make themselves more acceptable to anapaths. In spite of this, their attempts to establish working relations with the anapaths on the immunology of lymphomas have been largely unsuccessful (interview with M. C. Béné and G. Faure, CHU Nancy, February 1997).[11] While hematologists were also initially suspicious of the immunologists' lack of morphological experience, their mistrust quickly gave way to acceptance. Immunological methods are now tools that, in addition to morphology, cytogenetics and, most recently, molecular biology, make up the technological platform of a hematology center (interview with Françoise Valensi, Hôpital Necker, Paris, December 1996).

Things are different in the US. In addition to having a clinical status, pathologists, i.e. practitioners skilled in laboratory practices, control the lab, and hematologists rely on pathologists for the (often qualitative) interpretation of results. As long as the laboratory techniques amounted to microscopy, this division of labor was reasonably stable. But how can a pathologist now pretend to cover all the new technologies? Disturbing signs of change loom on the horizon. Some hospital-based, flow cytometric laboratories are directed by Ph.D.s who, in spite of not being M.D.s and not having a legal right to diagnose, claim to be able to work around the painstaking morphological examination of cells and to be able to come to a decisive conclusion. This happens not only within hospitals: large, private reference labs have been created that contain large assemblies of flow cytometric equipment and to which clinicians can send (sometimes from relatively distant sites) samples for testing. Pathologists claim that even high-tech technologies such as flow cytometry are more of an art than a science and require clinical experience. HIV testing with flow cytometry (one of the earliest and most widespread applications of this new technology) is seen as a routine, quantitative exercise; but not leukemias and lymphomas. Nor are technical developments limited to flow cytometry: as we pointed out, cytogenetics and molecular biology have joined in. Should one specialize in the flow cytometry or the cytogenetics or the molecular biology of everything, or should one specialize in integrating the contributions from these different techniques to one specific set of diseases, such as blood cancers, thus retaining a clinical, as opposed to a technical, edge?

Walking down the aisles of US hospitals, one now sees signs pointing to the department of hematopathology. This is a new and problematic breed of practitioner. They proliferate in the vicinity of laboratories equipped with a mix of the latest, most sophisticated technologies. The trusty microscope has been complemented with an array of instruments and the walls are covered with posters detailing antibodies and surface markers. According to some US hematopathologists, dramatic developments in new technologies have increased the gap both between the lab and the clinic and within laboratory sub-specialties. Is the clinical picture (the forest) lost in the proliferation of increasingly sophisticated details (the trees)? Or, to the contrary, are decisive contributions to better clinical practices lost because of the inability of clinicians to integrate the new data into their work? As we have seen in the section on the normal and the pathological, this is more than a turf struggle: it addresses significant clinical issues. The hematopathologist, at least in some US quarters, represents an attempt to tame technology and to master the division of work.

But what has all this to do with classifications? In a Quebec hematology service, one could witness the sense of excitement generated by the publication of the REAL classification. Copies of the article were posted at several places in the laboratory, and the clinician we interviewed spoke of it as the vindication of diagnostic and therapeutic decisions that they had been making for years and that had set them apart from other centers ("We went to that meeting in Toronto, and we were there, sitting all alone in our corner, so to speak"). Those divergent decisions were the result of differences between traditional, morphology-based classifications and the data the Quebec group obtained thanks to the latest laboratory techniques. REAL came as a legitimization of their clinical practice and was perceived as a more adequate classification because of that practice. Interestingly enough, when questioned about REAL, one of the American champions of both flow cytometry and hematopathology was far less enthusiastic. He noted that while members of ILSG were indeed using the latest antibody techniques, they were using them on microscope slides, not with flow cytometry. In other words, they were traditional tissue pathologists, not hematopathologists. Their classification fell short of both clinical demands as well as of the latest laboratory refinements that allegedly characterize hematopathology.

So far, our description seems to point to a somewhat untenable situation. Yet, outside the heated polemics in medical journals and conferences, the work of pathologists and clinicians proceeds smoothly: they routinely diagnose and treat leukemias and lymphomas. This apparent paradox can be resolved by looking at how they create a common ground on which to disagree.

The Accumulation of (Material) Data

It is difficult to classify diseases when individual experts observe only a limited number of cases and lymphomas are relatively rare cancers. The classification of lymphomas was thus profoundly transformed prior to and during the Second World War by the establishment of lymphoma banks containing data not only in written form but also in the form of tissue specimens. The Oxford Lymph Node Registry was founded in 1937 and published the results of its first 1,000 cases in 1947. In the US, the American Lymph Node Registry was founded in 1925 by the American Association of Pathologists and Bacteriologists. In the 1930s, it became the Lymphatic Tumor Division of the American Registry of

Pathology and managed to amass, in its first seven years of operation, 380 cases of lymphoma (Callendar 1943). The explosion of an American ship containing mustard gas in Bari (Italy) in 1943 and the resulting effects of the gas on the hematopoietic tissues of the conscripts led to the creation by the American Armed Forces Institute of Pathology of one of the larger banks centralizing biopsy material (Rhoads 1946). Robert J. Lukes, who gave his name to one of the major classificatory schemes of the lymphomas, grounded his proposal in his experience as Chief of the Hematopathology Section of the Armed Forces Institute of Pathology from 1954–62, and in his experience with over 5,000 autopsied cases of lymphoma and Hodgkin's disease (Lukes 1967).

From our previous discussion, one might have the impression that clinicians on the ward deal with patients whereas pathologists deal with body fragments. Yet the relation between the clinician and the patient is strongly mediated by the accumulated biopsy samples insofar as they are the grounds on which prognosis (and thus treatment) is made. Similarly, the work of pathologists is dependent on tissue banks that provide material for reference standards. Ultimately, pathologists and clinicians share a material world of common artifacts.

The importance of cell banks has not diminished. For instance, as we have shown elsewhere (Keating and Cambrosio 1994), the development of a collection of frozen cell specimens of lymphoid neoplasms at the Dana Farber Cancer Institute played an important role in the establishment of immunological techniques for the analysis of these diseases. Yet, material collections of patient specimens can, under certain conditions, be replaced by virtual collections of patient data. Indeed, just as lymphomas depend on the biopsy, the routine use of immunological tools in the diagnosis and therapy of leukemia is predicated upon the existence of an immunological framework establishing, for instance, the significance of a given marker or set of markers. Such a framework can only result from the analysis of large cohorts of patients. A single center has only a limited number of patients, and not even all its patients can be included in a research scheme, because, for instance, certain patient samples only provide a small number of cells.[12] It is only by pooling cases from different centers that one can achieve a statistically relevant collection of cases of leukemia covering the entire spectrum of disease manifestations. In collecting cases, one is referring here not to the concentration of bodies in a single location, nor even the centralization of samples in a collection, but, rather, to the collation of the results of the analyses performed on patients in a database. Thus, one needs to be sure that the same kind of data are being collected (a problem that can be solved by using a standard form), and that the data collected are reliable, i.e., that the methods, reagents and instruments used in laboratories are comparable.

GEIL's program, for example, is predicated upon methods for achieving inter-laboratory equivalencies (Keating and Cambrosio 1998) that involve both technical schemes, such as periodically circulating frozen, coded cells in a blind fashion to all members of the network to test inter-center agreement and organizational schemes that adopt, for instance, a loose network structure without a formal administration.[13] These methods are complemented by economic initiatives, such as the negotiation of better financial conditions from commercial distributors for the bulk supply of reagents so that every center can literally use the same antibodies.[14] In order for a group like GEIL to function then, two related, yet analytically distinct sets of practices must be instituted. The first, and most traditional, leads to the standardization of local routine practices, by allowing even small, marginal centers to align their practices on the protocols and reagents used in the more advanced centers;[15] the second results in a new approach to the conduct of research, namely the creation of a collective, multicenter authorship that ensures, *de facto*, the inter-center robustness of results.

Yet, even such a scheme is not perfect: centers outside the GEIL network are not necessarily willing to follow the group's prescriptions. Thus, the extension of GEIL's approach to the European arena through EGIL's proposal is not simply an attempt to achieve standardization on a larger geographic basis, but also an attempt to add internal weight to the national schemes that have apparently not shown impact beyond their own participants or users (Béné et al. 1996). This raises the issue of the variety of technologies deployed to reach consensus.

Consensus Technologies

As should by now be obvious, the history of leukemia and lymphoma classification is, in large part, a history of the establishment of competing classifications and of questions raised about their compatibility. Indeed, troubling medical and epistemological questions result from the proliferation of classifications. What is the nature of the differences? Is it merely a linguistic problem, a matter of mere terminology? Or, given the fact that the competing classifications are sometimes based on different principles, for instance morphological versus immunological criteria, do these differences correspond to deeper, biological problems? And what about the articulation of these differences with the practical problems of therapy? Consider the following example of how these questions are addressed.

In 1975, after the failure of various international meetings organized to solve the problem of incompatible classifications in the field of the lymphomas, the US National Cancer Institute grew increasingly alarmed at the proliferation of lymphoma classifications and by the consequences such a plurality would have on statistics and clinicians. The solution proposed by the NCI was to organize yet another conference not in order to choose a classification system (a delicate matter from any point of view) but to establish a basis of comparison between the systems. Alas, such a basis did not emerge, and the conference called for the production of an acceptable classification (Anonymous 1975). In an attempt to garner consensus, the NCI organized a retrospective study of biopsies of over 1,000 cases that were classified according to the competing systems: six different classification systems were played off against each other between September 1976 and June 1980. The six proponents of the six systems (termed experts) and six control pathologists classified 1,175 cases according to each system, the experts classifying according to their own system and the control pathologists according to all six.[16] The results of the showdown were discussed at conferences held at Stanford in 1979–80, and the participants agreed that no fundamental differences had surfaced. This opened the door to the establishment of a Working Formulation, the foundation of which was morphologic (pace the pathologists) but the central categories of which were prognostic (pace the clinicians): High Grade, Intermediate Grade and Low Grade (Anonymous 1982).

The REAL classification, the most recent attempt to displace/replace the Working Formulation, has, to a certain extent, resorted to similar procedures. First of all it should be noted that the Working Formulation (and the more distinctly European Kiel Classification) acted as the backdrop against which the REAL classification was devised, both in the sense that the presentation of the REAL classification includes tables comparing it to its two predecessors, and in the sense that the development of the former took into account requirements defined by the latter, such as the practicality of sub-classifying diffuse large cell lymphomas (as required by both the Kiel Classification and the Working Formulation) (Harris et al. 1994: 1362). Second, the production of the REAL classification included arrangements such as the circulation of slides among participants who were asked to classify the tumors, with the scoring sheets being returned to the conference site and collated before the meeting.

The circulation of material among experts is meant to achieve reproducibility but this kind of endeavor (reproducibility studies, proficiency

testing) while often presented as a means to assess the performance of
laboratories or practitioners can be seen as a way of achieving the very
reproducibility or proficiency that they allegedly test (Keating and Cambrosio 1998). Moreover, this kind of reproducibility is open to questioning by practitioners because of the gap between the doubly selective test
environment (participants are selected among the top practitioners and
they know that they are engaged in a reproducibility study) and daily
operations. Indeed, it is often noted that the percentage of diagnostic
agreement falls rapidly from around 70 percent to as low as 35 percent
when one goes from expert to practicing pathologists, with one study
showing that therapy relevant disagreements between the former and
the latter could be found in more than 30 percent of cases (Taylor 1993:
232). This, however, is not taken as a reason for abandoning the practice of pathology, but as the starting point of yet more reproducibility
studies aimed, precisely, at achieving better agreement.[17]

Consensus is often taken to mean 100 percent agreement, though –
as shown by expressions such as a large consensus – who is to be
included in the set of persons agreeing on something is an open question. Consensus is not necessarily present at the outset: several rounds
of discussion may be necessary in order to reach agreement and if dis-
senters persist in their (explicit) opposition, then according to conventional wisdom there is no agreement, and thus no consensus. Readers
may thus be surprised to learn that, in addition to the fact that various
formal techniques have been devised to reach consensus in medical matters (see, for example, the NIH consensus technology described in Kanouse 1989), the meaning of the term consensus has been statistically,
and pragmatically, redefined to mean, for instance, 80 percent agreement on a given topic between surveyed practitioners.

As we have seen, the validity of the REAL classification was questioned on the basis of the fact that the number of *major* (obviously an
important modality!)[18] pathologists involved in its production was not
large enough (Rosenberg 1994). The ILSG, in their reply to this criticism, in addition to pointing out that, for that matter, even previous
classifications, including the Working Formulation, "did not represent
a consensus because it was rejected by two of the twelve pathologists
involved . . . at the time of its publication," promised to work "with
other hematopathologists to broaden and build upon [the REAL classi-
fication] consensus" (Harris et al. 1995b: 857). Interestingly enough,
the REAL classification was presented as more of a true consensus than
previous classificatory attempts. Responsibility for this achievement was
shifted from humans to technology: when morphology was the only

classificatory criterion, human subjectivity led to controversy,[19] but a consensus is now possible thanks to the availability of objective immunophenotyping and genetics data (Harris et al. 1995b).

In spite of this alleged shift from subjectivity to objectivity, consensus technology is still a necessity. For instance, in November 1995 a group of pathologists and clinicians convened a Consensus Conference at the NIH in order to develop guidelines for the immunophenotyping of leukemias and lymphomas. Several remarkable things happened there. First, while no participant seemed to doubt that the new technology would confer more objectivity on the diagnosis of leukemias and lymphomas, the attempt to transfer responsibility for establishing a diagnosis to the machine or the technician or even the Ph.D. supervising the work of technicians was nonetheless resisted. The use of flow cytometry (immunophenotyping) in this domain, it was argued, was more an art than a science, and therefore was grounded in experience. Similarly, informal requests from industry representatives for a consensus on standardized minimal panels of antibodies that could be put on the market to diagnose various kinds of lymphomas and leukemias were resisted with the argument that such standardization would be a dangerous (for the patient) attempt to work around the diagnostic expertise of skillful practitioners. Industry could provide faster, more automated hardware, but the choice of antibodies and the interpretation of the visual patterns produced by the use of those antibodies should be left to the hematopathologist. The computer-generated, conventional displays of the flow cytometer acted here as the equivalent of morphologic images under the microscope. This, of course, constituted a criticism of approaches such as the one championed by EGIL, one that leads us back to the previously discussed quantity/quality issue.

Second, while one might expect that the new technique would displace traditional classifications and provide a basis for new ones, what happened looked more like an attempt to fit the new data into the older, established classifications. The new technology was, of course, a source of change. The increased use of flow cytometry, for instance, tended to make certain diagnoses more common. As one participant noted: "So far, flow is confirmatory. What should be done when it is at odds with morphology? Won't an increased use of flow make new diseases?" But the point is that those new diseases are only partly new, insofar as they are part of an older classification. In diagnostic practice, immunophenotyping follows on from a number of other procedures (clinical and morphological data) that have already eliminated other possibilities.

But what mechanisms are used to reach consensus? The method used by the committee on medical indications was as follows. The chairman formulated a series of general statements usually framed in the strongest manner possible and sent them out to members of the committee who scored the statements on a scale from one to seven and provided comments. References to the secondary literature for the statements were provided. The working document for the session resulted from a second round of consultation conducted along the same lines and included the comments made by the committee members. Of the original statements, only about half were retained at the end of the conference. Part of the attrition was due to the absorption of several statements by a more general proposition while part was also due to irreducible differences. Consensus was viewed as 80 percent, although during the course of the meeting statements were watered down in order to achieve unanimous consent.

Decision-making, thus, combined three distinct kinds of authority: the previously mentioned secondary literature (the latter, following our analysis of it, turned out to be often loosely or indirectly connected to the statements under discussion), the participants' own practical experience and a spontaneous sociology or philosophy of the science in question. All three could be and were, on occasion, contested. For example, it was possible to argue "We have literature on that," just as it was possible to say "The literature on minimal residual disease is a mess." Experience, of course, varied and the sociology revolved around just how far one could go with a statement before the speaker (in this case the committee) lost credibility.

Last, but not least, it should be noted that the consensus reached by any of the previously described schemes does not necessarily mean an end to controversy. Indeed, as we have seen in the case of leukemia immunophenotyping, several consensuses can coexist and thus be a sign of (at least latent) controversy. When asked about this kind of situation, actors react not only by, for instance, questioning the representativeness of a given consensus document (and thus its status as a real consensus) but also by mobilizing boundaries between, say, clinical and technical activities. So, for instance, EGIL's document on leukemia immunophenotyping was categorized as a clinical document, i.e., as a proposal the main purpose of which is to offer criteria for interpreting the results of the immunological analysis of white blood cells, whereas the corresponding German-based document (Rothe and Schmitz 1996) was characterized as a technical document, i.e., a text mainly devoted to a discussion of the various settings and parameters of the equipment and reagents used in the immunological analysis (interview with G. Rothe, Oslo, 27 May 1997). One can easily show that this distinction, if taken in an absolute sense, is hardly viable, not simply because of the presence of technical and clinical elements in both texts, but also because the articulation of the technical and clinical horizons is a condition of possibility and the ultimate *raison d'être* of this kind of undertaking. Yet to reduce the clinical/technical divide to a purely rhetorical move, to mere boundary work, would be to miss one of the constitutive dimensions of biomedical practice, namely the effective management of ongoing shifts between diagnostic, prognostic and therapeutic interventions as evidenced, for instance, in what in a previous section we have termed professional tactics.

Conclusion

Work on this paper started when informants told us that leukemia and lymphoma classification was a mess, but that the situation was improving thanks to the adoption of new technologies, such as flow cytometry. Here, it seemed, one would find a clinical culture (a set of beliefs and representations) in the process of being subverted by new biomedical technologies – or maybe an instance of the process whereby the new technology was being shaped by pre-existing clinical cultures. Not so. What we found was neither technological nor socio-cultural determinism but, rather, a complex set of issues and tactics, each of which mobilized pre-existing and newly invented elements as part of intersecting domains of practices.

Health care practitioners observe that there is a lack of consensus on lymphoma classification, and that this causes problems for practicing pathologists and clinicians, and creates difficulty in interpreting published studies (Harris et al. 1994: 1383). Should something be done about it? And, if so, what should and could be done? Update previous classifications? Find methods of translating between existing classifications? Create a new classification? But, if so, how? By relying on newly devised laboratory criteria? By combining old and new entities? By building on what experienced practitioners are actually doing in their daily practice (Harris et al. 1994)? The list could go on and no amount of sociological or anthropological imagination will succeed in reducing the open-ended nature of medical practices to a few, isolated factors. Yet, one should not be content with verifying the existence of differences (Berg and Mol 1998) or pointing to the mangle of practice (Pickering 1995). Although not transcendent, some patterns can be described.

A number of oppositions characterize the classifications discussed in this paper: solid tumor versus liquid tumor, morphology versus immunophenotype, microscopy versus cytometry, quantity versus quality, lym-

phoma versus leukemia, pathologists versus biologists. These divisions
are real, but the characterization is somewhat fictitious. Specimens
observed in the flow cytometer can be scrutinized under the microscope;
pathologists do biology and biologists are aware of clinical exigencies;
some immunophenotypes do have morphological correlates; lymphomas
may first appear as leukemias; solids can become liquids and vice versa.
While these divisions are at times the terms in which conflict is framed
in the field of the leukemias and lymphomas, they are not always so.
There is, in other words, no deep structure that divides the field in
clans or groups based on professional identity, technology or underlying
biological structures. There is, moreover, no simple division separating
the pathologist from the immunologist or the scientist from the clinician.

Nobody disputes the existence of leukemia and lymphoma, nor the
fact that there are important subdivisions. Similarly, nobody questions
the utility or the importance of the introduction of basic biological
(immunological) categories into the description of these two pathological processes. Conflict over the classification of the leukemias and the
lymphomas is based on the timing and circumstances of the introduction of new knowledge and techniques into standardized clinical practices. Deciding what is timely depends upon the definition of the present
state of science and technology. For that definition, there can be no
predefined consensus; it must be actively sought. But, and this is the
point, consensus is not sought because there is conflict, just as the lack
of consensus does not entail conflict. For instance, a consensus conference presupposes consensus about the present state of the art to the
extent that there is a clearly defined domain of diagnosis and therapeutic
intervention.

The variety of strategies pursued by pathologists and clinicians in the
quest for universally acceptable criteria for the diagnosis of leukemia
and lymphoma does not prevent the emergence of trends. For instance,
since the 1960s a general tendency can be perceived that seeks the generalization of pathological singularities by redescribing them as biological abnormalities. This trend, however, is consistently challenged by
divergent views on the tactics of description to be used in this project.
These views broach a variety of topics ranging from the epistemological – is morphological information equivalent to immunological information? – to the pragmatic – what sort of information enhances therapeutics? In view of the existence of competing technologies of
description and of their variable adaptation to local circumstances and
needs, the pursuit of consensus has itself become a goal. In other words,
consensus is not an external variable the presence or absence of which

can be assessed by epistemologically privileged analysts; rather, it is part and parcel of the socio-technical practices pursued by actors: no more, no less.

NOTES

Research for this paper has been made possible by a Social Sciences and Humanities Research Council of Canada grant 410-94-0352, and by a Fonds FCAR grant 95-ER-2220. We would like to thank Gavin Svensson for his invaluable assistance in collecting a large amount of material used in this article, as well as the scientists, clinicians and technicians who agreed to grant us interviews.

1. Non-Hodgkin's lymphomas represent the vast majority of lymphomas.
2. Dehner (1995) pointed out that there had been no previous European–American classification. The authors of the REAL classification argued that the acronym was justified in view of their effort to build on current European and American classifications (Harris et al. 1994).
3. A similar Dutch group, called SIHON, was created in the mid-1980s; other groups soon followed in other countries.
4. One could reserve the term "classification" for the finished product or for the establishment of a classificatory system, whereas the act of applying categories drawn from the general classification to individual patients would be called categorization. The term "categorization" could, in turn, be reserved for the act of assigning the patient to one of a few (often dichotomous) categories: e.g., low-grade versus high-grade lymphomas. Practice conflates these epistemological distinctions.
5. Any given group of diseases may be more readily classified by one principle rather than another, e.g., etiologic in the case of bacterial diseases, histopathological in the case of cancers. The etiologic principle is often held to be the gold standard, but attempts at comprehensive understanding or description of any class of diseases entail the mobilization of all four categories of cause. These four categories are the pillars of the Systematized Nomenclature of Medicine (SNOMED) promoted by the College of American Pathologists.
6. Note, in this respect, the pragmatic attitude of the ILSG: it is necessary to split before meaningful lumping can occur. If several morphologically, immunologically, and genetically distinct neoplasms prove to respond identically to currently available treatment, they can be lumped for the purpose of clinical treatment selection. However, if new forms of treatment become available it will be important to recognize and study each disease separately (Harris et al. 1994: 1384).
7. An alternative route, begun with the investigation of the role of the thymus in leukemia, involved thymectomized and irradiated mice; see Miller 1995.
8. Another main activity is to establish guidelines or good laboratory practices that will allow clinical laboratories involved in routine clinical work to produce an immunological diagnosis that can be fitted in the previously established immunological classification. Finally, the clinical relevance – in most cases: the prognostic value and thus the therapeutic strategy of the immunol-

ogical diagnosis – has to be established for all this to make sense, and large multi-center studies on this subject are one of GEIL's major preoccupations.

9. Pathology residents rotating through the flow cytometry laboratory at Rosewell Park are given a thick stack of images similar to those at the bottom of Figure 1 and are asked to learn to interpret the visual patterns shown on them (interview with Carleton Stewart, Bethesda, Maryland, November 1995).

10. In fact the slides are not the same: in a bone marrow biopsy, the first aspirate is of better quality than the following ones. Depending on your technological beliefs, you will save the better material for your technique of choice and send the material of lesser quality to the labs performing the test that you value or trust the least.

11. Interestingly enough, a look at the Nomenclature of Medical Biology Acts (the official list of all the diagnostic procedures that are reimbursed by the French medicare system and that is also used to assess hospital activities) shows that whereas the various tests from different specialties (microbiology, biochemistry, immunology, and so on) are all coded by the same letter, anatomopathological procedures are coded by a different letter, pointing to the fact that they are performed by clinicians who have a right to diagnose, as opposed to medical biologists.

12. From this point of view, according to GEIL, immunology lies somewhere between cytology/morphology (high number of successful studies) and cytogenetics (high number of unsuccessful karyotypic studies); see Béné et al. 1989.

13. This latter approach allows each hospital team to retain full ownership of the data provided to the group, a device aimed at decreasing fears of cannibalization by leading centers while ensuring access on request to locally archived, complementary clinical data, without which immunological information would be meaningless.

14. In fact, it appears that differences can still be observed among certain reagents belonging to the cluster but produced by different suppliers; see Béné et al. 1989; fieldnotes, Bethesda Consensus Conference.

15. To become a member of GEIL, a center has only to agree to participate in the overall endeavor by pooling its data in the collective database and by participating in periodical quality control studies. Poor performance in the latter does not lead to sanctions, since no administrative authority exists that could impose such sanctions. Yet, the (anonymous) exclusion of poor data from the cohort of cases analyzed for a given study, has apparently provided sufficient incentives for participating centers to seek the common standard.

16. The actual scheme involved a visit by the six experts to four participating institutions, where they were first asked to classify slides without any clinical information and then to revise their diagnosis after being given three pieces of clinical information (age, sex, site of biopsy). The control pathologists visited the same institutions and classified the same slides.

17. The authors of the REAL classification, after mentioning the poor reproducibility of prior classifications, argue that the addition of immunophenotyping data to morphology significantly improves reproducibility among

pathologists and state on that basis that they are "confident that a list of well-defined entities such as the one we proposed will be *more reproducibly* diagnosed than the more ambiguous categories of the working formulation" (Harris et al. 1995b). Reproducibility, here, is a matter of degree.
18. On the different weight of small versus large (i.e., expert) opinions, see the section on "The Democratic Process" in Taylor 1993: 232–3.
19. Controversy is indeed the right term. As noted by another author commenting on the 1970s period "the rhetoric had reached such a level that sarcastic wit found its way into the overheated debate" (Dehner 1995: 539).

REFERENCES

Anonymous 1975 "Workshop for the Classification of non-Hodgkin's Lymphomas." *Biomedicine* 22: 466–7.
    1982 "The National Cancer Institute Sponsored Study of Classifications of Non-Hodgkin's Lymphomas: Summary and Description of a Working Formulation for Clinical Usage. The Non-Hodgkin's Lymphoma Pathologic Classification Project." *Cancer* 49: 2112–35.
Atkinson, Paul 1995 *Medical Talk and Medical Work.* London: Sage Publications.
Béné, M. C., L. Boumsell, J.-P. Vannier, R. Garand, E. Solary, G. Faure and A. Bernard 1989 "Immunologic Analysis of a Thousand Cases of Acute Leukemia." *Nouvelle Revue Française d'Hématologie* 31: 133–6.
Béné, M. C., G. Castoldi, W. Knapp, W. D. Ludwig, E. Matutes, A. Orfao and MB van't Veer 1995 "Proposals for the Immunological Classification of Acute Leukemias. European Group for the Immunological Characterization of Leukemias (EGIL)." *Leukemia* 9: 1783–6.
    1996 "Classification of Acute Leukemias: Reply from EGIL to Dr. van Dongen." *Leukemia* 10: 1363–4.
Berg, Marc and Annemarie Mol 1998 *Differences in Medicine. Unraveling Practices, Techniques and Bodies.* Durham and London: Duke University Press.
Callendar, G. R. 1943 "Tumors and Tumor-Like Conditions of the Lymphocyte, the Myelocyte, the Erythrocyte and the Reticulum Cell." *American Journal of Pathology* 10: 443–65.
Dagognet, François 1970 *Le Catalogue de la Vie.* Paris: Presses Universitaires de France.
Dehner, Louis P. 1995 "Here We Go Again: A New Classification of Malignant Lymphomas." *American Journal of Clinical Pathology* 103: 539–40.
Good, Robert A. 1983 "Historic Aspects of Cellular Immunology." In John I. Gallin and Anthony S. Fauci (eds.), *Lymphoid Cells (Advances in Host Defense Mechanisms)* 2nd edition. New York: Raven Press, pp. 1–42.
Good, Robert A. and Joanne Finstad 1968 *The Association of Lymphoid Malignancy and Immunologic Functions. Proceedings of the International Conference on Leukemia-Lymphoma, 1967.* The Association of Lymphoid Malignancy and Immunologic Functions, Ann Arbor, MI: Lea & Febiger, pp. 175–97.
Griffin, J. D., R. J. Mayer, H. J. Weinstein, D. S. Rosenthal, F. S. Coral, R. P. Beveridge and S. F. Schlossman 1983 "Surface Marker Analysis of Acute

Myeloblastic Leukemia: Identification of Differentiation-Associated Phenotype." *Blood* 62: 557–63.

Hacking, Ian 1993 "Working in a New World: The Taxonomic Solution." In Paul Horwich (ed.), *World Changes: Thomas Kuhn and the Nature of Science.* Cambridge MA: MIT Press, pp. 275–310.

Hansen, John A. and Robert A. Good 1974 "Malignant Disease of the Lymphoid System in Immunological Perspective." *Human Pathology* 5: 567–99.

Harris, Nancy Lee 1995 "A Practical Approach to the Pathology of Lymphoid Neoplasms: A Revised European-American Classification from the International Lymphoma Study Group." *Important Advances in Oncology:* 111–40.

Harris, Nancy Lee, E. S. Jaffe, H. Stein, P. M. Banks, J. K. Chan, M. L. Cleary, G. Delsol, C. De Wolf-Peeters, B. Falini, K. C. Gatter, T. M. Grogan, P. G. Isaacson, D. M. Knowles, D. Y. Mason, H.-K. Muller-Hermelink, S. A. Pileri, M. A. Piris, E. Ralfkiaer, and R. A. Warnke 1994 "A Revised European-American Classification of Lymphoid Neoplasms: A Proposal from the International Lymphoma Study Group." *Blood* 84: 1361–92.

1995a "Lymphoma Classification Proposal: Clarification." *Blood* 85: 857–60.

Harris, Nancy Lee, Elaine S. Jaffe and Harald Stein 1995b "Response" [Letter]. *Blood* 85: 1973–4.

Henry, Kristin, M. H. Bennett and Geoffrey Farrer-Brown 1978 "Classification of the Non-Hodgkin's Lymphomas." In P. P. Anthony and N. Woolf (eds.), *Recent Advances in Histopathology 10.* Edinburgh: Churchill Livingston, pp. 274–302.

Kanouse, D. E. et al. 1989 *Changing Medical Practice Through Technology Assessment: An Evaluation of the NIH Consensus Development Program.* Ann Arbor, MI: Health Administration Press.

Keating, Peter and Alberto Cambrosio 1994 "Ours is an Engineering Approach: Flow Cytometry and the Constitution of Human T-cell Subsets." *Journal of the History of Biology* 27: 449–79.

1998 "Interlaboratory Life: Regulating Flow Cytometry." In Jean-Paul Gaudillière, Ilana Löwy and Dominique Pestre (eds.), *The Invisible Industrialist: Manufacturers and the Construction of Scientific Knowledge.* London: Macmillan, pp. 250–95.

Kuhn, Thomas 1993 "Afterwords." In Paul Horwich (ed.), *World Changes: Thomas Kuhn and the Nature of Science.* Cambridge MA: MIT Press, pp. 311–41.

Lévi-Strauss, Claude 1962 *Le Totémisme Aujourdhui.* Paris: Presses Universitaire de France.

Lukes, R. J. 1967 "A Review of the American Concept of Malignant Lymphoma." In A. Rüttiman (ed.), *Progress in Lymphology.* Stuttgart: Thieme Verlag, pp. 109–19.

Lukes, R. J. and R. D. Collins 1975 "New approaches to the Classification of the Lymphomata." In *Proceedings of the First International Symposium on the Non-Hodgkin's Lymphomata. Special issue. British Journal of Cancer* 31 (Supplement II): 1–28.

Mathé, G. and D. Belpomme 1974 "T and B Lymphocytic Nature of Leukemias and Lymphosarcomas: A New but Still Uncertain Parameter for their Classification." *Bioscience* 20: 81–5.

Meijer, C. J., P. van der Valk, P. C. de Bruin and R. Willemze 1995 "The Revised European-American Lymphoma (REAL) Classification of Non-Hodgkin's Lymphoma: A Missed Opportunity?" [Letter]. *Blood* 85: 1971–2.

MIC 1986 "First MIC Cooperative Study Group. Morphologic, Immunologic and Cytogenetic (MIC) Working Classification of Acute Lymphoblastic Leukemia." *Cancer Genetics and Cytogenetics* 23: 189–97.

   1988 "Second MIC Cooperative Study Group. Morphologic, Immunologic and Cytogenetic (MIC) Working Classification of the Acute Myeloid Leukemias." *British Journal of Haematology* 68: 487–4.

Miller, Jacques F. A. P. 1995 "The Discovery of Thymus Function." In Richard B. Gallagher, Jean Gilder, G. J. V. Nossal and Gaetano Salvatore (eds.), *Immunology: The Making of a Science.* New York: Academic Press, pp. 75–84.

Paietta, E. 1995 "Proposals for the Immunological Classification of Acute Leukemias." *Leukemia* 9: 147–8.

Pickering, Andrew 1995 *The Mangle of Practice. Time, Agency, and Science.* Chicago: University of Chicago Press.

Rhoads, C. P. 1946 "The Sword and the Ploughshare." *Journal of the Mount Sinai Hospital* 13: 299–309.

Rosenberg, Saul A. 1994 "Classification of Lymphoid Neoplasms." *Blood* 84: 1359–60.

Rothe, G. and G. Schmitz 1996 "Consensus Protocol for the Flow Cytometric Immunophenotyping of Hematopoietic Malignancies. Working Group on Flow Cytometry and Image Analysis." *Leukemia* 10: 877–95.

Schwarze, E. W. 1995 "Amerika, du Sollst es Besser Haben. Zur Diskussion um eine Aktuelle Lymphom-Klassification [America, You Deserve Better. On the Discussion Concerning Current Lymphoma Classification]." *Der Pathologe* 16: 241–4.

Taylor, Clive R. 1993 "An Exaltation of Experts: Concerted Efforts in the Standardization of Immunohistochemistry." *Applied Immunohistochemistry* 1: 232–43.

Terstappen, L. W., M Safford, S. Konemann, M. R. Loken, K. Zurlutter, T. Buchner, W. Hiddemann and B. Wormann 1991 "Flow Cytometric Characterization of Acute Myeloid Leukemia. Part 2. Phenotypic heterogeneity at diagnosis" [corrected version in *Leukemia* 6(1): 70–80, 1992]. *Leukemia* 5(9): 757–67.

van Dongen, J. J. M. 1995 "Proposals for the Immunological Classification of Acute Leukemias." *Leukemia* 9: 2149–50.

Willis, Rupert Allan 1948 *Pathology of Tumours.* London: Butterworth.

   1967 [1948] *Pathology of Tumours.* 4th edition. London: Butterworth.

7   History, hystery and psychiatric styles of reasoning

Allan Young

If we can begin to understand, accept, pity, and forgive ourselves for the psychological dynamics of hysteria, perhaps we can begin to work together to . . . avert the coming hysterical plague. (Showalter 1997: 207)

In her recent book, *Hysteries*, Elaine Showalter explains that episodes of hysteria occur among people who are exposed to emotional stress and mental conflict and have no effective means of putting their distress, desires and protests into words. Lacking permissible words, they express themselves through their bodies, in the "protolanguage" of symptoms. The process is unconscious and people are unaware of the meanings and messages they have produced:

stress/conflict ▷ unconscious processing ▷ meaningful symptoms

Hysteria "is a universal human response to emotional conflict" and is said to be part of everyday life. It has no constant appearance, no unvarying set of symptoms by which it can be easily recognized. Its function is to transmute knowledge and feelings – anger, pain, fear, resentment, self-loathing – into imitations of true disease and, *ipso facto*, into states of suffering and absolution. Yet the unconscious mind can mimic only what culture and history have provided. The protolanguage of symptoms is necessarily the language of the times. Without access to current nosologies and explanatory models of sickness, hysterical disorders would be meaningless and purposeless (Showalter 1997: 9, 11–13, 15, 17, 21).

Freud, Janet and their contemporaries were familiar with this process and, by the end of the nineteenth century, the disorder was a relatively common diagnosis ("hysteria," "hysterical neurosis," "traumatic hysteria"). During and immediately after the First World War, military doctors in England, Germany and France diagnosed tens of thousands of men as suffering from hysterical disorders ("shell shock," "war neurosis"). In the following years, the diagnosis gradually faded from medical discourse, nor was it revived during the Second World War. The phenomenon persisted, but without a clinical theater, a dialogic engagement (between patients and therapists), or its true name. By the 1980s, positivists and biological reductionists had reclaimed for themselves the leadership of American psychiatry. The American Psychiatric Association adopted a standardized diagnostic system (American Psychiatric Association 1980) that dispersed hysteria over multiple classifications – conversion disorder, somatization disorder, undifferentiated somatoform disorder, hypochondriasis, body dysmorphic disorder, factitious disorder, dissociative identity disorder. "Hysteria" was now merely history.

But history is full of surprises. According to Showalter, Americans are living through an epidemic of hysteria – an explosion of new and born-again psychogenic conditions that include multiple personality disorder, chronic fatigue syndrome, Gulf War syndrome, satanic ritual abuse syndrome, repressed memory syndrome, and a syndrome attributed to alien abductions. Showalter wants to make the epidemic visible in order to bring it under control. Writing about chronic fatigue syndrome (CFS), she quotes Arthur Kleinman, an anthropologist and psychiatrist:

Imagine being a chronic fatigue patient . . . We go to see a doctor and are sent on to a psychiatrist. [W]e are being asked about our families, our intimate personal life, our fears, our worries. We sense a distortion or incongruity about where our experience is [really] located: it's in the fatigue. And the psychiatrist . . . makes us feel that our experience, our primary grounding in our bodies, is unreal, imaginary. (Kleinman and Spiegel 1993 quoted in Showalter 1997: 130–1)

Kleinman's view of chronic fatigue syndrome is non-dualistic. He is further quoted as advising physicans to "work within a 'somatic' language" consonant with the patient's experience (Kleinman and Spiegel 1993: 329). In contrast, Showalter's approach to these syndromes is fundamentally dualistic. (In a short while, I will discuss how this difference is reflected in the ways in which writers connect symptoms to meanings, language, and intentionality.) It is not Kleinman's conflicting epistemology that captures her interest, however, but rather the *practical consequences* of taking his position:

[T]hese kindly, tolerant, and temporizing views do not address the ways that psychogenic epidemics escalate. Doctors may protect the self-esteem of their patients in the short run by prescribing placebos like vitamins and avoiding public statements about the history of effort syndromes [nineteenth-century precursor of CFS]. But in the long run, such acquiescence only creates more hystories [hysterical narratives]. Modern psychological epidemics feed endlessly on new disease theories, such as immunology. (Showalter 1997: 131)

By hiding hysteria behind a screen of false beliefs, the acquiescence of scholars-practitioners like Kleinman creates more hystories. Today, a century after the publication of *Studies on Hysteria* (Breuer and Freud 1955 [1893–5]), it is essential that we remember and reclaim the correct word:

[H]ysteria has not died. It has simply been relabeled for a new era ... In the 1990s, the United States has become the hot zone of psychogenic diseases, new and mutating forms of hysteria amplified by modern communications and fin de siècle anxiety. Contemporary hysterical patients blame external sources – a virus, sexual molestation, chemical warfare, satanic conspiracy, alien infiltration – for psychic problems. (Showalter 1997: 4)

This epidemic is nourished by an inexhaustible supply of psychologically vulnerable people and cadres of dedicated and (often) self-serving psychotherapists and trauma theorists. Why now? Showalter mentions the influence of religious fundamentalism, a growing "millenial panic," a paranoid style of political reasoning particular to American culture, the popularity and replicability of self-help groups, and a telecommunications industry that saturates the nation with hysterical fantasies and testimonials (Showalter 1997: 3, 5, 13, 15, 17).

Psychogenic Syndromes

Showalter traces the epidemiology and outward appearance of hysteria to the contingencies of culture and history. The distinctive psychogenic process that operates behind these appearances is, however, an endowment of human nature and not a construction. Take, as an example, this typical case of repressed memory syndrome. There is a woman who suffers a variety of medically unexplained symptoms, including persistent abdominal pain. Her psychotherapist, an expert in repressed memories of childhood sexual abuse, tells her that the pain is a "body memory" and the nature of her abusive event can be inferred from its location. Pain in the abdomen or groin is a memory of vaginal penetration, difficulty swallowing food and liquids is a memory of fellatio, etc. Showalter would say that the therapist's use of the concept of "body memory" is a construction, and particular to repressed memory syndrome. The patient's symptoms are nonetheless psychogenic; in contrast to what the psychotherapist says, the symptoms originate in strong emotions and psychic conflicts and not sexual acts, they mimic diseases and not etiological events.

Showalter's thesis consists of two propositions: (1) hysteria originates in this psychogenic process and (2) we are witnessing an epidemic of hysteria. Her point of departure, from which she proceeds to justify these claims, can be represented in the following formula:

mimicry : authenticity (disease) : : psychogenic : somatogenic

The formula implies a diagnostic logic of elimination: to learn if a given syndrome is an instance of hysteria, one first determines whether the symptoms are somatogenic or psychogenic. The logic presumes that there are techniques that allow experts to distinguish authentic somatic symptoms from mimicry. Without these techniques, there is no way to know whether rates of psychogenic disorders have increased, *sine qua non* for an epidemic. Indeed there are established techniques for diagnosing certain psychogenic symptoms. The standard diagnostic manual for psychiatric disorders (DSM-IV) alerts clinicians to pseudo-neurological symptoms and their modes of detection. Symptoms include anaesthesias (loss of tactile sensation, insensitivity to pain and extreme temperatures) that follow a pattern that matches folk conceptions rather than known anatomical pathways: "seizures" that vary from convulsion to convulsion and leave no trace on the EEG, "paralyzed" limbs that are moved inadvertently when the patient dresses or is distracted. Each act of detection demonstrates vividly how one might identify cases of hysteria or, as DSM-IV has it, conversion disorder. The problem here is that there are no comparable tests for the overwhelming majority of "hysterical" symptoms mentioned in Showalter's book.

Take the example of Gulf War syndrome (GWS). The "victims" of GWS associate their disorder with an extraordinary variety of symptoms, including headache, chronic fatigue, mood swings, memory loss, sleep problems, problems concentrating, sexual dysfunctions, bladder dysfunction, skin rashes, respiratory complaints, muscle pain, muscle spasms, swollen joints, bleeding gums, weight loss, nausea, vomiting, diarrhea and other digestive problems, birth defects (such as spina bifida), and pathologies affecting the reproductive organs of the veterans' spouses.

American and British medical authorities report that no one incident, toxin, virus, or disease entity is responsible for all the complaints that have been collected under the heading of "Gulf War syndrome" (Showalter 1997: 136, 137). This suggests four possibilities. The first possibility is that GWS is *psychogenic* (hysteria). The second possibility is that GWS is *somatogenic*, but medical science has yet to learn its cause and pathogenesis. Precedents for this conclusion can be found in the histories of multiple sclerosis, myasthenia gravis and porphyria. The third possibility is that GWS symptoms have *multiple* somatic origins. Soldiers were sprayed with insecticides that are chemically related to nerve gases; they were inoculated, vaccinated, and dosed with various combinations of possibly iatrogenic medical agents; some soldiers may have been exposed to poison gases and other troops were endangered by flea-borne parasites. It is clear that many of the medical problems that subsequently affected the soldiers would have developed anyway. In other words, the symptoms are truly somatogenic, but the disorder is sociogenic: "Gulf War syndrome" labels an assortment of medically unrelated conditions. The fourth possibility is that GWS, like other hysterias described in the book, *does not fit the dualistic formula*. That is, the syndrome does not mimic other disorders or diseases, and it does not fit a logic of elimination.

Showalter prefers the first possibility. GWS is precisely what she expects to find in cases of hysteria: a rag-bag of symptoms and a failure to find an inclusive somatic etiology. This psychogenic etiology, she adds, will be unpopular with many people, not least of all with the self-diagnosed victims of GWS. Even now, a half-century after Freud's death, "psychogenic" is a stigmatizing label for most Americans. For these veterans, it is evidence of mental fragility and moral weakness – a lack of virility and true grit. Likewise, psychogenic symptoms are perceived as a kind of pseudo-suffering, for which its "victims" must accept some responsibility. Showalter, a scholar with a mission, wants to change this conception. Hysteria can be made respectable:

The suffering of Gulf War syndrome *is* real by any measure and the symptoms caused by war neurosis are just as painful and incapacitating as those caused by chemicals, parasites, or smoke. But until we can acknowledge that strong and heroic men and women, fighting in a just cause, can be affected by the conversion of strong emotions into physical symptoms, no double-blind tests or expensive studies will change the likelihood that veterans of even the greatest military victories will continue to become sick. (Showalter 1997: 142–3)

Fear is pre-eminent among these "strong emotions." But only a very small minority of self-diagnosed patients were exposed to enemy fire. A larger fraction of patients recall being worried about the *possibility* of exposure to enemy weapons. Other patients recall that they were disturbed by the sight of dead enemy soldiers and animals. Finally, there are patients who have no recollections of strong fear and witnessed no dead bodies. A report prepared by the Department of Defense indicates how all of the veterans can be brought within the psychogenic circle:

Physical and psychological stressors were major characteristics of the Persian Gulf . . . US troops entered a bleak, physically demanding desert environment, where they were crowded into warehouses, storage buildings, and tents with little privacy and few amenities. No one knew that coalition forces would win a quick war with relatively few battle casualties. (Showalter 1997: 140)

This is followed by the comments of Simon Wessley, a British psychiatrist writing in the (London) *Times*:

[Having] to be ever alert for a silent attack by nerve gas or invisible deadly microbes must have taken a constant toll . . . The situation was made worse by the cumbersome protection suits, ill adapted for the desert heat, that had to be worn as a consequence. (Showalter 1997: 140)

Are these conditions stressful enough to produce emotions powerful enough to produce conversion symptoms? After long periods of latency? *Post hoc ergo propter hoc:* military service in the Persian Gulf was followed by an "epidemic" of conditions. No inclusive somatic cause is discovered. We ignore the possibility of multiple somatic origins, apply the logic of elimination, and reach the conclusion that the conditions are (mainly?) psychogenic conversions. Conversions are products of strong emotions and conflicts. But soldiers have both conscious and unconscious reasons to suppress their memories of these states, for instance, they do not want to delegitimize their symptoms and suffering.

Dualism

In Showalter's account, psychogenic symptoms begin with unspeakable meanings. In other words: first the meaning, then the symptom. Somatogenic symptoms, on the other hand, are products of pathoanatomy and pathophysiology. They are speechless because they are meaningless. The perspective is essentially dualistic, hence Showalter's insistence on mimicry and the logic of elimination.

There is one more way of connecting symptoms, meanings and language. The symptom develops first, and acquires its meaning only afterwards. This is completely unlike the relation described by Showalter: meanings are grafted onto symptoms, not encoded into them; meanings are expressed in language, not protolanguage; and meanings are products of the conscious mind, not the unconscious. Descriptions of this relation are often encountered in anthropologists' accounts of sickness and the body, but it is ignored in *Hysteries*. (Arthur Kleinman, mentioned above, has written on this subject at length and in detail. When Showalter discusses his work, her comments concern the political rather than epistemological implications of his ideas.)

To understand this process – *symptoms* ▷ *meanings* rather than *meanings* ▷ *symptoms* – one has to look beyond the two kinds of symptom formations described by Showalter:

1. Symptoms are *somatogenic.*
2. Symptoms are *psychogenic* and mimic somatic disorders.

There are at least three more symptom formations that can be found in the medical discourses of lay people and biomedical experts:

3. Symptoms are *psychosomatic*, a consequence of pathophysiological processes initiated by perceptions, mental conflicts and/or cognitive-emotional state. Psychosomatic processes were the basis for George Beard's notion of neurasthenia, Franz Alexander's theory of "organ neurosis," and Hans Selye's "general-adaptation-syndrome."[1] Today, it is the basis for neurohormonal and neuroimmunological theories that connect stressful life events to pathological outcomes.[2] In every case, it is said that symptoms may originate in psychological conflicts and stress. Unlike psychogenic disorders, however, the psychosomatic symptoms do not express or encode meanings.

4. Symptoms are modified through *amplification*. The patient is pre-occupied with vague or ambiguous bodily phenomena. She focuses her awareness on minor abnormalities and bodily functions and sensations (such as heartbeat, sweating and peristalsis) which she invests with meanings and emotions judged disproportionate or irrational by medical experts and other people. Some severe cases can be classified by psychiatric diagnosis as hypochondriasis, others can be associated with generalized anxiety disorder, obsessive-compulsive disorder, panic disorder, major depressive episode, and separation anxiety. In contrast to psychogenic disorders, the majority of cases encode no etiological conflict or meaning.

5. The individual's everyday language employs bodily organs, functions, and physiological and pathophysiological processes as a *mode of self-awareness* and an *idiom for communicating information* about her own (or someone else's) mental or emotional state, and life-world. The language of the body can be either self-consciously metaphorical (a psychological state is represented by a somatic state) or realistic (a somatic state is imagined to be integral to a psychological state). It can be employed expressively as an idiom of distress, as an instrument for managing and manipulating interpersonal relations, or as a medium for acquiring compensation and other kinds of desiderata. The conceptual boundary dividing these practices from psychogenic disorders is sometimes fuzzy, since symptoms are deployed instrumentally in both cases. Nevertheless, the distinction is generally clear and useful. The psychogenic process is said to operate at an unconscious level, while the language of the body is employed self-consciously. The psychogenic process is said to produce symptoms, while the language of the body is usually employed to define symptoms, link them to a preferred etiology, and situate them within a web of significance (a "semantic illness network"). Mimicry sometimes plays a role, as in cases of psychogenic disorders, but when it does, its emblematic expression is malingering, not hysteria.

Showalter writes that hysteria is a part of everyday life. How can this be true? If "hysteria" is identified with mimicry and the unconscious transmutation of cognitive-emotional states into symptoms, her claim must be rejected. There is simply no evidence that this kind of hysteria is a commonplace event. On the other hand, if someone wished to redefine "hysteria" to include *all* of the ways in which the body is used to make meanings – regardless of whether meanings are grafted onto symptoms or encoded into symptoms, or whether these meanings are unspeakable or articulated in words through somatic idioms – then it could justifiably be said that hysteria is part of everyday life. But why bother? What purpose would a watered-down version of hysteria serve? From an epidemiologist's point of view, the revised term would have good *sensitivity*: it identifies a feature that is shared by all of the populations included in Showalter's book. But it has zero *specificity*: everyone everywhere in the world is engaged in these practices, and there is absolutely no reason to suppose that the practices have accelerated.[3] Either way – high specificity, low specificity – it is useless to talk in this fashion about an epidemic of hysteria.

An Ideology of Traumatic Origins

Where does this leave Showalter's observations about Gulf War syndrome and its place in the epidemic of hysterical disorders? The visible expression of this epidemic would be rates of "functional syndromes." A case falls into this classification when it is medically unexplained. This means either of two things: no one knows if the case is psychogenic or somatogenic or, alternatively, the case is presumed to be somatogenic although its etiology and pathogenesis are unknown. An epidemic of hysterical disorders would imply an epidemic in psychogenic syndromes, not merely high rates of functional complaints. Currently there is no evidence of unusually high rates of functional complaints among Gulf War veterans. Furthermore, no one has proposed studying the ratio of psychogenic versus somatogenic cases occurring among these functional diagnoses. Where is the evidence for the epidemic? Gulf War syndrome is a significant event but, so far, it is entirely because of the meanings and emotions that veterans and others are attaching to their symptoms:

Although no single, recurring war-related disease has been identified, many aspects of the process used during the past 130 years to evaluate the health problems of veterans have been repeated with each war. The most important and consistent factor is that this process has involved medical evaluation after the critical event, thereby precluding a definitive demonstration of causality.

The problem of diagnostic labeling has [likewise] played a critical role in the evaluation of war syndromes. The naming of a syndrome has repeatedly exerted a powerful effect on the medical approach toward, official recognition of, and patient perception of these poorly understood conditions. A medically recognized diagnosis fundamentally alters the lives of . . . veterans, influencing . . . medical treatment, expectations of recovery, and eligibility for compensation. (Hyams et al. 1996: 402)

We are not witnesses to an epidemic of hysteria in the 1990s. No psychogenic thread connects the victims of Gulf War syndrome, multiple personality disorder, chronic fatigue syndrome, repressed memory syndrome, satanic ritual abuse and alien abductions. These populations *are* connected, but essentially through a set of family resemblances, or overlapping features. The most ubiquitous feature is the etiological starting point: multiple personality disorder, recovered memory syndrome, satanic ritual abuse syndrome, and (sometimes) Gulf War syndrome are all believed to originate in the victims' traumatic experiences and memories. They are differentiated from one another by the content of these traumas (satanic ritual abuse stands out for obvious reasons) and the victims' efforts to defend themselves (multiple personality disorder is linked to a distinctive kind of dissociation). And it is this story of traumatic origins, rather than a timeless psychogenic process, that connects these syndromes with the past, that is, to the hysterias described by Charcot, Breuer, Freud and Janet.

The story of traumatic origins is likewise an *ideology* – a standardized explanatory account routinely employed by clinicians, researchers, patients, and writers to translate (reduce, simplify, homogenize) patients' life-worlds into patterns (generally sequences) connecting stock causes with effects. It is published under the heading of *post-traumatic stress disorder* in the diagnostic manual of the American Psychiatric Association, and furnishes (1) a *representation* of invisible connections that are believed to underlie the tangle of visible circumstances and events and (2) a *blueprint* for identifying the phenomena that qualify as "trauma-related" circumstances and events.

This ideology is valued and preserved because it is *useful*. It permits clinicians and researchers to make discriminations that would otherwise be difficult or impossible: to differentiate victims of trauma from victims of depression and anxiety. The ideology is not merely useful, it is also *mandatory* – required for psychiatric record keeping, clinical communication, publication of research findings, and forensic decision-making relating to liability for patients' disabilities and culpability for their behavior. And thirdly, the ideology is valued because it is demonstrably *correct*: consonant with the relevant facts (products of the self-vindicating systems of reasoning employed in diagnosis, therapy and research) and the Western cultural implicit (taken-for-granted beliefs about self-identity, remembering and forgetting).

Memory and the Post-traumatic Syndrome

In most historical accounts, clinical interest in post-traumatic syndrome begins with John Erichsen's treatise on "railway spine" (Erichsen 1866). During the following two decades, the syndrome was commonly associated with events, such as railway collisions, producing shock, fright and physical and emotional perturbation. Symptoms were variable, but generally resembled effects associated with neurological injury. What made the new syndrome special was that (1) it occurred without significant external injury and (2) the putative victims often claimed compensation (from railway companies) for the pain, distress and loss of income said to result from their invisible injuries.

Opinion divided on the question of its pathogenesis. The majority view was that the vigorous jolts and shakes experienced on these occasions were sufficient to damage the nervous system. Pathogenesis could be understood by analogy with well-known neurological mechanism, especially concussion. Some physicians, notably Herbert Page (1883), suggested that the arousal of powerful emotions, specifically fear, might have similar effects. There was no obvious way to test the nerve-trauma hypothesis except by the pathoanatomical method, that is, by post-mortem examination. It was recognized that whatever interesting findings this mode of inquiry might eventually produce, it was diagnostically worthless for the present. Further, it was understood that the pathological alterations produced by these accidents might be submicroscopic or "nutritional" (pathophysiological) and therefore effectively invisible. Other physicians, including Jean-Martin Charcot (himself a celebrated neurologist), believed that only some cases of these disorders were attributable to nerve damage inflicted directly by the force of the accident. There were certain symptomatically similar cases that originated in a previously undetected mechanism, a kind of post-traumatic memory that was created at the time of the collision. The prevailing assumption was that, under ordinary conditions, memories are deposited in associative networks, within which they are connected to concomitant emotions, sensations and dispositions, and likewise to other memories. In contrast, the post-traumatic memories were isolated or dissociated. This explained the patients' characteristic inability to recall their traumatic events. Exactly how the characteristic symptoms were connected to the dissociated memory was a matter for speculation. Charcot and, at one point, Freud believed that the link might be explained in physical terms, wrapped up in action potentials and energy flows. In the course of time, the connection assumed a more symbolic quality (Charcot 1889). Thus Breuer and Freud (1955 [1893–5]) traced symptomatic neuralgia to a mental pain whose substance was hidden in amnesic memory. Whether the connection between memory and somatic symptoms was organic or symbolic or a combination of the two, the effect was the same. The symptoms were transformed into "mnemic symbols," that might lead experts back to memories to which patients had no ready access.

It is at this point, in the last decades of the nineteenth century, that the traumatic memory makes its appearance. Charcot portrayed it as "a coherent group of associated ideas which *install themselves in the mind in the fashion of a parasite*, remain isolated from all the reset, and may be explained outwardly by corresponding motor phenomena" (cited in Janet 1901: 267). It was an unprecedented kind of memory and it transformed the ways in which physicians thought about post-traumatic syndromes, and how the syndromes would be diagnosed and treated in the future. While no one denied that the symptoms could also be produced by mechanical forces, there was now a second possibility, a syndrome caused by moral perturbation (extreme psychological stress or conflict) rather than cerebral commotion.

During this period, post-traumatic syndromes were associated with amnesias of one kind or another. Almost without exception, patients are described as unable to recall the events that precipitated their illnesses. Many patients are also reported to suffer from retrograde amnesia (loss of pre-trauma memory) or anterograde amnesia (loss of post-trauma memory). In each of these instances, amnesia defines and confirms the unusual character of traumatic memory. In a monograph on *idées fixes*, Janet argued that patients continue to store memories acquired during the amnesic periods, but are unable to *assimilate* them. In this regard, they resemble the traumatic memory that has created this situation – they are disconnected from the network of memories that constitute the individual's personality and sense of self-awareness. "[Post-traumatic] personalities, blocked at a certain point, can no longer grow through the addition [and] assimilation of new elements" (Janet 1925: 138 cited in Roth 1996: 7–8). Over the following decades, the association of traumatic memory with retrograde and anterograde amnesias gradually uncoupled, and after the Second World War it is much less often reported. Nevertheless, the conclusions that Janet and other physicians had inferred from these forms of forgetting – traumatic memory constricts and distorts the self by imprisoning it in a timeless present – have endured and they continue to shape our understanding of the post-traumatic syndrome.

I want to briefly mention one more, obvious development that occurs during this formative period. In *Beyond the Pleasure Principle* (Freud 1955 [1920]), Freud linked traumatic memory to an unconscious compulsion to repeat. Patients were said to relive their etiological events in dreams, in an unconscious effort to anticipate and master the fright that had originally overwhelmed them. Janet's conception of traumatic memory had been essentially static: he described it as an *idée fixe* lodged in the psyche. Freud injected a dynamic aspect, by portraying the patient's relation to his traumatic memory as a series of encounters. While only a minority of clinicians and researchers would today accept Freud's claims about the function of traumatic dreams, his basic idea, that the post-traumatic syndrome is sustained by recurrent encounters with the traumatic memory (re-experiences) and by efforts to manage these encounters (avoidance and numbing), is generally taken for granted.

In a seminal account of post-traumatic syndromes, that combined Janet's and Freud's ideas, Mardi Horowitz (1976: chapters 3, 6, 7) described traumatized patients as people who are striving to metabolize their pathogenic memories through alternating phases of engagement (during which they work at assimilating and accommodating these memories) and withdrawal (an adaptive response to pain generated during the engagement phase). Here we have, in a nutshell, the post-traumatic syndrome that entered the official psychiatric nosology in DSM-III (American Psychiatric Association 1980) as Post-traumatic Stress Disorder. In this and subsequent editions (American Psychiatric Association 1987, 1994), the PTSD classification is defined by four diagnostic criteria: an etiological event, recurrent encounters with memories of this event, symptomatic avoidance and numbing, and physiological arousal. Remembering is said to occur in the form of intrusive recollections, during dreams, and on occasions when patients feel they are reliving their etiological experiences, for instance in "flashbacks." The act of remembering is also said to occur on occasions when patients react, either psychologically or somatically, to stimuli that are symbolically linked to their etiological events.

Today, as in the days of Charcot, Janet and Freud, memory is regarded as the key to understanding the origins and pathogenesis of the post-traumatic syndrome. A century after its discovery, the idea of a traumatic memory seems natural, even obvious. Indeed, one wonders why it took so long for the idea to come to mind and why, once it was proposed, some physicians resisted. Likewise, one wonders why an idea that now seems self-evident to most Westerners did not emerge spontaneously in other cultures and regions of the world. In the following pages, I want to show that these puzzles are not "academic," fit only for historians or anthropologists, but have interesting implications for clinicians and researchers. My thesis is that, while the idea of traumatic memory now seems self-evident, it is historically determined and rooted in culturally specific beliefs concerning the self and self-awareness. To grapple with this argument one must entertain the possibility that memory is malleable. I mean this in the obvious sense, that episodic memory is subject to a variety of "distortions," including retroactive interference – the influence of subsequent events on how one recollects earlier events. I mean to imply more than this though, namely that generic "memory" – *the assortment of things that experts and other people count as memories or evidence of memories* – is also malleable. And like traumatic memory, it needs to be seen in the context of history and culture.

History, Memory and Self-awareness

The association between episodic memory and the self has a long history in the West. St. Augustine wrote about it in his *Confessions,* at the end of the fourth century (Pelikan 1986). He portrays memory as a retrospective view through which someone might see the life journey that reveals the meaning of the self. Until a person grasps his memory of the past, he knows the self not in its wholeness, but in fragments, specific to time and place. Through the prism of memory, he discovers patterns and underlying meanings which, in Augustine's case, are consonant with Christian metaphysics. Memory reveals the self to consciousness but does not contribute to producing the self. This is a *modern* notion.

One of its earliest monuments is John Locke's concept of the *forensic self* – an entity identified with the individual's accountability for his intentional behavior (Locke 1959 [1694]: chapter 27). Intentionality and selfhood both presume consciousness, and consciousness is manifestly located in the present time. In what sense am I accountable for acts that I committed in long-ago acts of consciousness? What is the medium for the continuity of the forensic self? The answer is episodic memory. It connects moments of consciousness and renders acts in the past morally equivalent to acts in the present. David Hume's account of the self, written a century later, is still more recognizably modern. Like Locke, he discusses the continuity of the self in terms of episodic memory; unlike Locke, the existence of the self is not only forensic, but also psychological. Had we no memory, Hume writes, we would have no knowledge of the chains of causes and effects from which we produce our self-awareness and, perhaps, our very self-existence (Biro 1993).

These were the opinions of exceptional individuals, and one might argue that we can infer nothing from them about the self-awareness of ordinary people, either then or now. This would be a fair criticism if these ideas about self and memory did not pass beyond the circle of philosophers. In fact, however, Hume's ideas were taken up and elaborated by a Frenchman who profoundly influenced the thinking of Janet and Freud.

Théodore Ribot was a world-renowned psychologist and translator of British empiricist philosophy. In his widely read treatise on forgetting and remembering, *The Diseases of Memory*, first published in 1883, we encounter the self (*moi*) as something that is formed, nourished and renewed by its memory. Ribot describes it as being a protean phenomenon, ceaselessly passing through phases of growth, degeneration and reproduction. In his account, the self now acquires an economic dimension, since self-renewal is possible only because room is continually being made for new memories, new associations and new self-narratives. And room is available only when old memories are permitted to fade, and their ability to evoke the emotions with which they were first associated gradually weakens, to the point where these old memories are no more than the memories of memories. In other words, forgetting is both normal and necessary. Ribot writes:

To live is to acquire and lose; life consists of dissolution as well as assimilation. Forgetfulness is dissolution . . . Without the total obliteration of an immense number of states of consciousness, and the momentary repression of many more, recollection would be impossible. Forgetfulness, except in certain cases, is not a disease of memory, but a condition of health and life. (Ribot 1883: 61)

The Grammar of Forgetting and Remembering

Ribot's idea of a *self-narrated self*, held together by memories, found a receptive audience. It had a powerful effect on the thinking of Pierre Janet, who was Ribot's successor in the Seat of Psychology at the University of Paris. Marcel Proust had also been Ribot's student, and gratefully acknowledged his teacher's influence on his own thinking about time, memory and self-knowledge. When Sigmund Freud left Vienna for London in 1938, he brought a mere handful of books, included among which was his copy of Ribot's book on the diseases of memory (Young 1995: chapter 1).

Ribot believed that the self-narrated self is universal. He presumed that people naturally crave a sense of unity and wholeness that will incorporate memories of the personal past. Anthropologists and other investigators working in non-Western societies have no difficulty getting people to talk in autobiographical terms. Does this validate Ribot's claim? Before we can attempt an answer, we need to examine his other assumption, that self-narration is not only universally possible but it is also the predominant medium of self-consciousness. At this point, there is no compelling empirically based body of evidence to support this assumption, even if its truth is routinely taken for granted. Whether or not Ribot's ideas about the self and self-awareness are universal, one fact is undeniable. His notion of a self-narrated self is integral to the ways in which most clinicians and researchers think about traumatic memory and post-traumatic disorders.

It would be hard to exaggerate the importance of this concept of self for shaping psychiatric knowledge of PTSD. The disorder's pathology is said to reside in the fact that certain memories will neither fade nor submit to a process of assimilation. They refuse to make way for new constellations of memories and, because of this, the self loses its capacity for re-narrating itself. Disorders of traumatic memory are not self-destructive in the way of Alzheimer's disease and extreme cases of Korsakov's syndrome however. The self is distorted, crippled, even fragmented into part-selves, but it is not lost.

The last decades of the nineteenth century constituted the golden age of memory science, during which experts constructed the grammar of forgetting and remembering that is employed today to connect aberrations of memory to deformations of the self. In Ribot's scheme, the normal self occupies a space bounded on one side by *hypermnesia* – a "condition in which past acts, feelings, or ideas are brought vividly to the mind, which in its natural condition [would have] wholly lost the remembrance of these" – and on the other side by *amnesia*, remembering too little rather than too much (Young 1995: chapter 1).

Ribot is less interested in *cryptomnesia*, a condition in which a person remembers something from the past but forgets, or rather misremembers, the source of the memory. Théodore Flournoy (1994, [1899]), a Swiss psychologist and contemporary of Ribot, wrote about a spirit medium in this connection. The medium believed that she was a conduit for a group of spirits who had lived in fifteenth-century India. Flournoy was convinced that the information provided by the spirits was obtained from a history of India stored in the Geneva municipal library. Unfortunately, he could not learn the circumstances in which the medium had come across this book, nor could he explain why she easily recalled obscure details in the book but had no memory of their actual source. Freud self-diagnosed an episode of cryptomnesia, in which he confessed to unconsciously plagiarizing a colleague's ideas about bisexuality (Ceci 1995: 93–4). Cryptomnesia also labels the occasional cases of "factitious" PTSD among war veterans, in which men transform the combat experiences of other men into their own traumatic recollections. The most frequently reported cases of cryptomnesia today involve accusations, often raised during litigation, of traumatic recollections implanted in patients' minds by their therapists, in the pursuit of recovered memories of childhood incest.

The final ingredient in the grammar of forgetting and remembering consists of *phylogenetic memories*. In the early 1800s, the evolutionary biologist, Jean-Baptiste Lamarck, described a species of collective memory that was acquired biologically, over multiple generations. Phylogenetic memories are a basic part of Freud's *Totem and Taboo* (1952 [1912–13]) and *Moses and Monotheism* (1964 [1939]), and they are intrinsic to Jung's concept of racial archetypes (Young 1996). In each case, the memories incorporate huge amounts of information. Previous to these accounts, Herbert Spencer and Charles Darwin had suggested the possibility of a much simpler kind of phylogenetic memory, observed in "instinctual" reactions associated with fear and anger (Young 1996). Spencer argued that such memories had been engraved into the nervous system over the course of evolution. Countless repetitions – evidence of the survival value of the entailed behavior – would eventually produce neural pathways, along which perceptions and impulses could now race, no longer impeded by cognition or deliberation. The phylogenetic memories discussed by Freud and Jung fell victim to the Mendelian revolution. Their sheer complexity required a Lamarckian framework, as Freud himself acknowledged. On the other hand, the sorts of memories described by Spencer, accounting for instinctual fear and the fight or flight response, had no problem passing through this historical membrane, and emerged on the other side in pioneering research on the physiology of the autonomic nervous system, by George Crile, Walter Cannon and others (Young 1996). The subject of phylogenetic memory continued to be discussed well into the present century. For example, it is mentioned in Kurt Goldstein's book on holistic neurology, *The Organism* (1939). Over the subsequent decades, however, the term "phylogenetic memory" has entirely disappeared from psychiatry, neurology and physiology. At the same time, the adaptational structure that Darwin and Spencer described a century ago is a building block in our own understanding of the biology of extreme situations, and continuous with current PTSD research on the hypothalamic-pituitary-adrenal axis.

It is useful to know how this evolutionary structure entered scientific discourse on the post-traumatic syndrome. Beginning with Charcot, physicians recognized that, in some cases at least, the engine driving the post-traumatic syndrome might be an episodic memory. Even earlier, at the time of Erichsen's and Page's investigations, physicians had observed an association between the syndrome with experiences of fear. Most of these doctors limited the association to two points: intense fear might occur at the time of a patient's etiological experience, and fear in the form of a generalized fearfulness or anxiety might also occur as part of the syndrome. Janet went beyond this position, to argue that fear might also occur within a syndrome as a product of the patient's traumatic memory. That is to say, re-experiencing the etiological event would likewise elicit a fear response similar to the one that accompanied the original occasion. While Janet coupled the traumatic memory to the fear response, he did not connect the response to a discrete physiological mechanism. Interest in discovering this mechanism dates from the First World War, and it is at this point that we can say that the episodic memory responsible for the post-traumatic syndrome is intersected with the structure that Darwin and Spencer had characterized as phylogenetic memory, and that Cannon redescribed as an autonomic nervous system response (equally a product of the species' evolutionary history).

A New Science of Memory

The preceding pages describe a grammar of remembering and forgetting that emerged in the closing years of the nineteenth century. It was (and remains) associated with certain presumptions about the nature of the self and self-awareness. It created the possibility of a new psychiatric enterprise, organized around concealed memories (episodic, phylogenetic), mnemic symptoms, and the codes and procedures that have been developed for deciphering these clues. The symptoms are behavioral (compulsion to repeat, avoidance behavior), somatic (body memory, conversions, neurophysiological alterations, numbing), and cognitive (dreams, intrusive images and thoughts). They stand in a mnemic relation to the disorder – that is, they contain information about the traumatic memory and, in the right hands, can be read like a text.

These developments can be seen coinciding with the birth of a new political economy of memory, in which the person who owns the memory in question (the traumatic parasite that is stored in his brain and body) is not necessarily the same person who possesses the meaning of this memory or, in some cases, knowledge of the memory's very existence.

Opposition to Post-traumatic Stress Disorder

The PTSD classification was introduced into DSM-III in the face of opposition. A segment of the psychiatric establishment closely associated with the manual's editorial task force and its publicly affirmed neo-Kraepelinian principles, doubted the validity of the proposed classification. They believed that the PTSD syndrome was not a unitary phenomenon, and clinical cases were said to represent the co-occurrence of various combinations of established classifications – most commonly, depression, generalized anxiety disorder, and panic disorder.

The opponents argued that PTSD presupposes an etiology that is an unscientific relic of an age of psychiatric ignorance. A century ago traumatic disorders (including hysterias) were said to mimic neurological disorders. We believe that many of these cases had real organic origins, but that nineteenth-century physicians did not possess the technical means or knowledge required to correctly diagnose them. The proposed PTSD classification was seen to be an analogous phenomenon. The difference between the past and the present is that the underlying disorders are now psychiatric rather than neurological, and psychiatry possesses satisfactory ways of diagnosing these syndromes. Likewise, a century ago Charcot argued that traumatic hysteria is a unitary entity, comparable to multiple sclerosis or Parkinson's disease. To audiences at Salpetrière Hospital, he demonstrated that episodes of this disorder (*grande hystérie* or *hystero-épilepsie*) pass through invariable and well-defined stages. Yet we now know that Charcot's star performers acquired their symptom-complexes through subtle and unintended forms of suggestion in the clinic, and by auto-suggestion in the hospital ward, where they were domiciled alongside epileptic patients (Goetz et al. 1995: chapters 4–6). The opponents predicted that, once PTSD is integrated into diagnostic and therapeutic practices, similar effects can be expected – spurious or at least premature evidence of the existence of traumatic memory. This "evidence" will transform the pathognomonic meaning of the disorder's other features. Intrusive ruminations are a common symptom of major depression. Phobias, such as the irrational fear of crowds, are a common symptom of anxiety disorders. When either of these symptoms is connected, during diagnosis, to an antecedent trauma, its meaning is radically changed. Ruminations turn into intrusive "re-experiences" and phobias become "avoidance behavior" adjusted to the environmental stimuli that trigger re-experiences. Analogous transformations will account for the physiological symptoms – difficulty concentrating, irritability, explosions of aggressive behavior, emotional numbing – that were to be part of the proposed classification.

Advocacy for a PTSD Classification

The core advocacy group for the new diagnosis consisted of Vietnam War veterans and sympathetic psychiatrists (Scott 1990; Young 1995: chapter 3). They claimed that the Vietnam War created an epidemic of post-traumatic disorders. The afflicted veterans were habitually misdiagnosed (often with stigmatizing disorders, such as paranoid schizophrenia) and thus deprived of appropriate treatment. Further, their symptoms severely restricted the veterans' employability, precluded a normal social life, and engendered maladaptive social and psychological responses. The result was a pathogenic spiral, whose effects could be seen in the victims' high rates of suicide, parasuicide, and self-dosing with drugs and alcohol. A PTSD diagnostic classification, part of the new psychiatric nosology, was needed to bring this epidemic under control.

After some hesitation, the DSM-III editorial task force established a committee to draft a PTSD diagnostic classification. The committee's final draft, which appears in DSM-III, defined traumatic events as overwhelming experiences that can be expected to cause distress in nearly anyone. The definition brackets out the hereditary, congenital and developmental factors that had previously interested Charcot, Janet and Second World War military psychiatrists, and it allows only one interpretation regarding liability for veterans' post-traumatic disorders: if a patient's etiological event occurred in the course of military service, his consequent disorder is logically *service-connected*, since the diagnosis admits no prior condition. In effect, the definition establishes entitlement to appropriate medical treatment from the Veterans Administration Medical System. There are other implications, abundantly realized after 1980: if a VA disability rating board can be convinced that the veteran's symptoms have reduced or eliminated his ability to make a living, the new diagnosis makes him eligible for a disability pension, to last as long as his service-connected condition persists.

The Malleability of Memory

The neo-Krapelinian critics claimed that PTSD was essentially a traumatic neurosis and had no legitimate place in a diagnostic system dedicated to positivist principles (Young 1995: chapter 3). The critics focused on discrediting the disorder's mechanism – toxic memories, psychic conflicts, neurotic adaptations. They ignored a second criticism. To grasp this possibility, it is necessary to make certain assumptions rejected outright by the neo-Krapelinians. Assume that the pathogenic mechanism underlying PTSD is not an issue. And assume that horrible experiences can produce a syndrome similar to the one that is attributed to PTSD, and this syndrome can be satisfactorily distinguished from syndromes produced by other combinations of psychiatric disorders. Having made these assumptions, we come to the question that the neo-Kraepelinians ignored. Is it possible (or practicable) to consistently distinguish cases in which traumatic memory is the *cause* of the patient's syndrome from cases in which memory is simply the *reason* (or explanation) for the patient's condition?

The psychology of PTSD is based on memory: etiological events create pathogenic memories and it is these memories, rather than the events, that generate the disorder's characteristic symptoms. Ordinary memories are highly malleable. This is the memory expert's opinion. In popular culture, episodic memories are given a different appearance. They are routinely (and naively) compared with artifacts like photographs and videotapes. They are objects around which time flows in a single direction, from the past (an experience) to the present (storage of memory content of the experience) to the future (a progressive loss or degradation of memory content). To the memory expert, this comparison is profoundly misleading, since episodic memory is a process and not an object. Within this process, past and present interact and intermingle, producing multiple drafts of experiences, and not photographs (Schacter 1996). This is what makes traumatic memory so odd, that is, different from both the expert's and the lay person's conception of episodic memory. Traumatic memories are pathogenic precisely because they do not change or fade, they are immutable and indigestible. Further, time runs through them in just one direction. Or so it is said.

Questions concerning the malleability of traumatic memory are not new. A century ago, Janet explored the feasibility of altering these memories in the clinic – replacing a memory's pathogenic content with some innocuous content through the medium of hypnosis and suggestion (Van der Hart et al. 1993). Janet and certain of his contemporaries understood that memories were sometimes altered unintentionally, as a product of the clinician's tacit suggestions and the patient's unconscious desire to satisfy these expectations. Freud rejected Janet's idea of creating therapeutic fictions. According to Freud, it was partly his fear of creating fictions through suggestion that induced him to replace hypnosis and abreactive therapy with a new technique, free association. Freud and contemporary doctors, such as W. H. R. Rivers, recognized that memory alterations could also originate in the patient's own mind, in a process called "auto-suggestion," in which patients might unconsciously revise their memories in response to unacknowledged psychological needs or drives. In each of these cases (auto-suggestion, hetero-suggestion) a non-traumatic episodic memory acquires a traumatic or etiological potency at some point following the onset of the symptoms for which the memory is ostensibly responsible. Time flows in two directions, as it does in the case of ordinary memories (Young 1995: chapter 2).

In the years following the First World War, psychiatric interest in the malleability of traumatic memory declined. In his monograph on war neuroses, Kardiner (1941) essentially ignored this subject. During the Second World War, American and British military physicians relied on abreactive therapies and had no compelling interest in the constancy of traumatic memory. Nor did psychiatric attitudes change during the conflicts in Korea and Vietnam.

In the 1980s, this situation changed, partly in response to an "epidemic" of recovered memories of traumatic childhood sexual abuse. The most influential research consists of experiments aimed at producing a "misinformation effect" through heterosuggestion. In a recent review of this research, Elizabeth Loftus writes: "What do we know as a result of hundreds of studies of misinformation spanning two decades. . .? That misinformation can lead people to have false memories that they appear to believe in as much as some of their genuine memories." In a provocative series of experiments conducted with children, Loftus demonstrated that "a simple suggestion from a family member [colluding with Loftus] can create an entire autobiographical memory for an event that would have been mildly traumatic . . . [had it actually occurred]. Since it is relatively easy to produce the misinformation effect experimentally, "how much more powerful would be a combination of [clinical] techniques, over the course of years of therapy?" (Loftus et al. 1995: 65, 66; also Loftus and Ketcham 1994).

Almost no analogous research was conducted on PTSD *per se* during this period. (For a recent, important exception, see Southwick et al. 1997.) This is understandable. From the 1970s onwards, PTSD researchers struggled to establish and, following publication of DSM-III, to defend the validity of the disorder. Quite naturally, they had no incentive to undertake a research program that would draw attention to the epistemology of traumatic time. On the other hand, factitious memories (cases where patients invent or borrow their etiological events) are mentioned in the PTSD literature during this period. These memories represented only a technical problem – namely, the need for procedures for identifying fabrications – and they subverted no assumptions about the durability of traumatic memory. For many PTSD researchers, questions about the malleability of traumatic memory were a red herring. Changes in memory content could be explained in terms of the dynamics of PTSD, the patient's tendency to oscillate between periods in which he engages the traumatic content (remembering, processing) and, when the pain is too intense, disengages from it (suppressing or repressing painful elements). The therapist helped the patient modulate this process and, in this capacity, exerted no direct influence – conscious or unconscious – on the content of the patient's traumatic memory.

Clinical Reality versus Scientific Truth

For the moment, accept my claim that current diagnostic technology cannot distinguish between traumatic memories and distressful memories whose subjective significance is a product of antecedent psychiatric problems. Is this necessarily a bad thing? There are two equally valid answers to this question. For the researcher, committed to scientific standards of truth, the inability to make this distinction *is* a bad thing, since it is an obstacle to aggregating diagnostically homogeneous samples of subjects and to making valid epidemiological inferences. For the clinician, whose priority is to reduce distress and impairment, the distinction may be less critical.

PTSD's psychotherapeutic potential is rooted in an etiology that (1) relieves the patient of responsibility for his syndrome and its sequelae (unless it can be shown that he has deliberately or recklessly exposed himself to a traumatic stressor), and (2) posits a deeply rooted cultural association between memory and self-identity, described earlier in this chapter. Take the common case of the Vietnam War veteran whose pre-PTSD psychiatric history includes multiple stigmatizing disorders – alcohol and substance use disorders, paranoid schizophrenia, chronic depression. PTSD wipes his slate clean. Ruminations become re-experiences, chemical dependency becomes self-dosing, etc. Since PTSD is an exogenic disorder and a normal response to abnormal situations (a position recently contested in Yehuda and McFarlane 1995), onset imputes nothing negative about the patient's moral character or mental constitution (Young 1995: chapter 5).

It would be a mistake to argue that the PTSD diagnosis is inherently therapeutic. There are circumstances in which the diagnosis may contribute to a patient's chronicity and disability, especially when it establishes eligibility for compensation and other secondary gain. On the other hand, in cases where diagnosis and treatment function as therapeutic myth and ritual, the ability to distinguish between a traumatic memory and other kinds of distressful memory may be unimportant.

PTSD as a Style of Reasoning

Therapists are at liberty to either ignore or exploit the malleability of memory. Researchers are in a different position. They pursue scientific truths (timeless, universal, objective), not clinical realities (pragmatic, circumstantial, subjective). How, then, do we explain the credibility of methods and findings that ignore this fundamental quality of episodic memory?[4]

One answer is that research findings and methodologies relating to episodic memory have been supported by recent research on the neurobiology and neuroanatomy of PTSD (Yehuda and McFarlane 1995). At first glance, biological research appears to by-pass the problems associated with episodic memory, by focusing on non-malleable "phylogenetic memory" – a biologically programed physiological arousal (the fight-flight-freeze response described earlier) elicited by traumatic experiences and periodically renewed by the disorder's symptomatic re-experiences. Evidence of a trauma-triggered phylogenetic memory – e.g., abnormally depressed cortisol levels – confirms the traumatic (causal) quality of the patient's episodic memories. This is how biological evidence is generally interpreted within the PTSD community. However, the biological findings are themselves ambiguous and transparently vulnerable to criticism. By themselves, they do not account for the credibility of findings and assumptions relating to episodic memory.

"PTSD" can signify (1) a syndrome attributed to pathogenic mechanisms and patients' maladaptive efforts to control or limit their symptoms and distress; (2) experiential states, shaped by a patient's suffering, medical beliefs, self-narratives, clinical encounters, behavioral strategies, and social relations; and (3) a style of reasoning. I imagine that most anthropologists would favor either option two (a "person-centered" view of PTSD, simultaneously sensitive to the hegemonic discourses of psychiatry etc.) or a combination of options one and two (building on the psychiatric conception of PTSD). The first view sees PTSD as an epiphenomenon of people's psychological states, the second simply accepts the credibility of the psychiatric conception of PTSD. Neither view grasps the historical distinctiveness of PTSD, by which I mean not only its cultural origins (ideas about the self and self-identity), but also its recent transformation into something different from the post-traumatic disorders that preceded it. That is, PTSD has evolved into a style of reasoning.

I borrow the term from Ian Hacking (1992), who has used it to describe how knowledge is produced by laboratory researchers. The concept is likewise useful for describing how clinical knowledge is produced, and I want to use the term in this extended sense. A style of reasoning is composed of ideas, practices, raw materials, technologies and objects (e.g., clinical populations, episodic memories, avoidance symptoms, remissions). It is a characteristically *self-authenticating* way of making facts, in that it generates its own truth conditions. It determines for itself the kinds of perceptions that qualify as genuine "observations" and "data," the standards and tests that permit researchers and clinicians to distinguish between positive and negative outcomes, and the classes of events that count as "outcomes" in the first place.

Styles of reasoning are also *self-vindicating*, in that they adjust themselves to anomalies and to challenges to their authority, through a process of revising ideas and, more significantly, by tinkering with the physical conditions – raw materials, apparatuses, procedures, standards – with which researchers and clinicians create and manipulate their objects, and with whose help they devise, observe and interpret their outcomes.[5]

Psychiatry (research, clinical practice) intersects multiple styles of reasoning. The current mix is a product of developments over the past half-century, notably the biologization of mental illness (a process propelled by developments in psychopharmacology, neuroscience and imaging technologies), the meteoric rise of population-based epidemiological research, and the creation of the National Institute of Mental Health. DSM-III is the most conspicuous product of these developments. The manual's editorial task force set out, in a self-conscious way, to produce a disease-based diagnostic system that would be compatible with multiple styles of reasoning – epidemiological, statistical, clinical and experimental.

In PTSD, these styles have meshed with their subject, traumatic memory. Unlike the subjects of other diagnostic classifications – bipolar disorder, panic disorder, schizophrenia and so on – this "memory" is simultaneously a pathology and a program for making knowledge. This program has evolved over a century and consists of a characteristic logic, technologies, moral economy, discursive objects, and standards and tokens of authenticity. The result of this meshing (nurtured by the largess of the Veterans Administration Medical System) is a new, hybrid style of reasoning. Its products include diagnosed cases of PTSD, but likewise instances that do not fit the Aristotelian container erected by

the DSMs – cases of so-called "partial PTSD" and "complex PTSD."
(In this sense, PTSD and traumatic memory resemble the notion of
"neurosis," something that the DSM-III revolution was supposed to
relegate to the ash heap of history.) It is within this hybrid style of
reasoning that PTSD's curiously non-malleable episodic memories are
found, stabilized and standardized, on occasion quick frozen in bodily
fluids, and quite unlike the sorts of recollections that pop into the minds
of living people.

Conclusion

I repeat a point made earlier in this chapter. Despite the claims made
by Elaine Showalter in *Hysteries*, we are not witnessing an epidemic of
hysteria. No psychogenic thread connects the populations described in
her book. Rather, they are connected by family resemblances. The most
ubiquitous feature among these cases is an etiological starting point.
Multiple personality disorder, recovered memory syndrome, satanic
ritual abuse syndrome, and (sometimes) Gulf War syndrome are
believed, by patients and practitioners, to originate in the victims' traumatic experiences and memories. The big psychiatric story of the 1990s
is not an epidemic of psychogenic disorders. If there is a historical
moment worth recording, it is the transformation of traumatic memory
into PTSD. Reading about PTSD gives one a sense of *déja vu*.
Showalter is correct about that. But *déja vu* is a pseudo-memory, and it
is important not to confuse real historical continuities – a grammar that
provides indirect access to patients' memories via their behaviors and
somatic symptoms – with the kinds of pseudo-recurrences (hysteries)
described in her book. In reality, we have seen the last of hysteria.

NOTES

1. In *Psychosomatic Medicine* (1950), published in 1950, Alexander developed a
   theory of disease that is based on what people are inclined to do when they
   are confronted with anxiety-provoking situations. He writes about two kinds
   of people: those whose tendency is to attack the situation directly, and those
   who are inclined to retreat into increased dependence like the small child
   who turns to the mother for help instead of trying to meet the emergency
   himself. According to Alexander, the first tendency operates by means of the
   sympathetic nervous system, while the second operates through the parasympathetic system. When the consummation of these impulses is blocked, nervous excitation continues and leads to disturbances in the body's vegetative
   functions. These disturbances are etiologically specific, since each disposition
   and neural circuit has its particular target organs and functions. Sympathetic
   excitation leads to chronic hypertension, migraine, cardiac problems and

arthritis; parasympathetic excitation leads to colitis, peptic ulcer, asthma, chronic fatigue and constipation.

2. Showalter employs the term "psychosomatic" once or twice, but seems to be using the term as a synonym for "psychogenic."
3. It is unclear whether Showalter believes that "hysteria" in the specific (psychogenic) sense is *typical* of "hysteria" in the inclusive sense.
4. I am *not* referring to *my* standards of credibility, but the standards and perceptions of PTSD knowledge producers and their audiences.
5. The ongoing adjustment of practices, technologies and ideas helps to explain the relative stability of these systems, but does not entirely account for it. Moral economies are also a part of this process. They modulate the circulation, conservation and valorization of facts and findings, and they influence the choice of subject matter and procedures, the sifting of evidence and standards of explanation. Moral dispositions are grounded in sentiments and convictions, and also in calculation and self-interest. Two kinds of dispositions qualify as "moral" in relation to styles of reasoning: dispositions grounded in beliefs about normative social relations (rights and obligations) and dispositions grounded in ontological convictions (beliefs about what is real and the actions that ought, of necessity, to follow from having this knowledge). The moral economies and "affect-saturated values" of science (e.g., "objectivity") are fueled by combinations of both dispositions, normative and ontological (Daston 1995: 5–6). In her account of the moral economy of science, Daston refers to Ludwik Fleck's position that scientific research is the product of *Denkskollektivs* ("thought collectives" but not reducible to the aggregate mentalities of their members). Within each *Denkskollektiv*, members share emotional dispositions, and it is in this connection that Daston writes: "To extend Ludwik Fleck's terminology, what is meant here is a *Gefehls-* as well as *Denkskollektiv* . . . ways of feeling as well as ways of seeing, manipulating, and understanding. This is a psychology at the level of whole cultures, or at least subcultures, one that takes root and is shaped by quite particular historical circumstances" (Fleck, 1979 [935]: 5).

REFERENCES

Alexander, Franz 1950 *Psychosomatic Medicine: Its Principles and Applications.* New York: W. W. Norton.
American Psychiatric Association 1980 *Diagnostic and Statistical Manual of Mental Disorders.* 3rd edition. Washington, DC: American Psychiatric Association.
    1987 *Diagnostic and Statistical Manual of Mental Disorders.* 3rd, revised edition. Washington, DC: American Psychiatric Association.
    1994 *Diagnostic and Statistical Manual of Mental Disorders.* 4th edition. Washington, DC: American Psychiatric Association.
Biro, John I. 1993 "Hume's New Science of Mind." In D. F. Norton (ed.), *The Cambridge Companion to Hume.* Cambridge: Cambridge University Press, pp. 33–63.
Breuer, Josef and Sigmund Freud 1955 [1893–5] *Studies on Hysteria.* New York: Basic Books.

Ceci, Stephen J. 1995 "False Beliefs: Some Developmental and Clinical Considerations." In D. L. Schacter (ed.), *Memory Distortion: How Minds, Brains, and Societies Reconstruct the Past.* Cambridge, MA: Harvard University Press, pp. 91–125.

Charcot, Jean-Martin 1889 *Clinical Lectures on Diseases of the Nervous System Delivered at the Infirmary of La Salpetrière.* London: New Sydenham Society.

Daston, Lorraine 1995 "The Moral Economy of Science." *Orisis* 10: 3–24.

Erichsen, John E. 1866 *On Railway and Other Injuries of the Nervous System.* London: Walton and Maberly.

Fleck, Ludwik 1979 [1935] *Genesis and Development of a Scientific Fact.* Trans. Fred Bradley and Thaddeus J. Trenn. Chicago and London: University of Chicago Press.

Flournoy, Théodore 1994 [1889] *From India to the Planet Mars: A Case of Multiple Personality with Imaginary Languages.* Princeton: Princeton University Press.

Freud, Sigmund 1952 [1912–13] *Totem and Taboo.* Volume 13. *Standard Edition of the Complete Psychological Works of Sigmund Freud.* London: Hogarth Press.

    1955 [1920] *Beyond the Pleasure Principle.* Volume 18. *Standard Edition of the Complete Psychological Works of Sigmund Freud.* London: Hogarth Press.

    1964 [1939] *Moses and Monotheism.* Volume 23. *Standard Edition of the Complete Psychological Works of Sigmund Freud.* London: Hogarth Press.

Goetz, Christopher G., M. Bonduelle and T. Gelfand 1995 *Charcot: Constructing Neurology.* New York: Oxford University Press.

Goldstein, Kurt 1939 *The Organism: A Holistic Approach to Biology Derived from Pathological Data in Man.* Cincinnati: American Book Company.

Hacking, Ian 1992 "The Self-Vindication of the Laboratory Sciences." In Andrew Pickering (ed.), *Science as Practice and Culture.* Chicago: University of Chicago Press, pp. 29–64.

Horowitz, Mardi 1976 *Stress Response Syndromes.* New York: Jason Aronson.

Hyams, K. C., F. S. Wignall, and R. Roswell 1996 "War Syndromes and their Evaluations: From the US Civil War to the Persian Gulf War." *Annals of Internal Medicine* 125: 398–405.

Janet, Pierre 1901 *The Mental State of Hystericals: A Study of Mental Stigmata and Mental Accidents.* New York: G. P. Putnam.

    1925 *Neuroses et Idées Fixes.* 4th edition. Paris: Alcan.

Kardiner, Abram 1941 *The Traumatic Neuroses of War.* Washington, D.C.: National Research Council.

Kleinman, Arthur and H. Spiegel 1993 "Introduction." In Arthur Kleinman and H. Spiegel (eds.), *Chronic Fatigue Syndrome: Proceedings of a CIBA Conference, 12–14 May 1992.* London: Wiley.

Locke, John 1959 [1694] *An Essay Concerning Human Understanding.* Oxford: Oxford University Press.

Loftus, Elizabeth, J. Feldman and R. Dashiell 1995 "The Reality of Illusory Memories." In D. Schacter (ed.), *Memory Distortion: How Minds, Brains, and Societies Reconstruct the Past.* Cambridge, MA: Harvard University Press, pp. 47–68.

Loftus, Elizabeth F. and K. Ketcham 1994 *The Myth of Repressed Memory.* New York: St. Martin's Press.

Page, Herbert W. 1883 *Injuries of the Spine and Spinal Cord without Apparent Mechanical Lesion, and Nervous Shock, in their Surgical and Medico-Legal Aspects.* London: J. and A. Churchill.

Pelikan, Jaroslav 1986 *The Mystery of Continuity: Time and History, Memory and Eternity in the Thought of Saint Augustine.* Charlottesville, VA: University Press of Virginia.

Ribot, Théodore 1883 *Diseases of Memory: An Essay in Positive Psychology.* London: Kegan Paul, Trench.

Roth, Michale 1996 "Hysterical Remembering." *MODERNISM/modernity* 3: 1–30.

Schacter, Daniel 1996 *Searching for Memory: the Brain, the Mind, and the Past.* New York: Basic Books.

Scott, Wilber 1990 "PTSD in DSM-III: A Case in the Politics of Diagnosis and Disease." *Social Problems* 37: 294–310.

Showalter, Elaine 1997 *Hysteries: Hysterical Epidemics and Modern Culture.* New York: Columbia University Press.

Southwick, S. M., C. A. Morgan, A. L. Nicolaou and D. S. Charney 1997 "Consistency of Memory for Combat-Related Traumatic Events in Veterans of Operation Desert Storm." *American Journal of Psychiatry* 154: 173–7.

Van der Hart, Onno, K. Steele, S. Boon and P. Brown 1993 "The Treatment of Traumatic Memories: Synthesis, Realization, and Integration." *Dissociation* 6: 162–80.

Yehuda, Rachel and A. McFarlane 1995 "Conflict Between Current Knowledge about Post-traumatic Stress Disorder and its Original Conceptual Basis." *American Journal of Psychiatry* 152: 1705–13.

Young, Allan 1995 *The Harmony of Illusions: Inventing Post-Traumatic Stress Disorder.* Princeton, NJ: Princeton University Press.

1996 "Bodily Memory and Traumatic Memory." In Paul Antze and Michael Lambek (eds.), *Tense Past.* New York, London: Routledge, pp. 89–102.

Part III

Technologies and bodies: the extended networks of biomedicine

8 Screening the body: the pap smear and the mammogram

Patricia A. Kaufert

The field known as social studies of science is the province of those researchers who find science exciting at a philosophical and theoretical level, but who also are fascinated by scientists and what they do. Like the children and the governess in A. S. Byatt's story, "Morpho Eugenia" (1992), who watched and recorded the comings and goings and battles of the ant colonies, they observe the scientists. They sit in their laboratories, attend their meetings, collect their writings and persuade them to talk about their craft and their colleagues. If Latour's image of the black box is substituted for Byatt's ants, they want to lift the lid, peer inside the box, and make visible its contents. Once the period of observation is over, the researcher turns off the light, puts the lid back on the box and walks away. For understanding what goes on within the interior of the black box is an end in and of itself. How the box is sited in relation to the wider world seems of interest only insofar as this world impinges on events within the box. Hence, some critics have complained that too little attention is paid to the "processes of transmission of innovative knowledge from the benches of the laboratory scientist to the bedside of the patient" (Batchelor et al. 1996: 48).

Set against the complexity and diversity of the other chapters in this book, my characterization of social studies in science is clearly an over-simplification. Yet, like most over-simplifications, it is rooted in a grain of truth. Nell Oudshoorn describes much of the original research in this field as focused on a single university-based research laboratory or an industrial R & D unit (Oudshoorn 1997: 42). In her view: "This choice tended to restrict the scope of the analysis to the macro-sociological dynamics of laboratory work." "The world outside the laboratory comes into the picture only if it presents itself in the form of an actor enrolled by the scientists in the laboratory" (1997: 42).

Despite this criticism, the intensity of vision which was achieved by turning the laboratory into a restricted fieldwork site can equally be seen as a research strength rather than a weakness. Yet, whether admired or denigrated, this type of scientist-focused/laboratory-centered study is

165

increasingly rare. Most researchers now adopt a position somewhat outside the laboratory walls; for example, Vicky Singleton and Susan Leigh Star write out of a feminist tradition of women-centered rather than scientist-centered research (Singleton 1996; Star 1991), but others have stepped outside the confines of the laboratory simply because they are interested in a problem which takes them out into the wider world of the implemented technology.

My own interest is in the processes of transmission (Batchelor et al. 1996) of two screening tests – the mammogram and the Papanicolaou smear test – from the laboratory to the bedside, or rather from the laboratory and into the screening clinic. The fact that screening for cancer focused initially on the cervix and the breast is a reflection of a complex relationship between the site of the tumor, the nature of the technology, the perceived accessibility of the breast and the cervix, but also a particular understanding of the natural history of both these cancers. The concept of the hidden disease is not itself new; earlier versions appear in the literature on syphilis and consumption, but it was particularly well suited to cancer, imaged as spreading silently and invisibly within the body. Unlike other cancers, living and growing within the deeper recesses of the body, these two start out closer to the body's surface and are easier to access.

The actual idea for this essay originated in a period spent as a member of a Canadian provincial government committee planning the implementation of a breast cancer screening program. Other members of the committee – radiologists, oncologists, epidemiologists and bureaucrats – argued over which women should be screened, how screening should be organized, the exact costs and benefits of screening, and how these should be evaluated. Listening to these discussions made me aware of at least two conversations on women, risk and breast cancer going on simultaneously, but in different tones and using different languages. The first focused on the degree to which mammography satisfied the formal rules on screening. This conversation used the language of rates and ratios, survival times, the calculation of risk, mortality and cost-effectiveness. The second conversation dealt in issues of emotion, faith, responsibility, morality (both public and private) compliance, guilt, fear and death.

Listening to these conversations, I came to see screening as not simply a public health measure or an expression of corporate medicine, but as a philosophical and historical construct reflecting a very particular view of health and disease, and a very particular perspective on women and their bodies. I became increasingly interested in the implications for women of a definition of the female body as an object in constant need of monitoring, evaluation and surveillance, a body for screening. According to the public health literature, by the time women have evidence of what is happening within their bodies – whether by sight, touch or sensation – it will be too late. The skeleton will have started to disintegrate, the lump metastasized, the toxemia advanced on the body. Their best protection – or so women are warned – is to agree to a routine examination of their bodies for actual, or potential, signs of disease and decay. Being screened is a duty; evasion is tagged as irresponsible behavior, a moral dereliction.

Routine components in the medical care of most North American women, but lacking in the scientific glamor of screening for genetic disease, the Pap smear and the mammogram test have been largely ignored by medical anthropologists, except for a few feminist scholars. Adele Clarke and Monica Casper (Clarke and Casper 1996) have analyzed the evolution and development of the Pap smear test. In comparison to their more laboratory-based focus, Linda McKie's study of working-class women from the north of England takes the perspective of the woman screened (McKie 1995). Vicky Singleton concentrates on the organizational structure in which screening for cervical cancer is embedded (Singleton 1996).

The slightly surprising aspect of the relative neglect of these tests is that they are a constant in all women's lives, an annual reminder that their bodies are under surveillance. Admittedly, the levels of technology involved in the Pap smear and the mammogram are a long way from the present frontiers of medical knowledge. I had to read the medical rather than the social science literature to discover that screening for breast and cervical cancer has its own discourses, its own set of black boxes, its own scientists, epidemiologists and clinicians, its own relationships with women and the state, its own debates over scientific legitimacy, and its own emotional and ideological commitments. Reconstruing the mammogram and the Pap smear as prime examples of screening, intimate invasions of the female body by the medical gaze, I came to see them as an opportunity through which to think the topic of surveillance. Hence, the focus is neither the cancer, nor the test, nor the woman read in isolation from each other, but rather the complex web of ideas, practices, actors and ideologies which link all three together in the form of a screening program.

History and Surveillance

For Michel Foucault (1978 [1976]), surveillance was the expression of the power of the disciplinary regime, but David Armstrong (1995) has turned the term into a label, sorting the history of nineteenth- and twentieth-century medicine into three periods, "Bedside Medicine," "Hospital Medicine" and "Surveillance Medicine." Rather than leaving it as an abstract concept, Armstrong has effectively grounded surveillance in the day-to-day of screening programs, health promotion campaigns and the budgets allocated for public health and prevention. The effect is to strip away the slightly Kafka-esque overtones of Foucault's original concept, while also losing something of its moral and philosophical power and a sense of its historical roots.

Although Armstrong (1995) makes screening the defining characteristic of surveillance medicine in the late twentieth century, its origins lie in much older ideas of danger, stigma and contamination. The fear that someone might falsely pass as well, yet carry the plague or leprosy, or syphilis, or some form of contagious madness is an ancient thread running through the history of medicine. George Rosen (1993) tracks the origins of screening back to early attempts to find out and identify the diseased body and cast it out from the company of the non-diseased. He quotes Leviticus: "All the days wherein the plague shall be in him, he shall be defiled; he is unclean; he shall dwell alone; without the camp shall his habitation be." (*Leviticus* 14:6 in Rosen, 1993: 40) He also cites the Council of Lyons, which in 583 imposed restrictions on the free association of lepers with the healthy. Throughout the Middle Ages, church and state produced regulations on what lepers should wear, where they could live, and how they must identify themselves. The controls imposed on the leper provided a model for controlling the plague victim; the plague then served as a model for later campaigns against smallpox, cholera, typhoid and tuberculosis. Although each campaign was based on similar principles of isolation and exclusion, the attempts to control syphilis are the closest to modern practice in screening women for disease.

Rosen (1993) claims that syphilis was recognized as a sexually transmitted disease as early as 1507, referencing an Italian law passed in that year which required that any woman, who wanted to become a prostitute, should first be examined for signs of infection. Starting in Italian cities of the Renaissance but continuing in cities of the late nineteenth century – Metropolitan Toronto (MacDougall 1990), London (Smart 1992) and New York (Corea 1992) – civic authorities have acted as if control over prostitutes would ensure control over the disease. The New York state legislature, for example, passed a law in 1910 requiring: "The medical examination of women convicted of soliciting. Venereal infected women would be detained during treatment until they were noncontagious" (Corea 1992: 176).

Carol Smart has described the construction by Victorian physicians of the "lascivious working-class woman who could undermine the health of the nation both directly and indirectly" and who spread not only disease but foreign disease (1992: 28). The rhetoric of public health has changed and all women, not just those of the lascivious working class, are now targets for screening. Yet the same themes of sex, sin and blame have their echoes in the screening literature, particularly the literature on cervical cancer.

Screening acquired a new set of moral overtones in the late nineteenth and early twentieth centuries, when it was decided that the diseased and the unfit threatened the military and economic welfare of the state. According to Skrabanek, "Screening for disease was used as a sieve to separate the healthy and useful from the weak and useless, whether on behalf of insurance companies (to exclude poor risks), armies (to weed out weaklings) or employers (to keep up productivity)" (1990: 188).

As the public health movement gathered strength in the late nineteenth century, its officials took up the responsibility of protecting the health of the citizenry, albeit not without opposition. In Canada, the Toronto-based Medical Liberty League launched a vigorous legal challenge to vaccination for smallpox. Toronto physicians proved reluctant to report cases of tuberculosis, and the general public avoided testing whenever possible (MacDougall 1990). Despite resistance, public health officials gradually achieved a degree of public acceptance, political support and medical collaboration. By the 1930s, the stage was already set for the advent of surveillance medicine; then came the war accelerating the pace of change. Armstrong suggests that: "The main expansion in the techniques of monitoring occurred after World War II when an emphasis on comprehensive health care ... underpinned the deployments of explicit surveillance techniques such as screening" (1995: 398).

By the war's end, departments of public health had developed an array of surveillance mechanisms including mandatory case reporting, statistical record keeping and educational media programs. More recently, the electronization of information transformed the technological base of surveillance, facilitating the construction of vast banks of data, providing ways of sorting and linking together pieces of information from different sources but on the same individual. Thinking of the new genetics in combination with the new information capacity, screening for breast and cervical cancer are primitive prototypes of what is to come, but that is why they are so interesting to explore.

For Foucault (1978 [1976]) the advent of systematic record keeping added enormously to the power of the state to monitor the health of the citizenry. Yet, despite the very rapid escalation in the capacity to number and track every individual, one of the more surprising elements in the history of the Pap smear and the mammogram is the relatively slow pace taken by the health system in implementing mass screening programs. In the case of mammography and the United States, the barriers included a complex mix of political and economic factors (Kaufert 1996) but also a degree of resistance towards new ways of seeing disease and the body. For modern screening philosophy and practice requires agreement with a set of assumptions on the nature of disease which are in some ways counter-intuitive. Older, commonsense notions, which assume a relationship between feeling well and being well, needed to be replaced by the idea of the deceptive body, which may feel well, but is a hiding place for disease.

To convince clinicians of the value of screening for breast or cervical cancer, required persuading them, not only that the test would show them changes in the body before they could see these for themselves, but also that this visibility would enlarge their power to control or destroy the disease. Women had to be persuaded not only that a cancer could exist in their bodies yet outside their conscious awareness, but also that their lives depended on its early discovery. The state, or rather health policy-makers, had to be shown that screening was a worthwhile investment in which the returns could be calculated in terms of lives saved and health dollars not expended. The main champions of screening for breast and cervical cancer in Canada (as in the United States) have been researchers and practitioners committed to health promotion and community health, voluntary cancer societies, some public health officials and bureaucrats. Women have also been active but particularly in relation to mammography. Others (clinicians, technicians, owners of laboratories and equipment manufacturers) have seen to the actual implementation of screening and have been its financial beneficiaries.

It was the epidemiologists, however, who became the theologians, the high priests, the scientists of screening. They appear to have been motivated by the same conviction which drove the men who wrote *Malleus Maleficarum* (Kramer and Sprenger 1971 [1489]). Disturbed by the gullibility of the peasantry and the over-enthusiasm of the authorities, they developed a screening manual to bring order and standards to the detection of witches. Acting out of a similar commitment to bring order and standards to the detection of disease, epidemiologists have spent years on writing and refining the rule book on screening, defining its rules of evidence, setting up the criteria by which success is to be judged, arguing against gullibility and condemning those who act without evidence. Their rules vary slightly from one epidemiological text to another, but the essential elements are as follows: "The disease should be common and serious; its natural history should be understood; there should be a good screening test; acceptable treatment should be available; and this should favourably influence the outcome" (Mant and Fowler 1990: 916).

Many of the debates while I was a member of the provincial committee on screening mammography turned on the gap between the model of what a screening program should look like (as defined by these rules) and the realities of implementing a program to screen women for breast cancer. Following these debates gave me some insight not only into the gap itself, but also into the degree to which it is unavoidable because inherent in the nature of the screening process.

Out of the Laboratory and into the Screening Clinic

No one on the provincial committee disputed that breast cancer satisfied the first of Mant and Fowler's (1990) rules of screening; namely that the disease should be common and serious. Incidence rates had increased from 86.1 in 1981 to 102.7 per 100,000 Canadian women in 1995. Age standardized mortality rates had remained relatively static over time; they were 30.6 in 1970 and 30.6 in 1995 (National Cancer Institute of Canada 1995). The question for the committee was whether the rates of mortality attributable to breast cancer could be significantly reduced by implementing a province-wide mammography screening program. Supporters of the plan used the statistics on cervical cancer as evidence of the potential benefits of screening. The age standardized mortality rate for invasive carcinoma of the cervix in 1995 were 2.2 per 100,000 women relative to 7.4 in 1969; incidence rates were 7.8 in 1995 relative to 21.6 in 1969 (National Cancer Institute of Canada 1995). Crediting this decline to the use of the Pap smear they argued that the same result was possible with the mammogram. Sceptics supported screening in principle, but were mistrustful of its actual practice. Taking the evidence from the histories of mammography and screening for cervical cancer, they focused on the complexities of transferring tests from the laboratory to the diagnostic clinic, and from the clinic into the screening program.

Both the Pap smear and the mammogram began their lives as diagnostic tools, developed in the laboratory, then transferred to the diagnostic clinic. George Papanicolaou, for example, originally developed the Pap smear as an indicator of the estrous cycle in guinea pigs. A relatively simple technique, Papanicolaou saw it as easily transferable from one body cavity to another, one species to another. In 1941, he published a paper on the potential value of his procedure to the diagnosis of cervical cancer. A few gynecologists adopted the Pap smear as a diagnostic procedure but it remained confined within the black box of the scientific laboratory and research clinic for the next few years (Clarke and Casper 1996). The mammogram has a somewhat similar history. X-rays had been used in the diagnosis of breast cancer since the 1930s, but it was not until the 1950s that Kremens saw their potential value as a screening tool.

The American Cancer Society (ACS) was the catalyst in moving both tests out of the diagnostic clinic and into screening. Deeply committed to a search out and destroy philosophy, the idea of hunting down disease before it was visible had a strong theoretical and philosophical appeal for the ACS. Charles Cameron, a director of the society and a friend of Papanicolaou, recognized the potential of the Pap smear as a screening test; persuading the ACS to endorse the use of the vaginal smear as an effective cancer prevention for carcinoma of the uterine cervix in 1945 (Koss 1993).

The translation of mammography from a diagnostic to a screening test came later, influenced by the first randomized trial of screening for breast cancer, the HIP study. The epidemiological evidence that mammography would reduce mortality was slim but promising at the time the test was endorsed by the ACS (Kaufert 1996). Nothing even remotely equivalent to the HIP study had existed for cervical cancer. Even convinced advocates, such as Leopold Koss, admit that: "In the rush to apply the method rapidly to the largest possible number of women, no double-blind study of the efficacy of the cervical smear and its technical and clinical components has ever been conducted" (1993: 1407). In recommending them as screening tests, the ACS was enamored by their technical logic and fascinated by their ability to make disease visible. In other words, it chose them for their diagnostic qualities with very little sense of what might happen as they were transformed into screening tests.

The line between a diagnostic and a screening test is a fine one. A government document on screening for breast cancer proposes the following definition:

A screening mammogram is an x-ray of the breast in women who have no symptoms of breast cancer. A diagnostic mammogram is an x-ray of the breast taken when an abnormality is detected or suspected in the breast. (Canadian Breast Cancer Screening Initiative 1997: 5)

If a woman is referred to a radiology clinic for an investigation of a lump in her breast, then her mammogram is diagnostic. Its purpose is to confirm the existence and nature of something already known and suspicious. If she is referred for screening, the assumption is not that she is well, but rather that she has no visible signs of cancer. The distinction is both pedantic and yet at the heart of a philosophy of screening.

The difference between diagnosis and screening is partly a matter of words and a simple change in designation, but that is not the whole of the matter. The transition from diagnosis to screening set in place a process which transformed the character of the mammogram and the Pap smear, altered the natural history of both cancers, created a confrontation between radiologists and epidemiologists, and dramatically altered women's relationship with their bodies.

Scale is one of the more critical factors in this transformation. Women with symptoms to be diagnosed are vastly outnumbered by women who are symptom free but eligible for screening. The decision to screen results in a massive change in the size of the market with consequences which are sometimes obvious, sometimes hidden and sometimes unintended. As any business economist would predict, the creation of a larger and more competitive market stimulates changes in technology. Hence, as the demand for mammography machines expanded, the test became more accurate; the radiologist acquired more detailed information from better quality film, the machine became more consumer-friendly. At least in a technical sense, the impact of scale on mammography was positive, transforming the test into something other than, better than, the one initially sponsored by the ACS.

Yet the economist's prediction of technical change does not hold for the Pap smear which has changed relatively little since first developed by Papanicolaou. Relative to the mammogram which requires a machine, technicians to operate the machine and radiologists to read the film, the Pap smear is a simple technology. "The test consists of scraping cells from the cervix, the neck of the uterus onto a glass slide. The smear is then sent to the laboratory where it is stained and examined under a microscope for evidence of abnormal cells" (Russell 1994: 6). On the other hand, screening for cervical cancer reveals some of the other risks and benefits of the mass market. Relative to the specialist gynecology clinic in which it was first used as a diagnostic test, screening for cervical cancer now requires multiple armies of physicians and technicians. Quality control becomes a nightmare, as despite its simplicity the list of potential sources of error in the performance of the test is long:

The relevant part of the cervix may not be included in the smear, the important cells may not be transferred to the slide, the examination of the slides has to be undertaken by doctors or technicians and they may either miss abnormal cells or describe normal cells as abnormal. (Skrabanek and McCormick 1989:104)

A recent survey of physicians in the US reported critical gaps in their knowledge of the Pap smear and major inadequacies in their understanding the techniques needed to perform it adequately (Morrell et al. 1996). Competition and economies of scale have encouraged the development of large commercial, for-profit laboratories employing underpaid and ill-paid technicians. Positive results are sometimes missed; cancers are left untreated and women die. "In 1990, in the wake of articles in the *Wall Street Journal* on the inaccuracy of Pap smears, the federal government proposed new rules to improve test accuracy in labs participating in the Medicare and Medicaid programs" (Russell 1994: 101). Translating the problems of the misread Pap smear into the language of epidemiology, the question is whether a test, which worked well under the protected conditions of the diagnostic clinic, will function adequately, when carried out by people with lesser skills, working in poorer quality settings, and operating under different constraints of time and money. For women, the inefficiencies of the surveillance system may mean death or major and destructive surgery.

The problems of profit taking, the commercial laboratory, the ill-trained technician might appear solvable by removing capitalism and driving the health corporation out of health care. Revolution might help, except that the problem of the false negative is also inherent in the difference between diagnosis and screening. In diagnosis, there are already clues that something is amiss; the hand feels the lump or a woman reports pelvic pain. The test is done in the expectation of finding a cause. In screening, the usual experience of the physician doing the test or the technician taking the mammogram or reading the slide is that there is nothing to see; the breast and the cervix are normal. Screening hundreds of slides or films to find the few in which there is a sign of non-normalcy is time consuming and mind numbing. On the scale on which this has to be done, the mind and eye wander, something is missed. This is a consequence of scale, possibly unavoidable, but tragic for the women who did what they were told, but died nevertheless.

Screening and the Natural History of a Disease

Both cancers obviously exist independently of the diagnostic test and the screening program. Women have died from breast and cervical cancer without knowing the medical label for what is killing them, without having seen a physician and without having received any medical treatment. Both cancers are also real entities in the sense of having a tangible, measurable existence. A breast cancer can be removed, dissected and examined under a microscope. Malignant cells scraped from the neck of the uterus can be seen and counted. Yet, there is another sense in which each cancer is also what is "seen" on the diagnostic film or the slide. For example, a radiologist may "see" a particular breast as cancer-free looking at one image, but as diseased in another mammogram of the same breast but taken on newer equipment or by a better technician. One smear may be read as positive and the other as negative despite being taken from the same cervix, but because the cells were culled from a different place.

These examples happen in both diagnostic and screening clinics, and had a dramatic impact on clinical model building. The new natural history of cervical cancer is a product of information produced from hundreds and thousands of smears. The problem with this image is that each Pap smear is only the equivalent of a still photograph taken of a specific cervix at a specific point in time. The stringing of these images together to form a trajectory, anchored by normal at one end and by invasive carcinoma at the other, is a theoretical construct.

Medical texts are written as if the smear or the mammogram records the exact point reached in a natural line of transition from normal to full-blown disease, but the history of screening shows that it is not that simple. George Papanicolaou, as the scientist who developed the Pap smear, "saw" patterns in the cells, which he described as following a clear progression from normal to an advanced disease state. In his vision, this trajectory could be divided into five distinct classes. As the Pap smear moved out of his laboratory and became part of the general repertoire of screening, different laboratories gradually evolved their own criteria for separating one stage from another. The same smear might be read as class II in one place and class III in another. Some laboratories started to subdivide Papanicolaou's class II into three or four subclasses. In one sense, each laboratory was engaged in rewriting the history of the cervical cancer based on their own vision of how to recognize and define the divisions marking one stage off from another.

Screening has changed our understanding of both the past but also the future of these concerns. Prior to systematic screening, the history of any cancer started at the point it produced symptoms, became visible to the physician and could be diagnosed. Screening, as is suggested by these changes in classification systems, has given cervical cancer a prehistory marked off in stages and has relocated its point of origin much further back in time. In the following passage written some fifty years after George Papanicolaou's original paper, the critical transition from wellness to disease has been moved back "several decades" and the natural history of cervical cancer has been subdivided into an invasive and a non-invasive phase.

Most squamous epithelial cancers are preceded by a preinvasive phase lasting
several decades. Both in invasive cancer and in the preinvasive stage, abnormal
cells are shed from the cervix that can be recovered in a cervical-vaginal smear
and subsequently detected by microscopic examination of the material stained
with Papanicolaou technique. (Sedlis 1991: 107)

The future was once more certain in the sense that most women with
advanced symptoms died from their cancer. One of the dilemmas of
screening is the relationship between the theoretical model of what will
happen next and what would actually happen if nothing was done.
Would cervical changes reverse themselves in some women, but not
others? Does the pace of change vary from woman to woman? These
questions are speculative, because apart from a notorious study in New
Zealand (Sherwin 1992), clinicians are not supposed to observe how
trajectories vary from woman to woman, cervix to cervix. Once a particular pattern of cells is defined as potentially cancerous, they have
a moral obligation to act. By acting, they halt trajectory, but lose the
opportunity to verify whether the current disease model is correct. If left
alone, possibly the pattern may have evolved as predicted, but possibly
not.

The nature of this dilemma is illustrated by ductal carcinoma in situ
(DCIS). The US National Institute of Health organized a workshop on
DCIS in 1997 in response to a rapid rise in the number of cases, which
had increased from 742 women in 1983 to 4,676 in 1993. The general
assumption was that much of this increase was due to improvements in
the technology which meant that radiologists could see changes in the
breast, which were previously invisible or blurred. The question for
debate was whether or not these changes necessarily predicted breast
cancer. The following statement was issued after the workshop:

Ductal carcinoma in situ (DCIS) is frequently diagnosed in mammographically
screened women aged 40–49. DCIS is a heterogeneous entity for which the
natural history, clinical significance, prognostic factors and treatment are uncertain. Because some cases of DCIS may not progress to invasive cancer, a risk
of over treatment exists. (National Institute of Health Consensus Conference
Committee 1997: 4)

The problem is that screening is based on the premise that the earlier
disease is "discovered," the better are the chances of cure. The temp-
tation, particularly for clinicians, is to continually push back the boundaries and "find" the disease at an earlier and earlier stage. Epidemiologists worry and ask how far back a boundary may be pushed before
trespassing into the "normal" state and it is probably their views which
are reflected in the NIH statement. The dilemma for clinicians, however, is that once DCIS is defined as a precursor of cancer (even if only

in some rather than all women) then the obligation to treat becomes inescapable. The difficulties of reconciling these two very different views is a constant source of tension between clinician and epidemiologist.

Action Versus Evidence

During the period I was a member of the provincial committee on mammography, an intense battle was in process between epidemiologists and radiologists over the results of a large, Canadian randomized trial of mammography, the National Breast Screening Study. When the study's findings were published in 1992 (Miller et al. 1992a; Miller et al. 1992b), they showed a slight, but non-significant, benefit among women aged 50–59 randomized to an annual mammogram, but not among women aged 40–49. The implication was that screening programs should be restricted to women aged 50–59. Furious radiologists attacked the NBSS in the medical and popular press, on television, at medical conferences and in the special workshops called in the hope of finding consensus. They criticized the poor quality of the mammogram equipment used in the NBSS, the way in which the mammography was done, and the general conduct of the trial (Kopans 1993). They even hinted at scientific fraud, suggesting that the rules of randomization had been broken. Defenders of the NBSS answered in kind; for example, they implied that the study was the target of radiologists anxious to preserve a lucrative market in screening younger women (Kaufert 1996).

The end result of the battle, but not the war, was that the US National Cancer Institute withdrew its support for screening for women aged 40–49, but the ACS continued to advocate the screening of the younger age group. The debate rumbled on in the medical literature and at conferences for the next five years. Intense political pressure, coupled with new data from Swedish studies, finally persuaded NCI to reconsider. A committee was appointed to review the new evidence and report at a new consensus conference held in January 1997. To the surprise and anger of many clinicians, their report advised against a "universal recommendation for mammography for all women in their forties" (National Institute of Health Consensus Conference Committee 1997). Attacked at the meeting and later on television, the committee's findings were described as fraudulent and its members were accused of "condemning American women to death." The NIH had to defend the report before a Congressional committee, only to find that the US Senate subsequently voted in favor of mammography for younger women.

Susan Fletcher, the chair of the committee which had recommended against a resumption of screening in younger women wrote a commentary on her experience for the *New England Journal of Medicine* (Fletcher 1997) in which she refers to the involvement of "powerful financial interests" and to "billions of dollars in equipment and professional incomes." Claiming that "questions about health care are increasingly being distorted by emotional, political, financial and legal interests," she ends with the following comment on the times: "For those of us who have spent decades promoting the use of scientific evidence in the formulation of clinical policies, it is difficult not to view these events with sadness and even alarm" (Fletcher 1997: 1181). Caught up in a very political and public debate, her anger is very understandable. It is slightly more surprising that the *New England Journal* decided to provide a public forum to accusations which expose one of the aspects of screening that many of its advocates prefer to ignore, namely, its commercialization.

To pretend that screening is not influenced by corporate and commercial interests, the drive for profit rather than health, would be naïve. Yet, neither is it the whole story. Money was not the only motivating factor in the anger of the radiologists who attacked the NBSS or who lobbied in Washington against Susan Fletcher. Talking with radiologists and listening to them speak, it is evident that being able to see and show where the tumor lies has an intense reality, besides which the epidemiologists' statistics on changing mortality rates become mere manipulations of a series of numbers. Radiologists are convinced that without screening, women will die and that it is their technical skills and ability to interpret films which saves women's lives.

Numbers are truth, the ultimate reality for epidemiologists. Susan Fletcher's statement expressed many of the deeply held beliefs of others in her discipline. The source of her anger was the idea that women may be disfigured by treatment, emotionally and physically traumatized, *without* statistical evidence of benefit. Like many epidemiologists, she sees quantification as a virtue which protects against self-deception and is deeply troubled by the enthusiasm for screening among clinicians and in the general public. Louise Russell, an American, commenting on screening in the United States, writes:

These human costs – false positive tests and treatment that is not beneficial to the individual – are virtually ignored in the development of screening programs in the United States. The focus instead is on trying to ensure that no case of disease is missed, which leads to recommendations for more frequent screening – a practice that leads in turn to larger numbers of false positives and more treatment without benefit. That bias has probably been aided and abetted by a simple failure to calculate how many people will experience false positives or unnecessary treatment. (Russell 1994: 79)

Walter Holland, a British epidemiologist, expresses somewhat similar sentiments in a statement on the tendency to treat screening as a "good" in itself and ignore its darker side. He writes:

Screening for disease has become extremely popular. There seems to be an assumption in some quarters that if undiagnosed conditions exist it is the medical profession's responsibility to hunt them down. . . Such evangelism prevails despite the lack of evidence that some of the procedures are of benefit, and positive evidence that they may lead to increased anxiety, illness behavior, and the use of scarce health service resources. (Holland 1993:1222)

As these quotations from Fletcher, Holland and Russell suggest, epidemiologists are somewhat akin to medieval theologians in being fierce to defend truth as defined from within their rules and from their perspective, dismissive of the credulity of the commons, intensely angered by those they see as exploitative of gullibility, somewhat mistrustful of colleagues who may be tempted by money into acting without sufficient evidence. By contrast, clinicians see themselves as the searchers out and destroyers of disease, deeply mistrustful of those who would turn them from this task by using numbers and arguing the high costs of false positives. For them, the value of a life saved cannot be quantified whether in cash or pain suffered unnecessarily.

The debate between epidemiologists and radiologists turns on different definitions of visibility. For epidemiologists, screening was justifiable only if there was a visible benefit. "Visible" for the epidemiologist meant "statistically visible" and is expressed as a significant change in mortality rates at the population level. "Visibility" for the clinician, particularly the clinician/radiologist, means something quite different. When they talk about visibility, they are thinking in terms of the individual breast with its tumor seen and its position marked out for the surgeon.

While radiologists may act from a mixture of motives, some notion of the healer's responsibility to protect and cure the sick individual fuels the anger of their attacks on the NBSS or Susan Fletcher. In their turn, however, people like Fletcher, or Holland or Russell are motivated by equally old notions of the good of the community. In this sense, the debate between the clinician and the epidemiologist is part of a much broader confrontation in which the good of the individual is balanced against that of the group. Yet, while recognizing that each side to this debate acts out of its own form of emotional integrity, the costs of screening as well as its benefits fall most directly on women. In the final section, I want to return briefly to the point from which this essay first started out, the woman having the Pap smear or the mammogram.

Women and Screening

Terri Kapsalis (1997) has traced the process by which the cervix became a public rather than a private place, a venue for medical exploration, a piece of the body over which the gynecologist held rights of surveillance. She sees the pelvic examination as in effect the staging of sex and gender, arguing that the impropriety of the examination threatens the stability of its medicalization (1997: 14). The middle-class woman and her physician are trained in maintaining the proprieties in a situation which is both threatening and laughable, but the northern women in Linda McKie's study (1995) were more open in admitting both the implicit sexuality, but also the deep embarrassment of their experience. In marked contrast to the medical and public health literature, which is singularly Victorian in its ability to ignore the obvious, these northern women openly discussed the sexual connotations of the Pap smear, talking not only about the physical experience, but also about the problems of dealing with the interpretation which men give to the Pap smear.

It is the characterization of cervical cancer as a sexually transmitted disease which explains why the women in Linda McKie's study were reluctant to admit publicly that their smear test was positive. Like their Victorian counterparts described by Carol Smart (1992), women still fear the consequences of being labeled promiscuous. The public health and health education literature rarely acknowledges the complex symbolism of either the breast or the cervix. Screening is presented as a minimum cost, routine, piece of behavior, like dental check-ups. In the case of breast and cervical cancer, a woman risks not only death or disfigurement, but also an attack on her sense of identity as female. The breast is not only a site for cancer, but also a sexual object, a symbol of nurturing and motherhood. The cervix is not simply a body space into which a speculum can be inserted, but is heavy with meaning, the place of birth, but also sex, sin and dishonor. Every time a woman goes for a screening test, she sets her whole future life narrative in jeopardy. There is always the possibility that the test may be positive. A clinician pushing back the boundaries of the disease, for example, may be acting from the best clinical motives, but the effect as experienced by the woman may be devastating to her sense of survival and her sense of herself as a sexual being. One study comments on: "A significant alteration in sexual attitudes, behavior and response in young women after diagnosis and treatment of pre-invasive disease. . . Sexual intercourse becomes uncomfortable or less enjoyable, propagating negative feelings. Additionally women frequently developed hostility directed towards a sexual partner" (Campion et al. 1988: 180). These are identities spoiled, even if lives saved.

The woman told that her mammogram or her Pap test is positive cannot interrogate her own body to verify whether the statement is true. She has to accept that the mammogram has revealed a tumor lodged within the tissue of her breast, or that the laboratory has seen cell changes occurring within her cervix. Her experience of her body as being well comes into conflict with being told that her body is diseased. Innocence is lost and a woman is made aware that her body may betray her. Screening creates an uncertain relationship with the body. Nicky Britten, a British social scientist once wrote a piece for the *British Medical Journal* describing her experience of being told she had a positive smear: "Surprisingly, given my belief that early detection of cervical cancer carries an excellent prognosis, I reacted badly to the news. For several days, I could think of nothing but death" (1988: 1191) She continues:

It was as if, having allowed the possibility of one disease to enter my body, a host of other conditions have crowded in behind it. The slightest weight loss becomes sinister, stomach pains become ulcers and backache becomes kidney failure. I was changed: I had lost an innocence of outlook. (Britten 1988: 1191)

Conclusion

Deborah Lupton (1993) once suggested that it is difficult to challenge screening because of its benevolent goal of maintaining health. It is true that many women are alive, who might have died without benefit of the Pap smear or the mammogram. The purpose, that is, to detect the abnormal within a seemingly normal population, is well intentioned. But for Linda McKie (1995), the question is whether or not it is acceptable to intervene in the bodies and minds of the many in order to detect, and potentially control, abnormalities in the bodies of the few (McKie 1995). Each woman must find her own individual answer to this question (as Vicky Singleton (1996) suggests) but who can answer for the generality of women, the female commons? Women are told that being screened is an expression of virtue and that the punishment for those who resist is death and disfigurement. But the unanswered question is what does screening do by changing our sense of the body and the self, by introducing us to fear?

REFERENCES

Armstrong, David 1995 "The Rise of Surveillance Medicine." *Sociology of Health and Illness* 17(3): 393–404.

Batchelor, Claire, Evelyn Parsons and Paul Atkinson 1996 "The Career of a Medical Discovery." *Qualitative Health Research* 6(2): 48.

Britten, Nicky 1988 "Personal View: Colposcopy." *British Medical Journal* 296: 1191.

Byatt, A. S. 1992 *Angels and Insects.* London: Random House.

Campion, M., J. Brown, D. McCance, W. Atia, R. Edwards, J. Cuzick and A. Singer 1988 "Psychosexual Trauma of an Abnormal Cervical Smear." *British Journal of Obstetrics and Gynecology* 95(2): 175–81.

Canadian Breast Cancer Screening Initiative 1997 *Mammography Screening for Women under 50: Position Statement.* Ottawa: Disease Prevention Division, Health Canada.

Clarke, Adele E. and Monica J. Casper 1996 "From Simple Technology to Complex Arena: Classification of Pap Smears 1917–90." *Medical Anthropological Quarterly* 10: 601–23.

Corea, Gena 1992 *The Invisible Epidemic.* New York: HarperCollins.

Fletcher, Susan W. 1997 "Whither Scientific Deliberation in Health Policy Recommendations? Alice in the Wonderland of Breast-Cancer Screening." *New England Journal of Medicine* 336(16): 1180–3.

Foucault, Michel 1978 [1976] *The History of Sexuality: An Introduction.* Trans. Robert Hurley. Volume 1. New York: Pantheon.

Holland, Walter W. 1993 "Screening: Reasons to be Cautious [editorial]." *British Medical Journal* 306(6887): 1222–3.

Kapsalis, Terri 1997 *Public Privates: Performing Gynecology from Both Ends of the Speculum.* Durham: Duke University Press.

Kaufert, Patricia 1996 "Women and the Debate over Mammography: An Economic, Political and Moral History." In Carolyn S. Sargent and Caroline B. Brettell (eds.), *Gender and Health – An International Perspective.* New Jersey: Prentice Hall, pp. 167–86.

Kopans, Daniel 1993 "Breast Cancer Detection in an Institution." *Cancer* 72(4), Supplement: 1457–65.

Koss, L. G. 1993 "Cervical (Pap) Smear. New Directions." *Cancer* 71(4), Supplement: 1406–12.

Kramer, Heinrich, and James Sprenger 1971 [1489] *The Malleus Maleficarum of Heinrich Kramer and James Sprenger.* 2nd edition. Trans. Montague Summers. New York: Dover.

Lupton, Deborah 1993 "Risk as Moral Danger: The Social and Political Functions of Risk Discourse in Public Health." *International Journal of Health Services* 23(3): 425–35.

MacDougall, Heather 1990 *Activists and Advocates: Toronto's Health Department 1883–1983.* Toronto: Dundurn Press.

Mant, David and Godfrey Fowler 1990 "Mass Screening: Theory and Ethics." *British Medical Journal* 300: 916–18.

McKie, Linda 1995 "The Art of Surveillance or Reasonable Prevention? The Case of Cervical Screening." *Sociology of Health and Illness* 17(4): 441–57.

Miller, Anthony B., Cornelia J. Baines, Teresa To and Claus Wall 1992a "Canadian National Breast Screening Study: 1. Breast Cancer Detection and Death Rates Among Women Aged 40 to 49 Years." *Canadian Medical*

Association Journal 147(10): 1459–76. [Published erratum appears in *Canadian Medical Association Journal*, 1 March 1993, 148(5): 718.]

1992b "Canadian National Breast Screening Study: 2. Breast Cancer Detection and Death Rates Among Women Aged 50 to 59 years." *Canadian Medical Association Journal* 147(10): 1477–88. [Published erratum appears in *Canadian Medical Association Journal*, 1 March 1993; 148(5): 718.]

Morrell, D., P. Curtis, M. Mintzer, J. C. Resnick, S. Hendrix and B. F. Qaqish 1996 "Perceptions and Opinions on the Performance of Pap Smears: A Survey of Clinicians Using a Commercial Laboratory." *American Journal of Preventive Medicine* 12(4): 271–6.

National Cancer Institute of Canada 1995 *Canadian Cancer Statistics*. Toronto.

National Institute of Health Consensus Conference Committee 1997 "Consensus Conference on the Classification of Ductal Carcinoma In Situ." *Cancer* 80(9): 1798–1802.

Oudshoorn, Nelly 1997 "From Population Control Politics to Chemicals: The WHO as an Intermediary Organization in Contraceptive Development." *Social Studies of Science* 27: 41–72.

Rosen, George 1993 *A History of Public Health*. Expanded edition. Baltimore: Johns Hopkins University Press.

Russell, Louise 1994 *Educated Guesses: Making Policy About Medical Screening Tests*. Berkeley: University of California Press.

Sedlis, Alexander 1991 "The Pitfalls of Cervical Cancer Screening." *Contributions to Gynecology and Obstetrics* 18: 103–14.

Sherwin, Susan 1992 *No Longer Patient: Feminist Ethics and Health Care*. Philadelphia: Temple University Press.

Singleton, Vicky 1996 "Feminism, Sociology of Scientific Knowledge and Post-Modernism: Politics, Theory and Me." *Social Studies in Science* 26: 445–68.

Skrabanek, Petr 1990 "Why is Preventive Medicine Exempted from Ethical Constraints?" *Journal of Medical Ethics* 16(4): 187–90.

Skrabanek, Petr and McCormick, James 1989 *Follies and Fallacies in Medicine*. Glasgow: Tarragon Press.

Smart, Carol 1992 "Disruptive Bodies and Unruly Sex: The Regulation of Reproduction and Sexuality in the Nineteenth Century". In Carol Smart (ed.), *Disruptive Bodies and Unruly Sex: The Regulation of Reproduction and Sexuality in the Nineteenth Century*. London: Routledge, pp. 7–32.

Star, Susan Leigh 1991 "Power, Technology and the Phenomenology of Onions." *Sociological Review Monograph* 38: 25–6.

9 Extra chromosomes and blue tulips: medico-familial interpretations

Rayna Rapp

So they diagnosed Amelia right away, on the delivery table, she was barely out, I barely got a chance to catch my breath or marvel at my first baby when this doctor pours this bad news all over us. "She's got Down syndrome," he says to us, very coldly. And after he tells us about blood tests and confirmations and all this stuff, we say to him, "But what does that *mean*? What should we *expect*?" And just as coldly he says, "Don't expect much. Maybe she'll grow up to be an elevator operator. Don't expect much." So we clung to each other, and cried. (April Schwartz, white lawyer, mother of a four-year-old with Down syndrome)

My doctor was so angry with me, he couldn't believe I didn't take that test, "How could you let this happen?," he yelled at me, "you're 40!" But I think something else: Even though he's mentally retarded, he could be a good person... It's just like finding out you have a new job. You just do it, and you accept it, that's all there is to it. (Anna Morante, Puerto Rican nurse's aide, mother of a seven-year-old with Down syndrome)

In humans, the twenty-first chromosome suffers nondisjunction at a remarkably high frequency, with unfortunately rather tragic effect... These unfortunate children suffer mild to severe mental retardation and have a reduced life expectancy... We have no clue as to why an extra twenty-first chromosome should yield the highly specific set of abnormalities associated with trisomy-21. But at least it can be identified in utero by counting the chromosomes in fetal cells, providing an option for early abortion. (Gould 1980)

The smiling face of the Mongolian Imbecile suggests the possession of some secret source of joy. (Sutherland 1900: 23)

With the discovery of the complement of normal human chromosomes in 1958, and the development and widespread use of amniocentesis and related prenatal diagnostic technologies over the last twenty-five years, epidemiological knowledge and public health screening of Down syndrome have become routinized. In North America, Down's is the iconic condition described by geneticists and genetic counselors when explaining their diagnostic technologies to potential patients. Yet despite widespread popular recognition of this condition, expanded access to prenatal diagnosis, and a high rate of elective abortion following upon diagnosis, the birth of individual babies with Down syndrome is always a shock. It provides an occasion for intense medical and familial discussions of what "causes" the condition, and how children born with it are to be treated. There is a gap between epidemiological description, clinical services and individual understandings of affliction which is continuously open to speculation and practical intervention. Technologies of diagnosis, therapies of intervention, and systems of support are all enacted and interpreted within that gap.

This essay explores that gap, focusing on the traffic between biomedical and familial understandings of the presence of Down syndrome in newborns and children. It is based on two years' participant-observation in New York City in a support group for parents whose children have this condition, as well as interviews conducted through an early intervention program. The thirty-eight families who were kind enough to share their thoughts and family time with me are part of a larger study of the social impact and cultural meaning of prenatal diagnosis.[1]

Here, my analysis begins with the observation that the realm of technoscientific knowledge and practice is rapidly expanding: we all find ourselves increasingly inside of science, heir to its immense benefits and ambiguous burdens, whether as researchers, service providers, patients, and caretakers of patients, or anthropologists who occasionally occupy any and all of these roles. The clinicians and parents whose ideas fill this essay are differently located in relation to new technologies like prenatal diagnosis, chromosome karyotyping, and neonatal surgery, all of which are likely to loom large when a newborn is diagnosed as having Down syndrome. What counts as a new biomedical technology to one constituency may be quite routinized for another. And new technologies are deployed and understood by parents and practitioners in relation to their funds of social as well as individual knowledge. Thus medico-familial interpretations of the extra chromosome which produces Down syndrome are shaped at intersections which are unstable and continuously subject to claims of expert, expansive knowledge.

The Unexpected Baby

When parents narrate the natural history of learning to live with a child's hereditary disabilities, they almost always spontaneously begin by describing the birth, and whether or not a diagnosis was quickly made. As the first two stories which open this chapter suggest, the birth and diagnosis of a newborn with Down syndrome is an event which is vividly remembered not only by the birthing woman and her partner, but by medical practitioners as well. Indeed, the third quotation points toward a lengthy medical commentary on the mysterious nature of births gone awry: doctors may have strong personal and professional responses to delivering and treating babies who cannot be seen as normal, and whose ills cannot be cured, investing them with symbolic meaning which sometimes supersedes their individual characteristics. Birthing mothers recalled their attendants' words and deeds in great detail, judging the quality of response:

So I had a section and my doctor came in seven hours later and I was still pretty wiped out and he stood there with me and he says to me with tears in his eyes, he says, "Well, you have a Down syndrome child." And I didn't know what he meant, I says, "Is it a cold, does it go away, what the hell is it?" And he says, "Patsy, the baby is mongoloid." I mean, it hits home, it's like, "Are you for real?" And then he looks me square in the eye and he says, "We have some papers, you could award him to the state if you don't want him." And I looked at my doctor that just delivered my son, my doctor that I loved, we had such a friendship, and I says, "Get the hell out of this room." (Patsy DelVecchio, white bus driver, mother of a six-year-old with Down syndrome)

So my husband didn't make it home for the delivery but he called from the airport and the doctor got on the phone right away and gave him all this bad news. But you know it's like the doctor was more upset than we were, like he couldn't bring himself to say "here's this baby and we don't know for sure." It's very hard for professional people not to see the down side, you know, to see the worst possible, this could have been the Down's kid that was gonna have an IQ of 100 and make it to Harvard. We don't know the future when it's first born. But the doctor was seeing maybe his next door neighbor's kid who can't do anything, or something, so it was very hard that he painted this gloomy terrible picture. (Lydia Sellers, white homemaker and dressmaker, mother of a nine-year-old with Down syndrome)

She was tiny but she was great, like she was just the cutest thing and then my husband came in and he looked weird and immediately he said, "The baby, something's wrong. . ." And all I could think of was that she's blind, I guess that was probably the worst thing I could ever have imagined. But the doctor had just called him and told him that Rose was mongoloid. It took a half hour to get it out of him, like he couldn't finish telling me the story, and then the doctor came and said, "What your husband just told you is right." He was, like very down on the whole thing, very negative, he said, "The only blessing is they don't tend to live very long." So he thought it would be a good thing if our new baby would die. What more can I say? (Flora Taglitone, white homemaker, mother of a six-year-old with Down syndrome)

As such stories indicate, Down syndrome babies are "wrong babies," marked almost from the moment of birth by medical scrutiny as

incurably damaged. Many women across class lines and from diverse
ethnic backgrounds told similar stories of medical dismay at their children's births. It is not hard to spot the despair at having delivered a child
most people consider frighteningly marred, and for which technological
surveillance and interventions are available prenatally. Nor is it hard to
pick up (as Lydia Sellers's words suggest) the attitudes toward mental
retardation expressed by many medical professionals. I should also note
that while the majority of birth stories I collected pointed an accusatory
finger at awkward, cold or downright insensitive obstetricians, a few
families felt very well served by both obstetricians and pediatricians,
whose calm discretion they recalled with appreciation:

We're so lucky we had Robin at the Birthing Center, and not in the hospital. I
mean, in a hospital, he would have been examined to death by a cast of thousands, they surely would have picked it up. But at the Center, they missed it.
So I got to take him home, to nurse him, we stayed at home for four days
quietly, all together, and then we took him to meet the pediatrician. And he
made the diagnosis immediately. He was excellent, really excellent. It's such an
important thing, how the professional handles it, the initial comment, I can't
emphasize how important it is. . . He was just very positive and sensitive, he just
said, "I have to tell you this, there are some things I'm concerned about," and
I said, "Well, what?," and he said, "Well, let's look at his eyes and, of course,
there's this crease in his palm. It's a simian crease." I don't know how I knew
that, but I just knew what he was talking about, so I turned to my husband and
I said, "Do you know what he's talking about?," and Paul said, "No," and I
said, "Well, he's talking about Down syndrome." So I guess he didn't really
ever have to tell me, he just got me to the point where I knew for myself. And
then he hooked us up with all sorts of people, genetic counselors, heart specialists, and we always felt he just wanted the best for our son. (Polly Denton, white
actress, mother of a five-year-old with Down syndrome)

Laura and Dan Schulmann were also quite satisfied with the straightforward explanation their pediatrician offered when he made the diagnosis of Down syndrome one hour after Ashley's birth:

He caught Dan at the telephone, calling everyone, and stopped him. "Don't
make any more calls till after we've had a moment to talk," he said. And once
he was done explaining, he warned us, "Don't touch the literature. It's badly
out of date, it will only scare you." And he got us some other parents to talk to.

We should note the presence of the simian crease, a term of differential
diagnosis, to whose history I will return, and the auto-critique of the
medical literature in these very positive doctor/patient stories. Several
women went out of their way to also describe the sensitivity and compassion with which nurses, rather than doctors, embedded a diagnostic
situation in a more optimistic message that their babies would receive
help rather than judgement.

Medicalization

In the realm of biomedicine, newborns tentatively diagnosed with Down syndrome have their blood samples sent immediately for karyotyping. Once diagnosed, they are intensively and technologically scrutinized for specific conditions that range from mild to life-threatening. Regulation is considered key to normalizing the life-chances of babies and young children with Down syndrome. Whether the individual story of diagnosis is coded as negative or positive, virtually all parents of a newborn with Down syndrome find themselves stitched into medical networks. Because babies with this condition are at high risk for heart problems, intestinal blockages, and a host of less life-threatening disabilities, a diagnosed baby is a medicalized baby, tied to appointments with specialists, and scheduled for high-technology testing from the moment a diagnosis is tentatively made: geneticists, pediatric cardiologists, neurologists and pediatric surgeons are all likely to see the baby shortly after birth; audiology, ophthalmology, podiatry and behavioral psychology are among the services to which most parents of children with Down syndrome are routinely introduced. All are likely to be accompanied by a range of biomedical technologies. While some new parents find this attention reassuring, others find it invasive and disheartening:

Then they send you to the Heredity Department, that's when they give you the low-down, when you're at your lowest. That's when they say, "Heart problems. Leukemia. The works." (Johnella Cornell, African-American hairdresser, mother of an eighteen-month-old with Down syndrome)

Diagnosed babies and their parents are also likely to be "social worked," connected to early intervention services not only in the realm of medicine, but in educational, physical, occupational and speech therapies for infants and young children. These, too, include technologies which are likely to be new to families, whether as low tech as the physio balls physical therapists use with floppy newborns, or as cutting edge as computer learning programs for correcting toddler speech pathology. Funding for such interventions comes through the Family Court (in New York State, where my research was conducted), tying families into a bureaucratic web of services and paperwork from the moment of diagnosis. While we might want to note that all newborns are conscripts to modern bureaucratic record-keeping and discipline via birth records, immunization schedules, the establishment of contracts, wills and the like, diagnosed babies are fused with public services at an intense and often bewildering rate. This, too, is a realm where technology enters the lives of families with disabled newborns and older children.

For many of the families with whom I spoke, recommended services provide reassuring resources for dealing with what at first feels like an overwhelming dilemma: being able to "do something" to help an intensely vulnerable child sheds some rays of hope during the early weeks and months following the birth and diagnosis of a baby with Down syndrome. For some families, learning to speak the highly medicalized physical therapy language of hypotonia, proprioception, and subluxation provides a vocabulary around which early interventions may be effected. And exposure to the range of helping therapists available through early intervention programs also provides aid for families coming to terms with how to handle and what to expect from a "different" or "wrong" baby. As one physical therapist who works extensively with developmentally delayed newborns and young children put it, "With a handicapped baby, we now know how important it is to go all out, to shoot for the moon. That way, the kid will achieve whatever is best for them."

The optimistic energy and realistic sense of possibility expressed by such therapists are usually extremely beneficial to family members. Yet early intervention services also have shadow effects. When I praised the high-quality services available to parents of newborns and infants to the director of an early intervention program, herself the mother of a teenager with Down syndrome, she told me this story:

When Debbie was born, the pediatrician said, "Well, she has mongoloid tendencies." I knew what he meant. He knew that I knew. But no one talked about mental retardation or heart defects all the time. I went for weeks without anyone mentioning it; it was a keen eye that picked up Downs in babies then. I had a couple of years to grow into my baby, to grow with her. Now, every parent that's referred here is waiting for the results of chromosome studies, hoping it's "only mosaicism," and thinking about facial surgery. What kind of information do you really need to handle a six-week-old? I didn't look at my daughter every day and say, "She has Downs." Today, they get more services, and more support. But they've got less ability to forget it, to just get on with knowing the child.

New technical knowledge both opens and closes doors, a point forcefully made by Barbara Katz Rothman more than a decade ago, in speaking of amniocentesis (1986). Here, I underline the increasing biomedical routinization of diagnostic technological capacities such as chromosome karyotyping and cardiac echosonography of newborns which make both doctors and parents more quickly aware of the specificity of a newborn's membership in a taxonomy of pathology. In both positive and negative terms, I have been describing a system of continuous interventions marking difference in medical and kinship language.

In the shadow of such difference, establishing the child's *bone fide* presence inside a system of connection, that is, as a family member, is a major cultural accomplishment. There are many barriers – both subtle and overt – to normalizing kin ties with disabled children. Medical and other professional language may constitute the first barrier, for it often separates Down syndrome and other hereditarily disabled newborns from the category of normalcy, imposing descriptions that create distance. One Haitian mother, for example, who gave birth to a child with a rare and anomalous chromosomal diagnosis, a partial trisomy, was asked to bring her newborn son to the genetics laboratory. There, geneticists discussed the oblique palpebral fissure and micrognathia of her six-week-old which led them to label his condition as trisomy 9, while she genealogized his features, assimilating them to various aunts and uncles. Likewise, one white mother of a newly diagnosed Down syndrome baby boy kept insisting that his father was Black and had the same low-hung ears as the baby, linking the child to his familial heritage over the pathologizing discourse of the pediatricians. Another African-American mother said of her newly diagnosed baby, "They wanna talk about trisomy something, I need to deal with a sick kid. My kid's got a heart problem. Let me deal with that first, then I'll figure out what all this Down's business means." An interpretive clash on the terrain of medico-familial explication is always a strong possibility.

Alienated Kinship

When mothers of children with Down syndrome tell the story of their pregnancies, births and diagnoses, one common theme is explicit disconnection, or lack of familial resemblance, as orchestrated by medical attendants:

So I had a home delivery and the midwife was very cool. Like she suspected something, but she didn't want to say anything, she just wanted me to enjoy the birth, to bond with Laney. But he was too sleepy, so she knew something was wrong, she called the doctor, and the pediatrician came and she said, "I hate to bring this up, I just have the vague suspicion he doesn't look like he's related to anyone in this family, I just don't think he resembles any of you". . . At first, I just blocked what she was saying, and then I looked, and well, I had this uneasy feeling 'cause he didn't look like us. He looked like he belonged to some other family. (Judy Kaufman, white nurse)

The first thing the doctor said was, he said, "If you had a lot of Irish moon faces in your family, I'd be happier about seeing this child. But she doesn't look like you, she doesn't look like she's from your gene pool at all." Then he explained why he thought it was Down's. (April Schwartz, white lawyer)

An activist couple who were parents of a child with Down syndrome interrupted our interview in midstream when the mother exclaimed, "Shit! I just told you that Leslie doesn't have all the *stigmata* associated with Down's! There I go, sounding just like them!" The father commented that it was almost impossible to avoid pathological language, despite their pride in their daughter's accomplishments. And many families noted that the language used to diagnose and describe Down syndrome includes references to a "simian crease," obviously grouping its bearers with apes rather than humans. We will return to this problem of animal identification and a "throw-back" language of evolution below.

The claims of kinship must be articulated not only against the technicist diagnostic discourse of biomedicine, but sometimes against other kinsfolk and community members who blame mothers for giving birth to "wrong" babies: "My husband would have left me if I'd done that," said the mother-in-law of one mother of a newborn with Down's. Two African-American fathers believed that their babies caught mental retardation from retarded neighbors from whom they had warned their wives to keep a distance during their pregnancies lest it "mark the baby." Gloria Hurwitz, an Orthodox Jew, told almost none of her relatives that her baby had been diagnosed with mosaic trisomy 18. Beyond initial medical evaluations, she mainly consulted a geneticist who belonged to the same temple. "Jewish people don't accept mental retardation," she told me. But she expected to send Hershel to Hebrew school, along with her other children. Susan Lee, estranged from her parents after a religious conversion and marriage to someone of another faith, didn't initially tell her parents that their first grandchild had Down syndrome. "What's the point? They were already set to reject her, this will only make it worse," she reasoned. Marilyn Trainer (1991), whose widely published essays on life with a Down syndrome son present a consistent message of acceptance, never told her elderly parents that her fourth child had this disability. She didn't want to burden them with what she expected to be sorrowful news. Some women without privileged educational backgrounds had to convince their partners and other family members that they'd done nothing to "deserve" or "cause" the "wrong baby."

Indeed, the existential problem of what causes hereditary disabilities haunted many in the early days of parenting anomalous babies, when biomedical explanation often cannot assuage experiential confusion and pain. Susan Lee, newly fundamentalist Christian and anti-abortion, thought her prior abortion was being redressed by a Down syndrome birth; Patsy DelVecchio, a recovering alcoholic, believed that she was being punished for earlier drinking habits. Johnella Cornell told me she was refused amniocentesis at five City hospitals because she was too young; but in her recurrent dreams she gave birth to a damaged baby again and again, and she wanted the test to confirm the vision. When her son was born with Down syndrome, she considered it a sign, and was relieved to have discovered the root cause of the dream. Pat Carlson decided to keep a Down syndrome pregnancy after a positive prenatal diagnosis. She believed that her son Stevie was put on earth for a mysterious and only partly revealed reason; his mission will become clearer as he grows up. Many practicing Catholics and church-going Protestants told me, "God only gives burdens to the strong." Some parents used medical language against itself, to explain their children's special qualities:

I think it's like something positive, they're always feeding you all this negative stuff about the extra chromosome, all these disabilities, but I think it's something positive. Maybe the extra genetic stuff carries some mutation that causes positive things, too. I think that all that heart, that generosity, the lovingness, the feeling one with the world, those qualities, that's the positive side they never talk about. And it's got to be genetically built into them. Those are traits, too. (Judy Kaufman, white nurse, mother of a seven-year-old with Down syndrome)

My son just has a different brain, it's got different inhibitors built in to it. The point is not that he's stupid, that he can't learn. He learns really well, but really slowly. The brain connections are just different, he doesn't inhibit, he isn't limited, his brain just doesn't inhibit certain emotional expressions the way the rest of us do. His feelings are much more available to be expressed by this brain. What's so bad about that? (Bonnie D'Amato, mother of a five-year-old with Down syndrome)

Finding alternative meaning within biomedical discourses is a capacity exercised by many parents of youngsters with hereditary disabilities.

Acceptance of stigmatized difference is an achievement that surely belongs to parents, but it is also dependent on larger social groups and forces. Johnella Cornell's dream of a disabled baby, and her strong criticisms of "being sent to Heredity" after her son's birth should also be contextualized by her long-standing residence in Harlem. There, her mother received a White House commendation for having fostered twelve community children, many with disabilities. There, too, Johnella described dense interactions with neighbors who had non-specific mental retardation or cerebral palsy, both of which are diagnosed at high rates in poor communities. This working knowledge of disability gave Johnella pause to worry about how her son with Down syndrome might be teased as he grew up; but it also gave her confidence in his ability to survive as a member of his community. Likewise, three of the parents I interviewed through the Down Syndrome Parent Support Group were teachers of special education; they had considerable professional knowledge of mild mental retardation. Professional knowledge doesn't necessarily imply acceptance; among the fifty stories I collected of women who chose to abort after receiving what is so antiseptically labeled a "positive" diagnosis, teachers of special education are well-represented (Rapp 1999: chapter 9). But it does suggest that when babies are born with developmental delays, those with prior knowledge are likely to be quite resourceful about how to cope:

I spent the first month on the telephone. By that time, I had Amy connected to every retarded service in the Bronx and lower Westchester. There was never any question: my kid was gonna get the best special services the whole world had to offer. (Linda Hornstein, white special education consultant, mother of a six-year-old with Down syndrome)

When viewed from a wider context beyond the clinic, access to early intervention and its many services is a (relatively) new technology, too.[2]

Imagined Communities

The communities within which parents form alliances and receive support or judgement are not only geographically, professionally or religiously based: some are associational as well. Throughout this chapter, I have referred to some parents as activists; their particular activities, orientations and aspirations for their disabled children are powerfully reorganized by participation in support groups. Parents are encouraged by a host of professionals – geneticists and genetic counselors; pediatricians and social workers – to join voluntary family support groups. Such groups are historically rooted in at least three intersecting traditions. One historic precursor to these groups lies in the tradition of immigrant self-help groups of the late nineteenth century. These shared with Alcoholics Anonymous, a WASP invention of the 1930s, certain practices of what might be labeled "early-identity politics." A strong belief that "it takes one to know one", or, in this case, "to help one" was present in the birth of both those social movements. Endemic to this tradition is the valorization of "experience" (cf. Scott 1992) and the (often appropriately justified) suspicion of the availability or good-will of public agencies to solve what are widely perceived to be intractable problems and recurrent crises.

A second source of strategy and expertise initially emerged from the needs of disabled veterans with service-related chronic conditions. Many early charities and later research and service groups arose in conjunction with the Veterans' Administration (VA). Four major wars in the twentieth century have left the VA with both an enormous constituency, and a powerful, highly politicized budget-making process: expanding demands for medical care, pensions, employment and shelter have all been fueled by veterans' groups and the army of professionals who serve them (Young 1995). Developments in post-Second World War medicine also contributed dramatic resources: widespread use of antibiotics and rapid technical evolution in surgery and blood banking made survival after serious injury a common outcome. As these military experiments became successful, they diffused rapidly to the general population. There they had immense impact on accident survival rates (which affect young adults in disproportionate numbers), and babies born with hereditary conditions.

While many of the traditional service-related charities and organizations were fed by a decidedly masculinist ideology inflected through national military service, many of the care-takers and activists were mothers and wives, first of disabled veterans, and then of disabled children. As married women entered the paid labor force in greater numbers throughout the century, their voluntary and family-based care-taking became more visible; eventually, women became central activists in the movements which led to legislation guaranteeing not only medical but also educational resources for their disabled charges.

Additionally, national public interest in mental retardation was surely amplified by the well-publicized stories of the Kennedy family, beginning in the 1960s: an elder sister with mental retardation, and a child who died young with the same condition are part of the family legacy. So, too, are the scores of centers for research and clinical services to mentally retarded Americans which are found coast-to-coast. Many have been generously funded by the Kennedys, and some bear variants on their name. Legislative transformations in the Kennedy–Johnson years also affected the increase of Social Security coverage in the 1970s; and Section 504 of the National Rehabilitation Act of 1973 mandated that states cover an appropriate education for all handicapped children. The Americans with Disabilities Act of 1990, now winding its way into enforcement via federal and state regulations and court-based challenges, provides the most comprehensive protections to date.

Lay support groups clearly grew out of and responded to all these legal, medical and social developments. Self-help organizations for those with specific physical and mental health concerns (rather than generic veterans' groups, or research-service charities like the Easter Seal Society) are a relatively recent phenomenon, a product of the 1950s and 1960s, and becoming ever more specialized as more differentiating and disabling conditions take on specific medical nomenclature (Weiss and Mackta 1996). In this newer tradition of grouping and differentiating

support groups and networks according to diagnostic categories, there
are at least four important national organizations, and scores of state-
based and local associations, which grow from a fusion of familial and
professional concern with Down syndrome. The two largest national
organizations offer 800 telephone help-lines. The National Down Syndrome Congress was founded in 1971. It maintains a parent hotline,
publishes a newsletter, holds conventions and lobbies on national policy
issues. The National Down Syndrome Society, founded in 1979, raises
funds to support biomedical researchers whose work will enrich the
understanding of Down's. Both groups offer pamphlets, videos and
other resources which are widely available to parents of newly diagnosed
Down syndrome children. Local chapters of the ARC (formerly, the
Association of Retarded Citizens) and Down Syndrome Parent Support
Groups provide informal networks for parent-to-parent peer counseling.
Most early intervention programs have social workers and psychologists
on staff who specialize in the nuts and bolts of family support, including
the mazeway of medical and educational evaluations and paperwork
which accompanies access to the SSI and Medicaid funding to which
most disabled children are entitled. They also point parents toward the
local support groups (cf. Black and Weiss 1990). Ideally, by the time a
newly diagnosed baby leaves the hospital, the family should be hooked
up to such associational groups and services, where other parents and
professionals with long-standing experience will begin the process of
socializing them to life with a disabled child.

Local support groups offer rich and reassuring resources for parents
learning to normalize a child as a family member, not only as a medical
diagnosis. Paradoxically, as I hope to show, medical world-view and
resources figure large in the repertoire of such groups, even as they contest their exclusive dominion over definitions of disabled family members. New identities as well as new knowledge of services are modeled
by parent-activists for their recently conscripted peers. During the two
years in which I attended meetings of the Down Syndrome Parent Support Group of Manhattan and the Bronx, and occasional meetings of
other groups, I was particularly impressed by the many levels on which
parent peer support was mobilized and extended. For purposes of this
chapter, at least three should be mentioned. As its public face, the group
maintained a newsletter in which summaries of recent meetings and
announcements of future ones were publicized. In its pages, parents
might request specific information or help. At its monthly meetings, the
resources of cutting-edge biomedical research and scientific information
were regularly made available to the group. Researchers working on
chromosome 21, on the connection between Alzheimer and Down

syndrome, and on neuro-endocrinology all addressed the group. So did a host of clinical specialists and allied health professionals – neurologists, orthopedists, pediatric dentists, audiologists, speech therapists, physical and occupational therapists all gave presentations. Computer specialists in learning stimulation programs, behavioral psychologists, and representatives from state and municipal departments of education were among the invited speakers. With the aid of an array of professionals, activist parents tackled many problems in the realms of education and social services; cutting-edge medical and learning technologies were central to most of them. The group also sent representatives to various national conferences, sporting events and technology fairs from which they thought their membership could benefit. And they regularly heard reports on national legal and health policy issues affecting their families.

Of course, such projects involve far more work than can be accomplished by a few individuals at episodic meetings. In addition to countless hours clocked at subcommittee meetings, projects were also backed up by the existence and active use of a host of publications, including local newsletters, nationally distributed highly successful magazines like *Exceptional Parent* and *Exceptional Child*, and more vulnerable activist pulp magazines like *Disability Rag* and *This Mouth*. Technology, ranging from the most routinized – telephones, televisions, print media and fax machines – to the more elite – online services including chat groups, cyberspace newsletters, bibliographies and bulletin boards where regional, national and international conferences are announced (Ferguson 1996 for example) – is increasingly also part of the armamentarium of activist parental support. In all this work, the language of activism became deeply imbricated with that of science and technology.

This public face of activism was supplemented and transformed on at least two other levels. One concerned "human interest" meetings: adolescents with Down syndrome reporting on their aspirations for adulthood; a bar-mitzvah tape of a boy with Down syndrome whose successful speech therapy enabled him to participate in this congregational rite of passage; and a meeting on how to start a parent support group all drew large turn-outs. As several core activists told me, their own passionate concerns might lie in science-and-policy issues, but the crowd-drawing events were more likely to focus on uplifting experiences and success stories. The second transformatory activity of the group was not open to me directly, but I learned about it from the grateful stories parents of newly diagnosed babies told me: "old hands" were quickly mobilized whenever a social worker, relative, colleague or parent called for help. Using telephones, home visits, and occasionally, the offer of respite care, families who had made a successful adjustment to raising a child with Down syndrome offered empathic peer counseling to the newly afflicted. The first few weeks and months of family life with a diagnosed baby can be grim. Medical problems, some quite life-threatening, are likely to loom large. Until the advent of antibiotic drugs and infant surgery, 50 percent of children with Down syndrome died before their fifth birthday; 20 percent still do (Nadel and Rosenthal 1995). In addition to the stress and strain of "living on a medical roller coaster" (as several parents described it), there is the emotional strain of coming to terms with a child with a stigmatized difference. Peer counseling teaches parents how to cope with the ups and down of this transition. Using "been there" stories, "gallows humor," and the deep appreciation which comes from having survived something one could not otherwise have imagined, many parents provided a "buddy service" for newborns and their shocked families, making themselves available in creative ways. Collectively through their activism, parents of children with Down syndrome developed, deployed and transmitted a worldview in which difference could be accepted, and a new identity as parents of a different kind of child could be formulated and assumed.

Doubled Discourses

In attending public meetings, hearing uplifting success stories, and participating in peer counseling, parents who rely on support groups often come to speak a doubled discourse of both difference and normalization. On the one hand, they must individually come to terms with a baby who wasn't expected, a baby whose developmental trajectory is largely unknown, and known to be different from other family and community members. On the other hand, families in the support group are given a rich array of resources for the acceptance and incorporation of their Down syndrome children, and taught that they should have high aspirations for their success.

In describing this doubled trajectory of acceptance and normalization of difference, many parents told me a story which circulates widely among families with disabled children. I myself first heard it from activist Emily Kingsley at a parent support group. Some said an obstetrician or pediatrician first recounted the parable, while others attributed it to a caring nurse or social worker. It is xeroxed and distributed in many hospital pediatric wards:

Imagine you have planned a vacation to Italy, to see the rose gardens of Florence. You are totally excited, you have read all the guidebooks, your suitcases are packed, and off you go. As the plane lands, the pilot announces, "Sorry, ladies and gentlemen, but this flight has been rerouted to the Netherlands." At first you are very upset: the vacation you dreamed about has been canceled. But you get off the plane, determined to make the best of it. And you gradually discover that the blue tulips of Holland are every bit as pretty as the red roses you had hoped to see in Florence. They may not be as famous, but they are every bit as wonderful. You didn't get a red rose. But you got a blue tulip, and that's quite special, too.

This parable of acceptance glistens with metaphors of organic growth, planned and unplanned journeys, representational and contrastive colors, and evolving perception. Many parents shorthanded this parable when referring to something their disabled child had said or done, referring to "blue tulip" rewards. Nonetheless, even parents who accepted the language and constructs of "blue tulips" could also express the losses it entails:

I go along from day to day, marveling at what Stevie accomplishes. As long as he's home with me, I don't think he's slow, I just think he's growing and talking and learning. Now, he's counting to ten. Pretty soon, he's bound to be potty trained. Then once in a while, I'll take him to an office party or somewhere with other kids and I really get slapped in the face. Blue tulips, again and again. (Pat Carlson, white secretary, mother of a six-year-old with Down syndrome)

The parable of the blue tulip opens up for me a discussion of "doubled discourses," in which recognition of difference is substituted for judgements of abnormality, and enlightenment occurs. Like all metaphorical journeys of enlightenment, the one which many parents describe is time-consuming, fraught with tests and challenges and, of course, leads to great rewards. It entails a movement away from focusing on abnormality in their children to accepting differences variously described as physical, mental, emotional and, sometimes, spiritual. Thus the eye and facial bone structure, or low muscle tone so characteristic of Down syndrome becomes perceived as adorable and appealing rather than stigmatized in infants and toddlers; their eagerness and good humor are valued as signs of openness to experience rather than as simple-minded; their affectionate presence and ability to appeal to strangers are resignified as special "gifts" of a disabled child. In journeying narratives, doubled discourses provide maps, metaphors and images of the normal and abnormal, sometimes described in terms of sameness and difference, human and animal, or even innocence and savagery. Doubled discourses inform not only parental perceptions, but professional attitudes and activist aspirations as well.

As I became aware of these multiply sited doubled discourses expressed by a wide range of people among whom I worked in the course of this research, I initially tried to parse their grammar. But they

proved to be quite slippery. Their value statements may at first appear
to be starkly negative or positive, but explicitly or implicitly, they contain
a polarity marking the opposite value as well. They primarily rest on a
contrastive and exclusionary pair of images or processes in which ordinary common sense or hegemonic assumptions are embedded, marking
one element as normative and the other as abnormal. Intelligence in
children, to take an obvious example, is desirable and normal; mental
retardation is undesirable and problematic. Such polarized referents or
processes are highly malleable, providing linguistic resources for a wide
range of ideas and actions: mentally retarded children may be prized for
their "lack of guile" (to cite one parent). Most obviously, they may be
invoked to express dominant or hegemonic values like loathing or dis-
gust ("That child behaves like an animal!"); they may also be inverted
to mark an elevated, exceptional or romanticized status ("She's such an
innocent angel!"). At the same time, if less commonly, doubled discourses may provide the material from which resistant or new images
are forged. This is especially true when parents of disabled children
use the inclusive language of kinship to stake claims for their excluded
children's rights (Rapp 1995).

These ideas pertaining to doubled, hegemonic and resistant discourses are highly abstract, but the processes they describe are quite
concrete.[3] Nature/culture oppositions, for example, are commonly
found in the ordinary language with which mentally retarded children
are described by parents and professionals alike. Even those most committed to nurturing and serving developmentally delayed children spontaneously deploy nature/culture oppositions when they use the language
of animal imagery to merge them with other species:

Aleem was born with a lot of hair. I said, "Nurse, is this gonna fall off before I
bring him home from the hospital?" Because I didn't want nobody to look at
Aleem and think he was a little monkey, not a boy. (Johnella Cornell, African-
American hairdresser, mother of an infant with Down syndrome)

Having him in the house, it's like having a gorilla. (Cynthia Foreman, white law
professor, mother of a toddler with a chromosome anomaly)

Evolutionary Thought as Diagnostic Technology

Among the ten common characteristics used for medical diagnosis of
Down syndrome in newborns is the presence of a simian crease. The
label refers to a single deep fold which runs across the palm, common
among people with Down syndrome, in contrast to the multiple angular
folds which most people without this condition carry. The medical use
of the term "simian" carries with it a devolutionary implication: people

with Down syndrome share some physical characteristics with monkeys. Like the racial label of "mongol" to which I turn below, "simian" indexes similarities in its bearers which group and segregate them from people without this characteristic, recategorizing them as closer to the non-human primates than to their immediate human kin. Several parents alluded to the problem of "monkey business" in labeling this "stigmata" (another word still widely used in medical texts and practice to describe the signs of Down syndrome). One mother, however, inverted the discourse, resignifying the simian crease:

He's all heart, like he's such a lovely person, even now, he'll make me stop the car if his brother is crying, so he can get out of the car seat to hug him. He's pure love. He's right there in the moment, all 100 percent of him, which most normal people don't have that capacity . . . the simian crease, well, according to palmistry, there are two lines, the head and the heart. The two lines should go across, one's the head, one's the heart. And they (kids with Down syndrome) only have one. So it's like they're merged, the head and the heart, all in one line. And I think that's true of all Down syndrome people, right across the board. They're all heart. And it shows in the crease. (Judy Kaufman, white nurse, mother of a child with Down syndrome).

In her view, the purity of Down syndrome children's love, vested in their "heart," corresponds to the single, deep crease, when read through the counter-discourse of palmistry. A covertly negative label is thus reprocessed through an alternative grid to yield a positive attribute.

The idea that children with this condition are less evolved, hence closer to animals and to the "savage races" has a long history. Most famously, John Langdon Haydon Down, for whom the condition was medically named, served as the medical supervisor of the Earlswood Asylum for Idiots in Surrey, England for a decade beginning in 1858. Later, he ran a private home for retarded adults in Teddington until his death in 1897 (Brain 1967). In keeping with the humanist scientific fashions of his era, Down devoted considerable time to observing and categorizing his patients, whom he divided by what he perceived to be their similarities to various ethnic races. Some were classified as "Ethiopians," some as "Malay." But the largest group contained "Mongols," and it is worth considering Down's reasoning at some length:

A very large number of congenital idiots are typical Mongols. So marked is this that, when placed side by side, it is difficult to believe that the specimens compared are not children of the same parents . . . [He then describes hair, facial, skin and limb characteristics typical of the population under observation.]. . . The ethnic classification of idiocy which I indicated is of extreme interest philosophically as well as of value practically. Philosophically because it throws light on the question which very much agitated public opinion about the time of the American Civil War. The work of Nott and Glidden labored to prove that the various ethnic families were distinct species, and a strong argument was based on this to justify a certain domestic institution [RR: slavery]. If, however, it can be shown that from some deteriorating influence the children of Caucasian parents can be removed into another ethnic type, it is a strong corroborative argument that the difference is a variable and not a specific one. (Down, 1877 86: 210–17; 213)

Down's classification thus exhibits a doubled discourse which has perhaps "gone underground," but is by no means banished from popular understanding: on the one hand, "defectives" and "idiots" resemble races which are ranked (here, by the English) as inferior to "Caucasians." Retarded people and exotic races are thus condensed together as evolutionary throw-backs to a prior, intellectually inferior stage. This is the dominant message of the racial classification of retarded patients, and the one which continues to be projected whenever the label of "mongoloid" is used, as it was in the USA in medical books through the 1970s, and through the 1980s in analogous texts in England (Lippman and Brunger 1991; Gould 1980). While most educated people no longer use the term, it is widely recognized and carries with it the condensation of racial exoticism and mental inferiority. On the other hand, John Down's argument is entirely in the liberal universalist tradition, for he used the fantasized racial classification of his patients to argue for monogenism, a theory then in decline, that the human race was singular and unified. "Mongoloid idiots" (as he labeled them) illustrate a principle which weakens the justification for racially based slavery because those who appear to belong to a different race are actually offspring of Caucasians. When viewed from the end of the twentieth century, racial hierarchy dominates this scheme, and there remain pressing reasons for extinguishing the racial epithet "mongoloid" as inaccurate as well as deeply biased. But from a contemporary perspective, humanist inclusion as well as hierarchy also lay behind the racial connections Down traced out.[4] Likewise, other medical writers from the third quarter of the nineteenth century onward commented on the affectionate personalities and amiable humor of people with Down syndrome. Such commentary suggests that scientific practitioners and authors were no less heir to deeply held cultural imagery than were their less-educated contemporaries. To belabor an obvious point: we need to recognize that today's biomedical and social scientists, too, live through and in the socio-cultural horizons of their own times, including its genetic and prenatal testing technologies.

   If people with Down syndrome are metaphorized as closer to animals, nature, the "lower races" and mysterious innocents, they then also illustrate an older grand narrative scheme concerning the childhood of the human race. Elements of this narrative date back to the Greeks; aspects were reprocessed through the sieve of science to yield "ontogeny recapitulates phylogeny" in the nineteenth-century. Particular organisms can then be viewed as representing immature stages in a wider scheme of development. Metaphorically, certain adult groups may represent humanity's infancy: arrested in their development like fossil flies in amber, they are then thought to characterize a "purer" or more "original" state of being human. Pathological adults who are members of the dominant races may then be viewed as "throw backs" to prior developmental stages (Gould 1980). Like the "primitive societies" which fascinated nineteenth-century armchair anthropologists, infantilized populations condense many Western preoccupations: innocence before the Fall; or, in more secular parlance, pure feelings and perceptions rather than world-weary sophistication; or even states of permanent and childlike psychological and social dependency rather than the painful trade-offs involved in growth and development.

While I am claiming that the problem of infantilization is linked to pervasive evolutionary paradigms in the history of Western intellectual thought, many authors and activists concerned with disability rights contest a more straightforward present-day version of this problem. They have objected to the infantilization of disabled people in general: criticisms have been leveled against a wide range of "disabling images," including "Jerry's Kids"-style telethons; Poster Children as fundraisers; and, more grimly, the rigid and punitive practices of enforced dependency encoded in more than a century's history of institutions designed to both protect and contain disabled citizens; and in policies and laws limiting the autonomy and choices – in education, jobs, housing, and even sexual, reproductive and marital relations (Shapiro 1993; Finger 1990). This discourse of infantilization in all its complexity is particularly salient in representations of mentally retarded children, especially those with Down syndrome. Parents of disabled children fall heir to this complex discursive heritage for they spontaneously speak a doubled discourse of both accepting difference and actively working for normalization. Indeed, as many of the stories recounted in this essay suggest, activist parents are particularly articulate in deploying both sides of this world-view.

Activists and Non-Activists

But support groups do not reach or represent all parents of Down syndrome children. Indeed, during the two years in which I attended support group meetings, participation ranged from a "handful" of parents to audiences of thirty or forty adults in the room. Mothers from two-parent families were most likely to be in attendance; fewer fathers, and by far fewer single parents regularly came to meetings. Organizers told me that a core of about ten families did the work of the group, maintaining mailing lists of several hundred families who had requested information. At the time I conducted field research, similarly activist support groups were found in three of New York City's five boroughs. But most parents of children with Down syndrome do not participate in support groups. In New York City, active members are likely to be middle-class, most likely to be white, and parents of first children, or parents with the financial resources to use a host of commercial services, including nannies and babysitters. Parents whose child with Down syndrome is a younger sibling; who do not have much discretionary time or income; or who come from other community backgrounds where church or ethnic-group affiliation provide strong paths to social participation are far less likely to rely on the support groups as they integrate their disabled children. As these issues of discretionary time and income suggest, class-based differences surely figure in support group activism. But class is here mediated (and, sometimes, contradicted) through other, more "experience near" (Geertz 1967) sensibilities. As several social workers involved in Down syndrome services suggested, middle-class and professional parents are far more likely to take on a "voluntary" associational identity on behalf of their children than are working-class families. Perhaps middle-class comfort with "associational identity" is strengthened by prior professional experiences, or the proclivity to seek intellectually rational solutions to intractable personal problems. Some social workers, more comfortable than I am with a psychodynamic explanation, rendered the judgement that "those activists are too involved" with the issue of how Down syndrome has transformed their own identities: "Why don't they just get on with it?," was a question asked by several (cf. Bérubé 1996).[5]

Several marginally active members of parent support groups offered social analyses of their own, describing both the class leveling (of misfortune) and the class privilege (of resources) which united and separated them from many activist leaders:

You know, I just go to a few meetings a year, not too many. First of all, it's geared for new parents, the ones with babies and toddlers. I know all that stuff already. But second, I like to go because it really blows my mind, you know, if you think it was hard for us to accept a different kind of kid, imagine if you were like some of these people who thought you were gonna have a boy or girl with their lacrosse shirts, you know, that would go to Ivy League schools, that's how you always pictured it, and then this happened. . . I kind of like to be in a room with them once in a while because I think it changes them for the better.

It's not that I would hate them or despise them, it isn't that, at all. But if this thing that happened to them hadn't happened, well, we'd have absolutely nothing in common. (Judy Kaufman, white nurse, mother of a child with Down syndrome).

Patsy DelVecchio, a recovering alcoholic, offered both a class polemic and a commentary on the coercive, identity-encompassing aspects of support group membership when she said,

I'm very critical, you know. I cannot see myself sitting with a bunch of petty little women, talking about their children like they were some kind of topic of conversation. This is just life. You don't have to publicize, nor to condemn. You get a lot of mothers that's behaving just like in AA, like, "Yeah, I'm an alcoholic." "Yeah, I'm the mother of a Down's child that doesn't walk, doesn't talk, doesn't do this or that and I have no time." You make time, lady, I say, you just make time. As far as going to meetings for parents with Down's syndrome children, it's ludicrous. You get these Park Avenue high society women with charge accounts saying, "I have my daughter at the institute, I have a private tutor for my daughter." Just like they say, "I go shopping at Bloomies." [RR: Bloomingdale's.] Lady, I wish I could afford your nanny. Meanwhile, they sit at meetings talking, "I have a Down syndrome child, Oh my child has slanted eyes, well, my child's tongue curls." He's not a freak, you're talking about a human being. Right, wrong or indifferent, it's just life, and I wouldn't treat it any differently.

In addition to considerable class resentment, it is easy to spot a resistance to what Patsy DelVecchio takes to be self-promotion through identifying with difference. It is normalization through acceptance, not emphasis of difference, that she favors in this commentary.

Several working-class non-activists also expressed a rather different sensibility concerning aspirations for their children with Down syndrome. Unlike those who strategize for what they consider to be the best educational resources, nurse-aide Anna Morante replied to my questions concerning her son's future:

What does it mean to have this child? That I will be a mother forever, that this one will never leave home. That's ok, I'm glad I'll have him with me forever. Only I worry if I die before he does. I don't want anything else from the schools, there's no point in that. He's happiest right here at home, where I can take care of him.

And both an African-American welfare mother and a white secretary told me they didn't want help struggling with the Board of Education's bureaucracy to improve school placement: "Not everybody wants to fight City Hall," the secretary told me.

In offering these descriptions from the margins of parent activism, I should stress that the majority of non-activist parents remained deeply appreciative of support group resources. And they were as concerned about the health and happiness of their disabled children as their activist peers. Their strongest reasons for not attending meetings or participating in informal networks with other parents of children with Down syndrome were overwhelmingly focused on time constraints. But they were also far less likely to express mainstreaming aspirations for the futures of their Down syndrome children, and also less comfortable with the idea of representing themselves as parents of disabled children.

Bio-Techno-Sociality?

The connections between biomedical and technicist discourses and familial knowledge stand at the center of this chapter. I have implicitly argued that our understandings of new biomedical technologies are significantly enhanced when we examine them in a wide social framework, and do not confine our investigation to the clinic. This broader perspective enables us to see technologies in play, as they are understood, appropriated and occasionally resisted by the parties who deploy them. I am particularly interested in how a language of science (and social science) harking back to nineteenth-century evolutionary thought and forward to molecular biology is incorporated, and occasionally contested in the fund of social knowledge which families of children with Down syndrome develop. As I have tried to show throughout this essay, modern community-based public institutions like early intervention programs and parent support groups offer powerful resources for parents to become scientifically literate as they seek the best possible services and outcomes for their children. In the process, they also normalize biomedical definitions of the problems and solutions within which a disabling condition is assimilated into family and community life.

Parents (and children) who resculpt their identities using the resources of peer support groups are participating in a process which Paul Rabinow has labeled "biosociality," the forging of a collective identity under the emergent categories of biomedicine and allied sciences (1992). Throughout this chapter I have also tried to describe older and deeper traditions of doubled discourses through which children labeled abnormal or anomalous can be reconfigured and integrated into social life. Biomedicine provides discourses with hegemonic claims over this social territory, encouraging enrollment in the categories of biosociality. Its influential technologies provide precise diagnoses, clinical interventions and statistical pictures of risk and benefit for those who live under the sign of difference. In an emergent world-view of geneticization (Lippman 1991), new claims on identity are powerfully produced through biotechnical interventions. Yet these claims do not go uncontested. Religious orientations and practices, informal folk beliefs, class-based and ethnic traditions as well as scientifically inflected counter discourses also lay claim to the interpretation of extra chromosomes. Moreover, not all families of children with Down syndrome rely on support groups, nor are all families equally likely to traffic in scientific world-views and categories. At stake in the analysis of the traffic between biomedical and familial discourses is an understanding of the inherently uneven seepage of technoscience and its multiple uses and transformations into contemporary social life.

NOTES

Acknowledgements: funding for this study was provided by: the National Endowment for the Humanities, the National Science Foundation, the Rockefeller Foundation's "Changing Gender Roles Program," the Institute for Advanced Studies, the Spencer Foundation, and a semester's sabbatical from the Graduate Faculty, New School for Social Research. I am deeply grateful for their support, and absolve them from any responsibility for the uses to which I have put it. I especially thank the scores of pregnant women, health care providers and family members who took the time and energy to engage my research questions. Pseudonyms have been used when quoting directly from interviews and conversations.

1. Other aspects of this study are discussed in Rapp 1988, 1993, 1995, 1998, 1999; Marfatia et al. 1991.
2. The work of Alice Hayden and her colleagues which pioneered infant stimulation for developmentally delayed young children dates from the 1970s.
3. The influence of Raymond Williams's analysis (1977) of language-borne traditions of political and cultural agency deserves acknowledgement here.
4. A conversation with Susan Gal and Brackette Williams in 1993 suggested the importance of unraveling the racialized term "mongoloid." I thank them both for their recommendation.
5. In opening his stunningly philosophical and compellingly personal account of family life with a child who has Down syndrome, Michael Bérubé notes that on his son's neonatal intensive care unit chart, nurses had written, "parents intellectualizing." Reasonably enough, he asked, "Why not?," while beginning his discussion of the ever-expanding field of medical, educational and social knowledge he and his wife Janet Lyon had to learn as they came to grips with their son's condition (Bérubé 1996).

REFERENCES

Bérubé, Michael 1996 *Life as we Know It: A Father, a Family, and an Exceptional Child.* New York: Pantheon.
Black, R. B., and J. O. Weiss 1990 "Genetic Support Groups and Social Workers as Partners." *Health and Social Work* 15(2): 91–9.

Brain, L. 1967 "Chairman's Opening Remarks: Historical Introduction." In G. E. W. Wolstenholme and R. Porter (eds.), *Mongolism*. CIBA Foundation Study Group, 25. Boston: Little Brown and Company, pp. 1–5.

Ferguson, T. 1996 *Health Online: How to Find Health Information, Support Groups, and More in Cyberspace*. Reading, MA: Addison-Wesley.

Finger, A. 1990 *Past Due: A Story of Disability, Pregnancy and Birth*. Seattle: Seal Press.

Geertz, Clifford 1967 " 'From the Native's Point of View': On the Nature of Anthropological Understanding." In K. H. Basso and H. A. Selby (eds.), *Meaning in Anthropology*. Albuquerque, NM: School of American Research Press/University of New Mexico, pp. 221–38.

Gould, Stephen Jay 1980 "Dr. Down's Syndrome." In *The Panda's Thumb: More Reflections in Natural History*. New York: W. W. Norton, pp. 160–8.

Lippman, Abby 1991 "Prenatal Genetic Testing and Screening: Constructing Needs and Reinforcing Inequities." *American Journal of Law and Medicine* 17(1 & 2): 15–50.

Lippman, Abby and F. Brunger 1991 "Constructing Down Syndrome: Texts as Informants." *Santé Culture Health* 8(1–2): 109–31.

Marfatia, L., D. Punales-Morejon and R. Rapp 1990 "When an Old Reproductive Technology Becomes a New Reproductive Technology: Serving Underserved Populations". *Birth Defects* 26:109–126.

Nadel, L. and D. Rosenthal (eds.), 1995 *Down Syndrome: Living and Learning in the Community*. New York: John Wiley.

Rabinow, Paul 1992 "Artificiality and Enlightenment: From Sociobiology to Biosociality." In Jonathan Crary and Sanford Kwinter (eds.), *Incorporations*. New York: Zone (distrib: MIT Press), pp. 234–52.

Rapp, Rayna 1988 "Chromosomes and Communication: The Discourse of Genetic Counseling." *Medical Anthropology Quarterly* 2(1): 27–45.

(1993) "Accounting for Amniocentesis" In Shirley Lindenbaum and Margaret Lock (eds.), *Knowledge, Power and Practice: The Anthropology of Medicine and Everyday Life. Comparative Studies of Health Systems and Medical Care*. Berkeley, Los Angeles, London: University of California Press, pp 55–76.

1995 "Heredity, or: Revising the Facts of Life." In S. Yanagisako and C. Delaney (eds.), *Naturalizing Power: Essays in Feminist Cultural Analysis*. New York: Routledge, pp. 69–86.

1998 "Refusing Prenatal Diagnosis: The Uneven Meanings of Bioscience in a Multicultural World." *Science, Technology, and Human Values* 23(1): 45–70.

1999 *Testing Women, Testing the Fetus: the Social Impact of Amniocentesis in America*. New York: Routledge.

Rothman, B. K. 1986 *The Tentative Pregnancy: Prenatal Diagnosis and the Future of Motherhood*. New York: W. W. Norton.

Scott, Joan W. 1992 "Experience." In Judith Butler and Joan W. Scott (eds.), *Feminists Theorize the Political*. New York: Routledge, pp. 22–40.

Shapiro, J. 1993 *No Pity: How the Disability Rights Movement is Changing America*. New York: Times Books.

Sutherland, G. A. 1900 "The Differential Diagnosis of Mongolism and Cretinism in Infancy." *The Lancet* 6 January: 23–24.

Trainer, Marilyn 1991 *Differences in Common: Straight Talk on Mental Retardation, Down Syndrome, and Life*. Rockville, MD: Woodbine House.

Weiss, J. O. and J. Mackta 1996 *How to Start and Sustain Genetic Support Groups*. Baltimore: Johns Hopkins University Press.

Williams, Raymond 1977 *Marxism and Literature*. Oxford: Oxford University Press.

Young, Allan 1995 *The Harmony of Illusions: Inventing Post-Traumatic Stress Disorder*. Princeton, NJ: Princeton University Press.

10 When explanations rest: "good-enough" brain science and the new socio-medical disorders

Joseph Dumit

Explanations come to an end somewhere.
(Wittgenstein 1972 [1953]: 1)

Wittgenstein's opening to *Philosophical Investigations* points to a fundamental crisis in scientific and medical research: When is there enough explanation of a phenomenon to consider it settled and definable? If a cluster of symptoms – say dizziness, itching, extreme fatigue and weakness – afflicts a group of persons working together, what kind of explanation is good enough? Is finding a food they all ate, or common exposure to a rare gas, or a common brain pattern enough to say, "Okay, that is it"? Or is locating a certain gene they all share, or a drug that relieves some of the symptoms enough? What if only four out of five share the characteristic? Or yet again, do we need the entire pathophysiology of each symptom?

The fact that different people answer these questions differently points to the social location of these questions. The very meaning of "definable illness" and especially the entailments of that definition – whether a person with symptoms receives help or blame or dismissal – depend upon who is doing the assessing, where they are doing it from, and within what regime of social good and compassion they are operating. We may not like the implication that a person is sick in one place but not in another, but socially this may be a fact.

In this paper I begin an ethnographic characterization of what is *shared* across a set of contested fields I call the new socio-medical disorders. Under this name, I include Attention Deficit Disorder (ADD), Chronic Fatigue Syndrome (CFS), Gulf War Syndrome (GWS), Multiple Chemical Sensitivity or Environmental Illness (MCS) and, to a lesser extent, Post-Traumatic Stress Disorder (PTSD), schizophrenia and depression. Each of these has been and continues to be the object of anthropological, sociological and psychological studies. Each is very different from the others in terms of history, demographics and the social location of controversies.[1] Nonetheless, all of these conditions share the following characteristics:

1. They are "biomental": their nature and existence are contested as to whether they are primarily mental, psychiatric or biological.
2. They are causally undetermined: their etiology is likewise contested as to social, genetic, toxic and individual responsibilities.
3. They are "biosocial": persons having these conditions are organized, coordinated and feel a kinship based on their shared experience.[2]
4. They are legally explosive: each condition is caught up in court battles, administrative categorization and legislative maneuvering. Disability status, for instance, is haphazardly applied.
5. They are therapeutically diverse: the nature and reimbursement of competing therapies, including alternative medicine, is wide open.
6. They are cross-linked: each of these conditions has been linked to the other ones as subsets, mistaken diagnosis, and comorbid conditions.
7. Functional brain imaging is contested: brain scans (PET, SPECT and MRI)[3] play a significant role in staging the objectivity of each of the first six characteristics for each of these conditions, and is highly contested.

My interest in these disorders is in trying to understand how and why they have come to share these characteristics, and what this sharing implies about the landscape of biomedicine and suffering in the US today. The level of medical, social, legal, scientific and economic disorder implied by these seven characteristics must not be underestimated. Each of these conditions is a serious matter not only for the persons afflicted, but also for the thousands of physicians, researchers, corporations, insurance and administrative agencies having to deal with them. Yet, except perhaps for schizophrenia and depression, very little mainstream biomedical research has been carried out. Fights over definitions, diagnosis, response and prevention depend disproportionately on a small amount of research, much of it underfunded. In the absence of definitive answers, control of the very questions to be asked is also highly contested.

Drawing on studies of each individual illness, my project is to analyze the contested cultural field that helps to shape these illnesses from the outside as socio-medical disorders. By following the ways brain imaging circulates through the various sites of medicine, insurance, the Internet and courts, I begin to make explicit how scans and other biological evidence are usually not the final word on these disorders. Instead, they function *locally* as *temporary* resting places for explanations. At stake, even in my ethnographic descriptions, are the status of these brain imaging studies, and further, who has the right or ability to pass judgement on their status. What criterion, for instance, is sufficient to show significant differences between two groups? What method of analysis is good enough? Is PET or SPECT ready yet? I am not attempting to answer these questions here for two reasons. First, there are already *too many answers out there, competing*, and at best I could only echo one of these. Second, the *criteria for evaluation vary by site*. I am therefore trying to track the siting of the questions and the various attempts to frame and reframe the value and significance of different techniques within each site.

In this paper, I will first use the example of a particular contest over Boeing Corporation's role in defining and accounting for MCS in a factory in the state of Washington, to point out the many layers of social control that intersect in these illnesses. I then focus on the key role of brain imaging in these contests, how it comes to be so important and so controversial. I conclude with a discussion of how communities that have gathered around these disorders have become active participants in both the dissemination of research findings amongst themselves and publicly, and in the activity of research itself. In many cases, including the Boeing story below, the Internet has become a crucial medium for the exchange, collaboration and archiving of information and strategies regarding these illnesses. Where possible, I have provided Internet sites for locating these.

It's All in Boeing's Head

Disputes do not break out . . . over the question whether a rule has been obeyed or not. People don't come to blows over it, for example. That is part of the framework on which the working of our language is based. . .
"So you are saying that human agreement decides what is true and what is false?" – It is what human beings say that is true and false; and they agree in the language they use. That is not agreement in opinions but in form of life. (Wittgenstein 1972 [1953]: 240–1, my emphasis)

Between 1988 and 1989 at least 100 workers at a classified Boeing factory had enough symptoms including skin rashes, respiratory tract irritation, memory lapses and irritability to seek out medical attention.[4] At another plant, working with a known (to Boeing) toxic substance, many workers also came down with similar symptoms. In the worst of these cases, workers developed extreme sensitivity to many chemicals commonly used in cities and homes, necessitating elaborate precautions in terms of lifestyle. On top of trying to live with these symptoms, they also tried to obtain medical attention and diagnosis from their insurer's doctors. Since Washington is a self-insured state, Boeing was their insurer, and therefore Boeing decided what would count as a job-caused condition, as a disability, and as worker compensation. Most of the afflicted workers were examined and told that their symptoms were most likely "in their heads," directly implying that they were at fault for these symptoms, or certainly that Boeing was not at fault. Some women, for instance, were told that they were "just having a bad case of PMS" (Nelson and Worth 1994: 8). As they began to fight these diagnoses, often resorting to outside physicians and researchers, the workers became involved in a much larger struggle over the research and diagnosis of MCS. Two reporters from the *Washington Free Press* summarize the Kafka-esque situation of these workers.

the furious medical debate surrounding MCS has complicated matters for people who suffer from the condition. Because there's no medical consensus on what causes MCS, or how to diagnose or treat it, the state's "objectivity" test is nearly impossible for MCS patients to pass.

Plus, MCS is not recognized by the international body that categorizes diseases and illnesses. So even if a worker can "objectively" show that workplace chemicals caused him or her to contract MCS, Boeing and the Department of Labor and Industries [L&I] will reject the claim.

Making matters still worse, Boeing has a policy of refusing to pay for the tests customarily used by Dr. Gordon Baker and other specialists to diagnose MCS. This is because Boeing and the state Labor and Industries department do not recognize these tests as "objective" ways of diagnosing MCS, which is also not yet recognized by Boeing or L&I. (Nelson and Worth 1994)

As part of the attempt to diagnose MCS, many of the patients sought out SPECT scans (single photon emission computed tomography), a kind of functional brain imaging that produces three-dimensional images of bloodflow. These scans are similar to PET scans (positron emission tomography), but of much lower resolution and are less expensive to produce. There had been some published studies "showing" that SPECT found substantially more "abnormalities" in the brains of MCS patients compared with normal controls. Boeing, as the insurer, however, in most cases refused to pay for the scans and refused to accept the results.

In addition, Boeing, in collaboration with the University of Washington conducted a study led by Dr. Gregory Simon that concluded that MCS patients primarily suffered from psychological problems (Simon 1994; Nelson 1994a: 10).[5] Other researchers, also funded in part by Boeing, not only argued for the psychological nature of MCS, but also argued against the use of tests such as brain imaging to help diagnose it. For many MCS sufferers as well as some researchers and the *Washington Free Press*, it seemed that potentially critical tests were being excluded a priori.

At issue in this struggle is the existence of a syndrome or disease, the definitions of its diagnosis, treatments, and its etiology: Is it? What is it? How can it be treated? What causes it? At stake are legitimation of sick roles,[6] self-respect, research dollars, scientific careers, and millions of dollars in litigation. In this climate, the role of social constructionist arguments – that an illness is defined or manifested socially – often serve the conservative function of denying that the illnesses "really" exist, and preventing any resources from being allocated to those suffering. The problem is that there are too many answers but no consensus on the questions.

For example, at a 1994 conference on MCS attended by almost all of the major players on both sides of the Boeing case, one researcher presented a paper that first dismissed the possibility that MCS was "real" and then proceeded to argue that MCS symptoms were quite possibly the result of worker–management tensions.

Poor worker–management relations, interpersonal conflict at home, and other forms of stress or pressure can exacerbate physical symptoms. People in settings where they are unable to directly address the causes of their tension may be forced to look elsewhere to define their symptoms. For example, a person who has a specialized job with an abusive boss may not be able to acknowledge the tremendous tension brought about by his/her boss. *An alternative label for this tension might be illness or MCS.* (Pennebaker 1994: 505–7, emphasis added)

Significantly, Pennebaker is making an argument that is structurally identical to the one made by medical anthropologist Arthur Kleinman in *Social Origins of Distress and Disease* (1986). Kleinman argues that for many Chinese patients with neurasthenia, the mental, emotional and physical abuse they suffered during the Cultural Revolution may be the cause. The illness may be the manifestation of this abuse. Practically, however, the implications for these two views are opposed. Neurasthenia in China during Kleinman's fieldwork is considered by the state and general population as a real illness, and the abuse-as-illness receives sympathy and treatment, including compensation and rest. Pennebaker's analysis, however – speculative rather than empirical – reduces MCS to "nothing but stress" and thereby specifically disallows any but the most rudimentary care and little sympathy. Shadowing Pennebaker's statements is the clear implication that these supposed MCS sufferers are faking it.

Parallel to Pennebaker, the Boeing-paid psychologist Gregory Simon calls for an end to psychiatric studies including brain scans, "because they confuse the issue." He is apparently respecting the notion that mental illness categories can do more harm than good for those saddled with them. He then declares that the current political–legal–economic climate precluded objective research on MCS:

Current policies for compensating liability and disability claims are a definite impediment to research on neuropsychiatric aspects of chemical sensitivity. In many cases, toxic mechanisms of injury are compensable while behavioral mechanisms are not. Given these policies, most patients and treating clinicians have strong incentives to emphasize neurotoxicity as the explanation for symptoms of anxiety and depression. Employers, insurers, and industry have equally strong incentives to emphasize behavioral mechanisms or preexisting psychopathology in order to reduce costs of compensation. Those with vested interest may over-interpret research data on psychiatric symptoms in chemical sensitivity as proving or disproving particular theories of pathophysiology. This political environment leaves little room for impartial research. (Simon 1994: 494)

A cynical reading of this incisive passage is that it seeks to sustain current uncertainty over the status of MCS, denigrating existing SPECT studies along with Simon's own psychological studies. Such a strategy, if it succeeded, would thus continue to prevent MCS sufferers from obtaining "objective" proof of and compensation for their condition, especially since further research is not being pursued. As Buck Cameron, a member of the Department of Labor and Industries pointed out: "[Boeing's in-house Health and Safety] Institute is supposed to be studying the possible connections between the symptoms of sick workers and chemicals used in Boeing plants. So far, it hasn't happened" (Nelson and Worth 1994: 14).

Nelson and Worth also quote Meg Much, a former worker at the Institute: "The company is not interested in making that link. . . When you get down to finding scientific evidence, nobody wants to do it" (Nelson and Worth 1994: 14). These lines are drawn as follows: on one hand, the MCS sufferers are arguing that the preliminary evidence suggests (1) a need for further study, and (2) in the meantime, they should get the benefit of the doubt and some compassion and treatment. On the other hand, Boeing seems to be arguing that (1) in the absence of definitive (not preliminary) proof, it should not have to do anything; and (2) it has a right not to pursue research that risks its own financial loss.[7] The issue of companies and possibly governments or societies not wanting to research risks raises the issue of the right not to know. Though it may seem wrong to connect the issue of corporate knowledge with that of individuals at genetic risk for an illness (such as Huntington's), even unions representing workers are wary of the potential bankrupting of a company that employs hundreds of thousands of workers. Similarly, sympathetic research scientists within large companies must attend to the legal ramifications of their research.

The concern about the litigation consequences of doing research, from the law side of our corporation [a chemical industry carpet manufacturer], is a major stumbling block. I think that maybe, after looking at some well-conceived research protocols with good design, we scientist types can try and be persuasive to the legal types who are hysterical about it, and see if we can get them down off the chandelier. (*Toxicology and Industrial Health* 1994: 659)

In the absence of industry-funded research, and recognizing the meager, underfunded studies of MCS, sufferers are left in the dark as to where to go next. These passages point to the fundamental situation wherein money, explanations, research and theories become aligned and in opposition to each other. Wittgenstein's implication in the epigraph to this section is that people might come to blows where there is no agreement on forms of life and the language used to define the rules. "If language is to be a means of communication there must be agreement not only in definitions but also (queer as this may sound) in judgments" (Wittgenstein 1972 [1953]: 242). Each of the new socio-medical disorders involves a struggle toward a new language and for the establishment of a form of life of suffering from the disorder.

In the Boeing struggle, the scans are like words whose rules of usage are unclear and unsettled because the forms of life – the rules and judgements – are not agreed upon. Each institutional site – a doctor's office, an insurance agency, a health institute, a court – becomes a place where rules and judgements are made, not simply obeyed. These rules include what tests count as objective evidence. These judgements include whether or not a particular disease is worth studying. One consequence of this is that these non-scientific locations become local obligatory passage points for what counts as the facts of the matter.

Geography is Elsewhere

Biopolitical modes of fields of power are those which determine what counts in public life, what counts as a citizen, and so on. We cannot escape the salience of the biological discourses for determining life chances in the world – who's going to live and die, things like that . . . (Haraway interviewed in Penley and Andrew 1986: 11)[8]

I would like to use Donna Haraway's (1986) notion that geography is elsewhere to cut through the idea that facts can be settled in one place and be true once and for all everywhere. Rather, I think, it is often the case that the meaning of an event locally is decided somewhere else, that facts settled in one place are not settled in others, and that the venue of adjudication is often more important than the evidence available. In the case of the new socio-medical disorders, I am proposing that the reality of these illnesses as biological diseases is not settled by looking toward the geography of the brain, but elsewhere, in disability hearings, insurance companies and individual doctors' offices.

The Boeing/MCS case is not the only time when legal-insurance adjudication takes over the definition of illness and disease. Many health care regulations unfortunately still refuse to take mental illness seriously and embody a profound suspicion of malingering. Benefits for mental illness are often restricted in terms of time and cost. Recent research, especially brain imaging and genetics that demonstrate the biological nature of mental illness, have been creatively used by sufferers and their families.

For instance: in the first case of its type, a father sued Arkansas Blue Cross and Blue Shield for increased coverage for the care of his daughter, who was hospitalized for bipolar disorder. His insurance policy provided for extensive coverage for physical conditions but limited coverage for "mental, psychiatric or nervous" disorders. The plaintiff argued that bipolar disorder is a biological disorder and therefore should be considered "physical" under the terms of the policy. In this case, *Arkansas Blue Cross and Blue Shield v. Doe*, the courts ruled that bipolar disorder "is a physical condition within the meaning of the Blue Cross contract" (Office of Technology Assessment 1992: 161–2).

The institutional response to this litigation is perhaps predictable. After the court found in favor of the father, Blue Cross and Blue Shield rewrote their contract so that it explicitly defined bipolar disorder as a mental and not physical illness. In this case, contract law allows Blue Cross to make a list of what they will count as mental illness and include bipolar disorder on it. They can then cover it as such, regardless of popular or scientific definitions. Since another insurance carrier might treat bipolar disorder as a physical illness, it is clear that "facts" such as whether bipolar is physical or mental are not simply discovered and then universally known. Rather, they are quite unevenly known and even the criteria of proof can vary from site to site.

With regard to the new socio-medical disorders, these varieties of factual status are multiplied again by the different state-level and administrative court systems. Shelia Jasanoff (1995), for instance, has persuasively demonstrated that legal notions of scientific proof, consensus and implication differ considerably from most scientists' notions. Moreover, alongside Nelkin and Tancredi (1988), she has shown that (1) the courts' definition of scientific truth is historically variable and (2) it has tended toward a greater and greater emphasis on "hard," objective, neutral and automatically generated evidence. At the administrative level, for instance, the office of Housing and Urban Development (HUD) and the Social Security Administration (SSA) have already declared MCS as a kind of disability under the 1980 Americans with Disabilities Act (ADA), thus allowing MCS sufferers the right to live in toxic-free environments (Frisch 1994: 4). But disability law judges, like criminal court judges, demand objective findings, especially with emerging illnesses (Heuser and Heuser 1991). The relative autonomy of each administrative agency – SSA, HUD, insurance, HMO, Worker's Comp – and the fragmentation between federal and state authority in the US create a variegated landscape of opportunity and frustration for all parties involved in delimiting these socio-medical disorders.

For sufferers and their families, this landscape of differential diagnosis can provide an opportunity for them to help control the answers by *changing the venue* where the questions are asked. Biological definitions, especially the demonstrative proof of brain imaging, provide the objective basis for declaring a kind of kinship among sufferers. Similar to the genetic diseases Rabinow (1992) has discussed, each of the socio-medical disorders has its own organized support groups, lobbying efforts and other institutional forms for communicating and advocating kinship based on objectively shared biological attributes. Once organized, even in very loose networks, they are able to share strategies and tactics for responding to a generalized cultural and bureaucratic unwillingness to acknowledge their suffering. The Internet, for instance, is one of the key sites for this kind of dispersed organization.

For example, a 1990 article (Zametkin et al. 1990) showing brain abnormalities with PET in ADD adults sparked the construction of a Compuserve Forum dedicated to ADD that went online in 1993. It was immediately a huge success with 7,000 members in eight months and over 200 messages a day (Schwartz 1995). To provide some sense of the scale of this kind of interaction, the USENET online newsgroup <alt.med.cfs> (for CFS sufferers) received over 54,000 messages during the two years from mid-1995 to mid-1997. During that same time, the <alt.med.adhd> newsgroup (for Attention Deficit Disorder) received over 74,000 messages.[9] Each of the other disorders also has many other online support forums as well as more formal organizations.

The Internet, in these cases, provides a means for geographically dispersed sufferers to asynchronously share not only experiences, news, references and resources, but also *strategies* for dealing with physicians, insurance, HMOs and other bureaucracies. One Internet file, for instance, notes that sufferers of CFS in Canada can use SPECT findings of brain abnormalities to obtain a diagnosis of Major Acquired Brain Dysfunction, which insurers will pay for, rather than CFS which insurers do not cover (Carpman 1993: 2). Another source of information distribution is the Frequently-Asked-Questions document (FAQ). The FAQ for CFS runs to some thirty-five pages and is updated approximately every three months (Burns 1996). It includes a pointer to explicit instructions on "Dealing with Doctors When You Have CFS" (Cracchiolo 1995). This document instructs a sufferer in how to do homework on the condition and have citations and xeroxed articles organized and handy for the visit. It also suggests that one should remember that one may need to make a legal case for disability and therefore may be dependent upon the doctor's positive evaluation of one's illness; one should dress well because this will help avoid being diagnosed as having major depression; and in general one should treat the meeting as a business meeting between equals rather than as a helpless patient dealing with an omniscient doctor. This document and many others circulated through support groups, on and off the Internet, help sufferers to take control of their identities and their medical interactions. Other methods of disrupting the normal authority and business-as-usual of the biomedical community by support groups and illness organizations include attending medical research conferences as patients, and sponsoring conferences themselves (Burns 1994: 3–4).

In sum, because the authoritative facts for these disorders cannot be found in their bodies, nor with their doctors, sufferers have necessarily become activists. They have, in other words, been forced actively to advocate for the evidence of their illness in non-traditional medical settings: courtrooms, insurance offices, the mass media and the Internet. In the next section, I focus on the science and technology of brain imaging in order to point to both its immense value to our understanding of the brain and its power in presenting apparently unambiguous images of different kinds of brains. At issue are the meanings ascribed to these images by different groups in non-traditional medical and scientific settings where the explanations of these illnesses (temporarily) rest.

State of the Art Neuroscience and Controversy

[Even a teacher is not able to recognize exactly when a young child begins to read.] But isn't that only because of our too slight acquaintance with what goes on in the brain and the nervous system? If we had a more accurate knowledge of these things we should see what connexions were established by the training, and then we should be able to say when we looked into his brain: "Now he has read this word, now the reading connexion has been set up." – And it presumably must be like that – for otherwise how could we be so sure that there was such a connexion [in the brain]? That it is so is presumably a priori – or is it only probable? And how probable is it? Now ask yourself: what do you know about these things? – But if it is a priori, that means that it is a form of account which is very convincing to us. (Wittgenstein 1972 [1953]: 158)

Wittgenstein was fascinated with our apparent fixation on the idea that the head is the site of thinking and feeling, and that the brain is the site where answers to our human nature will be found. In this passage he addresses the fact that we appear to *know* that if we just had the right technology, we could determine from someone's brain patterns exactly what he or she was doing, thinking and feeling. Those who suffer from sociomedical disorders are put in the terrible position of having to contest bureaucracies and physicians as well as their friends, families and their own self-doubts. Even attaching a name to a set of symptoms is helpful and often therapeutic as it allows one to *have* a disease and not simply experience mysterious and troubling symptoms (Dumit 1997). Brain imaging offers the promise of *showing* that the disorder really is in their brain and not in their heads.

PET scanning and its less expensive cousin SPECT are recent technologies that produce images of living brain and body functions through the use of radioactive tracers.[10] Unlike CT (computed tomography) and MR (magnetic resonance), which provide images of the tissue and structure of the brain, PET and SPECT promise to provide images of the living brain in action, as it thinks, worries, gets sad, adds and goes mad. These functional imaging techniques represent a new paradigm in diagnosis and visualization, producing high resolution *functional* images through computer power.

There are many excellent sources for descriptions of how PET works (Posner and Raichle 1994; Roland 1993). The following brief description is intended to gesture toward the complexity of the process as both difficult and amazing. After an experiment is designed and representative subjects selected, radioactive isotopes must be obtained.[11] These isotopes are short-lived, their half-lives are from two minutes to two hours. They are immediately "tagged" or attached onto other chemicals to form radio-labeled substances, or radiopharmaceuticals. Fluorine-18, for instance, can be tagged onto glucose, and Oxygen-15 can be tagged onto water. These radiopharmaceuticals thus either mimic or are analogs of substances regularly circulating through the brain.

The next step is to set up the experiment, inject the person with the radiopharmaceutical, and place them in the scanner. While the person carries out some task (such as looking at words) or attempting to maintain some state (such as rest or anxiety), his or her brain is assumed to be using energy differentially in those regions involved in that activity or state. Scans can be taken quickly for a "picture" of blood flow during a thirty-second period, or they are taken after forty minutes for a "picture" of the glucose utilization up to the scan.

As the radiopharmaceutical decays in the brain, it emits particles that travel in relatively straight lines. The scanner consists of a ring of detectors connected to a computing system that reacts when they are struck by the particles. After collecting hundreds of thousands of data points, the computer attempts mathematically to reconstruct the approximate spatial density of the radiopharmaceutical, a process involving many assumptions about brain biochemistry and metabolism. The result is a simultaneously simple (in the sense of transparent) and complex image of a subject's brain at work.[12]

The use of PET to study the brain in action is a source of continuing controversy not because the technology is under almost continual revision, but because the referents of the images, theories of human behavior, of human cognition, and of how the human brain actually works are themselves sites of controversy.[13] Functional brain imaging studies have therefore been described as hypothesis generating rather than hypothesis confirming (Rapoport 1991). Nonetheless, the information that is provided by functional means is, quite simply, unavailable by other means, and certainly, any attempt to theorize the brain and cognition must be accountable to the results of such studies.

In addition to studying the history and community of functional brain imaging, however, I have also concentrated on *how* notions of brains and meaningful brain images come to be known outside of the relatively small group of biomedical researchers. To rephrase Wittgenstein: *How*, as a culture, do we come to know about these things? This question is vital since as Wittgenstein pointed out: if the result of our learning about brains and imaging technologies is as if a priori, then these are "a form of account which is very convincing to us" (Wittgenstein 1972 [1953]: 158). Consequently, as an ethnographer, in addition to fieldwork in PET scan laboratories, interviewing researchers and graduate students, and attending imaging conferences, I also studied the role of brain scans in popular culture, in courtrooms, and in the lives of those whose illnesses are presumed or suspected to lie in their heads.

One clear finding was that throughout these heterogeneous social worlds, the details behind the experiments were often left behind, and what remained was almost always two images, with ideal labels like "depressed person" and "normal control." In many cases, these labels were reduced to one word each: "depression" and "normal." The images thus appear to collapse a symptom – a brain abnormality correlated with a diagnosis of depression – into a referent – a depressed brain, or a depressed person.

This visually reductive practice, however, is not limited to popular culture. Researchers using PET almost exclusively conduct their studies on relatively small sample sizes (4–20 persons) and if they discover statistically significant differences between brain regions in sample versus controls, they report these numerical findings. In their scientific articles they also usually *show only two* images (or sets of images) that are almost always the most extremely different images. This provides a crystal clear visual referent implying diagnostic discrimination, even when the text of the article explicitly warns against it. This practice of showing extreme images even when the normal distributions of the two groups overlaps considerably is standard practice within the brain imaging community and within the life sciences in general. As one researcher stated:

If you are honestly and forthrightly trying to show something in the article, you try and take the data and the images and process them to point that what you know to be true you can see. So we take the extreme cases for the readers to be able to see them. You have the tabulated data to look at all cases. It is fine. (Michael Phelps, interviewed in Dumit 1995: 168)

The risk of such practices, of course, is that the images will travel without their accompanying graphs and caveats, and stand alone as visual arguments of the existence and extreme difference of one *kind* of person or brain state from another. In my previous work, I have treated this risk as a negative, as risking mistaking the scan – a statistical product – for diagnosis and kind of person. I repeat this argument here because in the case of mental illnesses and the new socio-medical disorders it is precisely this risk which sufferers are willing to take: they would prefer to be stereotyped biologically and to risk misdiagnosis rather than being excluded from diagnostics altogether. The alternative – that there is not yet enough evidence to decide one way or another regarding the reality and significance of their illness and therefore they should wait – is simply not livable given the current state of healthcare in the US.

Functional brain imaging, because of its construction as a device that shows differences between groups, plays a pivotal role in almost all of these new socio-medical disorders. Its advantage is that it not only provides statistically correlated differences between affected populations and normals, but it can "show that difference." Further, as opposed to graphs and other forms of visual displays of quantitative data, functional brain imaging is presented as a combination photograph and map of a person's brain in action. Photographically, it appears as an objective snapshot unmediated by subjective impressions or manipulations.

Cartographically, it points out specific areas of the brain that are not functioning normally, areas already mapped as relating to attention, memory, decision-making and so on. Together, these two discourses imply that a functional brain image not only shows the disorder itself (demonstrating its existence in general and within that particular brain or brains), but also show how it works (and therefore how it might be treated). Finally, within a biomedical culture, the demonstration that a disorder is in the brain implies that it is not (solely) in the mind. The brain in this sense can serve as etiology: e.g. a "brain-caused illness."

My contribution to this literature here is to survey the volatile, meaningful roles of brain imaging within the ongoing histories of these conditions. Brain imaging functions within each disorder as a "gold standard" of demonstrative proof of neurobiological involvement (Carpman 1993: 2), and also serves as a site for the intertwining of these various disorders. A "gold standard" in medical terminology is traditionally associated with a test that definitively identifies a biological marker for a disease (cf. Aronowitz 1998). In the case of the new socio-medical disorders, brain images repeatedly are taken from preliminary studies and iconically used as proof of the neurobiological nature and even cause of these conditions. The easy migration of this *basic* research in brain function and pathophysiology to the diagnosis and promotion of new disease categories is a function of the visual persuasiveness of brain images, one that is unmatched among other diagnostic tests.

Brain imaging scans are used as critical arguments by communities of all of the different socio-medical disorders. The scans for each illness are often done by the same relatively small group of researchers, and the larger imaging community is quite divided over the applicability and appropriateness of this use of scanning, with most researchers opposed. Significantly, those opposed most often have nothing at all to say about the application of brain imaging to these disorders. They would, quite simply, prefer the disorders not be studied at all with brain imaging. At best, they would prefer to wait until there is some agreement on precisely what a given disorder is, and some sense of its etiology. But again, for sufferers who see little mainstream attempt to put these disorders into research budgets, exploratory and peripheral research is preferable to no research at all. In the following, final section I trace some of this preliminary brain scan research on these socio-medical disorders as it is restricted by research budgets and specific cultures of meaning and accusation.

Good-enough Science and Political Economy

A picture is conjured up which seems to fix the sense unambiguously. The actual use, compared with that suggested by the picture, seems like something muddled... (Wittgenstein 1972 [1953]: 426)

Despite the small number of studies conducted on these socio-medical disorders, and despite being preliminary and underfunded, these brain images are powerful across social and cultural boundaries: they serve as insurance arguments, self-help diagnoses, legal claims for reparations, and popular arguments against the stigma of mental illnesses. And control of these images is most definitely not in the hands of the researchers who produce them.

Since there are not unlimited resources and money for labs and research, determining what to study is itself a social, political and economic issue. Not only must each disease or disorder compete with every other one for resources, so must each research method compete within each disorder. Consequently, one of the functions of national support groups is advocating for more research money for that particular disorder and for specific research directions.[14] Encouraging research into the neurobiological substrates and causes of mental illness, for instance, has been one of NAMI's chief tasks (National Alliance for the Mentally Ill). With regard to the new socio-medical disorders, there are precious few federally funded research studies at large, central research universities. Thus, the "debate" over brain imaging studies does not take place "in science" between mainstream and peripheral researchers, but across a purported science/non-science divide.[15]

Mental illness activist communities, for instance, such as the NAMI, have heavily supported and promoted functional brain imaging studies among other investigations into the biological basis of mental illness (e.g. genetics). They do this in direct response to a continuing stigma attached to mental illness, and a continuing history of reluctance by the state, communities and insurance agencies to adequately treat those suffering from it. Thus, not only do these studies offer the hope of designing specific psychopharmacological therapies (by identifying the particular brain areas affected by the illness), but they also visually demonstrate that specific mental illnesses such as depression are real neurobiological disorders. The Office of Technology Assessment book, *The Biology of Mental Disorders* sums up this argument:

Given that family members are often viewed as the agents of mental illness, it is understandable that they embrace biological theories of mental disorders. When families belonging to the National Alliance for the Mentally Ill (NAMI) were asked what had helped them to cope with stigma, 73.2 percent indicated that "research findings which establish a biological basis for mental illness helped much or very much in dealing with stigma." The concept that a biological defect causes a mental disorder largely exonerates family members and the individuals themselves from blame, placing it instead on a disease process. (Office of Technology Assessment 1992: 160)

Extreme brain images can also be used to redirect blame for criminal acts. In courtrooms, extreme images have been used to argue insanity defenses on the basis of a defendant's scan being more similar to published scans of schizophrenics, for instance, than published normals. Even though the peer review literature exclusively argues that in spite of the statistically significant correlates of certain brain features and schizophrenia, there is *no possibility* of going backward from scan to diagnosis, the visual argument presented in the form of the images remained compelling. The nature of this persuasion has been described by Zatz, who is referring to colored graphs:

Such "painting by numbers," Zatz contended, can have a tremendous impact [on juries]: "This is powerful testimony. It is simple, it is dramatic, and it is unforgettable. It makes allegedly subclinical injury almost visible to a jury that has come to expect a look at the amputated leg, a glimpse of the burnt flesh, a living reminder of a mistake in plastic surgery, or the proverbial x-ray of the surgical tool left inside the body. Practically speaking, it leaves the defense with an awful lot of explaining to do." . . . Represented by dots in a chart, test outcomes become mute "eyewitnesses to actual events." (Jasanoff 1995: 128–9, citing Zatz 1987)

With functional brain images, one is really "seeing the burnt flesh," a lesion in the brain is often made to appear as a black area in the scan, or a "hole." Some functional techniques consist in counting the "holes" in the brain. It must be noted that the use of images in courtrooms persists in spite of the furious opposition of over 90 percent of the imaging community (Mayberg 1992; Dumit 1995). It should be clear from these short descriptions of the roles of brain images of mental illnesses, however, that their status and their uses outside of laboratories are anything but settled (Kulynych 1997).

Surveying the available literature on socio-medical disorders, one is immediately struck by the ubiquity of compelling brain images. The Office of Technology Assessment's study of *The Biology of Mental Disorders* contains PET images for almost every mental disorder category (Office of Technology Assessment 1992). The oversized CFS conference book, *The Clinical and Scientific Basis of ME/CFS*, has PET, SPECT, EEG and MRI scans on its cover (Hyde et al. 1992). And, the

NIMH booklet on ADHD has only one scientific image (Neuwirth 1994). It contains two PET scans, ADHD vs. Normal. These scans are from the 1990 study by Zametkin et al. (1990), a study that Zametkin later failed to replicate and suggesting that the 1990 study was probably a false positive.

The underfunding of research into these socio-medical disorders has resulted in many cross-studies and low sample sizes. Researchers using functional brain imaging often study more than one of the disorders and either attempt to show that there are distinct differences between them, or argue that some disorders are variations of other ones. On the basis of SPECT brain pattern similarities, for instance, Staudenmeyer and Selner (1995) claimed that CFS was really depression. Komaroff and other researchers, however, counted defects in SPECT images among patient groups and distinguished CFS, dementia and depression (Carpman 1993: 7; Costa et al. 1995). Heuser et al. used SPECT to distinguish between MCS, CFS and depression (Heuser et al. 1991; *Toxicology and Industrial Health* 1994: 570). In other studies, one-third of CFS patients have been found to be chemically sensitive, as have many sufferers of Gulf War Syndrome (Deluca et al. 1994: 513; Simon et al. 1994: 573). A preliminary study of GWS with SPECT found six out of six patients had central nervous system damage. Many veterans of the Gulf War who are frustrated with their treatment by the Department of Veterans' Administration find outside MCS physicians who diagnose MCS (Miller 1994: 256). Major General Ronald Blanck, who has investigated GWS with SPECT, found it similar to CFS (even though the Department of Defense will not consider MCS or CFS as valid diagnoses) (Burns 1994: 10; Gulf War Organization 1995: 2). Jay Goldstein and Theodore Simon, two prominent SPECT researchers, have each studied breast implant silicone toxicity in addition to MCS and CFS (Carpman 1993: 2; *Toxicology and Industrial Health* 1994: 599). Regarding ADD, based on SPECT hypoperfusion patterns, Dr. Michael Goldberg hypothesized that many ADD children should really be diagnosed with CFS. He suggested that the widened DSM-IV category of ADD, which now includes an "ADD-quiet" subtype is causing misdiagnoses (Carpman 1993: 2, 6). This widespread cross-fertilization of brain imaging and brain theorizing often helps define and certify or decertify more than one socio-medical disorder at the same time.

For most sufferers, a single brain imaging study with statistical significance is more than enough proof that their disorder is not only real, but brain-based and neurobiological. This is especially true when the study shows an abnormal scan of a patient looking very different from a "normal" scan of a healthy individual. The Zametkin et al. PET study of ADD adults, cited above, has been characterized in the magazine *Wired* by a psychiatric researcher as providing "credibility for the adult form [of ADD]" (Schwartz 1995).[16] *Wired* continues, "Since the article was published, there has been a growing awareness of adult ADD in the medical community. And thousands of adults with attention problems have been coming out of the closet." Other sources refer to "the classic Zametkin study" (Diaz 1994: 4) as "the first clear evidence of a neurobiological difference between hyperactive and normal subjects" (Runge and Jaffe 1995). The visual impact of PET scanning thus plays directly into the metaphorics of proof such that evidence becomes clear with it.

According to Neenyah Ostrom, "Dr. Ismael Mena has studied CFS patients' brains using SPECT scans at the University of California-Los Angeles, where he is a professor of radiology. Over several years' investigation, Dr. Mena has consistently reported that 71 percent of CFS patients have a diminished flow of blood in their brains" (Ostrom 1990: chapter 20). These studies are cited as "breakthroughs . . . referenced by nearly all researchers" (Carpman 1993). Among these studies is one which showed that CFS was different from depression based on different patterns of brain abnormalities. "These data should end all speculation about CFS being a psycho-neurotic disease" (Wellness Web 1994). These claims are made in the face of only preliminary, and often underfunded studies. For instance, Paul Levine, an advocate for CFS, declared that "neural imaging as a whole is definitely showing abnormalities in CFS patients. Neural imaging techniques are being refined and are very promising, but they're not yet ready for clinical application" (Wellness Web 1994 citing Levine). In these sentences he stakes out a specific notion of objectivity for sufferers that allows definite *existence* of the disorder to be established based on these early mapping studies. Levine further characterizes the location of these disorders as *in the brain* while maintaining that the studies do not provide any diagnostic utility. This is a form of objectivity alien to most mainstream researchers who typically study conditions already known to exist in the brain. It is also a form of objectivity unfamiliar to many readers of this chapter.

With regard to this preliminary research however, there are many researchers who would like to keep the questions open while not jumping to any premature conclusions (Posner and Raichle 1994). Dr. Helen Mayberg, who attended the TIH conference as a respected mainstream PET researcher and neurologist, for example, urged caution with regard to the use of SPECT scans in MCS and CFS on the basis of the SPECT results being non-specific: what the scans show looks like more than one disease at the same time and is specific to none. She also noted that the apparent percent of abnormalities claimed to be found in sufferers (approximately 90 percent) is better than even the most well-characterized diseases such as epilepsy (70–80 percent), raising questions regarding the meaning of the results. Finally, she notes that since there is no pathophysiology known for MCS, there is no hypothesis being tested. She cautions that SPECT is therefore only useful for research, not diagnosis and that it is not appropriate for use in court (Mayberg 1992: 600).

A question thus arises: Are these preliminary underfunded studies, which are touted as proof, "bad science"? Are interest groups pressing for specific research agendas biasing otherwise objective work? Or, is it possible that there is a *need* for public relations research promoting these disorders as "brain disorders" (Office of Technology Assessment 1992; Neuwirth 1996 [1994]): 340)? Decisions as to what is important to study, and for whom, are made at many different levels of public culture, including Congress, the NIH and corporate funders. These decisions determine much of what truths get produced. Peripheral, underfunded science is not necessarily "bad science" but it is often "less good," less resourceful, even less rigorous (in no small part due to older machines, less sophisticated computers, smaller sample sizes). For purposes of advocacy, however, and keeping open questions that are not yet answered, these underfunded images look just as good and rigorous as the highly funded ones. These political and economic disadvantages produce worlds where truth is not unitary, nor simply hierarchical, but quite uneven.

If I want to underscore anything in this paper, it is this unevenness of objectivity, truth and meaning. Recalling for a moment the father who sued Blue Cross and Blue Shield, I want to call attention to the fact that despite the current state of BC/BS contracts that define bipolar disorder as a mental illness, the father's lawsuit nonetheless reconfigured the meaning and status of bipolar disorder *locally and temporarily*. It is quite possible, I suggest, that these temporary resting states of varying lengths of time are a much better empirical description of "truth" than atemporal, universal ones whose adjudication is not made clear. What good does a paper or study do that claims to have objective evidence that bipolar disorder is physical, if BC/BS does not have to listen, and a sufferer gets less treatment?

By unpacking the layers of conflicted judgements and experiences surrounding these socio-medical disorders, we can begin to understand how scientific and medical statements come to be central and yet nondecisive in many settings. Brain imaging – arguably the most ambiguously promising diagnostic technology – has and will continue to play a key role in resisting the easy assignment of blame, stigma and causation to the individual. But it appears that it will not do so by settling the matter once and for all in biology. Rather, the continual jostling of competing social, political and moral notions of nature and personhood that underpin our notions of biology and disease imply that these socio-medical disorders might only be "explained" temporarily and locally.

NOTES

Many thanks to the members of the Cambridge conference, my anonymous reviewers, and Hannah Landecker for their helpful feedback. Thanks also to the Wenner-Gren Foundation, the SSRC for funding the conference. Parts of this research were supported by the Smithsonian Institution, the NSF, and the NIMH Postdoctoral Fellowship program.

1. Useful overviews of ADD, also known as Attention Deficit Hyperactivity Disorder (ADHD), include Neuwirth 1996 [1994] and Harvard Mental Health Letter 1995. CFS is also known as Chronic Fatigue Immuno-Deficiency Syndrome (CFIDS) and has been studied by medical anthropologists Norma Ware and Arthur Kleinman (Ware 1993; Ware and Kleinman 1992). MCS is also known as Environmental Illness and is thoroughly debated in a special issue of *Toxicology and Industrial Health* (1994). For a history and summary of the many names for this condition, see Miller 1994. PTSD and Depression deserve inclusion because they continue to fulfill each of the seven conditions listed below. These latter two have also been the subject of medical anthropological scrutiny (Kleinman and Good 1985; Young 1995).

2. The concept of "biosociality" was coined by Rabinow 1992.

3. PET stands for "positron emission tomography," SPECT for "single-photon emission computed tomography," and MRI for "magnetic resonance imaging." See descriptions below.

4. This account is primarily drawn from the series of four articles in the *Washington Free Press* (Nelson 1994a, 1994b, 1994c; Nelson and Worth 1994).

5. For those interested in the full conspiracy account, far worse than one might imagine, please see the entire story at http://www.speakeasy.org/wfp/08/Boeing1.html.

6. On sick roles and chronic illness, see Charmaz 1991.

7. As the recent scandals regarding tobacco companies cynically show, it would have been better for those companies not to have conducted studies of cancer links in the first place, than to have done so and hidden them.

8. Haraway attributes this claim to "Foucault and others."

9. USENET is divided into a hierarchy of thousands of newsgroups. *All* of these newsgroup messages may currently be accessed (for free) at the Dejanews website, http://dejanews.com. I am currently analyzing the entire set of these messages from both groups with the assistance of Warren Sack, MIT Media Lab.

10. The acronym PET derives from PETT (positron emission transaxial tomography) developed at Washington University around 1974 (Dumit 1998).

11. With PET, a small but expensive and labor intensive cyclotron is needed to produce special isotopes.
12. There are many other uses of PET that deal with other organs (e.g. heart, lungs, liver), and with cancer.
13. See Poeppel 1996 and responses, and Gazzaniga 1997 for examples of some serious controversy over assumptions regarding the brain, imaging and language.
14. *Fortune* magazine recently ran three articles describing men coming to terms with prostate cancer and actively intervening in treatment decisions. One of the articles lamented the relative paucity of research dollars into prostate cancer relative to breast cancer. It cited efforts by men to emulate women's successful organizing around breast cancer, to the extent of hiring some of the same women to agitate for prostate cancer (Alexander 1996; Huey 1996; Grove 1996; Stipp 1996).
15. See studies of pseudoscience and other controversies (Wallis 1979).
16. Schwartz uses the acronym ADHD.

REFERENCES

Alexander, Tom 1996 "Still Waiting, Watchfully; A Former *Fortune* Writer Whose Unorthodox Choice in Facing Prostate Cancer Captivated Readers Reports on his Progress." *Fortune*. 13 May: 73.

Aronowitz, Robert A. 1998 *Making Sense of Illness: Science, Society, and Disease.* Cambridge: Cambridge University Press.

Burns, Roger 1994 Chronic Fatigue Syndrome Electronic Newsletter. Electronic document. ftp: //alternatives.com/library/hecfs/cfsn040.txt.

1996 CFS FAQ (archive). Electronic document. http://www.avana.net/pages/personal/hugman/Fibro_Docs/cfsfaq.htm.

Carpman, Vicki 1993 L.A. Conference Explores CFIDS Brain (#1). Electronic document. ftp: //alternatives.com/library/hecfs/cf93laa.txt File: "CFIDS 933 LACONF93."

Charmaz, Kathy 1991 *Good Days, Bad Days: The Self in Chronic Illness and Time.* New Brunswick, NJ: Rutgers University Press.

Costa, D. C., C. Tannock and F. J. Brostof 1995 "Brainstem Perfusion is Impaired in Chronic Fatigue Syndrome." *Quarterly Journal of Medicine* 88(11): 767–73.

Cracchiolo, Camilla 1995 Dealing with Doctors when you have Chronic Fatigue Syndrome. Electronic document. http: //www.cais.net/cfs-news/cfsdocs.txt.

Deluca, John, S. K. Johnson and B. H. Natelson 1994 "Neuropsychiatric Status of Patients with Chronic Fatigue Syndrome: An Overview." In Proceedings of the Conference on Low-Level Exposure to Chemicals and Neurobiologic Sensitivity. Special issue. *Toxicology and Industrial Health* 10: 513–22.

Diaz, Dan 1994 Russell Barkley Seminar on ADHD (newsposting). Electronic document. http: //www.realtime.net/cyanosis/add/barkley_seminar.html.

Dumit, Joe 1995 "Twenty-first-century PET: Looking for Mind and Morality Through the Eye of Technology." In George E. Marcus (ed.), *Technoscient-*

ific Imaginaries: Conversations, Profiles, and Memoirs. Chicago: Chicago University Press, pp. 87–128.

1997 "A Digital Image of the Category of the Person: PET Scanning and Objective Self-Fashioning." In G. L. Downey and Joe Dumit (eds.), *Cyborgs and Citadels: Anthropological Interventions in Emerging Sciences and Technologies.* Santa Fe: School of American Research Press, pp. 83–102.

1998 "PET Scanner." In R. Bud and D. J. Warner (eds.), *Instruments of Science: An Historical Encyclopedia.* New York: Garland Publishing, Inc, pp. 449–52.

Frisch 1994 MCS in the Workplace Task Force booklet (archive). Electronic document. http: //www.envirolink.org/action/news/toxics/MCS.html.

Gazzaniga, Michael S. (ed.) 1997 *Conversations in the Cognitive Neurosciences.* Cambridge, MA: MIT Press.

Grove, Andy 1996 "Taking on Prostate Cancer." *Fortune.* 13 May: 54.

Gulf War Organization 1995 Unexplained Illnesses among Desert Storm Veterans. Electronic document. http: //www.gulfwar.org/search.html.

Haraway, Donna 1986 "The Actors are Cyborg, Nature is Coyote, and the Geography is Elsewhere: Postscript to 'Cyborgs at Large.' " In Constance Penley and Ross Andrew (eds.), *Technoculture.* Minneapolis: University of Minnesota Press, pp. 21–6.

Harvard Mental Health Letter 1995 Internet Mental Health: ADD. Electronic document. http: //www.mentalhealth.com/mag1/p5h-add.html.

Heuser, Gunnar, A. Wojdani and S. Heuser 1992 "Diagnostic Markers of Multiple Chemical Sensitivity." In National Research Council, *Multiple Chemical Sensitivities: Addendum to Biologic Markers in Immunotoxicology.* Washington, DC: Natioal Academy Press. Also online: http/pompeii.nap.edu/books.030904736/html/index.html.

Huey, John W., Jr. 1996 "Our Reluctant Author Comes Forward." *Fortune.* 13 May: 8.

Hyde, B. M., J. Goldstein and P. Levine 1992 *The Clinical And Scientific Basis of Myalgic Encephalomyelitis/Chronic Fatigue Syndrome.* Ogdensburg, NY: Nightingale Research Foundation.

Jasanoff, Sheila 1995 *Science at the Bar: Law, Science, and Technology in America.* Cambridge, MA: Harvard University Press.

Kleinman, Arthur 1986 *Social Origins of Distress and Disease: Depression, Neurasthenia and Pain in Modern China.* New Haven, CT: Yale University Press.

Kleinman, Arthur, and Byron Good (eds.) 1985 *Culture and Depressions: Studies in the Anthropology and Cross-Cultural Psychiatry of Affect and Disorder.* Comparative Studies of Health Systems and Medical Care. Berkeley: University of California Press.

Kulynych, Jennifer 1997 "Psychiatric Neuroimaging Evidence: A High-Tech Crystal Ball?" *Stanford Law Review* 49: 1249–70.

Mayberg, Helen S. 1992 "Functional Brain Scans as Evidence in Criminal Court: An Argument for Caution." *The Journal of Nuclear Medicine* 33(6): 18N–19N, 25N.

Miller, Claudia S. 1994 "White Paper: Chemical Sensitivity, History and Phenomenology." In Proceedings of the Conference on Low-Level Exposure to Chemicals and Neurobiologic Sensitivity. Special issue. *Toxicology and Industrial Health* 10: 253–76.

Nelkin, Dorothy and Laurence Tancredi 1988 *Dangerous Diagnostics: The Social Power of Biological Information*. New York: Basic Books.

Nelson, Eric 1994a WFP "Boeing Story (No, not a retraction. A vindication)" (archive). http: //www.speakeasy.org/wfp/10/Follow_File.html *Washington Free Press*, Issue no. 10, June/July 1994.

1994b WFP "Disorder in the Courts" (archive) http: //www.speakeasy.org/wfp/08/Boeing5.html *Washington Free Press*, Issue no. 8, Feb./March 1994.

1994c WFP "The MCS Debate: A Medical Streetfight." http: //www.speakeasy.org/wfp/08/Boeing4.html *Washington Free Press*, Issue no. 8, Feb./March 1994.

Nelson, Eric and Mark Worth 1994 WFP "Boeing to Ill Workers: 'It's All in Your Head'." (archive) http: //www.speakeasy.org/wfp/08/Boeing1.html *Washington Free Press*, Issue no. 8, Feb./March 1994.

Neuwirth, Sharyn 1996 [1994] Attention Deficit Disorder. US Department of Health and Human Services Public Health Service, National Institutes of Health, National Institute of Mental Health. Electronic document. http: //www.nimh.nih.gov/publicat/adhd.htm.

Office of Technology Assessment 1992 *The Biology of Mental Disorders. New Developments in Neuroscience*. Washington, D.C.: Congress of the US, Office of Technology Assessment.

Ostrom, Neenyah 1990 Brain Waves article on CFS (archive). Electronic document. ftp: //alternatives.com/library/hecfs/brain1.txt.

Penley, Constance and Ross Andrew 1986 "Cyborgs at Large: An Interview with Donna Haraway." In Constance Penley and Ross Andrew (eds.), *Technoculture*. Minneapolis: University of Minnesota Press, pp. 1–20.

Pennebaker, J. W. 1994 "Psychological Bases of Symptom Reporting: Perceptual and Emotional Aspects of Chemical Sensitivity." In Proceedings of the Conference on Low-Level Exposure to Chemicals and Neurobiologic Sensitivity. Special issue. *Toxicology and Industrial Health*. 10: 4.

Poeppel, David 1996 "A Critical Review of PET Studies of Phonological Processing." *Brain and Language* 55: 317–51.

Posner, Michael I. and Raichle Marcus E. 1994 *Images of Mind*. New York: Scientific American Library.

Rabinow, Paul 1992 "Artificiality and Enlightenment: From Sociobiology to Biosociality." In Jonathan Crary and Sanford Kwinter (eds.), *Incorporations*. New York: Zone (distrib: MIT Press), pp. 234–52.

Rapoport, S. 1991 "Discussion of PET Workshop Reports, Including Recommendations of PET Data Analysis Working Group." *Journal of Cerebral Blood Flow and Metabolism* 11: 140–6.

Roland, Per E. 1993 *Brain Activation*. New York: Wiley-Liss.

Runge, D. and N. Jaffe 1995 The Neurological Bases of Attention Deficit Disorder. Electronic document. http: //www.generation.net/~dieter/adhd.html.

Schwartz, Evan I. 1995 Driven to distraction. *Wired* (Electonic version) 2(6): http: //www.hotwired.com/wired/2.06/departments/electrosphere/interrupt-driven.

Simon, Gregory E. 1994 "Psychiatric Symptoms in Multiple Chemical Sensitivity." In Proceedings of the Conference on Low-Level Exposure to Chemicals and Neurobiologic Sensitivity. Special issue. *Toxicology and Industrial Health*. 10: 487–96.

Simon, T. R., D. C. Hickey, C. E. Fincher, A. R. Johnson, G. H. Ross and W. J. Rea 1994 "Single Photon Emission Computed Tomography of the Brain in Patients with Chemical Sensitivities." In Proceedings of the Conference on Low-Level Exposure to Chemicals and Neurobiologic Sensitivity. Special issue. *Toxicology and Industrial Health* 10: 573–7.

Staudenmayer, H. and J. C. Selner 1995 "Failure to Assess Psychopathology in Patients Presenting with Chemical Sensitivities." *Journal of Occupational and Environmental Medicine* 37: 704–9, discussion at p. 710.

Stipp, David 1996 "The Gender Gap in Cancer Research; When it Comes to Mobilizing for a War on a Cancer that Threatens them Sexually, Men Have a Lot to Learn from Women." *Fortune*. 13 May: 74.

Toxicology and Industrial Health 1994 Proceedings of the Conference on Low-Level Exposure to Chemicals and Neurobiologic Sensitivity, Baltimore, 6–7 April 1994. Special issue. 10: 253–669.

Wallis, Roy (ed.) 1979 *On the Margins of Science: The Social Construction of Rejected Knowledge*. Keele: University of Keele.

Ware, Norma C. 1993 "Society, Mind and Body in Chronic Fatigue Syndrome: An Anthropological View." *Ciba Foundation Symposium* 173: 62–74.

Ware, Norma C. and Arthur Kleinman 1992 "Culture and Somatic Experience: The Social Course of Illness in Neurasthenia and Chronic Fatigue Syndrome." *Psychosomatic Medicine* 54: 546–60.

Wellness Web 1994 The Patient's Network: CFS. Electronic document. http: // wellweb.com/INDEX/QCHRONFS.HTM.

Wittgenstein, Ludwig 1972 [1953] *Philosophical Investigations*. New York: Macmillan.

Worth, Mark 1994a WFP "Suicide Solution – One Woman's Way Out." (archive) http://www.speakeasy.org/wfp/08.Boeing2.html *Washington Free Press*, Issue no. 8 Feb./March 1994.

    1994b WFP "Disunity among the Machinists." (archive) http://www. speakeasy.org/wfp/08.Boeing3.html *Washington Free Press*, Issue no. 8 Feb./ March 1994.

Young, Allan 1995 *The Harmony of Illusions: Inventing Post-Traumatic Stress Disorder*. Princeton, NJ: Princeton University Press.

Zametkin, Alan J., Thomas E. Nordahl, M. Gross, Anna C. King, W. E. Semple, Judith M. Rumsey, Susan D. Hamburger and Robert M. Cohen 1990 "Cerebral Glucose Metabolism in Adults with Hyperactivity of Childhood Onset." *New England Journal of Medicine* 323(20): 1361–66.

Zatz, C. 1987 "Unpublished Remarks. Immunotoxicology: From Lab to Law," Ithaca, Cornell University, Institute for Comparative and Environmental Toxicology, October.

11 On dying twice: culture, technology and the determination of death

Margaret Lock

The enterprise of organ transplantation is like no other among biomedical technologies in that the rapid conversion of the technologically managed death of one patient is transformed into the "gift of life" for a second dying patient. By far the majority of solid organ[1] transplants make use of what is known as a "brain dead donor." A three-year-old is hit by the neighbor's car as it swings into the driveway; a sixteen-year-old hangs himself when his girlfriend tells him she does not want to see him any more; a stray bullet lodges itself in the brain of an innocent passer-by at a bank robbery; a middle-aged woman falls unconscious with a massive brain hemorrhage – patients such as these are placed on the artificial ventilator, permitting them to breathe even though they have lost the spontaneous capacity to do so, and are subjected to a battery of tests, scans and clinical examinations. Certain of these individuals will make a partial or complete recovery, but the hearts of others will stop beating, or their blood pressure will drop irrevocably, and they will then die in spite of the ventilator.

There is a third class of patients, those who neither recover nor die but become brain dead. For these patients, resuscitative measures are only a "partial success" (Ad Hoc Committee of the Harvard Medical School to Examine the Definition of Death 1968) so that with the assistance of the ventilator, the heart and lungs of such patients continue to function, but the entire brain is irreversibly damaged. Brain dead patients exist betwixt and between, both alive and dead; breathing with technological assistance, but unconscious. Without the artificial ventilator the brain dead would not exist, and even with it, such patients survive for only a few hours, days or weeks, or very occasionally for months. Despite intensive care, the heart gives up, or the blood pressure cannot be sustained. Recently, however, with increased knowledge and experience, survival rates have lengthened, and one or two exceptional cases have been reported of over a year's duration (Shewmon, forthcoming), but there are no documented cases of anyone recovering from this state, *if* it has been accurately diagnosed.

233

"Accidental" deaths are untimely; senseless. In North America, even before the diagnosis is confirmed, patients are usually considered as potential organ donors. Once brain death is declared, if the patient's wish to donate is known, and with the consent of close relatives (although this is not legally required), the technologically maintained organs of brain dead patients can be used to "save the lives" of other patients whom the trauma victims never knew – patients whose hearts, livers, lungs, and/or kidneys have deteriorated beyond repair, and who have been selected as recipients by committees designated to allocate without prejudice the scarce supply of human organs. Aside from the benefit donation may bring to organ recipients, it is believed by many people who work in emergency medicine and by many families whose relatives have died of brain trauma, that the altruistic act of organ donation permits meaning to be created out of sudden death.

Becoming the recipient of an organ is a highly competitive endeavor, for we in Euro/America suffer from what is repeatedly characterized as a "shortage of organs." This shortage has been described as a "public health crisis" (Randall 1991). People whose work is associated with transplant technology are reminded repeatedly how many thousands of patients die each year waiting for an organ. In the United States, for example, roughly 30,000 potential recipients were waiting for transplants in 1993, and "every day six of these patients die prior to receiving a heart or liver transplant," while those who need kidneys continue on dialysis (Arnold et al. 1995: 1).

This shortage is exacerbated because people are more conscientious than formerly about buckling up seat belts and, over the past ten years, the number of automobile accidents has been reduced (Statistical Abstract of the United States 1997). At the same time, the "success rate" in obtaining agreement from patients and families to donate organs has remained unchanged (Caplan 1988; Prottas 1994). This is so even though the law demands "required request" of families in most parts of the United States, Canada and Europe. In certain European countries, including Spain and Belgium, "presumed consent" is legally recognized, that is, in theory permission is not needed from either donor or family in order to procure organs which will take place unless the family specifically "opts out." In practice, however, if families appear hesitant or are in opposition, no organs are taken routinely in any location in Europe or North America. Donation is not, therefore, based on individual autonomy, but on familial decisions, although surveys indicate that 90 percent of Americans, at least, claim that they will honor the wish of a relative to donate (Prottas 1994: 50).

An assumption is often made in North America and most of Europe that procuring organs from a brain dead body is in effect similar to performing an autopsy on a corpse – a brain dead body is a biological entity, but no longer legally alive. The results of comparative research with intensivists in North America and Japan to be reported below show that even among specialists who routinely work with brain dead patients, such patients are not likened to corpses. Furthermore, culturally informed knowledge infuses clinical practice in both locations, having a profound effect on the diagnosis of brain death, the time of signing of the death certificate, the procurement of organs, and the transplant enterprise, in both these locations. Even though brain dead bodies are not assumed to be biologically dead in either clinical space, organs are nevertheless taken from such patients routinely in North America, in contrast to Japan, where, over the past thirty years, very few organs indeed have been recovered, and then under duress.

Unstable Boundaries and the Moral Order

Death has become increasingly visible in recent years as a subject for media attention, whether it be a discussion about the moral status of euthanasia, or a lament at the increasing number of violent deaths that we are exposed to each day. Whatever form death takes, it conjures up that margin between culture and nature where mortality must be confronted.

The conceptualization of nature, including the specification of its relationship to human society and culture is, of course, contingent, and thus meanings attributed to it change through time and space. Latour (1993 [1991]) has discussed the way in which we "moderns" have placed nature "out there," in an ontological zone distinct from that of society and social relations. Conceptualized as neutral, nature is made into a domain entirely independent of the moral order. As a result it was possible to pass the Anatomy Act of 1832 in England, for example, so that dissections and autopsies of corpses could be legally carried out. In theory from that time on a corpse was reconceptualized as part of nature, no longer having social worth, and therefore available for scientific commodification. In practice, as Richardson (1989) has shown, corpses were not so easily divested of their meaning for families and social life. It is evident that nature continues to serve, as it did prior to the Enlightenment, as a hybrid[2] – a moral touchstone, the effects of which are especially apparent when we grapple with assigning the status of life or death to various entities (Lock 1995).

It is at sites of rupture and transition, of conversion from culture to nature, and life to death, or the reverse, where disputes often take place, and it is at these sites that a toehold can be found for critical and reflexive analyses about the development and application of technoscience in contemporary societies. Moralizing runs amok where efforts at purification (in Latour's idiom) – that is, claims about the epistemologically neutral status of nature – the non-human – and its rigorous separation from society – the human – are rigorously challenged. Examination of assertions at disputed sites about what is "natural" and what is "cultural" often reveals concerns about a destabilization of the moral order due to technological innovation.

Thus, while it is important to establish how any given technology is perceived to "enable" everyday life, it is equally important, as Strathern (1992) has shown, to monitor the flurry of voiced opposition that surrounds the introduction of many of the new biomedical technologies, for example. When widely accepted ontological statuses, such as those taken to constitute life and death, or basic human bonds, including those thought to be appropriate between parents and their children, come to be seen as under threat by the legitimization of technologically aided biomedical procedures, the resulting disputes provide a rich source of data for anthropological analyses. Such data are invaluable when attempting to understand what is believed to constitute social order and affiliation in contemporary life.

Moral disputes of this kind occur in so-called rational, secular, scientific societies, and in societies where other forms of cosmological order are in theory dominant. Where the process of purification takes place relatively smoothly – where silence resounds about any given innovation – this too is fertile ground for social scientists. In this instance, the initial task is, of course, to name the hybrid, for it will usually be camouflaged as though it is a natural entity.

Culture and Heterogeneity

Brain dead patients/cadavers clearly represent a "coupling between organism and machine, each conceived of as coded devices" (Haraway 1991: 150). The "boundary transgressions" exhibited by such cyborgs[3] present "dangerous possibilities" in part, suggests Haraway, because their development is related to an authoritarian need for control and universal domination. At the same time, she argues, cyborgs invite us to reconsider our relationship with and construction of the natural and mechanical worlds.

A comparative ethnography of technoscience (and I increasingly think comparison is a fruitful way to take on this daunting subject) must immediately confront the question of why in specific locales certain cyborgs raise little concern, while in others they create havoc. North American have been forced to engage with what it is about the manipulation of the fetus that triggers fury and violence. In many other locations this hybrid remains dormant, safely obscure, and in yet other situations, although recognized as a living, or potentially living entity, it causes little debate. As does a fetus, a brain dead patient/cadaver lurks on the margins of life and death, but in most of Euro/America a remarkable silence persists in connection with this new death, whereas turmoil has erupted in Japan over the past thirty years in connection with brain death and its associated technologies. It was only in the fall of 1997 that brain death was legally recognized in Japan as human death, and even then only for those patients who had made it clear that they wished to be organ donors, and whose families were in agreement. Where no prior wish to donate has been made, a brain dead body is legally alive.

So here we are, back in anthropology's favorite stamping ground of difference, seeking to understand why the Japanese, technologically sophisticated as they are, find themselves unable to recognize brain death as the end of life; why brain death and organ transplants, so dependent upon the recognition of brain death as the end of human life, signal danger, loud and clear, to many Japanese. This perceived danger has stimulated widespread public self-reflection over the past thirty years including in which disputes about the relationship of Japan to the West, tradition to modernity, and culture to technology all loom large. These disputes reveal the ambivalence certain Japanese experience in connection with technologies that radically intrude into what is taken to be the "natural order," together with a concern about the mixing of "self" and "other." But other issues are regularly voiced, including grave doubts about the integrity of the medical profession; concerns because informed consent is not formally institutionalized in Japan; worries that organ transplants are inherently non-egalitarian; and confusion about the status of dying patients, dead bodies, and their relationship to the living – all of which topics radiate out from the centrifugal trigger of brain dead entities (Lock 1995, 1996, 1997; Lock, forthcoming).

Of equal interest as an inquiry into the Japanese national debate is, I believe, to ask why the majority of Euro/Americans *apparently* sense so little danger emanating from this technological intrusion into death. Why has the focus in most of Euro/America been almost exclusively on the heroics of organ transplants and the gift of life, while deleting, it seems, almost all anxiety about the source of organs? This selective blindness has ensured that the second part of the equation only – the self/non-self hybrid of the organ recipient – has fully captivated public attention. In Japan, in contrast to the majority of Euro/American countries,[4] it has proved impossible from the time the new technologically mediated death was first discussed by the medical world in the late 1960s, to objectify brain dead patients as cadaver-like. Both the subjectivity and the social status of dying patients remain intact following a diagnosis of brain death, making it very difficult for families and many health care professionals alike to accept that this diagnosis represents the end of life.

Alan Feldman, following Adorno, argues for the possibility of "cultural anesthesia" – a condition produced by the objectification of certain individuals that increases the social capacity to inflict pain, while at the same time rendering that pain inadmissible to public discourse and cultural reflection (Feldman 1994: 406). While my argument is not that someone who is brain dead feels pain (such patients are deeply unconscious), a form of cultural anesthesia is apparently present in Euro/America such that public reflection has not taken place to any extent, nor has the pain and ambivalence in connection with the donation of organs experienced by almost all relatives of brain dead patients, and by many health care professionals, been recognized. This pain is well masked by the persuasive metaphors about saving lives associated with the transplant industry (Sharp 1995). This is not to suggest that organ transplants are not very effective in many cases, and increasingly so with improved drug technology. However, this success comes at a price, the death of the donor, a death that is rendered invisible, and then rapidly remade as the gift of life.

I agree with Haraway that the very existence of cyborgs, products of technological innovation, in this instance those entities diagnosed as brain dead and on ventilators, invites us to reconsider the way in which the fluid boundaries between nature and culture are created and defended, but I would qualify this assertion: The process of construction of such boundaries and the meanings attributed to them must be empirically established in light of the practices prevalent in specific historical and geographical locations if we are to understand why certain hybrids, the cause of endless trouble in some sites, go unrecognized in other times and places. Moreover, such boundaries, even when apparently agreed upon and beyond dispute, may become fluid once again within the space of months or years – the result of "second thoughts" after extensive experience with the technology, or alternatively of further technological modifications and concomitant changes in representations. Given the heterogeneity of contemporary societies, it is unlikely that such disputes can ever be considered as settled once and for all.

Clearly the meanings attributed to death vary depending upon whether one is close to death but still conscious, a close relative of a patient who is diagnosed as brain dead, a neurologist trying to subvert death, a transplant surgeon "in need" of organs, a cultural commentator writing for the media, someone who is devoutly religious or alternatively aggressively secular, an "average" Japanese or an "average" American, or some combination of the above. This chapter will show that heterogeneous constructions about the brain dead are created, as Casper (1994) suggests with reference to fetuses, through work practices. But they are also constructed in large part through culturally informed responses of individuals when confronted with brain death, whether as clients, patients, relatives or clinicians. Ultimately the treatment of brain dead bodies is dependent upon work practices in clinical practice, but work practices are not independent of culturally informed knowledge and values. In this chapter, attention will be focused on clinician conceptualizations and practices, and how their sensitivity to families in shock influences, in culturally informed ways, what is done to brain dead patients.

Pinning Death Down

Without the machine – the artificial ventilator – the condition of brain death would never have been marked, except on occasion as a brief period of time prior to cardio-pulmonary arrest, signaling the condition that most people living in the urbanized world intuitively understand as the end of life. Without the ventilator, then, brain death could not have been made into either a recognizable diagnosis or a construct for social analysis. The immediate precursor of the ventilator was the iron lung, invented in Denmark in the 1940s to assist polio patients, whose lungs had collapsed, to breathe. Created in the late 1950s, the artificial ventilator, with its delivery of oxygen under pressure was a great improvement on the iron lung, but polio was by then all but "conquered." One must meander through a veritable Latourian network of entanglements to tell the story of the ventilator. This particular network includes the emergence of the car as the prime mode of transport, and of fast roads, together with an accelerating number of automobile accidents, coupled, particularly in America, with escalating numbers (in absolute terms) of gunshot wounds, leading to increased incidents of traumatic injuries and deaths. These changes stimulated in part the development of emergency medicine as a specialty, and the institutionalization of intensive care units with specialized staff who work under pressure to get patients out of such units as speedily as possible, alive or dead. This is just one trajectory of the ventilator network; one must enter another domain to chart the emergence of an increasingly sophisticated immunology throughout the 1950s, permitting kidney transplants from both live donors and cadavers, and then follow the grandiose fancies of certain surgeons as they experimented on animals with liver and heart transplants. This technology took the world by storm, when the flamboyant South African surgeon Christiaan Barnard carried out what was announced in 1967 as the world's first heart transplant.

It was evident by the late 1950s that patient/ventilator entities were causing disquiet. For one thing, it was not clear what to call them: "living cadavers," "ventilator brain," and "heart-lung preparations" were just a few of the terms bandied about. In a 1966 CIBA Foundation symposium, the focus of which was on organ transplants, a certain impatience, characteristic of many professionals associated with the transplant world in connection with these new entities was apparent:

[F]or how long should "life" be maintained in a person with irrevocable damage of the brain? . . . [W]hen does death occur in an unconscious patient dependent on artificial aids to circulation and respiration? [A]re there ever circumstances where death may be mercifully advanced?. . . [D]oes the law permit operations which "mutilate" the donor for the advantage of another person? (Wolstenholme and O'Connor 1966: vii–viii)

The thrust of such questions becomes, in effect, a desire to know when individual patients whose organs have potential value for others, can be counted as dead enough to be transformed into commodified objects. After the Barnard heart transplant, it was clear that such questions needed answering urgently, particularly because more than one transplant surgeon was shortly thereafter summarily charged with murder for removal of a beating heart from a patient. In one case, in Texas, the charge was dropped when it was decided by the medical examiner that the donor had been murdered by an assailant when his head was smashed in, and not several hours later by the transplant surgeon (*Newsweek* 1968). In Japan a surgeon was also charged with murder. The case was dropped two years later, but it was clear that the doctor had lied at the hearing, and that the donor probably was able to breathe independently when his heart was removed (Nakajima 1985). This scandal contributed enormously to the fact that brain death has only recently been recognized in Japan, and then only for organ donors.

In May 1968 an Editorial appeared in the *Journal of the American Medical Association* (*JAMA*) in which the dilemma posed by vital organ transplants was clearly voiced: "It is obvious that if . . . organs [such as the liver and heart] are taken long after death, their chance of survival in another person is minimized. On the other hand, if they are removed before death can be said to have occurred by the strictest criteria that one can employ, murder has been done." The Editorial went on to state that it is therefore "mandatory that the moment of death be defined as precisely as possible" and concluded: "When all is said and done, it seems ironic that the end point of existence, which ought to be as clear and sharp as in a chemical titration, should so defy the power of words to describe it and the power of men to say with certainty, 'It is here'." (*JAMA* Editorial 1968: 220).

One month later, in August 1968, an Ad Hoc Committee composed primarily of physicians called together by the Harvard Medical School, published the findings of their meetings in the JAMA. The committee agreed that " 'irreversible coma' must be substituted for 'cessation of vital functions' as the criterion for death." Two principal reasons were given as to why there was a need for this new definition: improvements in resuscitative and supportive measures had led to increased efforts to save those who are desperately injured, sometimes with only partial success, so that someone with irreversible brain damage might continue to have a beating heart. It was argued that the burden of such patients was great on families, hospitals, and those in need of beds. A second reason given was that "obsolete criteria for the definition of death can lead to controversy in obtaining organs for transplantation" (Ad Hoc Committee of the Harvard Medical School to Examine the Definition of Death 1968: 337). The report noted that the first problem for the committee was to determine the "characteristics of a *permanently* nonfunctioning brain." It was emphasized that a decision to declare irreversible coma must be made only by the physician-in-charge, in consultation with one or more physicians directly involved with the case (implying that transplant surgeons should not be involved). The report continued, "it is unsound and undesirable to force the family to make the decision."

A legal commentary which followed this statement corroborated that judgement of death must be solely a medical issue, and that the patient be declared dead before any effort is made to take "him off a respirator," otherwise the physicians would be "turning off the respirator on a person who is, under the present strict, technical application of law, still alive" (Ad Hoc Committee of the Harvard Medical School to Examine the Definition of Death 1968: 86). The article also noted that Pope Pius XII had, in 1957, stated that it is "not within the competence of the Church" to determine death in cases where there is overwhelming brain damage, and that verification of death can be determined "if at all" only by a physician (*JAMA*, 1968: 362). In what seems to be, in retrospect, a surprising oversight, the impression was left by the Ad Hoc Committee that from now on *all* death would be determined by the condition of the brain; this position was modified when the Uniform Determination of Death Act was passed in America in 1981.

Standardized criteria for determining brain death in both Europe and North America have been in existence for nearly two decades (although they vary in small but significant ways from one country to another). A battery of clinical tests (which also vary within and among countries) are used to make the diagnosis. Guidelines recommend that two specialists perform the tests independently of each other, that transplant surgeons are not involved with making the diagnosis, and that a confirmatory set of tests be carried out between six and twenty-four hours after the first diagnosis.[5] However, when making clinical decisions on behalf of brain dead patients, this diagnosis provides little information that will incite any changes in the therapeutic regime, for nothing can be done, given our current state of knowledge, to reverse the situation once the brain stem is extensively damaged.

When an elderly or a very sick person on a ventilator starts to show signs of irreversible brain damage, very often no special effort is made to diagnose brain death. There is no pressure to bring about resolution to the situation. It is only for that relatively small number of patients who may become organ donors that a precision diagnosis is called for. Once it is confirmed that a donor has been located, then the assertive force of transplant technology comes into play, and attention is turned from the living cadaver to the condition of their organs (see also Hogle, 1999).

When Bodies Outlive Persons

It is striking that despite legal recognition of whole brain death as the end of life (or alternatively brain stem death in the United Kingdom and other locales), and the publication and distribution of recognized standardized guidelines for its determination by the various medical associations and hospitals, these guidelines are rarely referred to by the thirty-two intensivists[6] and eight nurses in ICUs whom I interviewed in 1997 and 1998 in Canada and the United States. Usually, intensivists are simply taught what to do at the bedside without referral to written guidelines and today, in contrast to the situation twenty years ago, there is a high degree of standardization (although not complete) across hospitals with respect to clinical tests (there is much less agreement about the value of certain confirmatory procedures such as use of the electroencephalograph).

All the intensive care specialists who were interviewed agree that the clinical examination for brain death is straightforward. The tests are described as "robust," "simple" and "solid" and, together with the apnea test which confirms whether or not the patient can breathe independently of the ventilator, they inform physicians about the condition of the lower brain – about the brain stem. If there is no response to this battery of tests, then whole brain death is diagnosed provisionally. Once the tests have been repeated for a second time, the diagnosis is confirmed (in practice, if the trauma is very severe, a second set of tests is dispensed with), the death certificate is signed, and the ventilator is turned off unless the patient is to become an organ donor.

Complete agreement exists among the intensivists interviewed that the clinical criteria for whole brain death (or brain stem death) are infallible *if* the tests are performed correctly. There is also agreement that whole brain death, properly diagnosed, is an irreversible state, from which no one in the experience of the informants has ever recovered, although five of those interviewed have been involved with cases where "errors" have occurred. However, although the physicians I talked to agree that a brain death diagnosis is robust, it does not follow that they believe that patients are biologically dead when sent for organ retrieval.

Not one thinks that a diagnosis of brain death signals the end of biological life, despite the presence of irreversible damage, and knowledge that this condition will lead, usually sooner rather than later, to complete biological death. As one intensivist puts it, "It's not death, but it is an irreversible diagnosis, which I accept." Despite massive technological intervention, a diagnosis of whole brain death indicates that the brain cannot continue to function as the site for the integration of biological activities in other parts of the body. At the same time a unanimous sentiment exists that the organs and cells of the body, including small portions of the brain, remain alive, thanks to the artificial brain stem created by the ventilator. Indeed, if organs are to be transplanted, then they *must* be kept alive and functioning as close to "normal" as is possible; as Youngner et al. note, "maintaining organs for transplantation actually necessitates treating dead patients in many respects as if they were alive" (Youngner, et al. 1985: 321).

The majority of intensivists are aware that infants have been delivered from brain dead bodies. It is not possible for them to disregard the fact that the brain dead are warm and usually retain a good color, that digestion, metabolism and excretion continues, and some know that the hair and nails continue to grow. Further, clusters of cells in the brain often remain active after brain death has been declared, and endocrine and other types of physiological activity continue for some time.

For almost all of those intensivists interviewed, although a brain dead patient is not biologically dead, the diagnosis indicates that the patient has entered into a *second* irreversible state, in that the "person" and/or "spirit" is no longer present in the body. The patient has, therefore, assumed a hybrid status – that of a dead-person-in-a-living-body. However, rather than dwell on ambiguities or engage in extended discussion about conceptual ideas about death, clinical practitioners are, not surprisingly, interested first and foremost in biological accuracy and certainty. In order to convey this certainty, namely that an irreversible biological condition has set in, in addition to explaining about tests and examinations to families, they emphasize that the "person" is no longer present in the body, even though the appearance of the entity lying in front of them does not give visual support to this argument.

Intensivists stated that they say things to families at the bedside such as: "the things that make her her are not there any more," or, "he's not going to recover. Death is inevitable." One doctor, who in common with many of his colleagues, chooses not to say simply that the patient is dead, because for him personally this is not the case, tells the family firmly that the patient is "*brain* dead" but that there is "absolutely no doubt but that things will get worse." A young physician doing a fellowship in intensive care pointed out that it is difficult to assess what is best to say to the family, because in most cases one does not know if the family has religious feelings or not:

I believe that a "humanistic" death happens at the same time as brain death. If I didn't believe this, then I couldn't take care of these patients and permit them to become organ donors. For me the child has gone to heaven or wherever, and I'm dealing with an organism, respectfully, of course, but that child's soul, or whatever you want to call it, is no longer there. I don't know, of course, whether the family believes in souls or not, although sometimes I can make a good guess. So I simply have to say that "Johnny," is no longer here.

Another intensivist thinks of the brain dead body as a vessel, and tells the family that what is left of their relative is only an empty container, because the "person has gone." For a doctor born in Latin America, the "essence" of the patient has gone, and this is what he tells the family. With only one exception, for all the intensivists, the absence of the person is evident *because* the brain is irreversibly damaged, thus ensuring a permanent lack of consciousness, no awareness, and no sensation of pain. In other words, a sensate, suffering, individual has ceased to exist.

More than one physician intimated that it is essential that the doctor takes control "a bit" when discussing brain death, both when it is immanent, and after the fact. As one of them put it, "families often find it difficult to accept that there is no possibility of reversibility, and this is where the doctor cannot afford to appear diffident or equivocating." Another insisted that "you can't go back to the family and say that their relative is brain dead, you've *got* to say that they are dead – you could be arrested for messing up on this." This intensivist recalled that during his training he had described a patient as "basically dead" to his supervisor, who had responded abruptly by insisting: "He's dead, that's what you mean, basically." The task for intensivists then is to convince the family that, even though their relative appears to be sleeping, they are in fact no longer *essentially* alive; what remains is an organism or vessel that has suffered a mortal blow.

Doubts Among the Certainty

It is clear that the intensivists have few second thoughts about reversibility, but it is also evident that many of them nevertheless harbor some doubts about the condition of a patient recently declared brain dead, and it is often those with the longest clinical experience who exhibit the most misgivings. An intensivist with over fifteen years of experience working in ICUs said that he often lies in bed at night after sending a brain dead body for organ procurement and asks himself, "Was that patient *really* dead? It is irreversible – I know that, and the clinical tests are infallible. My rational mind is sure, but some nagging, irrational doubt seeps in." This doctor, and the majority of other intensivists interviewed, take some consolation from their belief that to remain in a severely vegetative state is much worse than to be dead. *If* a mistake is made, and a patient is diagnosed prematurely, or treated as though brain dead when this is not the case, then it is assumed that either the patient would have become brain dead shortly thereafter, or permanent unconsciousness would have been their lot. But doubts continue to fester away at some people.

One intensivist, who came to North America from India as an immigrant when a child, stated that for him a brain dead body is "an in-between thing. It's neither a cadaver, nor a person, but then again, there is still somebody's precious child in front of me. The child is legally brain dead, has no awareness or connection with the world around him, but he's still a child, deserving of respect. I know the child is dead and feels no pain, is no longer suffering, that what's left is essentially a shell. I've done my tests, but there's still a child there." When asked by families, as he often is, if the patient has any consciousness, or feels pain, this intensivist has no difficulty in reassuring them that their child is dead, and is no longer suffering. He noted that it is especially hard for relatives when they take the hand of their child and sometimes the hand seems to respond and grasp back. This reflex response was noted by several of the intensivists and nurses as very disconcerting for families, especially when one is trying to convince them that the patient is dead.

One doctor professed to a belief in a spirit or soul that takes leave of the body at death. For her, if brain damage is involved, this moment happens when the patient's brain is irreversibly damaged, at the moment of trauma or shortly thereafter, that is, before the brain death diagnosis. Another intensivist insisted at first, as did many of the people interviewed, that he had no difficulty with the idea of brain death: "it seems pretty straightforward to me. Do the tests, allow a certain amount of time; a flat EEG and you're dead." Then, ten minutes later this doctor said: "I guess I equate the death of a person with the death of the spirit because I don't really know about anything else, like a hereafter. I'm not sure anyway, if a hereafter makes a difference or not." When asked what he meant by the word "spirit," this doctor replied: "I guess one would have to take it as meaning that part of a person which is different, sort of not in the physical realm. Outside the physical realm. It's not just the brain, or the mind, but something more than that. I don't really know. But anyway, a brain dead patient, someone's loved one, won't ever be the person they used to know. Sure their nails can grow and their hair can grow, but that's not the essence."

Another senior physician, struggling to express his feelings, imbued the physical body with a will: "the body *wants* to die, you can sense that when it becomes difficult to keep the blood pressure stable and so on." This intensivist, although he accepts that brain death is the end of meaningful life, revealed considerable confusion in going on to talk about the procurement of organs: "we don't want this patient to expire before we can harvest the organs, so it's important to keep them stable and alive, and that's why we keep up the same treatment after brain death." Yet another informant acknowledged that the "real" death happens when the heart stops: "the patient dies two deaths."

For these doctors, because there can be no argument about the liveliness of the principal body organs, aside from the brain, an organ donor is by definition biologically alive, or at least "partially" biologically alive when sent to the operating room for organ retrieval. Perhaps most pertinent of all is that, in addition to the confusion and occasional doubts expressed in connection with the status of a brain dead individual, among the thirty-two doctors interviewed, only six had signed their donor cards or left other forms of advanced directives, and one other wasn't sure whether he had done so or not. When I pressed for reasons for this hesitation, no one gave me very convincing answers. Some intensivists said that their family would know what to do, or else that they just didn't feel quite right about donating organs, or, alternatively, that they supposed they should get it sorted out.

Nursing the Brain Dead

Among the eight nurses I interviewed, all of them assume that brain death is a reliable, irreversible diagnosis, and claim that they have no difficulties in understanding what it signifies. When the first set of clinical tests indicate brain death, nurses think of their patients as "pretty much dead," because none of them have ever witnessed a reversal of the diagnosis when the second set of confirmatory tests are performed. However, they do not change their care or behavior towards a patient until after the second and final confirmation of brain death, and even then very little if the patient is to be an organ donor.

While carrying out their work between the two sets of diagnostic tests, nurses continue to talk to their patients and, in addition to keeping their eyes on the monitors, they pay careful attention, as they would with any patient, to the comfort and cleanliness of the body. Two nurses stated that they are acutely aware of the family at this time, and deliberately make their behavior around the patient as "normal" as possible, for the sake of the family. More often than not it is the nurse to whom the family has been putting their urgent questions, asking above all about the prognosis. In many cases nurses sense that patients are brain dead before the first set of tests are actually done, for they have been checking the pupils of the eyes regularly, looking for reflexes, and noting that the patient no longer responded to pain stimulation, nor shows any response when tubes are threaded into or taken out of their bodies.

Once whole brain death is confirmed, if the patient is going to be an organ donor, ongoing procedures do not change, except that the focus of attention is on the condition of individual organs, and not on the patient as a whole. The majority of the nurses now regard the patient in front of them as no longer fully human: "a brain dead body can't give you anything back; there's only an envelope of a person left, the machines are doing all the work." Some nurses continue to talk to brain dead bodies as they "care" for the organs, "out of habit," "just in case a soul is still there," or "because the soul is probably still in the room" (Youngner et al. 1985; see also Wolf 1991).

In common with the physicians interviewed, the majority of nurses think that "it is what goes on in your head that makes you a person." One nurse insisted that the idea that nails grow after brain death does not make her at all uncomfortable. Confusion is apparent, as we saw among some physicians, in the way in which nurses talk about the brain dead: "Once the patient has been declared brain dead you still keep them on all of the monitors and the ventilator, for two reasons: first of all, the family wants to go in and see the patient *still alive* and second, soon after, a few minutes after, we'll be asking them to consider organ donation" (emphasis added). One nurse insisted that brain death is not death, and that patients remain alive until the heart stops beating, which, if organs are to be procured, takes place in the operating room when the ventilator is finally turned off. Despite these ambiguities, the ICU nurses with whom I talked are more conscientious than are the physicians about signing their donor cards – all but one senior nurse had done so.

One group of medical specialists, anesthesiologists who are also intensivists, sometimes find themselves in disturbing circumstances in connection with organ procurement. As one woman who works in a children's hospital put it:

Occasionally there is a patient who I've been looking after over the weekend in the ICU, working with closely, hoping that things will improve. The following week I will be having my turn on anesthesiology, and so I don't go to the ICU, and I look up and see them wheeling in the child so as we can procure organs from him. The child has taken a turn for the worse and become brain dead in the day or so after I went off the ICU. For me, this is the most ghastly job that I have to do. (see also Youngner et al. 1985)

This same doctor added:

Procurements are not a pretty sight. I always get the hell out of the operating room as soon as I possibly can. As soon as they've got the heart out. Everyone starts to scrabble at that point. It's ghastly, absolutely ghastly. I sort of have to sit down by the machines and just keep checking the dials every couple of minutes so as I don't have to watch what's going on. It's ghoulish, but you just have to try and focus on the fact that those organs are going to do some good. In a way I *have* to think of them still as a patient because they are under my care, and I guess the most important thing is that they are treated with respect, which isn't normally a problem at all. But with procurements, there's this conflict between the whole body and the organs. I can't really let myself think of it as a person any more. On the other hand, certainly if I've had contact with the patient before, and have been caring for them, then it's really hard for me to just accept that that process has ended. There really is a conflict. So I have to think of the body as a vessel, partly because I'm trying to protect myself. It's a really unpleasant emotion, especially because often there's no external trauma, so it's really hard to realize that this young person is dead.

In summary, none of the clinicians whom I interviewed, physicians and nurses, were opposed in principle to the idea of organ transplants, and all of them believe that it is appropriate for individuals who have given prior consent to donate organs. Intensivists are more ambivalent than many of them care to admit, however, about the status of a living cadaver. While everyone agrees that brain death is irreversible, no one believes that brain dead individuals are biologically dead. Nevertheless, because they are convinced that no sentient being continues to exist once brain death is declared, they find themselves in good conscience able to send brain dead individuals off for organ procurement. Persons are clearly located in brains, that is, in minds.

In addition to ambiguous feelings about the ontological status of brain dead organ donors as alive or dead, are the more mundane but terrifying anxieties created by the possibility of errors, cases of which all the intensivists had heard about, and with which some have been directly associated. Among the intensivists interviewed, five of them had been involved with cases where there was confusion in connection with the apnea test, the test that confirms whether or not a patient can breathe independently of the ventilator. In one case, when the intensivist was still a resident, he had been part of a team that was trying to establish brain death very quickly:

I suppose we were working under pressure to procure organs for transplant. We did the apnea test for half a minute [a much shorter time than usual] and the patient didn't breathe. Then we sent the patient to the OR as a donor, and when they stopped the respirator, the patient started breathing. They brought him back to the ICU, and we kept supporting the patient. He finally died about two months later, but it was a complete nightmare. There were no excuses for that, but it was at the time before clear guidelines had been established for brain death – in the early 70s. I always tell my residents about this case, and I always teach people that they must *never* be in a hurry with this diagnosis.

One or two North American physicians have been actively opposed to the concept of brain death from the time it was first formulated in the late 1960s. In a review article Byrne and Nilges conclude that the requirement of the Uniform Determination of Death Act that "all functions of the entire brain" should have ceased before brain death can be declared, is not in fact met in clinical practice, and therefore "dying is confused with death." For these authors, "imminent" death is not sufficient or satisfactory as a criterion for organ donation. They also note that protocols put out by transplant coordinators and transplant surgeons emphasize the "*rapid* acquisition of *physiologically* sound organs," something that these authors insist "puts the donor at risk" (Byrne and Nilges 1993, emphasis in original).

On the basis of their review these authors claim that they are forced to bring up the "haunting question" of whether the "brain dead" really have an absence of all functions of the brain. Byrne and Nilges conclude that we should reverse our usual orientation, and that we should search not for signs of brain death but for signs of brain life. They are convinced that if this approach had been taken at the outset thirty years ago then greater efforts would have been made to save patients with major brain trauma:

Gunshot wounds of the brain have not been treated aggressively in the past twenty-five years. Pessimism as to outcome has led to withholding of adequate neurosurgical care (Kaufman 1990). We would suggest that to salvage some benefit out of such tragedies and to salve the consciences of those rendering care, these unfortunate patients (who are usually young and in previous good health) are used as organ donors without being given the benefit of at least an attempt at neurosurgical debridement. The period of lack of improvement in the care of gunshot wounds of the brain almost coincides with the rise of transplant surgery. (Byrne and Nilges 1993: 21)

During the interviews, several intensivists made their own anxieties quite clear about equivocal outcomes from severe brain trauma. They have all witnessed many patients who neither progress to brain death nor recover, but remain in a persistent vegetative state, and they themselves would rather be dead than in such a condition. While aggressive therapy may lead to something approaching a full recovery, the likelihood of this being so is very small. The experience of most intensivists is that partial recovery is the best that one should hope for. Some families want aggressive treatment, but many refuse this option, often on the grounds that they do not want to cause any more suffering for their dying relative. Today, a good number of intensivists and involved families alike believe that organ donation is the best way to create meaning out of sudden tragedy. Although I have no evidence for this, there is a possibility that a certain amount of collusion takes place at times between intensivists, nurses, transplant coordinators and families, so that slippage is made a little too quickly from being a patient for whom everything is being done, to becoming an organ donor. In Japan, it is just this kind of fear, that patients are being made into organ donors before they have died, that has created what is known nationally as the "brain death problem" (*nôshi no mondai*).

The Brain Death "Problem"

Tomoko Abe, a Japanese pediatrician employed for many years in a hospital that specializes in neurological disorders, has spent considerable energy during the past decade working with the grassroots movement in Japan against the legalization of brain death as the end of life. In discussing her position with me at one of our several meetings, she emphasized that the concept of brain death was created primarily for the purpose of facilitating organ transplants. She is emphatic that when a dying person is understood as the focus of both a concerned family and a caring medical team, then it is difficult to interpret brain death as the demise of an individual. Her opinion is derived, Abe states, from reflection on her own subjective feelings as a pediatrician: "The point is not whether the patient is conscious or unconscious, but whether one *intuitively* understands that the patient is dead. Someone whose color is good, who is still warm, bleeds when cut, and urinates and defecates, is not dead as far as I am concerned. Of course I know that cardiac arrest will follow some hours later – but I think even more significant is the transformation of the warm body into something that is cold and hard – only then do the Japanese really accept death." When asked why this is so, Abe replies that "it's something to do with Buddhism, I suppose, I'm not really a Buddhist but it's part of our tradition." Abe is completely opposed to organ transplants that are dependent on brain dead donors, and also has strong reservations about living related organ donations.

In 1985, the Japanese Ministry of Health and Welfare published guidelines for the diagnosis of brain death (*Kôseishô* 1985). The Ministry report is explicit, however, that "death cannot be judged by brain death" and it makes no claims to having any legal clout. Nevertheless, the diagnosis is frequently applied, and by 1987, 70 percent of the larger hospitals and university centers in Japan were making use of it, although patients were almost without exception maintained on ventilation even after the diagnosis "because relatives cannot accept the reality and medical personnel fear legal repercussions if they insist on discontinuing cardiopulmonary care" (Takeuchi et al. 1987: 98).

The three decades of debate and confusion about brain death in Japan *apparently* reached closure on 17 June 1997 when the Japanese government passed a bill just moments before parliament was dissolved for the year end recess. The bill, which became law in October 1997, is a compromise, however, and the long dispute over whether brain death represents human death remains unresolved because ambiguity is built into the wording of the new law. This states that organs may be retrieved from a patient diagnosed as brain dead provided that the patient (at least fifteen years of age) has left written consent to be a donor, and that the family does not overrule the declared wish of the patient. Consent should be obtained from *all* relatives who lived with the deceased, including grandparents and grandchildren, if appropriate. Caution is advised with patients who are mentally handicapped. If no advanced directives exist, then a brain dead patient will continue to receive medical care after such a diagnosis is made, until such time as the family and medical team agree to terminate treatment and turn off the ventilator, often several days after brain death is diagnosed.

In other words, brain death is legally recognized only for those patients who have made it clear that they wish to donate organs. For potential organ donors, the legal time of death is when brain death is confirmed. For all other patients, brain dead or not, it is when the heart stops beating. If organs are removed from the body, then this must be noted on the death certificate. The Act also stipulates that medical expenses for patients who continue to be ventilated after a diagnosis of brain death will be reimbursed through the health insurance system, "for the time being." The current law is subject to revision after three years. The law has been described as a "typically confusing Japanese compromise" by many commentators in Japan (Hirano: 1997). Under the new bill, physicians are not required by law to make routine requests for organs from the relatives of brain dead patients, nor can they be required by hospital administrators to do so. Initiation of inquiries about donation is thus left entirely up to the family.

Over the past thirty years, charges of murder have been laid against more than twenty doctors for procuring organs from brain dead, or purportedly brain dead patients. These charges were for the most part made by citizen activist groups, some of them led by physicians such as Tomoko Abe. Earlier this year all outstanding legal cases were dropped, and the assumption is that these decisions will facilitate the institutionalization of organ transplants using brain dead donors. However, despite the new law, to date not a single transplant has been performed making use of a brain dead donor. There have, however, been several "near misses." What might have been the first case of donation after the law was passed, by a man in his 50s, was brought to a halt because he had made a small error in filling out his donor card. The nation remains poised, still waiting for the first legal heart or liver transplant from a brain dead donor to be performed.[7]

A vast literature exists, mostly in Japanese, commenting on why there has been so much resistance to the recognition of brain death in Japan. There is no consensus, and explanations range from historical prohibitions about the dissection of human bodies, concerns about the souls of the dead, corruption in the Japanese medical system, to a lack of trust in doctors in tertiary care institutions, caused especially because the idea of informed consent is not fully recognized in Japan. All of these arguments have some validity, but Japan is a complex, pluralistic society about which sweeping generalizations cannot be made (even though many commentators are tempted to do so). Despite the thirty-year impasse about brain death, public opinion polls have shown for several years now that approximately 50 percent of people in Japan think of brain death as the end of human life, a figure that is not very different from those obtained from polls in North America (Nudeshima 1991).

Among the fifteen Japanese intensivists whom I interviewed, the majority of whom were neurosurgeons, I did not find anyone who took such an extreme position as Abe, although her sentiments and those of others who think as she does (including many physicians), are well known among the Japanese public because they have made numerous television appearances and published widely on the subject. Like the North American intensivists, all of the physicians with whom I talked believe that brain death is an irreversible condition, provided that no errors have been made, but that a brain dead body is not dead. They are not opposed to organ transplants, unlike Tomoko Abe, but none of them has ever actually been involved with procurement of organs for donation.

Although I conducted interviews in the year before the law was implemented, I would be surprised if the neurosurgeons working in departments of emergency medicine in Japan have changed their practices very much.[8] Their position, even though they are not in principle in opposition to organ donation, is that it is inappropriate to declare brain death and then abruptly ask the family about donation. If the family does not raise the question of donation independently, as they rarely do (although this is changing a little since the passing of the new law), then the matter will not be discussed. There is, therefore, no haste, no pressure, and no need for an accurate diagnosis. This situation remains even after the enactment of the law in most clinical settings because, aside from a relatively small number of designated, university hospitals, other hospitals are still not legally able to procure organs, and thus far a lack of cooperation among hospitals continues to be the usual state of affairs (Ikegami: 1989). Given the discursive background and the history of legal suits in connection with brain death in Japan, it might be assumed that doctors would tend to practice "defensive medicine" and that this would therefore account for their reluctance to approach families about donation. While there is some validity to such an interpretation, it is grossly oversimplified in my opinion, and underestimates to what extent doctors are active participants in their own cultural milieu.

Among the neurosurgeons interviewed, they all agree that they "more or less" follow the Takeuchi Criteria, that is, the standards set out by the Ministry of Health and Welfare in 1985 for determining brain death. However, several of them added comments to the effect, "we don't always make the diagnosis, even when we suspect brain death. We often guess, which is much easier for the patient and the family." What is implied is that, in severe cases, the attending neurosurgeon will do one or more clinical tests, on the basis of which he comes to the conclusion that the patient is either brain dead or very close to it. He then informs the family that their relative is *hobo nôshi no jotai* (almost brain dead), or alternatively that the situation looks *zetsubôteki* (hopeless). Despite the prognosis, the ventilator is not turned off until the family requests it, often several days after the diagnosis.

One physician commented, "perhaps this is unique to Japan, but we believe that it is best to tell the family that we are continuing to do our best for their relative even though brain death is 'approaching,' rather than to say as they do in America, 'the patient is brain dead, here are the test results, we are going to terminate all care.' " This same neurosurgeon went on to state that usually, once he is convinced of brain death, he will "gradually reduce the treatment," meaning that no more medications are administered, and that the amount of oxygen being delivered from the ventilator is reduced. In his own mind nothing more can be done for the patient, but this neurosurgeon continues catering to what he believes are legitimate family desires.

Another neurosurgeon commenting on the actions of his colleagues said that "brain death is a kind of 'end stage,' in other words, there is nothing more that we can do for the patient, but we are ambivalent because brain death is not human death. There was a case I had a while ago where a child stayed alive for six or seven days even when the ventilator had been turned down. If the family had said early on that they wanted to donate organs I would have stopped the ventilator at once, but there was no suggestion of this. As far as they were concerned, I would have been killing their child if I had turned off the ventilator – and in a way they are right. After all, we don't sign the death certificate until the heart stops beating."

A neurosurgeon with more than fifteen years of clinical experience said that he would never approach a family about donation, nor does he turn off the ventilator until the family requests it. This doctor reminded me that an extended family is often involved, and that if even one distantly related uncle telephones to say that he does not want the ventilator stopped, then it remains in place. In his experience the family usually waits for three or four days after they have been told that things look hopeless when, having come to terms with the situation, the ventilator is removed "and the patient dies." Like his colleagues, this neurosurgeon reduces the oxygen from the ventilator once he is convinced in his own mind that the patient is brain dead: "we do the basics and leave the rest to nature, we always leave room for a miracle, just in case someone comes back." This same doctor insists that he has recently been getting firmer with families who stubbornly refuse to accept that the situation is hopeless. However, he never tells families that their relative is dead, simply that their condition is irreversible, and that they can no longer breathe on their own. Among those specialists who were interviewed, only one emergency medicine doctor, a man who had worked for several years in America, believes that families should be told firmly that their relative is dead once brain death is diagnosed.

Of the four Japanese nurses whom I interviewed, in common with the neurosurgeons, none of them evinced any difficulty with turning down the supply of oxygen from the ventilator once it was clear to the medical staff that brain death was close. Nevertheless, as one nurse insisted, for the family a brain dead relative always remains alive. Like several of the doctors, the nurses insisted that "life" and "death" are not fully medical matters, and family sentiments must be considered. Further, they argued that although moral and ethical issues in connection with the brain dead are not the same as for the living, brain dead patients remain in a "micro world" of their own where "something continues to exist."

In complete contrast to the responses given in North America by medical professionals, although there is an acute sensitivity about the ambiguous nature of a living cadaver, no one in Japan described the shell of a body remaining once the person or the soul departs. There are three reasons for this, I think. One is that clinicians do not think it is appropriate to persuade families that their relative is no longer alive; second, although many of the doctors stated clearly that for them once consciousness is permanently lost a patient is as good as dead, they do not believe that most families think as they do. "Traditional" medical knowledge in Japan holds that life is diffused throughout the body in the substance of *ki* (*ch'i*, in Chinese), and it is assumed as a result that most Japanese are not willing to equate a permanent loss of consciousness with death; third, surveys have shown that in Japan a good number of families remain concerned about tampering with the newly deceased who will eventually attain immortality as ancestors, and therefore deserving of special respect. A small number of doctors participate in these sentiments, and those who are non-believers are reluctant to override families when they express some hesitation about donation; fourth, of most importance, perhaps, the idea of the person is not usually understood as an autonomous entity firmly encased inside a brain.

Japanese have never been overly concerned by something resembling a Cartesian dichotomy, nor is the concept of unique, clearly bounded individuals in whom rights are unequivocally invested part of their recent heritage, although both these topics are extensively debated in

Japan today. Among fifty Japanese I have talked to, only one-third locate the "center" of their bodies in the brain; the others, of varying ages, selected *kokoro* as the center, a very old metaphorical concept that represents a region in the thorax where "true" feelings are located.

The idea of individual rights is currently gaining a serious foothold in Japan, but has to battle against the still powerful flow of tradition in which an individual is conceptualized as residing at the center of a network of obligations, so that personhood is constructed out-of-mind, beyond body, in the space of ongoing human relationships. "Person" in Japan remains, for perhaps the majority, a dialogical creation, and what one does with and what is done to one's body are by no means limited to individual wishes. Moreover, self-determination is often thought of as essentially selfish (Lock 1998). In this climate, in which doctors themselves self-consciously participate to a greater or lesser degree, they are unlikely to impose their interests on families of dying patients, particularly when in the recent past the law has intruded with such force into medical practice.

Cultures of Technoscience

In North America, for intensivists, a brain dead body is alive, but no longer a person, whereas in Japan, such an entity is both living and a person, at least for several days after a declaration of brain death. Because, in the Japanese case, the social identity of brain dead patients remains intact, a brain dead body cannot be easily made into an object and commodified, but continues to be invested with "human rights." In North America, in contrast, a brain dead body takes on a cadaver-like status, deserving of the respect given to the dead, and, with family cooperation, is available for commodification, on the assumption that the procured organs will be transformed into the "gift of life." While these differing discursive backgrounds do not determine what happens in clinical settings, they nevertheless contribute profoundly to the way in which clinical signs and symptoms are interpreted and then acted upon. It must be emphasized that these are the dominant positions in these two geographical areas, and that in both locations ambiguities persist and are contested and resisted, particularly in Japan.

In North America a cultural anesthesia has prevailed, the dominant position was institutionalized with little trouble by powerful mediators in the medical world, backed up by the law, and given the stamp of approval of the Catholic Church. What few disputes arose were refocused by medicine and the media onto the heroics of organ transplants, an act deemed to promote social affiliation. In Japan, the medical world blundered. The infamous case of 1969 that resulted in a murder charge being laid against the physician, and others similar to it that followed, exposed corruption in medicine. Japanese lawyers were immediately opposed to recognition of brain death, religious bodies remained virtually silent, and the media for the most part participated in a campaign to bring down the profession they have repeatedly described as arrogant. Culturally shared ideas about dying and the importance of family involvement in the determination of death have been mobilized in Japan and put to use for political ends in creating these arguments (Lock, forthcoming), but these same ideas are also acted out at the clinical level, where preservation of family affiliation is usually given precedence over any promotion of the donation of organs to unknown others.

One other major difference between Japan and North America is that in North America those individuals who choose not to cooperate with the donation of the organs of their relatives tend to be thought of as aberrant. Organ donation is thoroughly normalized and, aside from the perennial concern about sales of organs, it is assumed that organ procurement and transplants should be promoted worldwide. In Japan, by contrast, there is a reflexivity and caution about these practices, caused not simply by the internal national difficulties that have arisen with these procedures, but also by an awareness that ideas about altruism, human relations and human solidarity, personhood, and autonomy are cultural constructs. It is believed in Japan that "Western" forms of these constructs function positively in connection with the donation and receiving of organs, and that this particular technology is not easily transportable to the cultural setting of Japan where ideas about human affiliation are on the whole different.

The Slippery Slope of Truth

Although the public is almost oblivious, in North America and Europe doubts persist among professional commentators on brain death, as they do in Japan, as to what actually constitutes human death (Arnold and Youngner 1993; Veatch 1993). Although it is frequently reiterated that debates about the concept of death must be kept entirely separate from the organ procurement enterprise, it is evident that in reality this has not been possible. The crisis created by the "shortage" of organs has caused the transplant world to cast around looking for other sources of organs. The question of redefining death once again, as the cessation of upper brain function alone, looms large as a result. Such a definition would permit patients in persistent vegetative state and possibly anencephalic infants (who lack part of the brain) to be counted as dead, or at least as dead enough to become organ donors if their relatives see fit. One effect of this re-examination of death, perhaps unforeseen, has been to cause a number of neurologists and associated specialists to reconsider the original brain death concept.

Robert Truog, a pediatric neurologist, argues that "despite its familiarity and widespread acceptance, the concept of 'brain death' remains incoherent in theory and confused in practice. Moreover, the only purpose served by the concept is to facilitate the procurement of transplantable organs" (Truog 1997: 29). Truog insists that it behooves us to maintain a "clear and simple distinction between the living and the dead" (Truog 1997: 34) and therefore we should return to the "traditional" cardio-respiratory standard but also permit retrieval of organs from those patients who have indicated their willingness in advanced directives, or have the permission of a recognized surrogate, when "no harm" will be done to the donor. This would include, according to Truog, those individuals who are permanently and irreversibly unconscious (but whose hearts still function either independently or through assistance from a respirator) and those who are imminently and irreversibly dying.

Robert Taylor, also a neurologist, comes to similar conclusions using an entirely different argument. He is emphatic that "death is a biological phenomenon, not a social construct." For Taylor a separation of nature from culture is complete, and must remain so for purposes of clarity. He continues, "the proper biological definition of death is 'the event that separates the process of dying from the process of disintegration' and the *proper* criterion of death in human beings is the "permanent cessation of the circulation of blood" (Taylor, forthcoming, emphasis added). Taylor, like Truog and others, finds the brain death definition of death unconvincing. However, together with Truog, he does not wish to undermine the transplant industry, and so he suggests that, similarly to "legal blindness" (a social construct designed to provide assistance to those who are not fully biologically blind), we could maintain brain death as a social construct and as a legal definition of a condition that, once entered, means that an individual, though living, could become an organ donor provided consent has been established.

Alan Shewmon, a pediatric neurologist from Los Angeles, in a letter circulated to certain participants of the Second International Conference on Brain Death that took place in Havana in February 1996, summed up the points of dispute that arose at the conference which struck him as most critical. His impression was that the majority of individuals who presented papers on various aspects of clinical diagnostics lacked a "coherent and universally accepted conceptual basis for why brain death should be equated with death." Shewmon is of the opinion that by the end of the conference there appeared to be virtually unanimous agreement that loss of all brain function is not equivalent to loss of biological life of the body as a whole, although obviously brain destruction is a fatal injury. The brain should be understood, therefore, as the organ critical to "consciousness and personhood." The question of its role in the "somatic integrative unity" of the body remains unsettled but, in any case, this should not be crucial in making a diagnosis of brain death. By extension Shewmon argues, as did at least one other conference participant, the philosopher Karen Gervais, that "*if* the brain dead patient is dead, then so is the PVS [persistent vegetative state] patient," because the only *coherent* argument that brain death is death [a lack of consciousness] logically applies to PVS as well" (emphasis in the original, unpublished letter). Shewmon argues that "we [society] tacitly adopted a new concept of human death, namely that human death is the permanent absence of consciousness" when we adopted the brain death criterion as signifying the end of life, even though this had been repeatedly denied in the medical literature. Shewmon is of the opinion that beyond that point, conference participants were seriously divided in their opinions because no agreement could be reached on the concept of "personhood" (personal communication, March 1996).

Truog, Taylor and Shewmon, together with an increasing number of their colleagues in neurology and related subjects, suggest that we should abandon what has informally been accepted as the axiom for organ donation: "the dead donor rule." However, they agree that organ donation will be severely curtailed if we can no longer obtain organs from brain dead donors, and hence these neurologists argue that individuals, with their prior consent, should be permitted to become donors while still alive, when it is clear that no chance exists for recovery. This position is not unlike that now legally recognized in Japan, except that in Japan families and not individuals have the last word. The debate continues, the transplant enterprise frets, and the hybrid of the brain dead body remains suspended, betwixt and between.

NOTES

1. By "solid organ" is meant those internal organs including the heart, liver, kidneys and lungs that have an obvious anatomical boundary in contrast to blood, bone marrow and so on.
2. The term "hybrid" is liberally used in contemporary cultural studies and cultural anthropology to signify the mixing and inversion of what are taken to be fundamental divisions and categories in society. When objects, languages and signifying practices recognized as coming from separate

domains are fused in practice then hybridity has occurred (Werbner and Madood 1997). In this paper I am following Latour (1993 [1991]), Strathern (1996) and others who have given particular emphasis to two things in connection with hybridity, namely that the dualistic categories of nature/culture, society/individual, subject/object and so on, characteristic of Euro/American thinking, are false dichotomies, cultural constructions that in practice cannot be readily divorced from one another. Second, a division between human and non-human cannot be specified because humans are materially constituted by objects, and objects of all kinds are prosthetic extensions of humans – thus the world is inhabited by hybrids, and heterogeneity is commonplace.

3. Haraway conceptualizes cyborgs as creatures that are both "organism and machine," entities that appear in science fiction but also populate the everyday world. She argues that cyborgs are ubiquitous, at once mythological and real. The cyborg is inevitably a politicized entity, in contrast to Latour's conception of a hybrid, and its recognition assists us in questioning that which is taken as "natural" and "normal" in hierarchic social relations (1990: 149). I make use of both hybrids and cyborgs in this paper when discussing bodies diagnosed as brain dead. Although these concepts come from different theoretical agendas I in effect use them interchangeably in the present discussion.

4. In Sweden, Denmark and Germany public debates about the recognition of brain death have taken place at various times over the past thirty years, setting these countries apart from the rest of Europe and North America.

5. The recommended time for waiting before confirming a brain death diagnosis varies depending upon local guidelines, and upon the cause of the brain trauma. With cases of hypothermia, for example, great caution is usually taken, and the wait may be up to 48 hours before brain death is confirmed.

6. The clinical tests to establish brain death inform one about the condition of the lower brain, or brain stem. In Great Britain, brain stem death is assumed to be equivalent to brain death because if the brain stem no longer functions then the upper brain must inevitably cease to function as well. In North America, France, Japan and other countries, confirmatory tests are often done to reveal the condition of the upper brain, and the diagnosis of brain death in these countries is understood as "whole brain death."

7. As of October 1999, four procurements have now taken place in Japan from brain dead donors.

8. I was told repeatedly while doing this research that the facilities in Japan for emergency medical care are not as up to date nor as efficient as those in America. Virtually no facilities have trauma units, accident victims are taken to general emergency medicine departments and centers. When a patient with a brain injury is brought in to such a unit a neurosurgeon, if not already on duty, will be called to assess the case. The specialty of intensive care is not highly developed, and very few physicians indeed describe themselves as intensivists.

REFERENCES

Ad Hoc Committee of the Harvard Medical School to Examine the Definition of Death 1968 "Definition of Irreversible Coma." *Journal of the American Medical Association* 205: 85–8.

Arnold, Robert, and Stuart Youngner 1993 "Back to the Future: Obtaining Organs from Non-Heart-Beating Cadavers." *Kennedy Institute of Ethics Journal* 3: 103–11.

Arnold, Robert, Stuart Youngner, Renie Shapiro and Carol Mason Spice 1995 *Procuring Organs for Transplant: The Debate Over Non-Heart-Beating Cadaver Protocols*. Baltimore: Johns Hopkins University Press.

Byrne, Paul and Richard Nilges 1993 "The Brain Stem in Brain Death: A Critical Review." *Issues in Law and Medicine* 9: 3–21.

Caplan, Arthur L. 1988 "Professional Arrogance and Public Misunderstanding." *Hastings Center Report* 18: 34–7.

Casper, Monica 1994 "At the Margins of Humanity: Fetal Positions in Science and Medicine." *Science, technology and human values* 19(3): 307–23.

Feldman, Allan 1994 "On Cultural Anaesthesia: From Desert Storm to Rodney King." *American Ethnologist* 21: 404–18.

Haraway, Donna 1990 "A Manifesto for Cyborgs: Science, Technology and Social Feminism in the 1980s." In Linda J. Nicholson, (ed.), *Feminism/ Postmodernism*. London: Routledge, pp. 190–233.

1991 *Simians, Cyborgs and Women: The Reinvention of Nature*. London: Free Association.

Hirano, Ryuichi 1997 "Sanpo ichiryôzon teki kaiketsu: 'soft landing' no tame no zanteki sochi" (A halfway settlement: tentative measures for a soft landing). *Jurist* 1121: 4–6.

Hogle, Linda F. 1999 *Recovering the Nation's Body: Cultural Memory, Medicine and the Politics of Redemption in Germany*. New Brunswick: Rutgers University Press.

Ikegami, Naoki 1989 "Health Technology Development in Japan." *International Journal of Technology Assessment in Health Care* 4: 239–54.

JAMA Editorial 1968 "Viruses and Renal Disease." *Journal of the American Medical Association* 204 (6 May): 6.

Kaufman, Howard H. 1990 "The Acute Care of Patients with Gunshot Wounds to the Head." *Neurotrauma Med. Rep.* (Spring): 1.

Kôseishô 1985 *Kôseishô kenkyûhan ni yoru nôshi no hantei kijun* (Brain death determination criteria of the Ministry of Health and Welfare). Tokyo: Government Publications.

Latour, Bruno 1993 [1991] *We Have Never Been Modern*. Trans. Catherine Porter. Cambridge, MA: Harvard University Press.

Lock, Margaret 1995 "Contesting the Natural in Japan: Moral Dilemmas and Technologies of Dying." *Culture, Medicine and Psychiatry* 19(1): 1–38.

1996 "Displacing Suffering: The Reconstruction of Death in North America and Japan." In *Social Suffering. Special Issue. Daedalus* 125: 207–44.

1997 "The Unnatural as Ideology: Contesting Brain Death in Japan." In Pamela Asquith and Arne Kalland (eds.), *Representing the Natural in Japan*. Cambridge: Cambridge University Press, pp. 121–44.

1998 "Perfecting Society: Reproductive Technologies, Genetic Testing and the Planned Family in Japan." In Margaret Lock and Patricia Kaufert (eds.), *Pragmatic Women and Body Power*. Cambridge Studies in Medical Anthropology, 5. Cambridge: Cambridge University Press, pp. 206–39.

(Forthcoming) "Situated Ethics, Culture, and the Brain Death 'Problem' in

Japan." In Barry Hoffmaster (ed.), *Bioethics in Context.* Cambridge: Cambridge University Press.

Lock, Margaret and Deborah Gordon (eds.), 1988 *Biomedicine Examined.* Dordrecht: Kluwer.

Nakajima, Michi 1985 *Mienai shi: Nôshi to zôki ishoku* (Invisible Death: Brain Death and Organ Transplants). Tokyo: Bungei Shunju.

Newsweek 1968 "Redefining death." 20 May: 68.

Nudeshima, Jiro 1991 *Nôshi, zôkiishoku to nihon shakai* (Brain death, organ transplants and Japanese society). Tokyo: Kôbundô.

Prottas, J. M. 1994 *The Most Useful Gift: Altruism and the Public Policy of Organ Transplants.* San Francisco: Jossey-Bass.

Randall, T. 1991 "Too Few Human Organs for Transplantation, Too Many in Need . . . and the Gap Widens." *Journal of the American Medical Association* 265 (13 March): 1223–7.

Richardson, Ruth 1989 *Death, Dissection and and the Destitute.* London: Penguin.

Sharp, Leslie 1995 "Organ Transplantation as a Transformative Experience: Anthropological Insights into the Restructuring of the Self." *Culture, Medicine and Psychiatry* 9: 357–81.

Shewmon, Alan (Forthcoming) "Chronic 'Brain Death': Meta-Analysis and Conceptual Consequences." *Neurology.*

Statistical Abstract of the United States 1997 *The National Data Book.* 117th edition. Washington: U.S. Department of Commerce.

Strathern, Marilyn 1992 *Reproducing the Future: Essays on Anthropology, Kinship and the New Reproductive Technologies.* New York: Routledge.

    1996 "Cutting the Network." *Journal of the Royal Anthropological Institute* 2 (n.s.): 517–35.

Takeuchi, K., H. Takeshita, K. Takakura, Y. Shimazono, H. Handa, F. Gotoh, S. Manaka and T. Shiogai 1987 "Evolution of Criteria for Determination of Brain Death in Japan." *Acta Neurochirurgica* 87: 93–8.

Taylor, Robert (Forthcoming) "Re-examining the Definition and Criteria of Death." *Neurology.*

Truog, Robert 1997 "Is it Time to Abandon Brain Death?" *Hastings Center Report* 27(1): 29–37.

Veatch, Robert M. 1993 "The Impending Collapse of the Whole-Brain Definition of Death." *Hastings Center Report* 23(4): 18–24.

Werbner, Pnina and Tariq Modood (eds.) 1997 *Debating Cultural Hybridity.* London: Zed Books.

Wolf, Zane Robinson 1991 "Nurses' Experiences Giving Post-Mortem Care to Patients who have Donated Organs: A Phenomenological Study." *Scholarly Inquiry for Nursing Practice: An International Journal* 5: 73–87.

Wolstenholme, G. E. W. and M. O'Connor 1966 *Ethics in Medical Progress: With Special Reference to Transplantation.* Boston: Little, Brown and Company.

Youngner, S. J., M. Allen, E. T. Bartlett, Helmut F. Cascorbi, Toni Hau, David L. Jackson, Mary B. Mahowald and Barbara J. Martin 1985 "Psychosocial and Ethical Implications of Organ Retrieval." *New England Journal of Medicine* 313 (1 August): 321–4.

12   The practice of organ transplants: networks, documents, translations

Veena Das

In a recent paper, Margaret Lock (1995b) reviews some of the programatic literature on transplant technology and finds a subtext through which this technology is sought to be "naturalized" and thus "the contradictions that inevitably arise from mixing self and other" are disguised, though not always self-consciously. "We have been warned," she says "about the Shiva like character of invasive biomedical technologies: potential creators of happiness but, at the same time, destroyers of society as we know it: for it is now possible to manipulate nature/culture and self/other dichotomies of long standing – projects confined thus far to the realm of fantasy" (1995b: 391).

In this chapter I try to trace the different and multiple genealogies that go in to make the object – the "transplant world" – as a set of practices. Following Foucault (1972) in his analysis of clinical discourse, I do not look for a synthesis or for the unifying function of a subject – instead, I consider the dispersions which occur over various statuses, sites and positions that can be occupied within this discourse. From its inception to its implementation, transplant technology traverses realms that are ethical, legal and medical. It forges relationships between the highly technical worlds of super speciality wards in hospitals, the worlds of organ procuring organizations and individuals; and the families within which decisions about gifting, selling, "cadaver donations" are taken. When considering the enunciative modalities within which to locate the transplant world we are faced with many sites including the international committees in which the standard setting normative exercises take place;[1] the national legislative bodies which enact laws; courts of law in which disputations occur; and the local worlds in which bodies, intimate or distant, come to be related through this technology.

In his provocative analysis of the constitution of modernity in the context of science and technology, Bruno Latour (1993 [1991]) gives us (in broad strokes) a schematic representation of the relation between scientific representation and political representation under this constitution. He argues that the birth of the idea of a political subject who is capable of being represented, the subject pole of modernity so to say, is conjoined to the simultaneous birth of "non-humanity" – the objects that are produced and mobilized through the intermediary of the laboratory. The modern constitution, he argues, masks the conjoined birth of both, "representation of things through the intermediary of the laboratory is forever dissociated from the representation of citizens through the intermediary of the social contract." Latour traces the proliferation of hybrids and the contradictory labours of mediation and purification through a fascinating series of contradictions through which nature and society come to be conceptualized within this framework.

The production of medical knowledge and its consumption, in contrast to the "pure" objects produced in the laboratory, has always involved the citizens as well as subjects in a much more direct manner than other kinds of scientific knowledge. This is partly because the tension between the experimental and the therapeutic that marks new innovations in biomedicine can lead even well intended physicians to take unacceptable risks on behalf of patients (Geison 1995). Thus the moment that a new innovation in medical technology (e.g., a vaccine) moves from the laboratory to the clinical trial, the question of the subject becomes integral to the production of this knowledge – hence the question of political representation comes to be folded into the production of scientific knowledge rather than being something which influences it from the outside. Two recent and telling examples of this process are, firstly, that of AIDS activism in challenging the design of randomized trials in the face of the catastrophic fate of AIDS victims who contest the practice of giving placebos[2] if the drug under experiment has a possibility of offering even short-term advantages (Epstein 1996); and secondly, the conflict between feminist critics and scientists engaged in conducting clinical trials of anti-fertility vaccines in several parts of the world (Viswanath and Kirbat 1998). All these have raised questions about the kind of rights that may be claimed by people suffering from terminal illness such as AIDS or from catastrophic social situations (e.g. the controversies on the use or not of a trial cholera vaccine for refugees of the Rwanda war) – some claiming a new category of rights entitled "catastrophic rights." In an opposite move women's groups have questioned whether a perceived global crisis of overpopulation should entitle the scientific establishment to treat individual women's bodies as bearers of less than the normal rights of citizens. All these are vexed questions that do not permit of simple answers. They do, however, point to the centrality of the issues that connect questions of political representation with scientific representation and invite anthropologists to trace the networks of practices, instruments, docu-

ments and translations in the new technologies that are redefining not
only notions of individuals and of society, but of life itself.[3] Clearly these
technoscapes, to use Appadurai's felicitious term, require innovation in
traditional anthropological methods as Appadurai (1996) and Marcus
(1995) have suggested. Even more important, one cannot assume that
the social relations between participants can provide a picture on which
the relations between the dispersed elements of a technoscape can be
seen. Some of these relations involve face-to-face interactions, as
between the transplant surgeons and the recipients of organs. Others
are explicitly modeled on norms carved within the disciplinary domains
of law or bioethics which forbid, for instance, any face-to-face interactions between those representing the organ donor and the recipient.
Thus the rules which come to govern the practices of organ transplants
are decisively shaped by ethical standards derived from theories of contract within the profession of bioethics as well as by their institutional
embodiments at different levels. Anthropologists, more used to speaking
from within the small face-to-face communities within which they
habitually work, are likely to be struck by the manner in which these
rules impinge on local moral worlds as Kleinman (1999) defines them.
Yet if one is to understand these technoscapes, then one is challenged
to conceptualize the configuration of these dispersed elements. This
raises both new challenges and an awareness of limits within which
anthropological knowledge is taking shape. For instance, rules about
confidentiality govern the anthropologist's access to patients as well as
to decision-making bodies in hospitals which frame substantive and pro-
cedural norms governing the new technologies. Thus weaving one's way
in the difficult boundaries between what is public knowledge and what
is private knowledge, the anthropologist becomes part of the discussion
on emergent ethics rather than someone whose eye can remain outside
the field of vision. It is within this complex configuration that I turn first
to the public discourse of shortage in transplant technology in the Western societies.[4]

The Rhetoric of Shortage

Transplant technology, especially the development of transplantation
immunobiology which vastly increased the chances of success of grafted
organs, has led to a perception among transplant surgeons, legislative
assemblies and the general public in many countries that there is a
"worldwide" shortage of organs needed to save lives. The picture of
suffering patients waiting to receive organs creates the notion of a crisis
and much debate has recently taken place on how to solve this "crisis."

As an example, consider the opening statement of a paper by William Dejong et al.:

Right now more than 37,000 Americans are waiting for an organ transplant to restore their good health. . . Sadly for their hopes of a medical miracle left unfulfilled, nine of these people will die today, and another nine every day this year. A shortage of organs exists despite the fact that there are more than enough potential organ donors to meet current needs. (Dejong et al. 1995: 463)

Though presented as a crisis facing the whole world, its implications for different parts of the world are in fact radically different. To take one example, whereas in countries such as the United States the crisis is to ensure that enough organ donors can be motivated to donate, in poor countries such as India the demand for organs has led to the development of black markets in organ procurement. These new kinds of markets are articulated to the informal economy in which effective legislative and administrative control is virtually absent. While I shall be exploring the different registers in which the crisis of the shortage of organs comes to be articulated cross-culturally, it may be useful to take a brief detour into the historical connections with perceived shortage of bodies for medical education and use in the West. This provides an important frame within which to view this problem.

Historical Antecedents

In an excellent historical analysis of the demand for the dead for purposes of dissection, Ruth Richardson (1989) has traced the interrelations between (a) legal provisions for procuring dead bodies for dissection; (b) the regulation of corpse costs and supplies by professional cartels; and (c) the popular resentments on the appropriation of the dead bodies of the poor, the criminal and the destitute elderly. In the sixteenth, seventeenth and much of the eighteenth centuries in the UK, it was the corpses of the gallows criminals which were supplied to "Companies of Barbers and Surgeons" to facilitate dissection. Popular resentment and gallows rebellions shifted the focus from executed criminals to the buried dead. Consequently, burial grounds were rifled for the freshly dead. The Anatomy Act of 1832 which defines the law regarding acquisition of dead bodies in many English-speaking countries, defined institutions such as workhouses and hospitals which housed the poor as "lawfully in possession" of the dead and permitted confiscation of bodies of those dying without relatives to claim the dead body or those without money for their funeral expenses.

These provisions showed that handing over dead bodies to medical schools for the advancement of knowledge was not seen as a legitimate way of dealing with the dead although exceptions were found in every period. This was why it was the poor and the destitute whose control over dying was taken away. As a category the poor came to replace criminals as suppliers of corpses. David Humphrey (1973) has observed that in practice, if not always in conception, the anatomy laws confined dissections to a voiceless, widely scorned section of society. Richardson highlights the affinity between the medical difficulty of obtaining human bodies for dissection in the past and for obtaining organs for transplantation in the present day.[5] This affinity, however, is precisely what poses serious ethical questions not only to those who are critics of transplant technologies but to the practitioners themselves. The enunciative modalities through which such questions are addressed show important variations across historical periods and across cultures.

How does the medical discourse in India address the problem of shortage of organs? In a series of workshops to examine public opinion on brain death and organ transplants in 1989 and 1990, held in Bombay, Madras and Calcutta, the ethical problems of organ transplant were formulated primarily in terms of resource allocation. For instance, Dr. Samiran Nundy, one of the major figures in transplant technology in India who gave direction to the legislation on the Brain Stem Death and Human Organs Transplant Act for the country, raised the following question (among many others) in the workshop in Calcutta:

Starting a transplant programme would involve a huge expenditure. But would it not be better to find the Indian answers to these problems and do the operation here rather than allow the rich to go to the USA and spend Rs.30 to 40 lakhs of foreign exchange for a transplant operation and let our poor die? (Nundy 1990: 13)

I reproduce part of the discussion which followed in response to these questions.

Dr. S. Mukherjee: Dr. Nundy, you should have stressed the fact that in our country we do not immunize all our children, we do not give full meals to all our people and we do not provide clean drinking water for all our people. These are real problems, while we are sitting in an airconditioned room and talking about transplants which cost scores of rupees.

Dr. Nundy: I think this is a very good point and Indians as people have to make up their minds about this important question. Should we allow a poor person who is dying of a liver disease to die and a rich person to go abroad for an operation? We already discriminate between the rich and the poor in practically every other way. Should this continue? Should we stick to doing hernia operations because these are the most inexpensive and economical and should we stop doing heart operations because so much more resources are involved? I think this is a very difficult decision for our society to take. But I agree that we should be continually reminded of this question.

Many other examples could be given to show that the question of shortage of organs was framed in these discussions in terms of issues of resource allocation and specifically in terms of the media coverage of poor Indians selling their organs to rich foreigners rather than in terms of a world-wide shortage of organs. The question of alternate use of resources – e.g. allocation of resources to public health measures versus expensive medical technologies – was raised frequently but the issues were not as simple as economic modeling in a pure world would assume. It seems to me that the question of resource allocation was posed in the specific context of the practices of organ transplants as they had already come into being and which were characteristically that of the poor selling their organs (i.e., their kidneys) to the rich. This is why the issues of resource allocation translated themselves into proposals for instituting transplant programs in selected government hospitals so that relatively poor persons could be recipients of organs; simultaneously there was pressure to regulate these practices in private hospitals and clinics. Although, to my knowledge, no local protocol was developed which explicitly stated that recipients for organs would be selected on the basis of economic criteria in government hospitals, this was emphasized in the media coverage of the first heart transplants which followed the legislation on brain death. It is also important to note that in the case of kidney transplants in private hospitals, recipients were selected on the basis of their financial ability to sustain post-transplant medication[6] thereby ruling out any access that the poor or even the moderately well off could have to this technology. We shall see later that the conflict that has developed between those who advocate the right to sell organs and those who believe that the encouragement of cadaver donation is the best way to counteract malpractices in the informal sector, is in no small way related to the different ways in which the question of "shortage" of organs is posed.

Redefining Death

For a successful program of transplant technology to be instituted in any country the boundaries between life and death need to be redefined. While kidney transplants can be sustained through live donor programs or through a market in kidneys, heart and liver transplant is not possible without the legislation to recognize brain stem death. Peter Singer states in this context that "Organ transplants are based on the idea that we

die when our brains are dead" (Singer 1994: 36). The classical definitions of death even in the clinical context were based upon permanent
cessation of the flows of vital fluids. But as the perceived need for more
organs and tissues arose the classical definition was sought to be redefined to meet this need. The first draft of the Harvard Brain Death
Committee appointed in the late 1960s whose recommendations on
how to define death came to be widely accepted and legislated upon,
talked about the great need for tissues and organs. This was later revised
and reference was made only to the life saving potential of this redefinition of death. A further report by the President's Commission in the
United States submitted a model statute of the Uniform Determination
of Death Act, in order to bring about uniformity in the different states
of the country for the certification of death. Clearly what is at stake is a
global negotiation on determining the moment of death in order to
facilitate a greater use of organs through methods of harvesting medically defined cadavers. This is apparent in the fact that the moment of
death does not simply occur any more – it has to be chosen.

As early as 1957, Pope Pius XII had stated in a speech that "death
was a complete and final separation of soul and body but it was for
doctors to define the precise moment" (Singer 1994: 29). The negotiated character of this moment is clear from the fact that Japan did not
until recently accept this clinical definition of death (Lock 1995a;
1995b, 1996, 1997). India has only recently passed the legislation to
recognize brain stem death as a definition of clinical death. Further, in
the actual hospital settings, patients who may be defined as dead from
the perspective of transplant surgeons, are not treated as dead either by
their loved ones or by the auxiliary staff of the hospital. That a deep
anxiety is created by these procedures is evident in surveys of health
care professionals, leading Stuart Young to state that we have created a
new class of dead persons in clinical medicine who are treated as dead
for some purposes and not dead for others. In the words of Peter Singer,
"The picture I have presented of brain death up to now suggests that it
is a convenient fiction. It is proposed and accepted because it makes it
possible for us to salvage organs that would otherwise be wasted and to
withdraw medical treatment when it is doing no good" (Singer 1994:
35). Singer is quite clear that repeated changes in the definition of death
may have to be made as transplant technology develops. He suggests
therefore that we should separate the question of when a human being
dies from the one which asks when is it permissible to remove organs
for transplantation from a person who is in "the irreversible process of
dying" (Singer 1994: 26).

While the cultural basis of medical technology has been emphasized by anthropologists such as Margaret Lock (1995b, 1997) and Ohnuki-Tierney (1994) in examining the case of Japan's resistance to the normalization of transplant technology in particular, the nature of public debate is informed by cultural assumptions as well as bureaucratic cultures. Even in countries such as India which have passed legislation on brain death and organ transplants, the process through which these laws came to be enacted is much more complicated than the final product. This complexity is indicative of the fact that there are important gaps between the rule and its execution: thus similarity of standards in the legislative enactments hides the entanglement of rules with customs and habits formulated through the interaction between bureaucratic rules and the larger environment.

I believe it was the shocking media revelations in the 1980s in India on the trading of organs, especially kidneys, which built public opinion against sale of organs. This led to important medical professionals and voluntary organizations dealing with health to petition the state for enactment of legislation that would curb and regulate this practice.

In a report on "Trading of Organs," the Voluntary Health Association of India (an important NGO dealing with all aspects of health), formulated the rationale behind the enactment of an Act to regulate sale of organs in the following manner:

The trading of organs has received much attention in the media of late and from all accounts the money involved in these transactions ranges from Rs.25,000 to over a lakh of rupees. One of the major organs being traded is the kidney. It is estimated that almost 2,000 or more are being sold every year. There is a considerable need for kidneys since nearly 80,000 people suffer from renal failure every year in India. Although the trading of organs is not a recent phenomenon, the last decade has seen a more prominent role of the private sector in the commercialization of the organ trade. It is difficult to estimate the number of transplants done in the major cities since most of them are conducted in small nursing homes and some large hospitals in the private sector. Similarly in the case of corneal transplants there have been reports of illegal sale of corneas.

In the light of criticism from professionals and foundations dealing with organ transplants, the Government has formulated the Transplantation of Human Organ Bill, 1992 "to provide for regulation of removal storage and transplantation of human organs for therapeutic purposes and for the prevention of commercial dealings in human organs." (Baru and Nanda 1993: 3)

An Expert Committee with Dr. L. M. Singhvi (a prominent lawyer and human rights worker)[7] had been appointed in 1991 to examine the proposal for enactment of legislation for use of human organs and their donation for therapeutic purposes. The committee had also been asked to examine the relevant changes which must be made in the definition of death. In the workshop in Calcutta held in 1990 (to which reference was made earlier), the problems of legalizing brain death had been discussed. Dr. A. Baghchi, one of the participants, stated quite clearly that "the definitions, the whole set up, the discussion – only applies to large hospitals in big cities." In the rural areas he said the doctor only had a stethoscope to diagnose death.

The Expert Committee drew heavily from a memorandum drawn by the Conference of the Royal Medical Colleges and their Faculties in the UK in 1979 which had stated that "It is now universally accepted by lay public as well as the medical profession that it is not possible to equate death itself with cessation of the heart beat." Pressing for a recognition of brain stem death, it stated that "it is not difficult or illogical in any way to equate this with the concept in many religions of the departure of the spirit from the body." Thus the Expert Committee also moved on the assumption of a societal consensus on the new legislation. It is interesting to note the style of argument which assumes that religious ideas about death need to be articulated in this context whereas it seems to me that such an articulation in the regulation of technology has rarely been made in the public culture in India. International concerns are simply grafted here on a presumed national discourse.

After languishing in Parliament for two years due to the pressure of the organ sale lobby, the bill was finally debated and accepted in 1994 although it received presidential assent only in February 1995. It could not acquire the force of law, however, until a notification from the relevant Ministry was issued. In fact it required strategic manipulation from the voluntary organizations and the media for the notification to be issued in September. Dr. Tamboli of the Transplant Society of India threatened to go on a hunger strike in September 1995 to press for the notification. He alleged that the notification was not issued because the organ lobby was using every tactic to delay the implementation of the Act. The media, including the electronic media, portrayed the plight of several patients waiting for transplant operations, especially liver transplants, in the All India Institute of Medical Sciences. Finally bowing under public pressure the Health Minister instructed his ministry to issue the relevant notification. While four states and the union territories adopted the law, other states are still to adopt the new law: the moment of death is therefore not uniform throughout the country.

The new legal definition of the moment of death departed from the commonsense understanding which, however, continues to inform the provisions of the Indian Penal Code. It states: "Death denotes the death of a human being unless the contrary appears from the context." Against this commonsense interpretation accepted in law, the new definition has relevance only in the transplant wards. Outside of these specialized contexts the boundaries between life and death continue to be determined by commonsense definitions and "normal" medical and legal practices. Yet these contexts too may come to be shaped in future by the changes introduced in the expert discourses on death.

The Transformation of the Local

An excellent example of the way in which standard protocols for organ procurement are "worked through" at the local level is provided by a recent paper by Linda Hogel (Hogel, 1995). She shows how cultural assumptions on the suitability of particular organs and the character of the "donors" seep into the local practices adopted by organ procurement agencies even when they are interpreting standard protocols. I illustrate a similar process which informed the initiation of transplant surgery based on cadaver donation in a premier government hospital in Delhi, the All India Institute of Medical Sciences (AIIMS).

Even before the notification on the new Act was issued by the government the first heart transplant was successfully accomplished in AIIMS by Dr. Venugopal, a renowned cardiac surgeon. The case was of a 46-year-old businessman who died in a road accident in July and was declared to be brain dead after two brain scans performed after an interval of 24 hours showed little brain activity. The recipient was a jawan (subaltern) in the Border Security Force who had been languishing in the same hospital with a condition diagnosed as "endstage ischemic cardio-myopathy" for which a heart transplant was the only hope. The characteristics of the donor and the recipient as they appeared in the public discourse may be seen from the following interview with the widow which appeared in the Sunday edition of the *Times of India* on 16 July 1995:

She gave away her husband's heart

It was not a difficult decision for her to make. Painful, but not something in which she faltered even once.

Ms. Neelam Narang had all the support from her family when she resolved to donate the heart of her "brain-dead" husband "so that another man could live."

"It is my fate. My husband was meant to die. The other man was meant to live," rationalized the wife of 46-year-old businessman O. P. Narang, victim of a road accident.

Mr. Narang's family, educated and aware, did not need much convincing. "My husband had already pledged his eyes when he was alive. When the doctors asked me if I was willing to donate his heart and other organs, I agreed. My husband would have also wanted it. His thinking was like that," said Ms. Narang, who had also pledged her eyes earlier.

"I lost my husband, but at least my children will get the blessings of the man who has got a second life," she added. Incidentally both her sons, Amit (18) and Sumit (14) backed their mother's decision. Amit is a first year Delhi University student and Sumit is studying in the Air Force School. Ms. Narang is happy her husband's heart is beating in a man who serves the country. "I have not met him yet but he has invited me. 1 am going to meet him in a day or two," she said. (*Times of India*, 16 July 1995)

In this interview, the characteristics of the donor and the recipient are constructed in terms of a narrative of national pride and the creation of legitimacy for the new medical technology. Thus the widow is said to be happy that at least her husband's heart is beating in a person who "serves the country." I am not suggesting that such assumptions are built into the structure of the new technology. At this historical moment, though, the idea of nation, altruism, and the claims to national pride on behalf of science, came together to create a public image of transplant technology. This image was the opposite of the stigmatizing image of the organ bazaars in which the poor were selling their kidneys to the rich, which was discussed earlier. The regulations regarding the anonymity of the recipient and the donor were ignored in that moment of claiming a new public space for this technology – thus political representation taking priority over scientific norms.

How did the new legislation alter the everyday practices of the hospital? In interviews conducted with junior doctors both in the cardiovascular and neurosurgery wards, I found considerable ambiguity about the nature of the transaction which had led to this nationally acclaimed outcome.

In the guidelines for harvesting organs from cadavers which were instituted in the hospital the following protocol was approved.[8] The Resident on duty in the neurosurgery ward was expected to enquire from relatives of accident victims who became brain dead as to whether they would consider donating the organs for transplantation. It was his or her task to explain the program of transplantation in the hospital but there was to be no pressure or offer of any monetary or other inducement. In this case the first relative of the patient to come to the hospital was the wife's brother.

The doctor on duty informed him that a brain scan revealed that the chances of survival for the patient were less than 1 percent. He was also informed that they would try to operate on him as soon as his condition stabilized a little. Unfortunately the blood pressure of the patient dropped to 70/50 and doctors could not take the decision to operate on him unless his blood pressure could be elevated.

Meanwhile the patient's wife had come to the hospital and was informed that surgery could not be performed at that time. She was also informed that the patient's chances of survival were small (*bachne ki ummid kam hai*). Despite the grim situation the wife sought out the Resident again. On her own initiative she informed him that her husband had pledged his eyes to the Times Foundation and had written it in his will. One of the doctors told me:

We do not normally remove the cornea till the person is dead. This is because unlike other organs the cornea does not deteriorate so fast. In the last moments relatives often want to see the person. People will relate to a dying person through his eyes – so although the person is legally dead when the brain stem function ceases, we don't treat him as dead and relatives don't treat him as dead. So when they come to see the person to say goodbye – they would be very shocked if the eyes were not there. With the other organs it is not so noticeable. Because you can remove the organs and stitch up the body.

Since the wife had approached this delicate and difficult question of the eye donation indicating that she was accepting the possibility of the imminent death – the Resident thought that the family may consider donating other organs too.

So I first talked to a relative of theirs who was a doctor. I explained about the transplantation programme and said that if his wife wanted to consider donating other organs too, then we will have to make the decision immediately because by the next day it may be too late. So this doctor (the relative) said that he will talk to the other relatives. I took the brain stem test at night. The blood pressure was still very low, also he was not breathing – he was on the respirator.

As I construct from the discussion that followed among the two junior doctors whom I interviewed, the wife initially refused to consider the Resident's request. Despite having brought up the question of the eye donation heself, the prospect of organ donations upset her enormously. She said that she was not going to allow her husband's body to be cut up into pieces. The doctor then took the eldest son to the café and explained to him that since this was a medico-legal case, an autopsy would have to be conducted in any case. So it was a choice between simply an autopsy or an autopsy and donation. The son was terrified of the economic ruin the family would face since his father was the only breadwinner. He asked if some reward in the form of a scholarship or financial help for his studies could be given if they agreed to the organ donation. According to the Resident, he then said something which could have been interpreted by the son to mean that he (the son) was bargaining over his father's body; though this is not what the Resident had intended to convey. In the highly charged atmosphere the boy started crying and the Resident immediately regretted what he had said. He told the boy that since this was the first heart transplant, the family would get a lot of media attention: perhaps some charitable foundation may help them financially. He explained that it was against the law and the regulations of the hospital to allow any financial rewards for the donations of organs.

Apparently the boy went back and discussed all this with his mother. They finally agreed to allow his father's organs to be harvested although no other organs except the heart could be used, for several reasons. The doctor who could have performed a liver transplant was not in the country and the kidneys also could not be harvested.

This entire episode led to much discussion among the junior doctors on the ethics of organ donation. One Resident in the neurosurgery ward told me that all the doctors were against financial incentives. However, they also felt that information about brain dead patients in the ICU would soon begin to be spread through the lower functionaries of the hospital and financial agreements may be secretly arrived at through the mediation of the peons and the wardboys. One doctor gave me the example of an accident victim whose wife had refused to consider the donation of cornea. Later the same day another relative came and enquired whether they could donate the kidneys of the patient if he died. "I felt that perhaps a deal was being struck behind the wife's back: if she had refused to donate the cornea how could she have changed her mind so fast and think of donating kidneys? I told this relative off saying that they were not suitable donors."

In order to locate this particular statement on a deal being struck behind the wife's back, we need to understand the well-developed system of informal transactions (which are violative of the formal rules) operative in most public hospitals. This aspect of the underlife of the hospital is much better understood by junior doctors who have to directly deal with the lower staff than by their senior colleagues. Many patients who come to the hospital as well as their relatives who accompany them are illiterate and poor: often they simply do not understand the regime of rules and regulations which stem from the moral life of the institution of which they are not a part. They depend upon the non-medical staff to negotiate these rules. For instance, in the hospital various kinds of forms have to be filled which assume a capacity to read and write; patients have to be taken for several diagnostic tests to offices and laboratories in different wings of the hospital which the relatives can negotiate only with difficulty; reports have to be collected;

sometimes medicines to meet an emergency have to be procured from private pharmacies. Sometimes family members who come from far away places wish to visit the patient outside of visiting hours; sometimes visiting passes are lost. The non-medical staff provide many of these services for a fee. Thus for the patients the rules are obstacles to be overcome while for the lower staff the rules are a form of resources which they can transform into monetary benefits by acting as intermediaries.[9]

Further, the staff bring their own cultural assumptions to bear upon the meaning of the rules. For example, relatives of accident victims may be told that the body would have to be cut up in any case, because of the medico-legal character of the case. The implied notion is that the circumstances have made this death into an event in which the religious norms regarding the integrity of the body cannot be respected. While the Resident may put this in the form of "why not change this 'waste' into a 'gift'?" – the other staff may tell the relatives that there is a way to mitigate the financial ruin facing the family by "donating" an organ for a financial reward. The junior doctors often expressed pessimism on their ability to prevent informal commercial transactions over organ donation, because they know the contours of the system within which the everyday life of the hospital is conducted.

Finally, the protocol forbids the doctors in the cardiovascular or other organ-receiving departments to seek consent for donation of the organs as this might lead to a conflict of interest. Thus the task of seeking consent falls upon the Residents in the neurosurgery department. This leads to a poignant situation in which many neurosurgeons feel a certain ambiguity about their task. As one attending surgeon said, the success of the cardiovascular department was a failure of their department. "Every time they save a life we have failed to save one."

I hope this description shows the density of interpretations within which the new legislation on brain stem death was actualized in the context of the hospital and thus illustrates the way in which the gap between rules and their execution appears even when the rules are followed.

The Interpretation of Failure

Unlike the initial success obtained in the heart transplant operations, the liver transplant project in AIIMS had to face many difficulties. Initially there were problems with appointing the appropriate authority in accordance with the requirement of the Act and inter-departmental rivalries came in the way of ensuring a program of identifying brain dead persons and receiving consent for the harvesting of organs. The two liver transplant surgeries that had been performed at the time of writing this paper (one at AIIMS and the other at the Apollo Hospital, Madras) did not succeed. In an interview with Dr. Nundy that I conducted in 1995, before a liver transplant operation had been conducted in the hospital, he stated that he was hopeful about a successful program of liver transplant in the hospital. He explained that the patients seeking liver transplants in India were often there because of a medical history of viral hepatitis B or C and not because of alcohol abuse. Consequently the patient profile was of considerably younger persons. Dr. Nundy therefore expected the outcomes of liver transplants in India to be relatively more successful than in other countries.

Despite this optimistic prediction, liver transplants, which are much more complicated than heart transplants, have not been successful in AIIMS. After the failure of the second operation at AIIMS, it was explained that the condition of the patient who was a young man suffering from hepatic encephalopathy, was so poor that he did not survive the operation beyond two days. Yet in an interview to the *Times of India* Dr. Nundy said that "I won't say it was not a success." Clearly the meaning of failure and success needs some exegesis.

I suggest that what we are seeing here is the tension between the therapeutic and the experimental, giving the impression of contradictory statements being made by the same surgeon. On the one hand, the hospital is gaining experience of both harvesting livers from cadavers and transplanting them, but on the other hand, the patients have not survived. Thus what is a step ahead in the gaining of experimental knowledge may be seen as aggravating the suffering of the patient and his or her relatives. Under these circumstances, the recipient (whose consent is as necessary as that of the donor or his/her relatives) may also refuse the process even after giving consent. This refusal comes to be seen also as a "failure" of the hospital authorities to ensure that organs are not "wasted." What is even more interesting is that such definitions of waste get strung into the discourses of other functionaries in the hospital and circulate as images of nation and of citizenship. I give one example of such enunciative modalities.

As I said earlier, one of the early attempts at harvesting a liver successfully was made in AIIMS in the month of October 1995. As it happened the liver was successfully harvested from the victim of a road accident but the recipient, a patient suffering from cirrhosis of the liver who had been shortlisted for a transplant, could not be traced that night.

One of the subordinate staff in the hospital who knew that a team of doctors had been trying to trace the whereabouts of the man, was indignant at what he saw as a dereliction of duty on the part of the recipient. As he said, "They found a donor but the recipient disappeared – he deceived us" (*dhoka de gaya*). He explained to me that illiterate or uneducated people did not understand the responsibility placed upon them when they were shortlisted as recipients. Drawing an analogy with service in the government he said that rules determine when a government servant could take leave. But in this case the person, though shortlisted as a recipient in a government hospital, had gone away without leaving any information about his whereabouts. "So all the efforts of the doctors were wasted, an organ was wasted," he said. Other employees were of the opinion that the family had probably lost confidence and hid him because they were scared for the person. "Although he may be dying," one person said, "they fear that he may die on the operation table – so why not buy a few more days?"

What was fascinating in this discussion was that notions of citizenship were evoked to explain both that the patient had a right to receive a costly therapeutic intervention free of cost because he was a government servant who worked in the Fire Brigade but conversely that he had duties, both as a citizen and a government servant, to comply by the rules laid out for him. The bits of knowledge that were stitched together by the subordinate staff of the hospital used ideas of state and citizenship as a glue. It was not informed consent which was evoked to mediate the experimental and the therapeutic: thus not ideas about the patient having consented to an experimental procedure in the terminal stage of his illness but his duty as a government servant to comply with the experimental procedures. I hasten to qualify that none of these formulations was shared by the medical professionals or by the senior administrative staff. The circulation of the images of state and citizenship here show rather how these ideas have been internalized in the lower echelons of the administrative hierarchy in the hospital.

So how is one to define the body and its components especially for the poor? As a property of the individual? As a property of the state? Let us turn to the discursive formations through which the body and its capabilities are articulated among the poor in a non-medical setting in order to ask – what, from the point of view of a poor person is an organ?

Organs in the Genealogies of the Poor

Some scholars hold it axiomatic that the body is the property of the individual. They then conclude that the individual "owns" his or her organs and hence is free to gift or sell them as he/she pleases. But while it is easy to conceptualize that one has a relation to one's body, it is difficult to think that one has a relation to one's kidneys or liver until one can conceptualize the context within which these have been made into objects of consciousness. Thus, for example, in a society where people believe in witchcraft and the use of body parts for such practices, one can readily see that rumors of body parts being stolen by witches may be part of the fabric of understandings of that society (White 1997). Similarly only if a technology develops in which organs can be extracted for transplantation can one even begin to speak of having "property" in one's organs. It is, therefore, important to inquire about the practices within which the body and its functions are viewed in the informal economy of the poor which assimilates the idea of organs becoming saleable commodities.

In one of the resettlement colonies in Delhi where I worked in 1984 after the riots against the Sikhs took place, different kinds of transactions for money or other goods were not uncommon. The resettlement colonies in Delhi were primarily the products of the Emergency of 1975 when the poor from shanty towns were forcibly uprooted and settled in these colonies so that they did not spoil the landscape of the city. In many resettlement colonies the condition under which one could obtain entitlement to a plot of land was to produce a sterilization certificate under the family program of the Health Ministry. The Delhi Development Authority which was the department authorized to provide land implemented this notorious policy.

In an excellent paper Emma Tarlo (Tarlo 1995) has described how this policy worked at the local level. She documents how people were forced to get themselves sterilized or to offer other members of the family for sterilization in order to get an allotment of land in one of the colonies in Delhi. Slowly a network of middlemen developed who could procure sterilization certificates for a fee by what came to be known as "motivating" others. One of the methods used by these middlemen to "motivate" was to inform the police about homeless persons sleeping on the pavements in old Delhi. The police would then arrest some of these persons on the grounds of creating public nuisance and agree to release them only on payment of a bribe. The middleman would then appear and offer to raise money in exchange for the prisoner offering his body for sterilization. Thus the Emergency made it possible to think of the body and sexuality as exchangeable for a plot of land under the programs instituted by the government. While many of the poor suffered enormously, others could use it as an opportunity. As Tarlo (1995) says, "The point is that when people purchased sterilization certificates in the open market, they did not know the history of the 'motivated' and it is no doubt this very ignorance that enabled them to ignore the more sordid aspects of the trade" (Tarlo 1995: 2).

In Sultanpuri when I did my work, the Sikhs had suffered enormous violence after the assassination of Mrs. Gandhi (Das 1990, 1996). They recalled the Emergency but not the sterilization programs since they had not directly participated in these. Instead, they had been offered plots through the mediation of one of the "big men" (*dada* in local parlance) who had risen to power during the Emergency. In exchange for the plots of land they received, their bodies were hostage to the underlife of the state. They willingly participated in such activities as providing crowds for political meetings, providing the manpower to intimidate the enemies of their patron, and the more powerful in the colony were known to be "raising" musclemen. When their own bodies were submitted to brutal violence during the riots and they were agitating to receive monetary compensation from the government, survivors would often comment that they were "eating the dead." The capability of the body, alive or dead, lay in its exchangeability within the volatile informal economy of the colony.

While in 1984 discussions about organ sales were not part of their world, in 1994 when I went back to survey the colony, I met an old friend, a Muslim man who had been relatively uninvolved in the riots. In 1984 he had been a petty thief.[10] He told me that when several civil rights groups working in the area had begun to put pressure for the guilty to be punished, he had run away because he was scared that people like him would be named in the first information reports by the henchman of the "big man." He was known to the police as a petty thief, he said, and it would be the easiest thing to pick him up as a "known bad character." He had made his way to Bombay where he lived with some relatives in Dharavi. After the demolition of the Babri mosque in 1992, there were terrible riots in his area and his relatives lost a small tea shop and their house. He came back to Sultanpuri to take up his old connections. At this stage of the narrative he lifted his shirt and displaying a scar dramatically in the manner in which the media has been portraying the pictures of people who have sold the kidneys he said "This is Hindustan." He did not want to give me a detailed story of how he had come to sell his kidney, so I shall have to leave the narrative here. I feel that it completes the story of the way in which concepts of national pride, citizenship and state have left their signatures at the several points traversed by the world of transplant technology. An organ too moves on these several points and acquires meaning that is different from its meaning for a transplant surgeon. A person constantly fleeing from one kind of violence to another is connected to the final transaction by becoming one of the points in the genealogy of the organ.

The Sacredness of Contract

The global standard setting exercises on questions of bioethics often depend upon philosophical discussions stemming from first principles regarding agency, rights over one's body, and the meaning of contract. In this section I wish to examine whether the ethnography of social contexts in which transactions over organs are actualized can give a different insight into the issues debated in the field of bioethics. While this might appear as a break in the flow of the argument since the discussion shifts to somewhat disembodied theoretical issues, I argue that these philosophical considerations get translated into local realities through complex, albeit discontinuous, links.

While the dominant opinion on the question of sale of organs rejects this option in favor of either live donation from related donors or programs of cadaver donation, several arguments are now being offered by philosophers and practising surgeons in favor of sale of organs in order to save lives of patients suffering from end stage renal failure.

Most proponents of the market solution do realize that markets for organs would, by their very nature, be highly regulated markets. But they see the ban on sale as a limitation on individual freedom to do what one pleases with one's body. Starting from the premise that people's bodies are their own private property (which some like Lloyd Cohen hold to be a moral canon [quoted in Fox (1996: 263)]), they argue that the poor should be free to contract the sale of their organs. A paternalistic attitude which would deem the state to be more knowledgeable about what preferences the poor should have is considered unacceptable. The real dangers to the poor, it is argued, arise from the unscrupulous practices of cheating them of the rightful returns for their organs and for failure to provide proper medical care.[11] The philosopher Janet R. Richards regards the prohibition on the sale of organs in the following manner:

in surprising contravention of our usual idea about individual liberty, we prevent adults from entering freely into contracts from which both sides expect to benefit, and with no obvious harm to anyone else. Our intervention, in other words, seems in direct conflict with all our usual concerns for life, liberty and the pursuit of happiness. (Richards n.d.: 3)

At first sight the argument seems compelling. After all, if one is free to sell one's labor as a commodity in a labor market, why not allow a market in organs to develop? It is true that under market conditions one can see a movement of organs from the bodies of the poor to the bodies of the rich but is that not equally true for other modes of deploying the body? To my mind there are two formidable problems in accepting this definition of the situation. First, in the case of labor markets in which the body is deployed in a seller–buyer relation we have some notion of the principle on which a just recompensation is based for the worker whose body gets depleted in the process of work. This is the notion of a "fair wage", premised on the idea that the worker should receive enough compensation to be able to renew himself not only as a biological being but also as a person in the social and cultural sense (Marx's famous distinction between a slave and a worker). Thus there is principle, however violated in practice it may be, which allows us to think of the person as being able to renew himself or herself over time. A system of exchange that led to irreversible damage to the body of the worker would in principle be unacceptable today. I am fully aware that these principles are not applied in practice and that industrial hazards continue to expose workers to ever new health hazards. That does not, however, detract from the fact that conceptually we know how to think about just and unjust wages, legitimate and illegitimate ways of deploying the worker's body; as well as regulation of the working day to allow for this renewability of the body.

In contradistinction to this, I suggest there are no principles that could allow us to think of just exchange in the case of organ transplants. This may be one reason why moral arguments on organ transplants are couched in terms of altruism rather than self-interest.

What about arguments on autonomy and contract? Richard argues that even if some people were not competent to enter into a contract about sale of organs, that is not a reason to legitimize a general prohibition. Yet many legal theorists (Unger 1983 especially) recognize that concrete legal rules and standards are connected to a set of background assumptions about the kinds of human associations that can and should prevail in different areas of social life. Because of this most legal principles have to be balanced by the argument of counter-principles which will keep the principles in place, preventing them from extending imperialistically to other areas of life. It is the relation between principles and counter-principles that allows what are larger visions of what are desirable forms of human association.

In the context of contract law, the first counter-principle that holds it in place even in fully fledged market situations is the limitation that the contractual relationship cannot be allowed to imprint a permanent character upon tangible or intangible things including the labor of other people. Hence a worker is entitled to compensation from industrial hazards that can be shown to have been incurred as a result of a work contract. The capitalist is not free to evoke the idea of consent in his defense.

Second, the law refuses to see the parties to a contract as high risk gamblers. In a high risk gamble things are worth only the value that parties place on them in particular transactions, but the law refuses to see contract in this light. In a game of poker it may be permissible to treat the value of cards in terms of the stakes one has put on them, but in any contractual situations the law is obliged to search for minimalist standards of equivalence that transcend those particular transactions.

In the case of organ sales both conditions are violated not only in practice but also in the principles of exchange. First, the sale of organs makes a permanent imprint on the body and is thus violative. It is certainly true that the removal of an organ from a related live donor results in the same situation. This is precisely why such a transaction would be valid only in the sphere of kinship which is not premised on the law of contract, but not in the context of a market. Second, as I have already stated, there is no principle by which an equivalence between the things being transacted may be found. This is why we get the situation in which Madras kidneys cost more than, say, Bombay kidneys. For the vendors, the sale of kidneys is a high risk gamble. We saw how the poor are compelled to use their body, their sexuality, their reproductive powers, and now their organs as commodities: they learn to convert all kinds of violence into opportunity. Whether they should do this under the guise of autonomy and rights is the question.

The proponents of contract theory do not look at accompanying labor laws which empower the poor through mechanisms of collective bargaining or the counter-principles to contract in which discharge due to changed circumstances as well as laws of duress protect those who are in unequal positions when they enter into contracts. What anthropologists can offer to bioethics is the means for overcoming the seductions of a highly abstract contract theory because it can be shown that what appears ethical at the level of an abstract discourse can be productive of violence at the level of local communities. Transplant technology raises questions about long-term dealings that cannot be solved by theories oriented towards one-shot, arm's length, low-trust transactions. In the present era it seems to me that the conferring of autonomy on the poor in order that they may be enabled to sell their organs from bodies already wasted from poverty, is a convenient fiction that masks new ways of recycling for the benefit of the rich what has always been conceptualized as a societal waste. A vocabulary of rights here simply masks the faces of social suffering – such techniques of survival are seen by the poor not as acts of autonomy but as part of their everyday life in which all kinds of violence has to be turned into opportunity. In order to understand their place in the transplant world one has to look not at gross human institutions but at the fine texture of life.

Concluding Observations

Let me reflect on Foucault's majestic questions on the law operating behind all the diverse statements that are to be found in the discourse of the nineteenth-century doctors and what links them together.

First question: who is speaking? Who, among the totality of speaking individuals, is accorded the right to use this sort of language (*langage*)? Who is qualified to do so? Who derives from it his own special quality, his prestige, and from whom, in turn, does he receive if not the assurance, at least the presumption that what he says is true? What is the status of the individuals who – alone – have the right sanctioned by law or tradition, juridically defined or spontaneously accepted, to proffer such a discourse? (Foucault 1972: 50)

Underlying these questions is the inspiration that even as a particular modality of speaking is instituted, other enunciative possibilities are excluded. In describing the transplant world from another place, I hope that I have been able to show the different sites which come together in creating this world. There are not only different statutes and laws but also different temporalities through which new kinds of subjects and objects are created in a tangled plurality. There is therefore no simple way of deciding *before* the investigation either the subjects or the objects of this "transplant world."

This mode of doing ethnography lacks the security of a locality to which the anthropologist can go leaving his or her normal academic world behind. Instead it tries to tread, at least part of the networks, that link subjects and objects in bringing the world of transplant technology into the social contexts in which it is embedded. This context cannot exclude the systems of expert knowledge any more than it can exclude the world of the donors and recipients of the technology. This gives the ethnography a fragmented character and invites further reflection on the picture of anthropology as it addresses the questions posed by new technologies.

NOTES

I am grateful to the Rajiv Gandhi Foundation for the award of a fellowship that allowed me to devote my attention to questions of biomedical technology from an anthropological perspective. I thank Kavita Misra for her help in getting the materials cited here and for assisting in conducting some of the interviews. Earlier versions of this paper have been presented at the University of California at Berkeley in April 1996 and at the SSRC seminar on the Culture of Biomedical Technologies at the University of Cambridge in July 1996. I am grateful to all participants for their critical comments.

1. For a summary of international proclamations on sale of organs as well as the gaps in these normative exercises, see Rothman et al. 1997.

2. The use of placebos in clinical trials on humans shows that the body is being treated both as subject and object – that in producing reactions under experimental conditions the body is capable of "lying." I am grateful to N. Harish for a discussion on this point.

3. Paul Rabinow makes the important distinction that while it was society that was the object of study and reform according to scientific techniques in the nineteenth century, the new knowledge of molecular biology – biotechnology's hallmark – as he puts it "lies in its potential to get away from nature, to construct artificial conditions in which specific variables can be known in such a way that they can be manipulated. The knowledge then forms the basis of remaking nature according to our norms" (1996: 20).

4. The landmark work of Renée C. Fox and Judith P. Swazey (1992) on organ transplants in American society shows the complex relation between academic research and the necessity to take positions on the ethical issues that new technologies raise.

5. There is some recent evidence that the US Atomic Energy Commission obtained human remains from several countries around the world, including India, to assess radiation levels from the US bomb test fallouts in the 1950s. The President's Advisory Committee on Human Radiation Experiments is said to have unearthed certain documents which showed that infant skeletons along with samples from soil, water and crops, were obtained in a clandestine manner under an undercover operation called Operation Sunshine. Reports of this appeared in the *Statesman*, 17 February 1995.

6. One 50 milligram tablet of cyclosporin costs Rs. 400. Many patients are required to take two tablets a day, thus incurring Rs. 24,000 a month as cost of medication. (An average university teacher's current salary would be in the range of Rs. 8,000 to Rs. 18,000 a month.) Dosage is determined on the basis of regular blood tests to ascertain the blood concentration. Thus it is not only the costs of operation but the ability to maintain post-operative medication which makes this option out of the reach of not only the poor but also of the middle classes. Further, the reagent for the blood test is expensive. It was recently reported that even in the state capitals like Patna, the Indira Gandhi Institute of Medical Sciences, a premier institution in the state of Bihar, had not been conducting the test for more than two years since it could not afford the cost of the reagent though it had all other facilities for conducting the test (*Times of India*, 30 June 1996: 272).

7. Mr. Singhvi later served as the Indian High Commissioner to Britain.

8. I am constructing this on the basis of interviews with some junior doctors. I was not able to obtain any document on this.

9. I do no mean to imply that the medical staff follow the rules strictly. They too can manipulate rules to offer advantages to their friends or relatives or be coerced into bending the rules of the organization under political pressure.

10. I myself discovered this when in all innocence I persuaded him to come and give testimony before the Police Departmental Enquiry Commission that had been set up to investigate allegations of either compliance with rioters or neglect of duty against police officers. He had not realized that the hearings would be in the headquarters of the Police Commissioner of Delhi. When I accompanied him there he became nervous and said, "Sister, don't you know our work is done at night – where have you brought me?"

11. For an extensive discussion on the complex set of issues from a sympathetic medical view, see Daar 1997.

REFERENCES

Appadurai, Arjun 1996 *Modernity at Large*. London: University of Minnesota Press.

Baru, Rama V. and Priya Nanda 1993 *Trading of Organs: Need for a Comprehensive Policy*. Delhi: Voluntary Health Association of India.

Daar, S. 1997 "Paid Organ Donation: Towards an Understanding of the Issues." In J. R. Chaperman, Mark Deirkoi, and Celia Wright (eds.), *Organ Tissue Donation for Transplantation*. London: Arnold.

Das, Veena 1990 *Mirrors of Violence. Communities, Riots, and Survivors in South Asia*. Delhi: Oxford University Press.
    1996 "The Spatialization of Violence: Case Study of a 'Communal Riot'." In Kaushik Basu and Sanjay Subrahmanyam (eds.), *Unravelling the Nation: Sectarian Conflict and India's Secular Identity*. Delhi: Penguin Books, pp. 157–204.

Dejong, William, J. Drachman and et al. 1995 "Options for Increasing Organ Donation: The Potential Role of Financial Incentives, Standardized Hospital Procedures, and Public Education to Promote Family Discussion." *Millbank Quarterly* 73(3): 463–79.

Epstein, Steven 1996 *Impure Science: AIDS Activism and the Politics of Knowledge*. Berkeley: University of California Press.

Foucault, Michel 1972 *The Archaeology of Knowledge and the Discourse on Language*. London: Tavistock Publications.

Fox, Renée C. 1996 "Afterthoughts: Continuing Reflections on Organ Transplantation." In Stuart J. Youngner, Renée C. Fox and Laurence J. O'Connel (eds.) *Organ Transplantation: Meanings and Realities* Wisconsin: The University of Wisconsin Press, pp. 252–275.

Fox, Renée C. and Judith P. Swazey 1992 *Spare Parts: Organ Replacement in American Society*. New York: Oxford University Press.

Geison, Gerald L. 1995 *The Private Science of Louis Pasteur*. New Jersey: Princeton University Press.

Hogel, Linda F. 1995 "Standardization Across Non-standard Domains: The Case of Organ Procurement." *Science, Technology and Human Values* 20(4): 482–500.

Humphrey, David 1973. "Dissection and Discrimination: The Social Origins of Cadavers in America, 1760–1915." *Bulletin of the New York Academy of Medicine* (49): 819–827.

Kleinman, Arthur 1999 *Experience and its Moral Modes: Culture, Human Conditions, and Disorder.* The Tanner Lectures on Human Values. Salt Lake: Utah Press: 357–420.

Latour, Bruno 1993 [1991] *We Have Never Been Modern.* Trans. Catherine Porter. Cambridge, MA: Harvard University Press.

Lock, Margaret 1995a "Contesting the Natural in Japan: Moral Dilemmas and Technologies of Dying." *Culture, Medicine and Psychiatry* 19(1): 1–38.

  1995b "Transcending Mortality: Organ Transplants and the Practice of Contradictions." *Medical Anthropology Quarterly* 9(3): 390–3.

  1996 "Death in Technological Time: Locating the End of Meaningful Life." *Medical Anthropology Quarterly* 10(4): 575–600.

  1997 "Displacing Suffering: The Reconstruction of Death in North America and Japan." In Arthur Kleinman, Veena Das and Margaret Lock (eds.), *Social Suffering.* Berkeley, Los Angeles, London: University of California Press, pp. 207–44.

Marcus, George E. 1995 "Ethnography in/of the World System: The Emergence of Multi-Sited Ethnography." *Annual Review of Anthropology* 24: 95–117.

Nundy, Samiran. 1990 "Ethical Problems in Organ Transplantation." In Brain Death and Organ Transplantation in India. Theme Issue. *National Medical Journal of India.*

Ohnuki-Tierney, Emiko 1994 "Brain Death and Organ Transplantation: Cultural Bases of Medical Technology." *Current Anthropology* 35(3): 233–42.

Rabinow, Paul 1996 "Artificiality and Enlightenment: From Sociobiology to Biosociality. In Jonathan Crary and Sanford Kwinter (eds.), *Inforporations.* New York: Zone (distrib: MIT Press), pp. 234–52.

Richards, Janet Radcliffe. n.d. "Organs for sale."

Richardson, Ruth 1989 *Death, Dissection and and the Destitute.* London: Penguin.

Rothman, D. J., E. Rose., T. Awaya et al. 1997 "The Bellagio Task Force Report on Transplantation, Bodily Integrity, and the International Traffic in Organs." *Transplantation Proceedings* 29: 2739–45.

Singer, Peter 1994 *Life and Death: The Collapse of Our Traditional Ethics.* New York: St. Martin's Press.

Tarlo, Emma. 1995 "Body and Space in a Time of Crisis." *Economic and Political Weekly.*: 46.

Times of India 1995 "She Gave Away her Husband's Heart." 15 July.

Viswanath, Kalpana and Preeti Kirbat 1998 "The Campaign of the Women's Movement Against New Contraceptive Technologies." Working Paper 18, *Social Science and Immunization.* Centre for Development Economics, Delhi.

White, Luise 1997 "The Traffic in Heads: Bodies, Borders, and the Articulation of Regional Histories." *Journal of Southern African Studies* 23(2): 325–38.

Index

A small 'n' following a page reference indicates a footnote number.